LIBRARY IN A BOOK

CAPITAL PUNISHMENT

Revised Edition

Harry Henderson

Original edition by Stephen A. Flanders

Facts On File, Inc.

CAPITAL PUNISHMENT, Revised Edition

Facts On File, Inc.
11 Penn Plaza
New York NY 10001

Library of Congress Cataloging-in-Publication Data
Henderson, Harry
    Capital punishment / Harry Henderson.—Rev. ed.
        p. cm.—(Library in a book)
    Rev. ed. of: Capital punishment / Stephen A. Flanders, c1991.
    Includes bibliographical references and index.
    ISBN 0-8160-4193-8
    1. Capital punishment—United States. 2. Capital punishment. I. Flanders, Stephen A. Capital punishment. II. Title. III. Series.
KF9227.C2 F53 2000
345.73'0773—dc21   00-028775

Facts On File books are available at special discounts when purchased in bulk quantities for businesses, associations, institutions or sales promotions. Please call our Special Sales Department in New York at 212/967-8800 or 800/322-8755.

You can find Facts On File on the World Wide Web at http://www.factsonfile.com

Text design by Ron Monteleone

Maps and graphs by Jeremy Eagle

Printed in the United States of America.

MP Hermitage 10 9 8 7 6 5 4 3 2 1

This book is printed on acid-free paper.

CONTENTS

PART I
OVERVIEW OF THE TOPIC

Chapter 1
Introduction to Capital Punishment   **3**

Chapter 2
The Law of Capital Punishment   **40**

Chapter 3
Chronology   **90**

Chapter 4
Biographical Listing   **117**

Chapter 5
Glossary   **127**

PART II
GUIDE TO FURTHER RESEARCH

Chapter 6
How to Research Capital Punishment   **133**

Chapter 7
Annotated Bibliography   **150**

Chapter 8
Organizations and Agencies   **225**

PART III
APPENDICES

Appendix A
Statistics on Capital Punishment   **249**

Appendix B
Polls and Surveys   **255**

Appendix C
Overview of Research Studies   **258**

Appendix D
Extract from U.S. Supreme Court Ruling:
Furman v. Georgia, 1972   **266**

Appendix E
Extract from U.S. Supreme Court Ruling:
McCleskey v. Kemp, 1987   **279**

Index   **291**

PART I

OVERVIEW OF THE TOPIC

CHAPTER 1

INTRODUCTION TO CAPITAL PUNISHMENT

In 1972 the Supreme Court halted executions in the United States. Four years later, the Court authorized their resumption. Between 1977 and 1999, 596 prisoners were put to death, most of them in the 1990s as the pace of executions picked up with a record of 96 in 1999. The nation's death row population now numbers more than 3,335 inmates.[1] Capital punishment, or the death penalty, has again become a basic fact of American criminal justice.

In simple terms, capital punishment is the lawful taking of a person's life after conviction for a crime. However, the use of death as a punishment is highly controversial. It has raised difficult ethical, practical, and legal issues. The debate over capital punishment continues to be waged in both the courts and the political arena. The debate can be crystallized around several questions:

- Is it ever morally justified to deliberately take the life of any person, even a person who has killed another?

- Is an ultimate retribution for an ultimate crime necessary for justice, or for society's upholding of the value of life?

- Is the death penalty actually effective in deterring crime? Is it necessary for the incapacitation of dangerous criminals?

- Would a sentence of life without parole be as effective as the death penalty in deterring crime and protecting society from criminals?

- How often are innocent persons executed by mistake? Is the execution of the innocent a necessary price to pay for the security of society?

- Does the value of capital punishment justify its cost and the diversion of scarce resources from efforts to fight crime or rehabilitate criminals?

- Does the U.S. Constitution's prohibition of "cruel and unusual punishment" apply to the death penalty?

- What is the role of racism in the disproportionate sentencing of blacks and other minorities to death? Can the death penalty ever be administered fairly?
- How can judges and jurors be given enough discretion to consider the individual merits of each case without decisions appearing to be "arbitrary and capricious"?
- Should the United States follow the lead of the many other developed nations that have abolished capital punishment?

In exploring these questions, this chapter presents five major sections. American ideas of justice are deeply rooted in the long tradition of Western culture. The first section, Historical Background, begins by briefly tracing the development and use of capital punishment from earliest times to the British political tradition, the influence of the 18th-century Enlightenment, and the beginning of the American republic. Developments in capital punishment in the United States and the movement to reform or abolish it are then discussed in detail. These include 19th-century penal reform, the established practices of the first half of the 20th century, the legal and sociological challenges of the 1960s and 1970s culminating in the temporary abolition of the death penalty, the return of capital punishment after 1976, and the growth in both the number of executions and the organized opposition to the practice today.

The second major section, The Pragmatic Debate, looks at the hotly contested assertion that the death penalty deters crime and other possible effects including those on the allocation of resources in the criminal justice system.

The third major section, The Religious Debate, considers the clash of ultimate values that motivates much of the controversy about capital punishment. Both abolitionists* (people who want to end capital punishment) and retentionists (those who want to continue the practice) draw upon the Bible and other religious traditions as well as philosophical perspectives—theories of justice, the role of the state, and the worth of individual life.

Even if one concludes that capital punishment is justified under some circumstances, the question then arises of whether it does more good or harm to society as a whole. If one concludes that capital punishment is both right and efficacious, the next question is whether the system can be administered in a way that is compatible with the values of individual rights and fairness that are enshrined in our Constitution and legal tradition. The fourth major section, Legal Issues, is an overview of how the courts have confronted and tried to settle these issues, including what constitutes a capital offense, who

---

* For the purposes of this book, the terms *abolition* and *abolitionist* refer strictly to the capital punishment debate.

can be charged with one, what kinds of evidence must be considered by the judge or jury, how procedures are to be carried out, and the extent to which a convicted person can appeal the verdict to higher courts.

Finally the concluding section, The Future of Capital Punishment, looks at current American trends, the role capital punishment plays in American politics, and an international context in which many developed nations have abolished capital punishment and many international organizations continue to work toward its abolition.

HISTORICAL BACKGROUND

The infliction of death for the purpose of retribution has been a facet of human existence since earliest times. Even before the emergence of organized societies, individuals killed to avenge wrongs done to them and their families. These killings were acts of private retribution. There was no code that specified wrongful conduct or the penalties such behavior would incur.

The first criminal laws were an outgrowth of this practice of personal justice. These laws evolved as a means of codifying the compensation one individual or family owed another in order to right a personal wrong. The idea that this restitution involved a punishment imposed on behalf of the society as a whole, however, was yet to come.

As larger-scale social structures developed, wrongs or crimes were divided into public and private offenses. Public offenses, such as witchcraft or blasphemy against the official religion, were punished by the state, while private offenses were still answered by acts of personal retribution. This split system of justice eventually yielded to a unified scheme in which private retaliation was replaced by a concept of public justice. Behind the shift was an emerging recognition that every crime committed by any member of society was harmful to the interests of the entire society. With the public-private distinction removed, the individual relinquished the right to personal revenge. In return, the state assumed responsibility for the punishment of all crimes, including personal offenses. For ultimate crimes against the person, such as murder, personal vengeance had given way to lawfully derived and administered death sentences.

ANCIENT AND MEDIEVAL WORLD

Capital punishment was common throughout the ancient world. Death sentences were imposed for a wide variety of offenses. One of the earliest recorded sets of laws known to Western society, the Babylonian Hammurabi Code (ca. 1700 B.C.), decreed the death penalty for crimes as minor as the fraudulent sale of beer. Egyptians could be killed for disclosing sacred burial places. The Athenian leader Draco in the seventh century B.C. fashioned a criminal code that described the death penalty for most offenses. The severity of this code gave rise to the word "draconian." Socrates' suicide several hundred years later to escape execution for the crime of flouting social mores is among the most famous events in Western intellectual history. The Torah, the law of the Hebrews, authorized death for more than a dozen offenses. And in the most famous execution in history, Jesus Christ was crucified as a rebel under the laws of the Roman Empire.

The Middle Ages and Renaissance saw little change in the widespread use of capital punishment. Death was the standard penalty for major crimes across Europe. The methods of execution used frequently were cruel and barbaric by modern standards, often involving some form of torture. The condemned were subject to such ordeals as burning at the stake, being broken on a wheel, or being crushed under heavy stones. Execution, in fact, represented the ultimate point in a continuum of corporal punishment that for minor offenses involved branding or flogging.

The reign of King Henry VIII was illustrative of this period. Apart from the famous beheading of several of the monarch's wives, as well as of Sir Thomas More, more than 70,000 executions took place during the first half of the 16th century in England. Over the next several centuries, Great Britain continued to add to its already large number of crimes punishable by death. By 1789, the British criminal law contained 350 capital crimes. The statutes were known popularly as the "Bloody Code." Interestingly, the actual number of executions dropped substantially throughout this era. The reasons for this decline included the reluctance of judges and juries to convict persons of minor offenses that required the death penalty. (Britain also began to experiment with transportation to places such as Australia as an alternative to death for serious crimes.)

THE ENLIGHTENMENT

The emphasis on reason and humanity that marked the 18th-century Enlightenment brought about a transformation in the way capital punishment was viewed. The extensive use of the death penalty and the brutal manner in which it was administered were denounced by such leading thinkers as the French philosophers Montesquieu and Voltaire. In 1764, the Italian jurist Cesare Beccaria greatly advanced the entire field of criminal justice when he published his *Essay on Crimes and Punishment*. Widely translated and read, his book had an immediate and dramatic impact.

Beccaria criticized the use of torture, the imposition of harsh penalties for minor offenses, and the archaic state of the criminal law in general. He argued that the certainty of punishment was much more important to deterring crime than the severity of the sanction. He favored instead incarceration and hard labor for persons convicted of capital crimes.

Beccaria's writing served as the theoretical foundation for the major reforms in criminal law that occurred in the late 18th and early 19th centuries. In England, his ideas were taken up by the philosopher Jeremy Bentham, who advocated a complete revision of the British criminal code. Bentham's proposals, such as a reduction in the number of designated capital crimes, were presented in Parliament by another preeminent legal reformer, Sir Samuel Romilly. Although neither lived to see the result, their efforts sparked a reform movement that brought the number of capital crimes in Britain down to four by the mid-1800s.

EARLY REFORM MOVEMENTS IN AMERICA

The American colonies inherited the British system of law. Each of the colonies had its own criminal code, reflecting the distinctive circumstances of its founding. In early Puritan Massachusetts, the list of capital crimes included witchcraft, blasphemy, and adultery. In contrast, the Quaker influence in Pennsylvania limited the death penalty to crimes of murder and treason. Paralleling the trend in criminal law in the mother country, the number of criminal offenses in each of the colonies increased throughout their development. By the time of the American Revolution, all the colonies had severe criminal laws. However legal historians, noting the relatively low rate of actual executions across the colonies, point out that these criminal codes were far harsher in word than in practice.

Americans in the first years of the nation were familiar with the new ideas on criminal justice taking hold in Europe. Beccaria's book had been published in New York City in 1773. In 1787 Dr. Benjamin Rush, a signer of the Declaration of Independence and surgeon general to the Continental Army, delivered an address at the home of Benjamin Franklin in Philadelphia. Rush called for an end to public executions as part of an overall reform of the criminal justice system. The same year he helped found the Philadelphia Society for Alleviating the Miseries of Public Prisons.

The society was instrumental in the development of the prison system in the United States. In 1790 the Walnut Street Jail in Philadelphia was converted into the nation's first modern penitentiary. The emergence of such penal institutions had a major impact on the use of capital punishment. Historically, one of the reasons societies had relied so heavily on the death penalty was that other punishment options sufficient to incapacitate serious offenders did not exist. The new prison facilities, funded by the state and staffed by professionals, changed this. For the first time, confinement became a realistic alternative punishment for many crimes.

Rush was the first prominent American to publicly urge the abolition of the death penalty. He published several influential essays in which he maintained that capital punishment was indefensible on either rational or religious grounds. Rush was joined by other legal reformers, most notably the state's attorney general, William Bradford, in a campaign to modernize Pennsylvania's criminal code. In 1794 the state became the first political entity to differentiate among degrees of homicide when it made first-degree murder its only capital offense.

Other states followed suit in a general movement to update the criminal law. Over the next two decades, state penitentiaries were constructed, and the number of capital offenses was cut considerably. While the efforts of those opposed to capital punishment helped make these reforms possible, the primary impetus for their implementation was the perceived need to curb excesses in the criminal justice system. The death penalty itself was widely accepted and remained in effect throughout the country.

THE FIRST AMERICAN ABOLITION MOVEMENT

Capital punishment in the United States has undergone many modifications since the early 1800s. Its use gradually has become more limited and constrained. However, the death penalty has endured as a basic fact of American jurisprudence. The debate over capital punishment throughout American history has been characterized by the struggle of a relative handful of groups and individuals to change the nation's broad and consistent support for the sanction. The level of opposition has varied greatly. More often than not, its strength and success have been affected by other historical events.

The first concerted nationwide campaign against the death penalty took hold in the 1830s and 1840s. The movement initially formed around a desire to halt public executions. Public hangings of the time normally drew large crowds. Disturbed by the drunkenness and riots that often accompanied these events, by 1835 legislatures in five states had passed laws providing for private executions. A growing antigallows sentiment over the next 15 years caused another 10 states to enact similar measures.

This sentiment was fueled by a new generation of abolitionist leaders. Many had been inspired by the ideas and writings of the politician and lawyer Edward Livingston. In the early 1820s, Livingston had drafted a new criminal code for the Louisiana Assembly that eliminated capital punishment. Although his proposals were not approved, his arguments against the death penalty were published and read throughout the nation.

The abolitionist cause was joined by such prominent reformers as Robert Rantoul, Jr., and John L. O'Sullivan and the writers John Greenleaf Whittier and Walt Whitman. The period also saw the formation of the first abolitionist organizations, most notably the American Society for the Abolition of Capital Punishment. The movement was effective in communicating its message to the American public. Written appeals, speeches, lectures, meetings, and debates were all part of the effort to generate understanding and support for abolitionist goals. Supporters William Cullen Bryant, editor of the *New York Post*, and Horace Greeley, founder of the *New York Tribune*, used their newspapers to reach a nationwide audience.

The campaign met with limited success. Maine implemented what was in effect a moratorium on executions in 1837. Ten years later, abolitionist forces achieved their most important victory to date when Michigan became the first state to completely abolish capital punishment. The sense that the movement was gaining momentum was short-lived, however. Although Rhode Island and Wisconsin repealed their death penalty statutes in the early 1850s, the attention of the country had turned elsewhere. After 1846, abolitionist activity faded as the Mexican War, the growing struggle over slavery, and the Civil War dominated the national agenda.

The diminished abolitionist movement made little real headway in the decades following the Civil War. Led by the dedicated reformer Marvin H. Bovee, opponents of capital punishment were able to persuade many state legislatures that mandatory death sentences for certain crimes should be replaced by discretionary sentencing procedures. By the 1890s, 21 states had switched to discretionary capital sentences. The abolitionists had believed that, given the option, courts would be more lenient in their sentencing patterns. In practice, the actual number of executions did not drop as juries continued to impose the death sentence.

The Progressive Era around the turn of the 20th century witnessed a burst of renewed abolitionist activity. In 1897 Congress approved a measure submitted by Representative Newton M. Curtis (R-N.Y.) that reduced the number of federal capital offenses to four. The first years of the 20th century saw a rejuvenation of abolitionist organizations. The ranks of capital punishment opponents included representatives from the new field of penology. The development of a more scientific approach to understanding criminal behavior contributed to the general inclination of the time for criminal law reform. Between 1907 and 1917, eight states repealed capital punishment, bringing the total number of abolitionist states to 12, or one-quarter of the Union.

CAPITAL PUNISHMENT AS STATUS QUO: THE 1920S TO THE 1950S

Abolitionist gains were halted by America's entry into World War I and then reversed. Historians believe that a series of sensational crimes in the years just after the war caused the reinstatement of the death penalty in four states. Members of the law enforcement community moved to the forefront of efforts to retain capital punishment.

Since the early 1920s, an interesting pattern has emerged in the debate over capital punishment. Certain kinds of events have tended to build support for the death penalty and others to generate opposition to the sanction. Not surprisingly, public support for capital punishment has been highest in the aftermath of particularly horrid or brazen crimes. Conversely, controversial executions have led to an upsurge in abolitionist activity.

In 1924, the renowned lawyer Clarence Darrow, an ardent foe of capital punishment, undertook to defend two young men, Nathan Leopold and Richard Loeb, accused of killing a neighborhood child. His stirring plea against their execution, which ultimately resulted in terms of life imprisonment, inspired abolitionists across the country. The following year Darrow, Sing Sing prison warden Lewis E. Lawes and other leading opponents of the death penalty formed the American League to Abolish Capital Punishment. Membership picked up dramatically two years later following the execution of the Italian-born anarchists Sacco and Vanzetti. Supporters of the two men, alleging their murder convictions were politically motivated, fought an unsuccessful six-year legal battle to reverse their sentences. Their executions sparked worldwide protests. A picture secretly taken by a news photographer during the electrocution of Ruth Snyder in 1928 also raised many doubts as to the wisdom of capital punishment.

The revitalized abolitionist activity was quickly matched by growing cries for greater use of the death penalty. These pleas were driven by widespread alarm over a rise in violent crime. The St. Valentine's Day Massacre in 1929 became a symbol of the gangster violence of the Prohibition period. The kidnapping and murder of the Lindbergh baby in 1932 led to both federal and numerous state statutes making kidnapping a capital offense. In the wake of violent crime sprees in their states, Kansas and then South Dakota legislators restored the death penalty.

As the United States entered World War II, the federal government and 42 of the 48 states had authorized capital punishment. This status did not change for almost 20 years. During this time, there was no real debate over the merits of the death penalty as the nation was preoccupied with the difficult challenges of the war, its cold war aftermath, and the conflict in Korea. The execution of Julius and Ethel Rosenberg for espionage in 1953 met with opposition, but at issue were their death sentences rather than the death penalty itself.

As the 1950s progressed, however, there was some resurgence of interest in the death penalty issue. The catalyst for resumed abolitionist efforts was the publication in 1954 of *Cell 2455 Death Row* by California death row inmate Caryl Chessman. The book, which characterized the prison system as a virtual school for crime and condemned the death penalty as little more than an act of vengeance, provoked a sympathetic response. Chessman, who published two more books about death row before his eventual execution in 1960, became a celebrated author as well as an international cause célèbre. His case served to galvanize a new affiliation of organizations and individuals opposed to capital punishment.

The territories of Alaska and Hawaii ended the death penalty in 1957. The following year, Delaware became the first state in 40 years to abolish capital punishment. In 1959 the American Law Institute, in its Model Penal Code, proposed significant changes in the way capital punishment was administered in the criminal justice system. Campaigns were mounted to eliminate the death penalty in California, New Jersey, Ohio, and Oregon.

In each state, however, abolitionist forces were unable to convince a majority of the public that the death penalty should go. Law enforcement organizations and officials, political figures, and others in favor of retaining capital punishment frequently cited statistics showing a steady increase in violent crime. In 1961 Delaware restored the death penalty after a series of highly publicized murders of elderly citizens. The same year Congress added skyjacking to the list of federal capital offenses.

BATTLE IN THE COURTS

Historically, opponents of capital punishment had worked to eliminate the practice through the legislative repeal of death penalty statutes. To even the most optimistic abolitionist, though, it was increasingly evident there was little chance capital punishment would be ended through the legislative process in the foreseeable future. But as the strength of the civil rights movement grew during the early 1960s, it inspired a major switch in tactics on the part of the abolitionist movement. This shift was led by a small group of lawyers at the NAACP's Legal Defense and Education Fund (LDF). The new strategy was to move the struggle over capital punishment to the judicial arena.

The LDF was established in 1939 as a nonprofit organization to litigate civil rights issues and provide legal services to the poor. LDF lawyers were deeply involved in the civil rights movement, particularly in the South, where they frequently represented black defendants accused of capital crimes. Firsthand experience with the criminal justice system had convinced many of the attorneys that the death penalty was unfair and unworkable as well as morally wrong.

By 1965, the LDF, under director Jack Greenberg, had launched a nationwide legal attack on capital punishment. The immediate goal was to block every execution in America through a combination of lawsuits, appeals, and other court actions. At the same time LDF lawyers, headed by law professor Anthony G. Amsterdam, undertook a series of test cases designed to challenge the constitutionality of the death penalty. Their hope was that the Supreme Court would consent to hear one or more of these cases, rule the death penalty unconstitutional, and thus in one stroke outlaw capital punishment in the United States.

The LDF was subsequently joined by the American Civil Liberties Union (ACLU) and other legal organizations committed to ending the death penalty. Within two years, a coordinated series of legal actions across the country had achieved a freeze on executions in the United States. For the first time since the federal government started keeping statistics in 1930, no one was put to death in 1968. The moratorium continued over the next four years as the courts struggled to resolve the different legal challenges raised against capital punishment.

The legal campaign to have the death penalty declared unconstitutional seemingly had succeeded in 1972. In *Furman v. Georgia*, the Supreme Court struck down the nation's capital punishment laws. As Justice William O. Douglas noted in his opinion (and quoting former Attorney General Ramsey Clark):

It is the poor, the sick, the ignorant, the powerless, and the hated who are executed. . . . [The law] leaves to the uncontrolled discretion of judges and juries the determination of whether defendants committing these crimes should die or be imprisoned. . . . These discretionary statutes are unconstitutional.[2]

The court found that the statutes as written permitted the death penalty to be imposed in an arbitrary and capricious manner in violation of the Eighth Amendment's ban on cruel and unusual punishment.

The decision met with immediate criticism. President Richard Nixon and California governor Ronald Reagan were two of the most outspoken of the many political figures across the nation who denounced the ruling as an unwarranted intrusion on the prerogatives of the legislative branch of government. The Supreme Court was characterized as thwarting the will of the majority as expressed through its elected representatives. The Court, it was argued, had usurped to itself the right to make rather than interpret law.

THE REVIVAL OF CAPITAL PUNISHMENT

What seemed to be a sweeping abolitionist triumph would prove to be short lived. In *Furman*, the Court had not gone so far as to rule that capital punishment itself was unconstitutional but only that the haphazard way in which it was administered was constitutionally impermissible. Many states moved quickly to amend their capital punishment laws to conform to the procedural guidelines outlined in the *Furman* decision. In 1976, these revised laws received their crucial test when the case of *Gregg v. Georgia* reached the Supreme Court. In their decision, the justices held that the new statutes provided sufficient safeguards to ensure that the death penalty was employed in a constitutionally acceptable manner. The Court's ruling thus reinstated capital punishment in America. The nation's first execution in 10 years took place in January 1977 when Gary Gilmore was put to death in Utah by a firing squad.

Since that time, the Supreme Court has reaffirmed the principles in its *Gregg* decision and has failed to find any constitutional defect broad enough to sweep away all the state and federal death penalty statutes. However, as will be described later, the Court has invalidated a number of individual aspects of death penalty statutes on various grounds for not meeting the high standard of fairness and due process that is required before the ultimate sanction is imposed.

ABOLITIONIST EFFORTS CONTINUE

The failure to achieve a legal knockout of capital punishment also meant that abolitionists would return to the political arena. The death penalty was a major issue in the 1988 presidential campaign, where Republican George W. Bush attacked Democrat Michael Dukakis for being an opponent of capital punishment. During the 1990s, the number of executions would climb along with the crime rate. Political support for capital punishment was strong enough to compel leaders to demonstrate their public support for the sanction, such as when Arkansas governor and presidential candidate Bill Clinton, interrupted his campaigning in 1992 in New Hampshire to return to the statehouse and deny the final appeal for clemency on behalf of Ricky Ray Rector, a man apparently suffering from serious brain damage.

Abolitionists have responded to this climate by organizing vigorously. In 1976, following the restoration of capital punishment, participants in the ACLU's Capital Punishment Project formed a new umbrella organization, the National Coalition to Abolish the Death Penalty (NCADP). Formed as a resource, coalition, and support agency for a nationwide campaign against capital punishment, the coalition now numbers nearly 140 affiliated organizations. A substantial number of the members are religious organizations. Most of the nation's major religious denominations have voiced their opposition to capital punishment. Additionally, many civil rights groups have long condemned what they view as the discriminatory manner in which the death penalty is disproportionately imposed on minorities in general and blacks in particular.

against capital punishment in America has also become part
onal human rights movement. Despite these efforts, neither
islatures seemed inclined to overturn the death penalty in the
foresee   uture. The issue would continue to flare into public view when
high profile cases mixed the death penalty with race (the case of black journalist and death row convict Mumia Abu-Jamal) or with religion (Texas
murderer turned born-again Christian Karla Faye Tucker).

THE PRAGMATIC DEBATE:
DOES CAPITAL PUNISHMENT WORK?

Even if one grants that capital punishment is moral, there would still be the
question of its effectiveness. What is the purpose of the sanction, and does
it accomplish that purpose at a cost (financial or otherwise) that is acceptable to society?

DETERRENCE

Deterrence is the idea that punishments imposed by society for criminal activity discourage its members from engaging in such behavior. Advocates of
capital punishment contend that fear of death deters people from committing murder and other serious crimes. The average person will think twice
before running the risk of possible execution. In addition, the death penalty
is viewed by some as the only sanction severe enough to keep professional
criminals from taking part in violent acts.

Deterrence is the most frequently made and most widely accepted argument in favor of the death penalty. It has generated intense debate and controversy. Opponents of capital punishment have attacked the deterrent
value of the death penalty on a number of grounds.

They argue first that there is no conclusive evidence the death penalty
has any impact on the rate of violent crime. At the least, they suggest, capital punishment is no more effective a deterrent than prolonged incarceration. Numerous studies have been conducted to gauge the actual
effectiveness of the death penalty as a deterrent. Most often, murder rates
are examined in states that have abolished capital punishment, or in states
that have recently reinstated the sanction. The rate of murders prior to abolition or reinstatement is compared to the rate in subsequent years. The
problem with this methodology is that many other variables can be involved. A general rise in the crime rate, a change in the state's demographics, or new types of violent crimes, such as gang wars, may complicate the
picture. At any rate most experts agree that studies to date have not been
able to conclusively ascertain the deterrent value of capital punishment.

Abolitionists also stress that with deterrence, the certainty of is much more important than the severity. Any fear of death they contend, by the long delays between conviction and execution, the fact death sentences are carried out in private and the relatively low number of executions. Some proponents suggest that if this is a problem, it is caused by the abolitionists' own efforts to block executions by any means possible, and that the solution is to streamline the process and allow the number of executions to reach the point where the risk to the individual criminal is significant. But abolitionists, in turn, question whether Americans would truly want to live in a society where hundreds of people were executed each month.

Abolitionists cite statistics showing that in a majority of murders the killer knew the victim. A rational consideration of future penalties has little or no bearing on situations where murders occur as a result of family quarrels or other emotional disturbances. Proponents respond that the death penalty is not applicable to these kinds of homicide but to premeditated first-degree murder. Crimes such as killing a police officer or a rival drug dealer are those which are said to be deterred by capital punishment.

If one assumes that capital punishment does produce some deterrence, another question that arises is how much more deterrence does capital punishment provide than another severe sanction such as life in prison without possibility of parole. How many of the "rational" criminals who would be deterred by death would not be deterred by the prospect of spending a lifetime in prison? This "incremental deterrence" also proves difficult to measure.

Finally, abolitionists argue that even if the deterrent effect of the death penalty were established, this would not in itself justify retaining capital punishment. They point out that if, as retentionists say, the specter of electrocution or lethal injection deters murder, then logically it should follow that burning at the stake or drawing and quartering would be even more effective at discouraging potential killers. But society has long renounced these methods of execution as barbaric. From the abolitionist perspective, if society can forego the deterrent value of these means of executions, its "evolving standard of decency" (frequently cited by the Supreme Court) ought to impel it to do without more modern, but still uncivilized, ways of putting people to death.

PROTECTING SOCIETY

In addition to deterrence there is the related concept of social protection. Both advocates and opponents of capital punishment agree that society has a right to protect itself from criminal activity. The debate is over the effectiveness of the death penalty as one of the means of protection.

15

Capital Punishment

Proponents claim that by imposing the death sentence for certain offenses, the law is sending a clear message about types of behavior that will
not be tolerated. Capital punishment is a statement by society that it is willing and able to protect itself from brutal, violent crimes. The educational
value of the death penalty is also noted. By defining premeditated murder as
a capital offense, the law serves to develop a general abhorrence for the
crime.

Abolitionists maintain that the selective and often arbitrary way in which
the death penalty is administered undermines any message its use may be
meant to deliver. They contend that death sentence statistics reveal that the
criminal justice system disproportionately singles out the least advantaged
members of society for execution. Those who are wealthier, more educated,
and more socially connected rarely, if ever, receive the death penalty. In
their view the message actually conveyed is that America has two standards
of justice.

Finally, another aspect of social protection cited by death penalty advocates is its ability to incapacitate most violent offenders, ensuring that they
can never commit another brutal crime. Opponents counter that the rate of
recidivism, or return to criminality, among convicted murderers is very low.
Moreover, dangerous individuals are just as incapacitated by life imprisonment without parole as by death (except for the possibility of killing a fellow inmate or a guard, of course).

RETRIBUTION

Retribution refers to the penalty a society exacts for wrongful behavior. It is
the idea that persons should pay for their crimes.

The criminal law of a society reflects its value system or moral code. Proponents of capital punishment believe that the law should place less value on
the life of a convicted murderer than on the life of an innocent victim. The
law recognizes the necessity of this kind of distinction, justifying killings
committed in self-defense or during the arrest of a dangerous felon. They
conclude that the state has the right to execute certain grievous offenders in
order to uphold and preserve greater societal values. This can be viewed
both as a form of collective self-defense and as a declaration that the only fit
restitution for taking a life in cold blood is the giving up of one's own life.

Proponents insist that there is no valid substitute for the death penalty.
More serious offenses should be met with more severe penalties. If varying
lengths of imprisonment are used to punish all crimes, then society risks los-
ing sight of the distinction between murder and misappropriation of funds.
Proponents insist that retribution is not revenge. The individual desire for
revenge has been replaced in modern society by a concept of lawful punish-

ment. It is important that the penalty for a crime fulfills society justice has been served. For certain horrifying and heinous cri the 1995 Oklahoma City bombing or the cruel dragging death   black man or the brutal beating of a gay man in a hate crime, only the execution of the offender will satisfy the public that justice has been attained. Furthermore, continuing failure to satisfy the public's sense of justice may well lead to loss of respect for authority and persons starting to take justice into their own hands, such as through lynching.

Opponents of the death penalty do agree that retribution is an essential part of justice. However, the penalties imposed by society should not be based on vindictive or bloodthirsty motives that really amount to revenge masquerading as retribution. In a civilized society, the brutal nature of violent crime should not determine the limits of appropriate punishments. To do so would be to brutalize society itself. They contend that long periods of confinement will meet society's need for justice, while affording the offender some opportunity to become rehabilitated and possibly provide some form of restitution, however inadequate.

In an argument that parallels their attack on the deterrent value of capital punishment, abolitionists reiterate that the death penalty is not imposed in a uniform manner. Society is not protecting higher values or distinguishing between the relative seriousness of different offenses if it executes one person for murder but spares another for the same crime.

PROPORTIONALITY

Retribution also involves the issue of proportionality. In simple terms, the sentence should fit the crime. As for capital punishment, is death ever warranted as a penalty? If so, are there only certain crimes that merit its imposition?

Opponents of capital punishment would obviously answer no to the first question and thus consider the second question to be irrelevant. From the abolitionist perspective, an eye for an eye or a life for a life is neither a sound nor a workable principle of criminal justice. Punishments should correspond to the moral culpability of the offender, not the harm suffered by the victim.

Advocates of capital punishment point out, however, that moral culpability is related under the law to the impact a crime has on a victim. A person who commits murder is guilty of a more serious offense than an individual who merely injures another. Proponents maintain that death is the only form of retribution that matches the grievousness of certain crimes. Proponents are less in agreement about whether serious crimes that do not involve killing should nevertheless be subject to the death penalty. (In recent years, American courts have tended to restrict capital punishment to crimes that involve homicide, but the issue remains unresolved.)

BARBARITY

While opponents of capital punishment have tended to react to the arguments of proponents with regard to the social necessity of the death penalty, abolitionists also have taken the offensive by insisting that capital punishment, in any form and used for any reason, is inherently barbaric. The infliction of death, they maintain, has no place in an enlightened society. An execution, no matter how swift and painless, is still psychological, if not physical, torture. As opponents also observe, no method of execution is foolproof. For example, during the electrocution of Pedro Medina on March 25, 1997, a malfunction caused sparks, flame, and smoke to erupt from his head. Lethal injection has also run into problems when the condemned person, because of drug abuse, no longer has an easily accessible vein. Many abolitionist publications contain graphic accounts of such botched executions that caused evident pain and suffering to the condemned.

It is alleged that capital punishment brutalizes a society. Executions are seen as a form of institutionalized violence. In this view, use of the death penalty accustoms a society to violence, upholds violence as a way to solve social problems, and hardens people to the suffering of others.

Proponents counter that it is violent, wanton crime that tears apart the social fabric. Abolitionists are criticized for seeming at times to be concerned with the punishment of criminals but indifferent to the impact their actions have on society. The fact a given punishment may cause a prisoner anguish is not sufficient reason to abandon its use. After all, a life sentence without parole is also likely to produce anguish and psychological torture.

PUBLIC OPINION AND DEMOCRACY

Public opinion surveys consistently show high levels of support for capital punishment. Should this matter in the decision whether to retain or abolish the death penalty?

Many opponents of capital punishment believe it should not. They argue that public policy should lead public opinion on issues of justice and the law. Capital punishment should be eliminated on the merits of the arguments against it. It is suggested that opinion polls actually reveal a fear of rising crime rates more than they reflect inherent support for the death penalty. Fears in times of crisis are not a good basis for making public policy, as can be seen retrospectively in the Red Scares of the 1920s and 1950s and the incarceration of Japanese Americans after Pearl Harbor. Abolitionists also suggest that if the public were more informed about capital punishment and its alternatives, then the sanction's popularity would diminish significantly.

Death penalty advocates characterize these views as elitist and self-righteous. In a democracy, citizens, through their elected representatives, have the right and duty to determine the appropriateness of a given punishment. Judges and other experts who may not have personally experienced the devastation of violent crime should not function as self-appointed arbiters of right and wrong. Public opinion polls simply document the decision that the public continues to make, and that is reflected in the enactment and continued use of the death penalty across the nation. Retentionists also accuse abolitionists of hypocrisy. They note that in the 1960s, when surveys indicated an almost evenly divided public on the issue of capital punishment, abolitionists were quick to cite the results.

A number of abolitionists, while sharing the perception the public is uninformed about the realities of the capital punishment system, stop short of discounting the importance of public opinion to the functioning of the criminal justice system. They believe that they must continue the long struggle to educate and persuade a majority of Americans that the death penalty is unworkable and wrong. As this occurs, they expect the nation to gradually abandon capital punishment.

IRREVERSIBILITY

The risk of executing an innocent person is generally considered the strongest practical argument against capital punishment. Abolitionists condemn the death penalty for its irreversibility. The death sentence, once carried out, is irrevocable. If society executes an innocent prisoner, there is no way to undo the error. In contrast, imprisonment always leaves the possibility of overturning a wrongful conviction. Although years lost to incarceration cannot be restored, it is possible to make some sort of compensation (although this is seldom done).

The possibility that innocent persons may be sentenced to death exists. In 1987 professors Hugo Adam Bedau and Michael L. Radelet, both strong opponents of capital punishment, published in the *Stanford Law Review* a detailed study of death sentences in 20th-century America. They concluded that, between 1900 and 1985, 349 persons were incorrectly convicted of capital offenses and 23 innocent prisoners were actually executed. Abolitionists cite this and later studies, and the instances of persons wrongly sentenced since 1973 in particular, as proof that no amount of procedural safeguards can ensure innocent persons will not be executed.

Proponents make three points in rebuttal. They dispute the work of Bedau, Radelet, and others, saying that they overstate the number of cases where persons were demonstrably, factually innocent. They argue that the extensive safeguards now surrounding a capital trial in fact do work. The recent instances where it was found that innocent persons were sentenced to death, and their sentences overturned while they waited on death row, are taken as evidence of the effectiveness of the criminal justice system in catching such errors. Finally, they insist that even the theoretical possibility (indeed, likelihood) that at least a few innocent prisoners are being put to death is not sufficient grounds to abandon the death penalty. After all, innocent persons are also occasionally killed as a result of accidents during hot pursuits by police or by errors in judgment by law enforcement officers. Just as this is not a reason to abandon law enforcement, execution of the innocent is not a reason to abandon capital punishment. Society cannot place its concern for the wrongly condemned person above its legitimate and compelling interest in administering the death sentence for heinous crimes. Of course it is just the "compelling" nature of this societal interest that abolitionists challenge on all grounds discussed throughout this chapter.

FAIRNESS, CLASS, AND RACE

One of the most complex aspects of the debate over capital punishment is the question of fairness. The issues involved go to the very structure and nature of the American criminal justice system, and invoke some of the most apparently intractable problems in our society.

Abolitionists charge that the death penalty is not applied in an even remotely impartial manner in the United States. Because the way it is administered is so fundamentally unfair, the practice of capital punishment should be discontinued. Moreover, abolitionists assert that the discretion built into the criminal justice system makes it impossible to ever achieve a truly consistent and unbiased use of the sanction.

Opponents of capital punishment point first to the fact that the death penalty is disproportionately imposed on the less advantaged members of society. The poor, the uneducated, and the socially unacceptable are more likely to face execution than those of more privileged backgrounds.

Abolitionists contend that justice is not blind where the death sentence is concerned. Juries are less sympathetic to persons from society's lower strata. Those of lesser means do not have access to the same quality of defense counsel as persons who can afford private representation. Key procedural issues may be overlooked by an inexperienced or overworked public defender.

The problem of the uneven distribution of justice becomes even more pronounced in the case of racial minorities. At the start of 1998, blacks in particular made up a much larger share of the death row population (41 percent) than the percentage of the population as a whole (about 12 percent).

Further, as shown by a study of 2,000 murders committed in Georgia during the 1970s by professors David Baldus, George Woodworth, and Charles Pulanski, the race of offender and victim strongly influenced the likelihood of a death sentence. In cases in which someone who was black was convicted of killing someone who was white, the death penalty was given 22 percent of the time. When both offender and victim were white, the death penalty rate was only 8 percent, and only 1 percent when both participants were black. When someone who was white killed someone who was black, the rate of being given the death penalty was also only 3 percent.

Abolitionists cite such statistics as striking evidence that the racism that still infects American society is manifested in harsher penalties for blacks than for whites. More importantly, because the criminal justice system allows district attorneys, judges, and juries great latitude in determining the fate of a given prisoner, there is no way to guarantee that bias or prejudice does not play a part in the decision made.

Some advocates of the death penalty believe that that the statistics may exaggerate the role of racism and that other factors (such as the differing proportions of different kinds of homicide, such as drug-gang murders or street robberies versus domestic murders) may account for blacks committing a higher proportion of murders that qualify for the death penalty.

In general, advocates argue that the procedural safeguards built into the process for capital cases, such as bifurcated trials and appellate review, will diminish the effect of remaining racism.

Furthermore, proponents reject the idea that allowing the criminal justice system the discretion necessary to reach an individualized determination in each case (as required by the Supreme Court) results in unfair verdicts. This assertion is seen as an attack on a fundamental principle of American jurisprudence. If it were true, then all punishments arrived at under current procedures, and not just death sentences, potentially would have to be abandoned as fatally flawed. Rejecting the notion that capital sentences are inherently unfair, proponents stress the need for full enforcement of the safeguards already in place.

EXPENSE

The issue of expense is the most recent addition to the debate over capital punishment. It is commonly assumed that it costs less to execute a person than it does to imprison that individual for life. The reverse, however, is true.

The costs of capital cases have soared in recent years. There are several reasons for this. Capital trials take longer to litigate since a second, penalty phase is required if a guilty verdict is returned. A protracted appeals process normally follows all death sentences. Death row facilities where defendants often wait execution for 10 years or longer require more money to staff and maintain than regular prison facilities. The result is that capital cases are significantly more expensive over their entire course than cases of serious felonies that don't involve the death penalty. As a result, incarceration of a prisoner for 40 years is substantially less costly than going through the full legal process necessary to put a person to death.

Many localities are having difficulty meeting the costs involved in capital cases. Recognizing the growing concern over the availability of funding for the criminal justice system, the abolitionist movement has argued that capital punishment doesn't make economic sense. Instead of dedicating scarce resources to executing a relative handful of prisoners, it would be more worthwhile to sentence capital offenders to long prison terms and use the money saved to fully fund efforts such as victim-assistance programs.

Many advocates of the death penalty label these arguments as insincere. In their view, the high costs of capital punishment that abolitionists cite are due to the inordinate number of appeals filed by the abolitionists themselves as part of their campaign to block executions. Other proponents accept that procedural safeguards involved in capital punishment are necessarily more expensive, but insist that capital punishment's importance to the administration of justice is such that it should be underwritten regardless of the cost.

THE RELIGIOUS DEBATE: AN EYE FOR AN EYE?

Although religion has no formal role in the governance of the nation, American institutions are deeply rooted in the Judeo-Christian tradition. Both abolitionists and death penalty supporters often appeal to religious ideas and values in the political debate over the future of capital punishment.

Capital punishment and religion have been linked since the first use of death as a sanction. The earliest laws and criminal codes were religious in nature. Throughout much of Western history, many religious offenses were punishable by death. As recently as the 18th century, witchcraft was a capital crime in the American colonies. The differentiation between civil and religious crimes is a comparatively modern development. As Western societies evolved, gradually the idea took hold that religious offenses were not properly the province of a civil government. In the United States, the First Amendment to the Constitution established a separation between church and state that has been strengthened by court interpretations during the 20th century.

Introduction to Capital Punishment

The relationship of organized religion in the American experience has thus been an advisory one. Religious leaders have spoken from a position of moral authority in the public debate over questions of right and wrong, crime and punishment, and justice and mercy.

In the 19th century, the major religious denominations uniformly supported the notion of capital punishment. Members of the clergy, particularly from the Congregationalist and Presbyterian denominations, publicly opposed efforts to abolish the death penalty. They based their arguments mainly on statements from the Bible, such as "Whosoever sheddeth a man's blood, so shall his blood be shed" (Genesis 9:6).

By the middle of the 20th century, this kind of literal biblical interpretation no longer had much force in an increasingly secular society or among the more liberal clergy. Reflecting the growing concern over social issues, many churches became active both in the civil rights movement and in efforts to help the disadvantaged and needy. While the New Testament does not explicitly condemn capital punishment, some contemporary theologians have insisted on the incompatibility of human execution with Jesus Christ's message of forgiveness and redemption. The death penalty is called a fundamental departure from this message and from Christianity's commitment to the sanctity and dignity of human life. Also citing the fundamental dignity of human life, the Catholic Church has in recent years moved strongly into the forefront of the abolition movement. In 1995, Pope John Paul II issued an encyclical *Evangelium Vitae* (the Gospel of Life) that strongly condemned capital punishment, together with abortion and euthanasia, as offenses against the divine gift of life.

Certain religious groups, such as the Quakers, have long opposed capital punishment within the context of an overall pacifism. Within the last 40 years, representative organizations of almost all of the nation's major denominations have issued statements calling for an end to the death penalty. Many religious groups are active in the abolitionist movement.

However, a number of more conservative religious organizations continue to endorse capital punishment. These include Mormons, Jehovah's Witnesses, and certain fundamentalist Christian and orthodox Jewish groups. While religious supporters of capital punishment lack the visibility of many abolitionist groups, the high proportion of overall public support for the death penalty suggests that many people do not oppose capital punishment on religious grounds.

The case of Karla Faye Tucker in Texas changed the perspectives of some religious conservatives who had been staunch supporters of the death penalty. Tucker, convicted of murder in Texas, declared while on death row that she had become a born-again Christian. Many supporters believed she was sincere, and religious leaders ranging from Pope John Paul II to

Reverend Pat Robertson sought unsuccessfully to have her sentence commuted. The case brought into conflict two fundamental religious values: divine justice and the possibility of forgiveness.

LEGAL ISSUES: CAN IT BE FAIR?

Capital punishment is inseparable from the law. The law defines the death penalty, authorizes its use, and specifies the circumstances under which it can be applied. Before considering the many legal issues that have arisen concerning capital punishment, it is useful to give a quick overview of the criminal justice system itself.

THE CRIMINAL JUSTICE SYSTEM

Capital punishment cannot exist outside of a criminal justice system. A person may kill another to avenge a wrong, but this is an act of private revenge. The idea of punishment implies there is an established standard of behavior to which persons are able and expected to conform. It suggests, as well, that society has both a means to determine whether a person has violated this standard and what penalties should be applied depending on the infraction. The basic judicial system required to impose a punishment is necessarily the product of an organized society.

In a modern political state, such as the United States, the rules governing unacceptable behavior are specified in the law. In America, the law has two components. The first is statutory law. This refers to the statutes, or laws, that are enacted by a legislature, which can range from the Congress of the United States all the way down to a town council. These laws reflect the public policy wishes of the people as expressed by their elected representatives. What crimes are and the penalties for these crimes are defined by the statutory law.

This law, however, does not function in a vacuum. The courts modify and shape the law as they apply it to specific cases. The legal rules fashioned by courts in the process of deciding cases is known as common law. This second component of American law evolves over time as judges refer to prior cases and the precedents set by other justices to help them determine the appropriate ruling to make in a given instance.

America also has two distinct sets of laws. Each state has its own unique body of laws passed by its legislature. Historically, the preponderance of criminal activity has been a matter for state law. State criminal codes address offenses such as murder, rape, and kidnapping—all of which have merited the death penalty in a majority of states at one time or another. Today, court decisions have eliminated state capital offenses that do not involve murder.

Federal law, which is enacted by the U.S. Congress, tr dealt with crimes that cross state lines (such as some kidnappin, fect the federal government or interstate commerce. Such offe. cluded espionage, assassination of the president or other high o ...s, and air piracy. In 1994, Congress considerably expanded the range of federal offenses subject to the death penalty, including drug-related offenses. These new capital offenses include murders involving such factors as bomb attacks on government facilities, denial of civil rights, kidnapping or hostage-taking, killing of federal witnesses or informants, bank robbery, carjacking, murder for hire, racketeering, drug-related drive-by shootings, and sexual molestation of children. (See Chapter 2, The Law of Capital Punishment, for more details about what is covered by federal and state capital crimes legislation.)

The courts are where determinations of guilt or innocence are made and punishments meted out to the convicted. Corresponding to the distinction between state and federal law, there are state and federal court systems. Both systems are organized like a pyramid, with local, lower courts at the bottom, appeals courts above them, and a supreme court at the very top.

In most states, criminal cases are heard in local trial courts. (In some jurisdictions, more serious offenses are tried in statewide criminal courts rather than at the local or county level.) The appellate level of courts is the first stage where appeals of trial court rulings are heard. The appellate courts normally are concerned with issues of law. The decisions of the trial courts on issues of fact (and thus of the actual guilt or innocence of the defendant) are almost always considered final.

The state supreme court is the highest court in the state system. It reviews appeals from the lower courts, most often in connection with state constitutional issues. A state's supreme court is the final authority on its constitution. However, the rights guaranteed in the federal Constitution (such as the right to due process in the Fifth Amendment, the ban on "cruel and unusual punishment" in the Eighth Amendment, and the right to equal protection of the laws in the Fourteenth Amendment) take precedence over state constitutions and statutes. When such a constitutional question or a question of conflict between federal and state law arises, state court rulings can be appealed to the federal court system.

The federal court system has a similar structure. The basic trial court is the federal district court. Each state has at least one federal district court. These courts hear both federal cases and appeals from state courts involving questions of federal law and the Constitution.

The next level, the U.S. Court of Appeals, handles appeals of the decisions of the district courts. The United States is divided into 12 circuits, each of which takes appeals from several districts in a particular region of the country. As with the state appeals courts, the focus is on interpretation of the law. Findings of fact are ordinarily presumed complete and are not reviewed.

The U.S. Supreme Court is the court of last resort for the nation. Its decisions are binding on all federal and state courts. The Supreme Court hears limited appeals from the lower federal courts and from the highest state courts where a federal question is presented. The Court has the authority, through judicial review, to strike down legislation that it deems unconstitutional. (In such cases legislators have only two recourses: they can either revise their statutes to conform with the Court's guidelines, or try to pass an amendment to the Constitution.)

WHAT IS A CAPITAL OFFENSE?

A capital case begins of course with the arrest of a person for a serious crime (nearly always, murder). The district attorney reviews the facts of the case and decides whether it meets the jurisdiction's definition of a capital crime. This means determining whether the murder is a first-degree murder (or equivalent) in which the offender acted with deliberate intent, rather than spontaneously (as in a "crime of passion"). The crime must also have one or more "aggravating circumstances" to raise it to the status of capital offense. Such circumstances are specified in state and federal statutes. Some typical aggravating circumstances include:

- The crime was particularly vile, atrocious, or cruel.
- There were multiple victims.
- The crime occurred during the commission of another felony.
- The victim was a police or correctional officer in the line of duty.
- The offender was previously convicted of a capital offense or violent crime.
- The offender directed an accomplice to commit the murder or committed the murder at the direction of another person.

The death penalty is imposed most often for murders committed during the course of another major felony. These homicides are usually termed felony-murders. In most states there is no need for the prosecution to prove intent on the part of the killer in a felony murder. The law assumes that persons who engage in serious felonies are responsible for the consequences of their actions and the dangerous situations they create. Defendants who kill, even accidentally, in the course of another felony may be found guilty of first-degree murder. It is only necessary to show that the offender intended to commit the original crime.

Introduction to Capital Punishment

Historically, many states held accomplices to a felony-murder to be equally liable for the crime, even if they did not participate in the actual homicide. In 1982, however, the Supreme Court, in *Enmund v. Florida*, prohibited states from sentencing to death accomplices to a felony-murder unless it was shown that the accomplices took part in the killing, intended that the killing occur, or were involved in the employment of lethal force. (The Court later broadened its rule to make a defendant who was intimately involved with the crime and who showed "reckless disregard" for the victim's life to be liable to capital punishment even if the defendant did not directly use force.)

A few states still have death penalty statutes for crimes not involving homicide, such as kidnapping and child rape. However, recent Supreme Court decisions linking the death penalty to offenses involving the death of the victim make it extremely unlikely anyone will ever be sentenced under these laws.

Federal law provides for the death penalty for murder under a variety of special circumstances, including air piracy (skyjacking), certain drug-related murders, and sexual assault against children.

THE ROLE OF THE JURY

Most defendants opt to have their case heard by a jury. During the jury selection process (called *voir dire*), prospective jurors will be asked their opinions on the death penalty. The courts have ruled that mere opposition to the death penalty is not sufficient for someone to be automatically excluded from the jury, but if a juror's opposition is strong enough that it might affect his or her ability to determine the defendant's guilt, the juror will be excluded.

If the defendant is convicted of a capital offense, the Supreme Court has decreed that there must be a separate hearing called the penalty phase. This is like a mini-trial in which the issue is not guilt or innocence, but whether the defendant is to be sentenced to death or to some lesser sanction (usually life in prison). As in the main trial, the prosecutor and defense counsel both make opening statements, introduce and examine witnesses, and make closing arguments. The prosecution will try to show the aggravating circumstances that justify imposing the ultimate penalty. These are similar to the circumstances that justify making a capital charge in the first place, but are usually presented in an attempt to show the defendant acted in a particularly cruel or depraved way. The defense counsel try to counter the aggravating circumstances by introducing mitigating circumstances, such as the defendant's youth, lack of previous criminal record, extreme emotional circumstances, or lack of direct involvement in the crime. (For more on statutory aggravating and mitigating circumstances, see Chapter 2, The Law of Capital Punishment.)

Assuming the jury imposes the death penalty (and, depending on the state, the judge approves the sentence), the postconviction appeals process begins. Capital punishment statutes provide for an automatic review of every death sentence by a state appeals court. If this court upholds the death penalty, the defendant still has two other possible avenues of appeal. The first is postconviction proceedings in the state court system. Normally, these appeals culminate in a ruling by the state's highest court. However, if federal questions of law are involved, the defendant has the right to petition the federal courts for review. Appeals based on issues of federal law have the potential to reach the Supreme Court, and this is how the major issues involving capital punishment are ultimately settled. This entire appeals process may, and almost invariably does, extend over a number of years, even with recent Supreme Court rulings that have cut down on the number of appeals allowed and the ways in which issues can be raised.

There are three other important elements of the criminal justice system as it pertains to capital punishment. In criminal trials, the government's case is presented by a prosecuting attorney. Prosecutors have a substantial amount of discretion in the performance of their duties. A criminal proceeding has a number of key decision points. These include what charges to bring, whether to plea bargain, and what sentence, if any, to offer a defendant in return for a guilty plea. The choices a prosecuting attorney makes in a potential capital trial have a direct impact on the likelihood of a person facing a possible death sentence.

The ability of the prosecutor to influence a capital proceeding is balanced, at least theoretically, by the defendant's right to legal representation. It is a basic tenet of American jurisprudence that each person accused of a crime is entitled to a defense counsel. The capabilities of the defense attorney can have a major bearing on the outcome of the trial.

Finally, there is the penal system. Prisons fulfill several obvious roles in the administration of capital punishment. The area in which prisoners are held pending their execution, commonly known as death row, has held a certain fascination in American culture and lore. Since the 1930s, executions in America have been carried out within the relative privacy of prison walls. Less readily apparent is the fact that the development of modern penal institutions has provided society a range of possible punishments for serious crimes. It would not be possible, for instance, to advocate mandatory life sentences in lieu of the death penalty if appropriate confinement facilities were not available.

Introduction to Capital Punishment

CRUEL AND UNUSUAL?

The debate over capital punishment for the last 35 years has been waged primarily in the judicial system. In a series of court cases extending from 1972 to about 1990 (with a few later refinements), the Supreme Court has effectively set the parameters of capital punishment in America today. Summaries of the most significant Supreme Court decisions are provided in Chapter 2. Presented here are the basic issues that have driven the legal struggle over the role of capital punishment in American society.

The most basic legal controversy centers on whether capital punishment is inherently constitutional. This issue raises an even more fundamental legal question. How is the constitutionality of any given law determined? Since the early 19th century, the Supreme Court has exercised a power of judicial review or what is in essence the authority to strike down statutes it deems unconstitutional. The Court has the final say as to whether a legal measure conforms to the Constitution. Two elements normally are necessary for the Supreme Court to declare a law unconstitutional. The first is a clear and convincing argument that the law violates a specific constitutional provision. Historically, the Court has been reluctant to rule against the expressed will of the legislative branch of government without a compelling reason to do so. Second, the constitutional provision must be applicable to the law in question.

Most of the constitutional challenges to the death penalty have been based on one or more of the first 10 amendments. When these amendments, the Bill of Rights, were added to the U.S. Constitution in 1791, it was with the understanding that they applied only to federal law. State laws were beyond their reach.

As legal challenges to capital punishment mounted in the 1960s, one of the first issues that had to be resolved was whether the Bill of Rights could appropriately be applied to state death penalty statutes. The answer was found in the Fourteenth Amendment. This amendment, which was passed in 1868 in the aftermath of the Civil War, stipulates that states shall not "deprive any person of life, liberty, or property, without due process of law." In the course of the 20th century, the Supreme Court gradually interpreted this due process clause as extending all the due process guarantees in the Constitution, the first 10 amendments included, to state laws. In other words, the Supreme Court was empowered to review state laws for adherence to the fundamental individual rights articulated in the Bill of Rights.

In 1972, in *Furman v. Georgia*, the Supreme Court did precisely this when it held that the nation's capital punishment laws, both federal and state, were in violation of the Eighth Amendment. The Court found that the arbitrary and capricious way in which the death penalty was administered constituted cruel and unusual punishment, which the amendment bans. The Court, however, did not rule that capital punishment itself was unconstitutional. Only the random and freakish employment of the death penalty, and not the sanction itself, was ruled constitutionally indefensible. Many states quickly revised their death penalty statutes to respond to the objections raised in the *Furman* decision. Four years later, in *Gregg v. Georgia*, the Court reinstated capital punishment, holding that the new death penalty statutes contained safeguards that would ensure the sanction's use in a rational and fair manner.

APPROPRIATE APPLICATION OF THE DEATH PENALTY

Since 1976, the Supreme Court has declined to reconsider the basic legality of capital punishment itself. Instead, the Court has concentrated on narrower (but still very important) constitutional questions: what crimes merit the death penalty, and which members of society, if any, are eligible to receive a death sentence.

The Supreme Court has emphasized that a punishment must be proportionate to the crime committed. In applying this standard to the death penalty, the Court has overturned capital punishment statutes that allowed the death penalty to be imposed for rape and kidnapping. The Court indicated that the death penalty was a disproportionate and excessive response to offenses that did not involve the death of the victim. In apparently restricting the death penalty to crimes involving homicide, the Court has raised doubts as to the constitutionality of capital punishment for offenses such as espionage and treason, or for some of the many capital crimes newly created by Congress during the 1990s. Whether the death penalty is disproportionate for all nonhomicidal crimes has yet to be litigated.

Another tenet of American jurisprudence that has guided the Supreme Court's thinking on the death penalty is the belief that punishment should be related to the culpability of the defendant. Within a legal context, culpability implies the ability to exercise and take responsibility for one's conduct. There is widespread consensus in American society that juveniles are not sufficiently mature or informed to be held fully accountable for their actions. However, a debate has been waged over the age at which a juvenile may be considered an adult for the purposes of a capital trial. In a series of controversial decisions on this issue, the Court effectively has set the age of 16 as the minimum age at which a person can be held responsible and executed for criminal offenses.

The Court likewise has ruled that it is unconstitutional to execute persons who are insane. The development of guidelines governing the execution of the mentally retarded has proven to be more difficult. The degree of mental retardation and its impact on a person's ability to act responsibly are difficult to measure. The Court has essentially held that if a mentally impaired person is unable to distinguish right from wrong and behave accordingly, then that individual is not subject to the death penalty.

The constitutionality of different methods of execution has also been litigated. The basic issue here is whether a method of execution is cruel enough or inflicts gratuitous pain to the extent it violates the Eighth Amendment ban on cruel and unusual punishment. In 1890 the Supreme Court decided the use of the newly invented electric chair was not cruel and unusual punishment. Interestingly, in 1925 the federal government substituted electrocution for hanging because it was viewed as more humane. The 1920s also saw several unsuccessful challenges to the introduction of the gas chamber. Proponents of lethal gas defended it as a swift and painless method of execution. More recently, inmates facing death by lethal injection sought unsuccessfully to block the procedure on the novel grounds that the Federal Drug Administration (FDA) had not approved the fatal drugs to be used.

The Supreme Court has consistently taken the position that a given method of execution is not unconstitutionally cruel if it does not involve torture, barbarism, or the infliction of unnecessary pain and suffering.

THE DEATH PENALTY AND RACE

One of the major roots to the movement beginning in the 1960s to challenge the death penalty in the courts was the civil rights movement. The question of race in capital sentencing came to a head in 1987 with the case of *McCleskey v. Kemp*. In its decision, the Supreme Court turned aside arguments that capital punishment in the United States was administered in a racially discriminatory manner in violation of the Fourteenth Amendment's requirement that the law be applied in a nondiscriminatory manner to all citizens. These arguments were based on statistical evidence that showed that blacks were significantly more likely than whites to receive the death penalty for similar crimes. (Although opponents suggested that the studies underplayed the importance of comparing crimes with similar aggravating factors and defendants with similar criminal records.)

The Court accepted the general accuracy of the information, but found that broad statistical studies were insufficient to prove racial discrimination in a given specific case. *McCleskey* raised a line of questioning that goes to the very core of the American criminal justice system. In its decision, the Supreme Court indicated that in order to establish that racism played a part in a person receiving a death sentence, it was necessary to prove actual discrimination in the case at hand. As several of the dissenting justices pointed out, that was much easier said than done. In their view, the wide discretion

31

provided prosecutors, judges, and juries frequently served to mask and give scope to the institutional racism that still infects the criminal justice process. How is it possible to prove that a certain prosecutor is more likely to offer a plea bargain agreement to a white defendant than to a black? The Court majority acknowledged this problem but suggested that short of changing the entire American system of justice, which was both unreasonable and undesirable, the best answer was to surround the administration of capital punishment with extensive procedural safeguards.

PROCEDURAL ISSUES

The net effect of the Supreme Court's major rulings on capital punishment has been twofold. It is clear that the death penalty, at least from a legal perspective, is here to stay. After affirming that capital punishment is itself constitutional, the Court has gone on to define more precisely the circumstances and conditions under which it may be imposed. The Court as it is currently constituted has shown no inclination to reverse this course. In dealing with the various broad constitutional challenges to the administration of the death penalty, the Court gradually removed the remaining legal obstacles to a full resumption of executions in the United States. It is generally agreed that there are few if any remaining legal arguments against the death penalty that will affect more than a relative handful of death row inmates.

In recent years, a great deal of the legal debate over capital punishment has centered on procedural questions. There are several reasons for this. First, and most importantly, has been a growing recognition throughout the criminal justice system that the death penalty is substantively different from other criminal sanctions. This has meant an enhanced focus on the procedural safeguards necessary to ensure that capital punishment is administered in a fair and appropriate way. Secondly, as broad or far-reaching constitutional challenges to the death penalty were whittled down following the reinstatement of the sanction in 1976, the only recourse left to defense attorneys was to challenge their clients' death sentences on technical or procedural grounds.

The Supreme Court has long taken the position that death is different from other punishments. The irrevocable nature of the death penalty has caused the Court to pay particular attention to procedural safeguards in capital cases. As early as 1932, the Court ruled that an indigent defendant had the right to a lawyer in a capital trial—a right only later emphasized as belonging to criminal defendants in all cases. Since the reinstatement of the death penalty in 1976, the Court has insisted on clear and objective standards to guide the administration of capital punishment.

Introduction to Capital Punishment

In response to Supreme Court rulings, death penalty statutes across the nation now share several features. They all require a bifurcated, or split, trial proceeding. The bifurcated trial, as discussed earlier in this chapter, separates the determination of guilt or innocence from the decision as to what penalty will be imposed. This is done to ensure a convicted defendant has an opportunity to present mitigating evidence prior to sentencing. Death penalty statutes also require an automatic review of every death sentence by an appeals court.

The Court has effectively barred mandatory capital punishment laws, holding that automatic death sentences for certain crimes do not allow for individualized consideration of all the circumstances involved in a particular case. This same reasoning has led the Court to maintain that trial courts must permit defendants to introduce a wide range of evidence concerning mitigating factors on their behalf.

Much contention has centered around the kinds of evidence the prosecution in a capital case should be allowed to introduce to argue for the appropriateness of the death penalty and to counteract any mitigating factors. Generally, the Court has required that aggravating factors introduced by the prosecution be more narrowly defined and more directly relevant to the question of sentencing. In addition, if the prosecution tries to show that a defendant is particularly violent and likely to be dangerous in the future, the Court requires that the jury also be informed of any state law that would prohibit releasing the defendant on parole—that is, that a true "life without parole" sentence is available.

Another kind of prosecution evidence, victim impact statements that seek to show the extent of the harm done by a murder to the victim's relatives, received less consistent treatment by the Court. In *Booth v. Maryland* (1987), a 5-4 majority ruled that victim impact statements were unconstitutional because a jury must make an "individualized determination" based on the offender's particular circumstances, not those of the victim. Further, the idea that the killing of victims who were well loved and considered to be particular assets to the community should be punished more harshly than the killing of persons considered to be more marginal in society was repugnant to the majority.

However, in the 1991 case of *Payne v. Tennessee*, a 6-3 majority of the Court reversed its earlier finding. The justices now looked at the broad principle that crimes that cause more harm are typically punished more severely (a theft of $50 may be a petty theft, while a theft of $50,000 is grand larceny). In this view, the victim impact statement is simply another piece of evidence that the jury can consider when weighing the seriousness of the offense against the mitigating factors.

The most contentious procedural issue today concerns the misuse of the appeals process. The sheer volume of death penalty appeals threatens to overwhelm the criminal justice system. This volume can partly be attributed to the steady growth in the size of the death row population. It is also due to a deliberate strategy on the part of many opponents of capital punishment. It is their hope that by paralyzing the appeals courts with an excess of legal actions, the nation will eventually conclude capital punishment is unworkable. Many observers have seen a fundamental contradiction between the Court's insistence on the one hand that jurors and judges have the broad discretion they need in order to give each defendant individualized consideration and on the other hand that patterns of capital sentencing be rational and consistent rather than arbitrary and capricious.

In 1994, in his dissent in the case of *Callins v. Collins*, Supreme Court Justice Harry Blackmun declared that

> *From this day forward, I no longer shall tinker with the machinery of death. For more than 20 years I have endeavored . . . along with a majority of this Court, to develop procedural and substantive rules that would lend more than the mere appearance of fairness to the death penalty endeavor. Rather than continue to coddle the Court's delusion that the desired level of fairness has been achieved and the need for regulation eviscerated, I feel morally and intellectually obligated simply to concede that the death penalty experiment has failed. It is virtually self-evident to me now that no combination of procedural rules or substantive regulations ever can save the death penalty from its inherent constitutional deficiencies.*[3]

The majority of the Court however, has not agreed that the search for a truly fair capital justice system is hopeless. Throughout the 1990s executions continued at an increasing rate. In its recent procedural decisions, the Court has narrowed the circumstances under which defendants can file habeas corpus petitions, the appeal enshrined in the common law to require that authorities "bring forth the body" of a prisoner so that a judge can inquire into a possible miscarriage of justice. Such litigation raises one of the most fundamental questions of all: can a person be executed if convincing evidence of his or her innocence emerges after conviction?

In the 1993 case of *Herrera v. Collins*, the Supreme Court ruled by a 7-3 majority that it was constitutional to execute the defendant without the appeals court having to reopen the question of guilt or innocence. In his majority opinion, Chief Justice Rehnquist pointed out that while a defendant starts the legal process with a "presumption of innocence," this presumption disappears after conviction. Appeals courts exist, he said, "to ensure that individuals are not imprisoned in violation of the Constitution—not to correct errors of fact." No doubt practical considerations also played a role in the decision. After all, if defendants had a right to raise endless appeals based on supposed new evidence of innocence, they could postpone their execution indefinitely as each appeal received due consideration.

However, executing someone after being confronted by convincing evidence of his or her innocence is repugnant to most people. Speaking for the minority, Justice Blackmun insisted that

> *The Eighth Amendment prohibits "cruel and unusual punishments." This proscription is not static but rather reflects evolving standards of decency. I think it is crystal clear that the execution of an innocent person is "at odds with contemporary standards of fairness and decency." . . . [T]he protection of the Eighth Amendment does not end once a defendant has been validly convicted and sentenced.*[4]

The upshot of this decision and those that followed is that there must be a constitutional error, not just new evidence before an appeal will be considered. Further, the Court set a high standard for overturning a conviction due to an error that prevented consideration of evidence of innocence. The evidence must be so convincing that "no reasonable juror" would have voted to convict if the evidence had been presented to the jury.

THE FUTURE OF CAPITAL PUNISHMENT

The future of capital punishment in the 21st century will depend not only on court decisions but more fundamentally on popular opinion, the political process, and possibly, international trends in criminal justice.

PUBLIC ATTITUDES

In general, Americans have overwhelmingly approved of capital punishment. This support, which opponents of the death penalty readily grant, is reflected in the fact that 38, or roughly three-quarters, of the states currently have death penalty statutes. These laws have all been enacted since 1973. In most instances, capital punishment bills have been passed by the state legislatures. (In 1995, New York became the 38th state to impose capital punishment when Governor George Pataki signed death penalty legislation that had been vetoed year after year by his more liberal predecessors.) In the five states that held public referenda on the death penalty, four favored capital punishment by a substantial margin. The only exception was Kansas, where voters rejected a reimposition of the death penalty in 1987.

Capital Punishment

Public opinion polls consistently document the high levels of support for capital punishment. This support has increased significantly over the past 35 years. In the mid-1960s, the population was almost evenly divided between those who favored and those who opposed the death penalty for murder. By the mid-1970s, Americans advocated the death penalty for murder by a margin of two to one. In 1985, the percentage had risen to 75 percent, or three to one. At the close of the century, this margin seems to be holding steady. Support for the death penalty remains at its highest point since formal studies on American attitudes about capital punishment were first conducted prior to World War II.

Attitudes about capital punishment are based on individuals' values, convictions, and, to a lesser degree, experiences and perceptions. The data about the relationship between demographic factors and a given position on the death penalty are imprecise. In very general terms, men support the death penalty more than women do, and support for the death penalty increases along with income up to about $60,000, then begins to decline. The region of the country, size of the community, educational level, and type of occupation seem to have little correlation with attitudes toward the death penalty. However, while whites strongly favor the death penalty, blacks and Hispanics are more divided on this issue, favoring capital punishment by about 60 percent to 40 percent. This is perhaps a result of the continuing public attention to racial disparities in death sentencing patterns. (For more information, see Appendix B, Polls and Surveys.)

Social scientists are wary of generalizations about why Americans support capital punishment. The most commonly advanced theory is that the average citizen is deeply concerned about the steady rise in the nation's crime rate. Sensational crimes are extensively covered in the media (including, in recent years, mass shootings in schools and churches, vicious hate crimes, and the Oklahoma City bombing). Many individuals have had a direct experience with less serious but still frightening violent crimes such as robbery or muggings. Support for the death penalty is seen as an expression of the desire to deal firmly with the violence and lawlessness in American society.

As the new century begins, it will be interesting to see whether current trends support this theory. Since the mid-1990s, the crime rate (and the murder rate in particular) have begun to decline. The economy, another source of social anxiety, has undergone a remarkable stretch of sustained growth. Will these trends lead to a decline in support for the death penalty, or will they be offset by other factors, such as the "tabloidization" of the media where sensational crimes are covered incessantly?

Opponents of capital punishment cite what is known as the "Marshall hypothesis." Supreme Court Justice Thurgood Marshall has argued that people who favor the death penalty are frequently uninformed about the actual nature and use of the sanction in America. It is Marshall's contention, shared by many abolitionists, that as the public becomes more educated about the issue, the general attitude will change from support to opposition. It is difficult to evaluate this hypothesis, but polling does suggest that awareness of alternatives reduces support for the death penalty. When death penalty supporters are offered the alternative of life without parole in various surveys, 20–40 percent of them say they would not continue to support the death penalty (the addition of victim restitution further erodes support for the death penalty). Finally, according to a report by the Death Penalty Information Center, 58 percent of the people polled said that the possibility of innocent persons being executed raised doubts about the death penalty.[5]

THE DEATH PENALTY IN POLITICS

Capital punishment first became a national political issue in the 1960 presidential campaign. The movement to spare California death row inmate Caryl Chessman had raised the level of public discussion on the issue. Of the major candidates canvassed on the subject during the primary season, only Senator Hubert H. Humphrey (D-Minn.) went on record as opposing the death penalty.

President Lyndon B. Johnson's administration became the first, and only, presidential administration to recommend ending the death penalty for federal crimes. Attorney General Ramsey Clark, in testimony before Congress, called on the United States to join the growing worldwide trend toward abandonment of the sanction. All of the presidential administrations since, however, have supported capital punishment.

Most political figures and public officeholders endorse capital punishment. The relatively few public figures who oppose the death penalty are normally found on the more liberal end of the political spectrum while those who are more conservative are often its staunchest advocates. Political analysts believe that when the death penalty becomes an issue in a campaign, the candidate favoring capital punishment almost inevitably will benefit.

Most often, the death penalty has not been a dominant issue in major campaigns. The 1988 presidential race was an exception. Then vice president George Bush, the Republican nominee, campaigned extensively on his advocacy of the death penalty for the killers of law enforcement officers. He contrasted his position with the strong abolitionist stance of his Democratic opponent, Massachusetts governor Michael S. Dukakis. When Dukakis was asked during a presidential debate whether he would favor capital punishment if his wife were raped and murdered, his answer sounded weak and unconvincing to many viewers. Political experts agree that Bush's active support of capital punishment contributed to his eventual victory, as did his use of ads featuring Willie Horton, a furloughed convict who committed beatings and rapes while outside the prison.

State legislatures have been the primary battlefield in the political fight over capital punishment. State legislators, who are responsible for fashioning the criminal codes that address most homicide offenses, are more immediately and directly affected by the views of their constituents on capital punishment. The most intense political debate over the death penalty took place in New York during the 1980s and early 1990s. For eight years, Governor Mario Cuomo, a staunch liberal Democrat, regularly used his veto pen to turn back death penalty legislation. In 1994, however, Republican George Pataki won the governor's seat, and in 1995 he signed a bill restoring capital punishment in New York, resulting in a major setback for the abolitionist cause.

INTERNATIONAL PERSPECTIVES

The trend worldwide among developed nations is toward a gradual decrease in the use of the death penalty. The United Nations has become increasingly active on the issue of capital punishment. Although the organization has not taken a formal abolitionist position, many studies, reports, and resolutions have called on member nations to progressively restrict the number of offenses for which the death penalty may be imposed. In 1971 the General Assembly adopted a resolution that articulated an ultimate goal of eliminating capital punishment in all countries. In 1997 the U.N. Commission on Human Rights voted to call upon member countries to abolish their death penalty. (The United States was among the eight nations voting in opposition.)

This worldwide abolitionist effort seems to have made considerable progress in the past 30 years. As of 1997, 58 countries had no penalties of capital punishment for any crime, while 26 countries still had laws on the books but had not executed anyone for the past 10 years. Ninety-four countries continue to actively use capital punishment. According to Amnesty International (the international human rights organization), the four most prolific users of the death penalty in 1996 were China (4,367 executions), the Ukraine (167), the Russian Federation (140), and Iran (110). The United States executed 45 prisoners that same year.

The United States is now the only Western nation that routinely practices capital punishment. In recent years, Amnesty International thus focused much of its abolition effort on ending the death penalty in the United States.

Introduction to Capital Punishment

Many Americans cherish what they consider to be a distinctively American approach to individual liberty and responsibility. To some extent the capital punishment parallels the debate over gun control. Conservatives believe in giving the individual the means to kill another person, but hold the individual accountable with his or her life for the misuses of that liberty. Liberals take a more utilitarian approach and argue for restricting both the state's and the individual's capacity to kill.

While there are strong beliefs on both sides of the capital punishment debate, factors such as the decline in the crime rate, the publicity about mistaken convictions, and the growing cost of the criminal justice system may ultimately favor the abolitionist cause, but the issue is volatile and outcomes are very difficult to predict. An outbreak of terrorism, urban unrest, or economic chaos could easily reverse any trend toward abolition.

Barring a drastic change in the composition of the Supreme Court, it is unlikely that the legal shape of the capital punishment system will radically change again the way it did between 1972 and 1976. This means that any changes are likely to be gradual and will take place on a state-by-state basis.

---

[1] Bureau of Criminal Justice Statistics, Table 6.80, *Sourcebook of Bureau of Criminal Justice Statistics, 1998.* Available online. URL: http://www.albany.edu/sourcebook/1995/pdf/t680.pdf.

[2] Justice William O. Douglas, majority opinion, *Furman v. Georgia*, 408 U.S. 238 (1972).

[3] *Callins v. Collins*, 510 U.S. 1141, p. 1,128–1,130 (1994).

[4] *Herrera v. Collins*, 113 U.S. 853 (1993).

[5] Alan Berlow. "The Wrong Man." *Atlantic Monthly*, November 1999. Available online. URL: http://www.theatlantic.com/issues/99nov/9911wrongman.htm. Also see Richard Dieter. "Sentencing for Life: Americans Embrace Alternatives to the Death Penalty." Death Penalty Information Center. Available online. URL: http://www.essential.org/dpic/dpic.r07.html.

CHAPTER 2

THE LAW OF CAPITAL PUNISHMENT

This chapter begins by summarizing the main factors that are considered in deciding to impose the death penalty. This is followed by a summary of federal offenses for which the death penalty can be imposed. (This list was greatly expanded by Congress in the 1994 Omnibus Crime Bill.) Next comes a summary of the status of capital punishment in the 38 states that currently have the death penalty. (See Chapter 6, How to Research Capital Punishment, to learn how to find the latest information and statistics on capital punishment.) The remainder of the chapter presents summaries of the key Supreme Court decisions that have provided the guidelines that have shaped the administration of capital punishment during the past 30 years.

FACTORS IN IMPOSING THE DEATH PENALTY

One of the implications of the Supreme Court's decision in *Furman v. Georgia* (1972) was that if a procedure for capital sentencing was not unconstitutionally "arbitrary and capricious," it had to be systematic in its protection of the rights of the defendant. In practice, the states tried to meet this requirement by establishing a "bifurcated" procedure in capital trials. In this scheme, if the defendant is convicted of a capital offense during the "guilt phase" (the main trial), a separate hearing called the sentencing phase is then held. During this second "mini-trial" the prosecution and defense counsel first give opening statements (although the defense can reserve its statement until after the prosecution presents its evidence). Following the opening statements is the "case-in-chief," in which first the prosecution and then the defense present their witnesses and evidence. As in the main trial, each side has the right to cross-examine opposing witnesses.

AGGRAVATING AND MITIGATING FACTORS

The purpose of the witnesses and evidence presented during the penalty phase is to establish aggravating and mitigating factors (or circumstances) for the "factfinder" to consider in deciding whether to impose a death sentence or a sentence of life in prison. (The factfinder is usually a jury, but a judge or panel of judges perform this function in some states.)

The prosecution tries to demonstrate the existence of one or more aggravating factors that allow and justify imposition of the ultimate penalty of death. Aggravating factors can involve the circumstances of the offense, the status of the victim, or the attitude or state of mind of the offender. Each state's penal code specifies the aggravating factors that can be used. For example, the fact that a murder was committed in the course of another major felony such as robbery or rape is nearly always considered an aggravating circumstance.

The defense, in turn, tries to offer mitigating factors that, while not absolving the convicted defendant of culpability for the crime, reduce his or her culpability to the point where death is not an appropriate sanction. For example, a defendant's suffering from a serious mental or emotional disorder (although short of legal insanity) can be considered a mitigating circumstance in virtually all jurisdictions.

The justification for considering mitigating factors was expressed by Supreme Court Justice Sandra Day O'Connor in her concurring opinion in *California v. Brown* (1987), when she noted that

evidence about the defendant's background and character is relevant because of the belief, long held by this society, that defendants who commit criminal acts that are attributable to a disadvantaged background, or to emotional and mental problems, may be less culpable than defendants that have no such excuse. The sentence imposed at the penalty stage should reflect a reasoned moral response to the defendant's background, character, and crime.

WEIGHING THE FACTORS

After closing statements the jury or judge must determine whether any aggravating or mitigating factors have been established by the evidence and testimony presented. Most states require that at least one aggravating circumstance must be proven beyond a reasonable doubt in order for the jury to consider imposing the death penalty. For mitigating factors, however, the standard in 12 states and the federal system is simply that "the preponderance of the evidence" show the existence of a mitigating circumstance. The remaining states have no explicit standard.

Once aggravating and mitigating circumstances have been established, the jury or judge must weigh them in order to determine the appropriate sentence. This is not a simple process of counting to see whether there are more aggravating than mitigating circumstances, but rather, a consideration of how credible, important, substantial, or persuasive the factors on each side are in their totality. The Supreme Court has left it to the states to determine exactly how this is to be done. In eight states and the federal system, a death sentence is indicated if the aggravating circumstances outweigh the mitigating circumstances. (The burden of proof is on the prosecutor, but there is no specific standard of proof, just the judgment of the jury or judge.) In 12 states a death sentence is to be imposed unless the mitigating factors outweigh the aggravating factors. The burden of proof is thus on the defense, although again, there is no specific standard of proof.

The majority of states require that the factfinder impose a death sentence if the aggravating factors outweigh the mitigating ones. However, a considerable number of states allow for discretion such that the death penalty can be rejected even if the weighing process would indicate its appropriateness.

STATUTORY AGGRAVATING CIRCUMSTANCES

The following statutory aggravating circumstances have been enacted by the legislatures of one or more states. In order for a death sentence to be imposed, the penalty phase factfinder must find that one or more of these circumstances apply to the murder in question.

These "aggravators" are divided into three categories: those relating to the nature or circumstances of the offense, those relating to the identity of the victim, and miscellaneous other factors.

Nature or Circumstances of Offense

arson   intentional burning of an occupied dwelling, commercial building, vehicle, or other property

battery, aggravated   beating that causes serious injury to the victim

burglary   breaking and entering with intent to commit a felony (usually theft)

carjacking   forcibly taking a vehicle from its owner or possessor

drug trafficking   buying or selling of narcotics, often as part of a conspiracy

escape   from the custody of a law enforcement officer or correctional facility

hijacking   forcibly seizing control of a car, bus, aircraft, ship, or train (sometimes specifically called carjacking, bus hijacking, plane hijacking, ship hijacking, or train hijacking)

kidnapping   unlawful seizing or holding of a person, often for ransom

robbery   use of force or threat of force to commit larceny (theft)

sexual offenses   such as rape, statutory rape, compelled anal or oral intercourse, sodomy, and deviant sexual behavior with a minor

train wrecking   damaging or destroying railway equipment or deliberately causing a railroad accident

Note that the general crimes of arson, burglary, kidnapping, rape, and robbery are considered aggravating offenses in the majority of death penalty states. The more esoteric offenses such as carjacking are considered aggravators in only a few states at this time.

IDENTITY OF VICTIM

elected official	victim was an elected state or local official
firefighter	victim was a firefighter or paramedic
handicapped person	victim had a physical or mental disability
hate crime	victim was targeted because of race, religion, ethnicity, or, in some states, sexual orientation
informant	victim was a police informant killed in connection with information
judge	victim was a judge or magistrate
juror	victim was a juror killed in connection with a case
law enforcement officer	victim was a police or correctional officer
parole or probation officer	victim was a parole or probation officer
pregnant woman	victim was pregnant
prosecutor	victim was a prosecutor killed in connection with a case
witness	victim was killed for being witness or potential witness to a crime
youth victim	victim was a youth (age varies by state but is generally considered 11 years of age or younger)

Note that murder of law enforcement officers, firefighters, witnesses, prosecutors, and judges is an aggravating circumstance in a majority or substantial minority of states. Among the other victim characteristics, age is the most common aggravator.

OTHER

assault weapon	use of automatic (or certain semiautomatic) firearm
authorized release from custody	defendant on work-release, leave, etc. from prison
disrupting government function	when resulting in death
drive-by shooting	(sometimes specified as gang-related)
explosives	used in commission of offense
great risk to others	defendant should have realized action caused extreme danger
in custody	defendant already in custody at time of offense
lying-in-wait	attacked from ambush or hiding
multiple homicides	mass murder or serial killing
ordered killing	committed upon the order of another person
parole or probation	defendant on parole or probation at time of offense
pecuniary (monetary) gain	murder motivated by desire for money
prior felony or homicide	defendant has serious prior conviction
torture	defendant inflicted great pain or suffering on victim
unlawfully at liberty	defendant failed to return from authorized release

STATUTORY MITIGATING CIRCUMSTANCES

Mitigating circumstances authorized by one or more states include the following. Note that a mitigating circumstance is considered by the penalty factfinder only if deemed relevant and if evidence of its existence is offered in court. The Supreme Court has required that the factfinder consider a wide range of relevant mitigating evidence before imposing sentence.

age   usually applies to defendants under 18 or over 75 years old

another proximate cause   a factor other than defendant's action had a direct role in causing the victim's death

codefendant spared death penalty   equally culpable codefendant was not sentenced to death

cooperation with authorities   defendant cooperated with authorities in investigating this offense or another one

extreme duress   defendant subject to extreme force or domination by another person

extreme mental or emotional disturbance   defendant is not retarded or insane, but is under the influence of an extreme, temporary mental state or emotion such as anger

impaired capacity   substantial mental impairment, due to mental disease or defect sufficient to prevent defendant from appreciating the wrongfulness of conduct or from conforming conduct to the law; some jurisdictions include impairment brought about by alcohol or drug intoxication

mentally retarded   not insane, but substantially limited in mental capacity

minor participation   defendant played little role in the actual killing

moral justification   defendant believed killing was morally justified

no future threat   defendant unlikely to commit another murder if given life in prison

no reasonable forseeability   defendant could not reasonably foresee that the conduct would cause harm

no significant prior criminal history   defendant does not have a conviction for a serious crime

traumatic-stress syndrome   defendant suffers from mental disorientation caused by extreme stress or abuse; can be mitigating if trauma had been previously caused to the defendant by the victim or through wartime service

victim's consent   victim consented to being killed or to participating in activity that led to his or her death

FEDERAL CAPITAL OFFENSES

The following federal crimes are punishable by death. Citations in parentheses refer to the United States Code. (Many of these provisions were added by Congress as part of the 1994 Omnibus Crime Bill.) In all cases except treason and espionage, the activity must involve murder or the causing

Capital Punishment

of death. Note that this summary is adapted from the Bureau of Justice Statistics's report *Capital Punishment 1997*.

Provisions are divided into three categories: those relating to the status of the victim, those involving the status of the offender, and those involving the nature of the criminal offense itself.

VICTIM STATUS

children, molestation of, murder related to (18 U.S.C. § 2245)
children, sexual exploitation of, murder related to (18 U.S.C. § 2251)
court officer or juror, murder of (18 U.S.C. § 1503)
federal judge or law enforcement official, murder of (18 U.S.C. § 1114)
foreign official, murder of (18 U.S.C. § 1116)
law enforcement official, family member, retaliation murder (18 U.S.C. § 115(b)(3) by cross-reference to 18 U.S.C. § 1111)
law enforcement official, state or local, or other person aiding federal investigation, murder of (18 U.S.C. § 1121)
law enforcement official, state or local, murder of, related to continuing criminal enterprise (21 U.S.C. § 848(e))
member of Congress, important executive official, or Supreme Court Justice, murder of (18 U.S.C. § 351 by cross-reference to 18 U.S.C. § 1111)
president or vice president, assassination of, or kidnapping resulting in death of, (18 U.S.C. § 1751 by cross-reference to 18 U.S.C. § 1111)
U.S. national, murder of in foreign country (18 U.S.C. § 1119)
U.S. national, murder of in foreign country, related to terrorism (18 U.S.C. § 2332)
witness, victim, or informant, murder to prevent testimony by, (18 U.S.C. § 1512)

DEFENDANT STATUS

federal prisoner, murder by (18 U.S.C. § 1118)
federal prisoner, escaped and sentenced to life, murder by (18 U.S.C. § 1120)

STATUS OF ACTIVITY

aircraft hijacking, death resulting from (49 U.S.C. §§ 1472–1473)
aircraft, motor vehicles, or related facilities, destruction of, resulting in death (18 U.S.C. §§ 32–34)
airport, international, killing in (18 U.S.C. § 37)

aliens, smuggling of, murder related to (8 U.S.C. § 1342)

bank robbery, murder or kidnapping related to (18 U.S.C. § 2113)

carjacking, murder related to (18 U.S.C. § 2119)

civil rights offenses, resulting in death (18 U.S.C. §§ 241–242, 245, 247)

commerce, foreign or domestic, destruction of property in, resulting in death (18 U.S.C. § 844 (i))

continuing criminal enterprise, murder related to (21 U.S.C. § 848 (e))

drug-related drive-by shooting, murder committed during (18 U.S.C. § 36)

espionage (18 U.S.C. § 794)

explosives, transportation of, death resulting from (18 U.S.C. § 844 (d))

federal government facility, murder committed in (18 U.S.C. § 930)

firearm, use of during violent or drug-trafficking crime, murder committed during (18 U.S.C. § 924 (i))

first-degree murder, involving federal jurisdiction (18 U.S.C. § 1111)

genocide (18 U.S.C. § 1091)

government property, destruction of, resulting in death (18 U.S.C. § 844 (f))

hire, murder for (18 U.S.C. § 1958)

hostage-taking, murder during (18 U.S.C. § 1203)

injurious articles, mailing of with intent to kill or resulting in death (18 U.S.C. § 1716)

kidnapping, murder during (18 U.S.C. § 1201)

maritime platform, murder committed during offense relating to (18 U.S.C. § 2281)

maritime navigation, murder committed during offense relating to (18 U.S.C. § 2280)

racketeering offense, murder during (18 U.S.C. § 1959)

rape, murder related to (18 U.S.C. § 2245)

torture, murder involving (18 U.S.C. § 2340)

treason (18 U.S.C. § 2381)

train, willful wrecking of, resulting in death (18 U.S.C. § 1992)

weapon of mass destruction, murder by use of (18 U.S.C. § 2332a)

SUMMARY OF CAPITAL PUNISHMENT BY STATE

The following section summarizes information about capital punishment for each of the 38 states that have the death penalty. Each entry consists of the following:

- offenses for which the state can ask for the death penalty: "First-degree murder" generally means premeditated or deliberated murder; "felony murder" means murder committed in the course of another felony. References to "aggravating factors" or "aggravating circumstances" refer to one or more of the aggravating circumstances discussed earlier. Some factors, such as killing a police officer, are recognized in most states, while others, such as an incarcerated person killing a fellow inmate, are found in only a few states. Note that while some states don't specify first-degree murder, in practice, the offense must generally meet the standards for first-degree murder.

- minimum age at which a person can commit a crime eligible for the death penalty (the Supreme Court in *Thompson v. Oklahoma* ruled it cannot be younger than sixteen)

- whether the state forbids execution of persons who are sufficiently mentally disabled (definition varies with state)

- whether the state also has life without parole (this is included because life without parole is frequently considered an alternative to capital punishment)

- whether the final decision is made by the jury or a judge

- the state's method of execution (A few states offer alternative methods.)

Note that this material is drawn from information supplied by the Bureau of Justice Statistics's *Capital Punishment 1997*, the Death Penalty Information Center, and other sources.

ALABAMA

Capital offenses: intentional murder with one of 18 aggravating factors
Minimum age: 16
Mentally disabled: no
Life without parole: yes
Who decides: judge can override jury's recommendation
Method of execution: electrocution

ARIZONA

Capital offenses: first-degree murder with at least one of 10 aggravating factors

Minimum age: 16
Mentally disabled: no
Life without parole: yes
Who decides: judge
Method of execution: lethal injection; persons sentenced before 11/15/92 can choose lethal gas instead

ARKANSAS

Capital offenses: capital murder with at least one of nine aggravating circumstances; treason
Minimum age: 16
Mentally disabled: yes
Life without parole: yes

Who decides: jury
Method of execution: lethal injection; persons whose offense was committed before 7/4/83 may choose electrocution instead

CALIFORNIA

Capital offenses: first-degree murder with special circumstances; perjury causing execution; train-wrecking; treason
Minimum age: 18
Mentally disabled: no
Life without parole: yes
Who decides: jury
Method of execution: lethal injection unless inmate chooses lethal gas (subject to possible review by U.S. Supreme Court in wake of *Fierro v. Gomez*)

COLORADO

Capital offenses: first-degree murder with at least one of 13 aggravating factors; treason
Minimum age: 18
Mentally disabled: yes
Life without parole: yes
Who decides: panel of three judges
Method of execution: lethal injection

CONNECTICUT

Capital offenses: capital felony with nine categories of aggravated homicide
Minimum age: 18
Mentally disabled: no
Life without parole: yes

DELAWARE

Capital offenses: first-degree murder with aggravating circumstances
Minimum age: 16
Mentally disabled: no
Life without parole: yes
Who decides: judge may overrule jury's recommendation
Method of execution: lethal injection; persons who committed the offense before 6/13/86 may choose hanging instead

FLORIDA

Capital offenses: first-degree murder; felony murder; capital drug-trafficking
Minimum age: 17
Mentally disabled: no
Life without parole: yes
Who decides: judge may overrule jury's recommendation
Method of execution: electrocution; lethal injection to be used if electric chair found unconstitutional

GEORGIA

Capital offenses: murder; kidnapping with bodily injury or ransom where the victim dies; aircraft hijacking; treason
Minimum age: 17
Mentally disabled: yes
Life without parole: yes

Who decides: jury
Method of execution: electrocution

IDAHO

Capital offenses: first-degree murder; aggravated kidnapping
Minimum age: 16
Mentally disabled: no
Life without parole: yes
Who decides: judge
Method of execution: lethal injection or firing squad selected by the director of the Department of Corrections; firing squad will be used if lethal injection is "impractical"

ILLINOIS

Capital offenses: first-degree murder with one of 15 aggravating circumstances
Minimum age: 18
Mentally disabled: no
Life without parole: yes
Who decides: jury
Method of execution: lethal injection

INDIANA

Capital offenses: murder with one of 15 aggravating circumstances
Minimum age: 16
Mentally disabled: yes
Life without parole: yes
Who decides: judge may override jury's recommendation
Method of execution: lethal injection

KANSAS

Capital offenses: capital murder with one of seven aggravating circumstances
Minimum age: 18
Mentally disabled: yes
Life without parole: no, except if governor commutes a death sentence
Who decides: jury
Method of execution: lethal injection

KENTUCKY

Capital offenses: murder with aggravating factors; kidnapping with aggravated factors
Minimum age: 16
Mentally disabled: yes
Life without parole: yes
Who decides: jury
Method of execution: choice between lethal injection and electrocution; persons sentenced after 3/31/98 will receive lethal injection

LOUISIANA

Capital offenses: first-degree murder; aggravated rape of victim under age 12; treason
Minimum age: 16
Mentally disabled: no
Life without parole: yes
Who decides: jury
Method of execution: lethal injection

MARYLAND

Capital offenses: first-degree murder either premeditated or during commission of a felony
Minimum age: 18
Mentally disabled: yes
Life without parole: yes
Who decides: jury
Method of execution: lethal injection; persons whose offenses occurred before 3/25/94 may choose lethal gas instead

MISSISSIPPI

Capital offenses: capital murder; capital rape; aircraft piracy
Minimum age: 16
Mentally disabled: no
Life without parole: yes
Who decides: jury
Method of execution: lethal injection

MISSOURI

Capital offenses: first-degree murder
Minimum age: 16
Mentally disabled: no
Life without parole: yes
Who decides: jury, but judge decides if jury is deadlocked
Method of execution: lethal injection or lethal gas

MONTANA

Capital offenses: capital murder with one of nine aggravating circumstances; rape with serious bodily injury (second conviction)
Minimum age: 16
Mentally disabled: no
Life without parole: yes
Who decides: judge
Method of execution: lethal injection (hanging eliminated March 1997)

NEBRASKA

Capital offenses: first-degree murder with a finding of at least one statutorily defined aggravating circumstance
Minimum age: 18
Mentally disabled: yes
Life without parole: yes
Who decides: panel of judges
Method of execution: electrocution

NEVADA

Capital offenses: first-degree murder with one of 10 aggravating circumstances
Minimum age: 16
Mentally disabled: no
Life without parole: yes
Who decides: jury
Method of execution: lethal injection

NEW HAMPSHIRE

Capital offenses: capital murder
Minimum age: 17
Mentally disabled: no
Life without parole: yes
Who decides: jury
Method of execution: lethal injection; lethal gas if lethal injection cannot be given

NEW JERSEY

Capital offenses: purposeful or knowing murder by one's own conduct; contract murder; solicitation by command or threat in furtherance of a narcotics conspiracy
Minimum age: 18
Mentally disabled: no
Life without parole: no
Who decides: jury
Method of execution: lethal injection

NEW MEXICO

Capital offenses: first-degree murder
Minimum age: 18
Mentally disabled: yes
Life without parole: no
Who decides: jury
Method of execution: lethal injection

NEW YORK

Capital offenses: first-degree murder with one of 10 aggravating factors
Minimum age: 18
Mentally disabled: yes, except for murder by a prisoner
Life without parole: yes
Who decides: jury
Method of execution: lethal injection

NORTH CAROLINA

Capital offenses: first-degree murder
Minimum age: 17

Mentally disabled: no
Life without parole: yes
Who decides: jury
Method of execution: lethal injection

OHIO

Capital offenses: aggravated murder with at least one of eight aggravating circumstances
Minimum age: 18
Mentally disabled: no
Life without parole: yes
Who decides: jury
Method of execution: inmate's choice of lethal injection or electrocution; electrocution will be used if inmate fails to choose a method

OKLAHOMA

Capital offenses: first-degree murder with at least one of eight aggravating circumstances
Minimum age: 16
Mentally disabled: no
Life without parole: yes
Who decides: jury
Method of execution: lethal injection; electrocution if lethal injection is found unconstitutional; firing squad if electrocution is held unconstitutional

OREGON

Capital offenses: aggravated murder
Minimum age: 18
Mentally disabled: no

Life without parole: yes
Who decides: jury
Method of execution: lethal injection

PENNSYLVANIA

Capital offenses: first-degree murder with one of 17 aggravating circumstances
Minimum age: 16
Mentally disabled: no
Life without parole: yes
Who decides: jury
Method of execution: lethal injection

SOUTH CAROLINA

Capital offenses: murder with one of 10 aggravating circumstances
Minimum age: 16
Mentally disabled: no, but mental disability can be considered as a mitigating factor
Life without parole: yes, for certain repeat offenders
Who decides: jury
Method of execution: lethal injection or electrocution

SOUTH DAKOTA

Capital offenses: first-degree murder with one of 10 aggravating circumstances
Minimum age: 16
Mentally disabled: no
Life without parole: yes
Who decides: jury
Method of execution: lethal injection

TENNESSEE

Capital offenses: first-degree murder
Minimum age: 18
Mentally disabled: yes
Life without parole: yes
Who decides: jury
Method of execution: lethal injection for persons sentenced after 1/1/99; persons sentenced prior to that date can choose electrocution instead

TEXAS

Capital offenses: criminal homicide with one of eight aggravating circumstances
Minimum age: 17
Mentally disabled: no
Life without parole: no
Who decides: jury
Method of execution: lethal injection

UTAH

Capital offenses: aggravated murder; aggravated assault by a prisoner serving a life sentence if serious bodily injury is intentionally caused
Minimum age: 16
Mentally disabled: no
Life without parole: yes
Who decides: jury
Method of execution: lethal injection or firing squad

VIRGINIA

Capital offenses: first-degree murder with one of nine aggravating circumstances

Minimum age: 16
Mentally disabled: no
Life without parole: yes
Who decides: jury
Method of execution: inmate may choose lethal injection or electrocution; lethal injection is used if inmate fails to choose

WASHINGTON

Capital offenses: aggravated first-degree murder
Minimum age: 18
Mentally disabled: yes
Life without parole: yes
Who decides: jury

Method of execution: inmate may choose lethal injection or hanging; lethal injection used if inmate fails to choose

WYOMING

Capital offenses: first-degree murder
Minimum age: 16
Mentally disabled: no
Life without parole: yes
Who decides: jury
Method of execution: lethal injection; lethal gas to be used if lethal injection is held to be unconstitutional

REPRESENTATIVE SUPREME COURT DECISIONS

In the case of *Furman v. Georgia* (1972) the U.S. Supreme Court declared that the "arbitrary and capricious" administration of capital punishment violated the Eighth Amendment's ban on "cruel and unusual punishment." Those states that had death penalty statutes quickly revised them in an attempt to satisfy the requirements implied in the Court's decision. The Court's decision in *Gregg v. Georgia* broadly affirmed that the revisions were sufficient to allow executions to proceed. In the ensuing decades, however, several important constitutional challenges were made concerning particular aspects of the legal procedures in capital cases. In the cases described below, these challenges were decided, sometimes resulting in further procedural safeguards for defendants during the sentencing and appeals process.

The following list summarizes the main issues dealt with in these cases. Decisions in boldface are discussed in separate entries in this chapter, while others are mentioned briefly:

accomplice, capital punishment for: ***Enmund v. Florida***, *Tison v. Arizona*
aggravating circumstances: *Blystone v. Pennsylvania*, ***Godfrey v. Georgia***
assistance of counsel, ineffective: ***Burger v. Kemp***, *Strickland v. Washington*

54

Eighth amendment, cruel and unusual punishment (general):
Furman v. Georgia, Gregg v. Georgia

future dangerousness and parole: *Barefoot v. Estelle, Simmons v. South Carolina*

innocence, actual as basis for appeal: *Herrera v. Collins*

juveniles, capital punishment for: *Thompson v. Oklahoma*

jury qualifications for capital cases: *Witherspoon v. Illinois,* Davis *v. Georgia, Adams v. Texas, Wainwright v. Witt, Lockhart v. McRee*

mandatory death sentences: *Woodson v. North Carolina,* Roberts *v. Louisiana* (1977), *Summer v. Shuman*

mental incompetence or retardation: *Ford v. Wainwright, Penry v. Lynaugh, Payne v. Tennessee*

mitigating circumstances: *Lockett v. Ohio,* Eddings v. Oklahoma, *Skipper v. South Carolina, Mills v. Maryland, McKoy v. North Carolina, Buchanan v. Angelone*

proportionality review: *Pulley v. Harris*

non-murder crime, capital punishment for: *Coker v. Georgia,* Eberheart v. Georgia

race discrimination in death sentencing: *McCleskey v. Kemp,* Ham *v. South Carolina, Ristaino v. Ross, Turner v. Murray*

victim impact statements: *Booth v. Maryland,* South Carolina v. Gathers, *Payne v. Tennessee*

WITHERSPOON V. ILLINOIS, 391 U.S. 510 (1968)

Background

William G. Witherspoon was convicted in 1960 for the murder of a Chicago police officer. An Illinois law specified that persons could be excluded from serving on a jury for a capital crime if they opposed or had "conscientious scruples" against the death penalty. This "scrupled juror" rule was invoked by the prosecutor at Witherspoon's trial to dismiss any prospective members of the jury who voiced misgivings about capital punishment. Witherspoon contested his conviction and challenged the constitutionality of the procedure by which Illinois selected juries in capital cases. After Illinois courts rejected his appeals, the Supreme Court granted his request for review.

Legal Issues

Witherspoon's counsel maintained that—in violation of the Sixth Amendment—the question of his client's guilt or innocence had not been determined by an impartial jury. His argument rested on the contention that jurors without scruples against capital punishment are more inclined to vote for guilt than those with qualms about the sanction. He asked the Court to overturn Witherspoon's conviction on the grounds that it was obtained from a biased or "prosecution prone" jury.

The attorney general of Illinois responded that a state had a right to ensure that jurors were able to meet their responsibilities under the law. In defense of the scrupled juror statute, it was alleged that jurors who opposed capital punishment would be reluctant to convict a defendant of a capital offense out of concern the death penalty would be imposed. It was also noted that there was no substantive evidence that "death qualified" juries that excluded opponents of capital punishment were more likely to convict.

Decision

In a decision announced June 3, 1968, the Supreme Court did not specifically address Witherspoon's claim that his conviction was the result of a biased jury. As Justice Potter Stewart noted in his majority opinion, available data was "too tentative and fragmentary" to conclude that death qualified juries were more likely to find a defendant guilty. The Court instead focused on the narrower question of Witherspoon's punishment. Justice Stewart declared that the Constitution did not permit jury selection procedures that in effect produced a "hanging jury." The Court reversed Witherspoon's death sentence, ruling in his case that the systematic exclusion of jurors who had merely voiced ambiguous feelings about the death penalty had deprived him of his constitutional right to an impartial hearing. The Court concluded that an appropriate inquiry had to be conducted to determine a potential juror's level of opposition to capital punishment before that person could be excluded from jury duty. Only those persons who indicated that they would automatically vote against imposition of the death penalty could legitimately be disqualified.

Impact

Witherspoon was the first time the Supreme Court significantly impacted the procedures by which states administered the death penalty. The decision raised the hopes of abolitionists who looked to the Court to eventually outlaw capital punishment. The immediate impact of the *Witherspoon* ruling, because it applied retroactively, was to open a new avenue of appeal for many of the approximately 430 persons under death sentence nationwide at the time. However, it was quickly recognized that the ruling left their actual convictions intact affecting only the penalty, and many states moved to implement new, constitutionally acceptable jury selection procedures with the intent of resentencing their death row inmates. These efforts were superseded in 1971 when the Court held, in *Furman v. Georgia*, that the nation's death penalty statutes as written were unconstitutional.

After the restoration of the death penalty in 1976, the Court returned to the issue of juror selection at capital trials in a number of subsequent decisions. That same year the Court stated in *Davis v. Georgia* that the exclusion of even a single juror in violation of the principles determined in *Witherspoon* invalidated the death sentence imposed.

In response to the requirements outlined in *Furman*, capital trials had been bifurcated, or split into two separate parts: the regular trial, in which the guilt of the defendant was determined, and (if the defendant was convicted) a separate sentencing phase. While *Witherspoon* had declared that jurors could not be removed simply for opposing capital punishment, what degree of opposition was tolerable in the sentencing phase? In *Adams v. Texas*, 448 U.S. 38 (1980), the Court ruled that jurors could not be excluded simply because they could not take an oath guaranteeing that their beliefs about capital punishment would have *no* effect on their deliberations.

However, in *Wainwright v. Witt*, 469 U.S. 412 (1985) the Court ruled that a juror who was not absolutely opposed to capital punishment could still be removed if he or she appeared to have a degree of opposition sufficient to "prevent or substantially impair the performance of his duties in accordance with his instructions and his oath."

Defense attorneys then raised an argument that exclusion of jurors who were strongly opposed to the death penalty would result in a jury unacceptably biased toward death. In *Lockhart v. McRee*, 476 U.S. 162 (1986), the Court rejected this argument. It ruled that the practice of striking jurors who were unequivocally (or too strongly) opposed to the death penalty from the guilt phase of a capital trial did not abridge a defendant's Sixth Amendment rights, even if it were established that death qualified juries were somewhat more "prosecution prone" than average juries.

Furman v. Georgia, 408 U.S. 238 (1972)

Background

In 1965 the NAACP Legal Defense and Education Fund (LDF) launched a campaign to have the death penalty declared unconstitutional. By 1967 a series of legal challenges to death sentences across the nation had succeeded in halting all executions while the courts grappled with the difficult constitutional issues involved. After the Supreme Court ruled against several major challenges to capital punishment in May 1971, many in the abolitionist legal movement worried that the moratorium on executions was about to end.

However, the following month the Court announced it would review four cases to determine whether the death penalty constituted "cruel and unusual punishment in violation of the Eighth and Fourteenth Amendments." In two cases, *Aikens v. California* and *Furman v. Georgia,* the defendants contested their death sentences under state law for murder. The other two cases, *Jackson v. Georgia* and *Branch v. Texas,* questioned the constitutionality of imposing the death penalty for rape. Underscoring LDF arguments about racial discrimination in the imposition of capital punishment was the fact that in each of the four cases the defendant was black and the victim was white.

Legal Issues

LDF lawyers, who represented three of the defendants, presented a progression of interconnected arguments against the death penalty. They noted the Supreme Court's understandable reluctance to overturn well-established death penalty statutes in forty-one states but urged the Court to do so because the laws violated the cruel and unusual punishment clause of the Eighth Amendment. They called on the Court to continue its practice, first articulated in 1958, of viewing the amendment's prohibition of cruel and unusual punishment within the context of "evolving standards of decency."

Acknowledging that the existence of the death penalty in so many states suggested its use was acceptable to contemporary society, they contended that the public tolerated the sanction only because it was so infrequently imposed. A mere fraction of those who committed capital offenses were actually put to death. Those who were executed were disproportionately the poor, the disadvantaged, and minorities. They concluded that it was cruel and unusual to randomly single out a handful of persons for a penalty which society would not condone if evenhandedly and extensively applied.

Attorneys for the states responded that the people, through their elected representatives, should decide what penalties a state might employ. There was no clear and compelling reason for the Court to impose its judgment on legislative bodies. By any measure of contemporary standards, the death penalty could not be construed as cruel and unusual punishment. The idea that Americans in reality opposed capital punishment was characterized as a way to explain away the fact that the federal government and the majority of states had death penalty laws. If there were discriminatory practices in the actual imposition of the death sentence, then the issue was not capital punishment but equal protection under the laws as guaranteed by the Fourteenth Amendment. The small number of executions reflected the care with which the death penalty was used.

Recognizing the importance of the pending Supreme Court decision, numerous groups filed friend-of-the-court briefs. These included arguments against capital punishment from a range of civil rights and religious organizations.

Decision

The case from California had subsequently been dismissed after the California Supreme Court ruled the state's capital punishment statute unconstitutional in February 1972. The remaining three cases, officially reported under the name *Furman v. Georgia*, were decided on June 29, 1972. In a brief general opinion, the Court declared that the imposition of the death penalty in these cases would constitute cruel and unusual punishment.

In a departure from normal practice that reflected the widely divergent views of the justices on the issues involved, there was no majority opinion that explained the Court's reasoning. Instead, each of the five justices who voted for abolition wrote a separate concurring opinion. Justices Brennan and Marshall believed capital punishment in general was prohibited under the Eighth Amendment. The other members of the majority did not address the constitutionality of capital punishment itself, but rather the way in which current laws caused the death penalty to be imposed. Justices Douglas, Stewart, and White agreed that the nation's capital punishment statutes resulted in cruel and unusual punishment because of the arbitrary and capricious manner in which the death penalty was imposed.

Each of the dissenting justices likewise issued a separate opinion. Their general conclusion was that the majority had gone too far in trying to find a judicial solution to the troubling aspects of capital punishment. They believed the Court through judicial review had encroached upon the powers constitutionally provided to legislatures.

Impact

At the same time it announced the *Furman* decision, the Supreme Court issued orders that similarly reversed the death sentences in more than 100 other capital cases under appeal. The effect of *Furman* was to render the nation's capital punishment laws, as written, unconstitutional. The ruling spared from execution the approximately 630 persons on death row across the country.

The *Furman* decision provoked widespread reactions. Although abolitionists hailed the landmark judgment, the prevailing response was negative. Political leaders nationwide, most notably President Richard Nixon and California governor Ronald Reagan, strongly criticized the Court's action. Many stated their intention to find a way to reinstate capital punishment.

In his dissent, Chief Justice Burger noted that the lack of a clear majority consensus on the ultimate constitutionality of the death penalty meant that the full scope of the *Furman* ruling was unclear. He suggested that legislatures could enact capital punishment measures tailored to satisfy the objections stated in *Furman* by "providing standards for juries and judges to follow in determining the sentence in capital cases or by more narrowly defining the crimes for which the penalty is to be imposed." Over the next several years numerous states followed this course in amending their death penalty laws. In 1976, in *Gregg v. Georgia*, the Supreme Court restored capital punishment by upholding the constitutionality of the revised statutes.

GREGG V. GEORGIA, 428 U.S. 153 (1976)

Background

In 1972 the Supreme Court struck down the nation's capital punishment laws. These statutes had allowed juries in capital cases an essentially unrestricted discretion to determine whether a person received the death sentence. The Court found in *Furman v. Georgia* that the resulting arbitrary and capricious manner in which the death penalty was imposed violated the Eighth Amendment ban on cruel and unusual punishment.

By 1976, 35 states had enacted death penalty measures that attempted to conform to the guidelines established in the *Furman* decision. That same year the Supreme Court agreed to review five cases that challenged the constitutionality of the new laws in several states. Its ruling would possibly determine whether capital punishment would be reinstated in the United States. Two of the cases concerned mandatory death sentences and are reviewed separately under *Woodson v. North Carolina*. The other three cases, *Gregg v. Georgia*, *Profitt v. Florida*, and *Jurek v. Texas*, involved defendants convicted of murder.

Legal Issues

In *Furman*, the Supreme Court had stopped short of concluding that capital punishment was inherently unconstitutional. This left open the possibility that death penalty statutes could be designed that would pass judicial scrutiny. The states argued that they had implemented procedures that met the Court's requirement for clear sentencing standards in capital cases. These included a bifurcated, or split, trial proceeding in which guilt or innocence was determined during a first phase and the sentence then imposed during a separate second phase. Juries were provided certain criteria to follow in deciding which convicted capital offenders would receive the death penalty.

Attorneys for the defendants contended that neither these nor any other procedures that could be adopted by the states would ensure capital punishment was administered in a rational and fair way. They asserted the Court should take the final step of declaring the death penalty itself unconstitutional, alleging the sanction was no longer compatible with contemporary standards of decency and as such was a violation of the Eighth Amendment ban on cruel and unusual punishment.

Decision

In a historic judgment delivered on July 2, 1976, the Court ruled that capital punishment did not invariably violate the Constitution and upheld death penalty laws that set objective standards for juries to follow in their sentencing decisions. The Florida, Georgia, and Texas statutes were found to be within constitutional limits. The Court chose to present its basic reasoning in *Gregg v. Georgia*, making it the lead case that would be cited for the decision.

The seven members of the majority were unable to agree on an opinion. In the Court's ruling, Justices Stewart, Powell, and Stevens noted that passage of the death penalty measures by so many states after *Furman* undercut the argument that society no longer endorsed the sanction. The different majority opinions in general indicated the Court would uphold capital punishment laws that met several key conditions: clear standards to guide juries in their sentencing decisions; consideration of any mitigating factors prior to sentencing; and automatic review of each death sentence in a state appellate court.

Impact

Although *Gregg v. Georgia* reinstated the death penalty, the ruling did not overturn *Furman*. Instead, the decision reflected the Supreme Court's judgment that the defects previously identified in the administration of the death penalty had been remedied. More than 460 persons had been sentenced to death under post-*Furman* statutes, and *Gregg* cleared the way for a resumption of executions. The first execution in 10 years was carried out in 1977.

On the same day the *Gregg* decision was released, the Supreme Court determined in *Woodson v. North Carolina* that mandatory death sentences were unconstitutional. Together, *Furman* and *Woodson* made it clear the Court would not consent to giving a capital jury either too much or too little discretion in arriving at a sentence. Other states consequently moved to amend their death penalty laws to conform to the guided-discretion statutes approved in *Gregg*.

The 7-2 vote in *Gregg* suggested the Supreme Court was not likely to significantly modify its core stance on capital punishment in the foreseeable future. In subsequent decisions, the Court has focused on further defining the circumstances under which the death penalty is a constitutionally acceptable punishment.

WOODSON V. NORTH CAROLINA, 428 U.S. 280 (1976)

Background

In 1972 the Supreme Court ruled that death penalty statutes that did not contain specific sentencing standards were unconstitutional. Relying on the precedent established in *Furman v. Georgia*, the North Carolina Supreme Court overturned the provision of that state's capital punishment law that granted the jury tremendous leeway on when to impose the death penalty. In 1974 the North Carolina legislature attempted to resolve the question of sentencing procedures in capital trials by passing a new statute that removed all discretion, making the death penalty mandatory for first-degree murder. The state's highest court subsequently upheld death sentences two defendants had received under the new law following their murder convictions. The defendants appealed, and in 1976 the U.S. Supreme Court agreed to hear their case, *Woodson v. North Carolina*, as part of a broad review of the constitutionality of various state capital punishment laws enacted in response to the *Furman* decision.

Legal Issues

The basic question before the Supreme Court was whether mandatory death statutes provided a constitutionally acceptable response to the rejection in *Furman* of unbridled jury discretion in sentencing decisions. Attorneys for the states involved argued that mandatory sentences would prevent arbitrary and freakish inconsistencies in the imposition of capital punishment. Defense lawyers countered that mandatory statutes did not take into account the unique circumstances of a given case and would still result in indiscriminate sentencing patterns. They further contended that there was no workable way to address the concern raised in *Furman* and called upon the Court to abolish capital punishment outright.

The Law of Capital Punishment

Decision

The Supreme Court announced its decision in *Woodson v. North Carolina* on July 2, 1976, the same day it delivered its landmark *Gregg v. Georgia* ruling. The court declared North Carolina's capital punishment law unconstitutional because it did not provide "objective standards to guide, regularize, and make rationally reviewable the process for imposing a sentence of death." In a companion case, *Roberts v. Louisiana*, 428 U.S. 242 (1976), the Court struck down that state's mandatory death penalty statute for similar reasons.

The 5-4 majority in *Woodson* stressed the fact that since the early 19th century the United States had gradually moved away from mandatory sentences. An automatic death sentence was seen as inconsistent with "evolving standards of decency" and consequently constituted cruel and unusual punishment under the Eighth Amendment. The Court stated that "particularized" consideration had to be given to the relevant aspects of a convicted defendant's character and record before a death sentence could be imposed.

Impact

In its simultaneous release of the *Gregg* and *Woodson* decisions, the Supreme Court staked out a carefully defined position on capital punishment. In *Gregg*, the Court found that the death penalty per se was not unconstitutional and upheld death penalty statutes that provided for guided jury discretion in sentencing decisions. With its ruling against mandatory sentences in *Woodson*, the Court, in effect, had endorsed a bifurcated, or split, trial process in capital cases where conviction and punishment were determined in separate hearings.

Woodson established the important precedent that a defendant was entitled to an individualized sentencing determination. In later decisions the Supreme Court extended this principle to include a defendant's right to present a broad range of mitigating evidence prior to sentencing. The Court continued to rule against mandatory death sentences. The following year, in *Roberts v. Louisiana*, 431 U.S. 633 (1977)—a different Roberts—a Louisiana statute that mandated the death penalty for persons convicted of killing a police officer was overturned. The Court did not accept the argument that the process of convicting a person of a special and narrowly drawn category of crime could serve as a substitute for "particularized" consideration. In 1987, the Court nullified, in *Summer v. Shuman*, a Nevada law that required the death penalty for murders committed by prisoners serving life sentences without possibility of parole.

While mandatory death sentences for particular crime circumstances had been banned by the Court, the justices took a different position with regard to mandating a death penalty based on aggravating circumstances found at the time of sentencing. In *Blystone v. Pennsylvania*, 494 U.S. 299 (1990), the Court ruled by a 5-4 margin that providing for a mandatory death sentence if the jury finds one aggravating circumstance and no mitigating circumstances was not a violation of the Eighth Amendment. Such a system did not interfere with the consideration of all relevant mitigating evidence, but only directed what was to be done if none was found. The dissenters objected, saying that any such mandatory aspect of the sentencing process deprived the jurors of the ability to make an individual determination of whether any aggravating circumstance they found was sufficient to warrant imposing the death penalty.

COKER V. GEORGIA,
433 U.S. 584 (1977)

Background

Anthony Coker escaped from a Georgia correctional institution where he was serving consecutive life sentences for murder, rape, and kidnapping. He subsequently raped an adult woman during an armed robbery. Georgia's death penalty statutes authorized capital punishment for rape if one or more of the following aggravating circumstances was present: the defendant had previously been convicted of a capital offense; the rape occurred during the commission of another capital felony (including armed robbery); or the crime was particularly vile or horrible, involving torture, depravity, or aggravated battery. After his conviction for rape and armed robbery, Coker was sentenced to death by a jury that found the first two aggravating factors applied. When Georgia's highest court affirmed the sentence on automatic appeal, Coker petitioned the Supreme Court to declare the death penalty for rape unconstitutional.

Legal Issues

In *Gregg v. Georgia* the Supreme Court upheld the constitutionality of capital punishment laws that provided for a consideration of aggravating and mitigating circumstances prior to sentencing. The question in *Coker v. Georgia* was not whether Georgia's statutes were procedurally flawed but whether death was an appropriate punishment for rape, even with aggravating circumstances. Coker's counsel noted that the rape had not involved the loss of life and contended the sentence was disproportionate to the crime committed. Such an excessively harsh penalty violated the Eighth Amendment's ban on cruel and unusual punishment.

State attorneys argued the case was beyond the reach of proper judicial review. The Court should not substitute its policy judgment for that of the state legislature. Rape was not a minor crime, and it was the considered reasoning of Georgia's elected representatives that there were times the offense merited the ultimate sanction.

Decision

The Supreme Court ruled in favor of Coker on June 29, 1977. The Court followed its normal practice of determining the constitutionality of a given punishment. A punishment was cruel and unusual under the Eighth Amendment if it was incompatible with "evolving standards of decency." Measured against contemporary American sensibilities, a sentence of death was wholly disproportionate to the offense of raping an adult woman. The Court cited the fact that Georgia was the only state to authorize the death sentence for rape. The 7-2 majority also underscored the difference between murder and crimes such as rape where the defendant, whatever the aggravating circumstances, had not taken the victim's life.

Impact

Coker was the first time the Supreme Court specifically limited the authority of either federal or state government to impose the death penalty for a specific type of crime. In a summary opinion released at the same time, *Eberheart v. Georgia*, the Court also overturned the death penalty for kidnapping when homicide was not involved. The two decisions served to suggest the Court was drawing a clear link between death as a punishment and crimes involving loss of life. This apparent linkage raised serious doubts about the constitutionality of capital punishment for other crimes such as treason, espionage, and airplane hijacking that might not result in immediate death. The Court has yet to rule on these questions.

LOCKETT V. OHIO,
438 U.S. 586 (1978)

Background

Sandra Lockett drove the getaway car in a pawnshop robbery during which the owner was killed. Ohio laws required the death penalty for a conviction of aggravated murder (such as murder in the course of committing a robbery), unless the sentencing authority determined that at least one of the following three mitigating circumstances existed: the victim induced or facilitated the crime; the defendant was under duress, coercion, or strong provocation; or the crime resulted from the defendant's mental deficiency short of actual legal insanity. Lockett was found guilty of committing murder during the course of another major felony. At the penalty phase of her trial, the judge determined that none of the mitigating factors applied and imposed the death penalty. After the state courts turned down her appeals, Lockett successfully petitioned the Supreme Court to review the constitutionality of Ohio's sentencing procedures.

Legal Issues

The applicable Ohio statute attempted to conform to the requirement for individualized sentencing determinations mandated by the Supreme Court in *Woodson v. North Carolina*. The state contended that its procedures allowed for a balanced weighing of aggravating and mitigating elements prior to sentencing. Defense lawyers argued that Ohio's limited list of mitigating factors actually denied their client a fair hearing by preventing her from offering a wide range of pertinent information on her own behalf. For example, the court had not learned of Lockett's youth, her history of drug addiction, or her lack of previous serious criminal activity. As a consequence, her rights to due process and an individualized sentence had not been guaranteed.

Decision

The Supreme Court overturned Lockett's death sentence on July 3, 1978. The Court held that the Ohio statute in question unconstitutionally limited the presentation of mitigating evidence in violation of the Eighth and Fourteenth Amendments. In a related ruling, the justices left standing lower court orders that struck down comparable laws in New York and Pennsylvania.

In the principal opinion for the majority, Chief Justice Warren E. Burger stated that a death penalty statute could not preclude a sentencing authority from considering "as a mitigating factor, any aspect of the defendant's character or record or any of the circumstances of the offense that the defendant proffers as a basis for a sentence less than death." In keeping with the Court's traditional emphasis on the unique nature of capital cases, Burger observed that the death sentence differed profoundly from other penalties in its irreversibility. The nonavailability of corrective remedies once the sentence was carried out underscored the need for individualized treatment in the imposition of the death penalty.

Impact

The immediate effect of *Lockett v. Ohio* was to invalidate the death sentences of approximately 100 inmates on Ohio's death row. The decision cast serious doubts as to the validity of capital punishment laws in two dozen other states. State legislatures subsequently moved to align their statutes with the principle established in *Lockett*.

In later rulings, the Supreme Court continued to insist on the broadest possible consideration of mitigating factors prior to sentencing. In *Eddings v. Oklahoma* (1982), the Court nullified a death sentence on the grounds the sentencing judge had refused to consider the defendant's history of emotional disturbance and turbulent family background. Exclusion of testimony that the defendant would adjust well to prison life was cause for reversing the death sentence in *Skipper v. South Carolina* (1986). In 1988 the Court found, in *Mills v. Maryland*, that a jury did not have to unanimously agree a mitigating circumstance existed before considering it in sentencing. When some confusion arose concerning the latter ruling, the Court reaffirmed it in *McKoy v. North Carolina* (1990).

In *Buchanan v. Angelone* (1998), the Court was faced with the question of whether the jury must be explicitly told to consider any mitigating evidence that had been presented and must be instructed as to the meaning and use of such evidence. The Court decided by a 6-3 majority that such instructions were not required, that it was sufficient that the jury had been instructed to consider "all the evidence" in arriving at its sentence.

GODFREY V. GEORGIA,
446 U.S. 240 (1980)

Background

In *Gregg v. Georgia* the Supreme Court found that a provision of the Georgia code that allowed a person convicted of murder to be sentenced to death if the offense was "outrageously or wantonly vile, horrible or inhuman in that it involved torture, depravity of mind, or aggravated battery to the victim" was not unconstitutional. Robert Godfrey was subsequently found guilty of two counts of murder and a single count of aggravated assault. The defendant, experiencing marital difficulties, had shot his wife and his mother-in-law, killing both instantly. He also struck and injured his fleeing daughter with the barrel of a shotgun. At the sentencing phase of the trial, the jury relied on the provision in question in imposing the death penalty for each murder. The sentence was upheld by Georgia's highest court. The Supreme Court then agreed to consider Godfrey's charge that the definition of the aggravating circumstances for which he had received the death penalty was unconstitutionally vague.

Legal Issues

Godfrey v. Georgia presented the Supreme Court with two interrelated questions. The first was whether the Georgia law had been correctly applied in Godfrey's case. The court could rule that the evidence did not support the jury's finding of the aggravated circumstance without overturning the provision on which it was based. The Court could also hold that the language in the statute was so broad and imprecise, or unconstitutionally vague, that it violated a defendant's right to clear sentencing standards.

Decision

On May 19, 1980, the Supreme Court left standing the Georgia law but set aside Godfrey's death sentence imposed under the statute. In a plurality opinion announcing the judgment of the 6-3 majority, Justice Potter Stewart emphasized that a state that authorized capital punishment had a constitutional responsibility to design and apply its laws so as to avoid arbitrary and capricious infliction of the death penalty. In previous decisions, the Georgia Supreme Court had constrained use of the provision under which Godfrey was sentenced to instances involving serious physical abuse of the victim before death. The statute, however, had not been similarly limited in the case at hand. The Court concluded that there was "no principled way to distinguish this case, in which the death penalty was imposed, from the many cases in which it was not" and the sentence was thus improperly derived.

Impact

Godfrey marked the first time the Supreme Court directly addressed the constitutionality of a given aggravating circumstance. Although the Court did not overturn the provision in question, *Godfrey* made clear that the Court was exercising particular care to ensure the administration of capital punishment did not revert to the kinds of standardless death sentence determinations ruled unconstitutional in *Furman v. Georgia*. The Court established a very different yardstick for aggravating circumstances than it had for mitigating circumstances in *Lockett v. Ohio*. The two decisions indicated that constitutional safeguards for a defendant facing a possible death sentence required the widest possible consideration of mitigating factors and a very precisely drawn and applied set of aggravating conditions.

ENMUND V. FLORIDA,
458 U.S. 782 (1982)

Background

Under Florida law, a killing committed during another major crime was a "felony murder" for which all the participants in the crime were legally responsible. Earl Enmund was convicted of the murder of two persons during the course of a robbery at their farmhouse. The Supreme Court of Florida upheld his death sentence, although the trial record revealed that Enmund's involvement in the crime was limited to waiting outside in a car for his two accomplices at the time the killings occurred. The state's highest court ruled this was sufficient to establish Enmund as a principal in the first-degree murder. Enmund's appeal that the Eighth Amendment barred capital punishment in cases where the defendant did not intend to take life was accepted by the Supreme Court.

Legal Issues

The question was not whether Enmund should have been convicted of a felony murder but whether he should receive the same sentence as those who were directly involved in the killing. Enmund maintained his punishment was disproportionate to his peripheral role in the crime. Florida's counsel noted that the law has long recognized the joint responsibility borne by all accomplices to a given crime. Enmund actively took part in a felony that resulted in murder and then assisted the actual killers to escape.

Decision

By a 5-4 margin, the Supreme Court on July 2, 1982, reversed Enmund's death sentence. Writing for the majority, Justice Byron White stated that death was an excessive and disproportionate punishment for a defendant who aided and abetted in the commission of a felony that resulted in murder but who neither killed, attempted to kill, nor intended to kill the victim. Enmund's sentence was impermissibly cruel and unusual under the Eighth Amendment.

Impact

On its face, *Enmund v. Florida* seemed to establish a major new precedent that only those who were directly responsible for a homicide could receive the death sentence for the crime. Although the language of the decision was somewhat ambiguous, *Enmund* was widely viewed as prohibiting the execution of felons who neither actively participated in murder committed by

69

their accomplices nor intended that the offense occur. Still, the Court's exact meaning in its use of the legal concept of intent was unclear.

The Supreme Court returned to the issue of intent in 1987. In *Tison v. Arizona* the Court held that an accomplice to felony murder was legally responsible for the crime if the person demonstrated a "reckless disregard for human life implicit in knowingly engaging in criminal activity known to carry a grave risk of death." Participation in such activity represented a "highly culpable mental state" which could be taken into account in capital sentencing judgments. While not exactly reversing *Enmund*, the new decision seemed to offer a standard that would be relatively easy for the prosecution to meet in many cases. Based on the fact that 26 states authorized capital sentences for accomplices to felony murders, many saw the decision as leading to an expanded use of the death penalty.

BAREFOOT V. ESTELLE, 463 U.S. 880 (1983)

Background

In 1978 Thomas A. Barefoot was convicted of the murder of a police officer in Texas. At a separate sentencing hearing, the jury decided that the death penalty should be imposed. The Texas Court of Criminal Appeals rejected Barefoot's contention that the state's use of psychiatric testimony to predict the future dangerousness of capital defendants was unconstitutional. Successive appeals to the U.S. Supreme Court, again to the Texas Court of Criminal Appeals and then to a federal district court for the western part of Texas were likewise denied. Although the district court ruled against Barefoot's claim, it granted him a certificate of probable cause to appeal its judgment to the Fifth Circuit Court of Appeals. This appeal was filed in November 1982.

Texas authorities meanwhile set a new execution date of January 25, 1983. Another request for review and motion for stay of execution were subsequently turned down by the Texas Court of Criminal Appeals. In early January 1983, Barefoot petitioned the Fifth Circuit Court of Appeals for a stay of execution pending its consideration of his appeal of the district court ruling. The court of appeals heard arguments on this motion and, in turn, issued an order denying the stay.

On January 24, 1983, the Supreme Court agreed to consider Barefoot's contention that the court of appeals had erred in not granting a stay of execution while the appeal of the lower court's ruling was still pending. The Supreme Court's action halted the execution less than 11 hours before the scheduled time.

Legal Issues

Barefoot v. Estelle specifically addressed the narrow procedural question of the circuit court's actions in not issuing a stay of execution during a pending appeal. In a broader sense, however, the case illustrated the serious problems the mounting number of appeals in capital cases posed to the fair and timely administration of justice. The federal court system was struggling to distinguish substantive from frivolous appeals and to respond correctly to last-minute requests for stays of execution. The Supreme Court had to consider how best to balance the rights of defendants, the need for particular care in capital cases, and the necessity of workable appeals procedures.

Decision

On July 6, 1983, the Supreme Court ruled that the court of appeals had acted properly in its refusal to grant Barefoot a stay of execution even though the death row inmate's constitutional challenge to his sentence was technically still pending. In his majority opinion, Justice Byron R. White noted that the federal law governing the right to appeal prevented a prisoner from presenting his case to a federal appeals court unless the federal district court issued a certificate of probable cause (certifying that the appeal had substantial merit and was not frivolous). Once the certificate was granted, the appeals court "was obligated to decide the merits of the appeal." The appeals court was also required to issue a stay of execution if necessary to provide sufficient time to properly dispose of the appeal.

The majority found that the court of appeals had clearly considered the merits of Barefoot's appeal as part of its decision to deny his request for a stay of execution. The expedited process used by the appeals court, condensing the motions for appeal and stay of execution into one proceeding, was an acceptable handling of the case. Although the court of appeals had not specifically affirmed the fact it had ruled on Barefoot's appeal in its opinion, to conclude that the defendant had not had a full hearing "would be an unwarranted exaltation of form over substance."

The Supreme Court used *Barefoot v. Estelle* as a vehicle for issuing guidelines to the lower federal courts for the handling of appeals in death penalty cases. The subordinate courts were authorized to enact local rules that would implement these guidelines. In a general sense, the Court observed that appeals in the federal court system were only appropriate when a federal question was involved. Federal courts were not "forums in which to relitigate state trials." Similarly, repetitive appeals were not meant to function as a mechanism by which a defendant could delay an execution indefinitely.

The appeals process was not a "legal entitlement" that a defendant had a right to pursue regardless of the substance of the issue in question.

The Court tightened the standards for separating meritorious from frivolous appeals. The different nature of the death penalty was a relevant consideration in deciding whether or not to grant an appeal, but the severity of the sanction did not justify automatic approval of an appeal in every case. A lower court should only allow an appeal to go forward if the petitioner had made a "substantial showing of the denial of a federal right" where the issues involved were at least "debatable among jurists of reason." When a court determined that these conditions were met, then the petitioner was entitled to a full hearing on the merits of the appeal. Circuit courts were encouraged to adopt and make known rules that would speed the appeals process. Expedited procedures were particularly appropriate in instances of second and successive appeals.

Impact

Barefoot was intended at least in part to relieve the burden on the Supreme Court of last-minute appeals in capital cases. The guidelines established by the Court, however, did not succeed in appreciably reducing either these appeals or the volume of death penalty–related legal actions in general. In subsequent years a number of justices, most notably William H. Rehnquist and Lewis F. Powell, Jr., have expressed their concern over the impact the growing number of appeals in death penalty cases was having on the entire criminal justice system. On several occasions, Justice Powell suggested publicly that if the issue could not be resolved, then the death penalty itself should be abandoned as unworkable.

In 1988, Chief Justice Rehnquist appointed then-retired Justice Powell to head a commission charged with finding ways to expedite the handling of capital appeals. The panel submitted its proposal for strict new limits on multiple appeals by death row inmates in 1989. Its recommendations have been incorporated into deliberations in the Senate over possible federal legislation in this area.

Underlying the debate over death-penalty appeals is the more basic struggle between proponents and opponents of capital punishment. Lawyers for death row inmates have a professional responsibility to pursue every possible avenue on the behalf of their clients. At the same time, many abolitionist groups believe that the generation of time-consuming and costly litigation will eventually lead the public to conclude that capital punishment is not worth the trouble its imposition causes. (Of course it could also lead to a political backlash resulting in legislation that seeks to drastically streamline the appeals process.)

While the Court had not overturned the use of "future dangerousness" testimony, it did require a balancing consideration. In *Simmons v. South Carolina* (1994), the petitioner had been sentenced to death. His attorney had asked the judge to instruct the jury that Simmons would be ineligible for parole because of his two previous convictions for violent crime. The judge refused to give this instruction, and when the jury spontaneously asked about it, he told them that parole "was not a proper issue for your consideration" and that "the terms life imprisonment and death sentence are to be understood in their plan [sic] and ordinary meaning." By a vote of 7-2 the Supreme Court overturned the conviction, noting that since the state had raised the issue of the defendant's future dangerousness in the first place, fairness required that the jury also be informed about the alternative of life without parole.

PULLEY V. HARRIS,
465 U.S. 37 (1984)

Background

Robert A. Harris was convicted by a California court of killing two teenage boys to use their car for a bank robbery. He was sentenced to death. California's capital punishment statute did not require that a state appellate court conduct a "proportionality review" to ensure that a given sentence was in line with other sentences imposed in the state for similar crimes. The California Supreme Court rejected Harris' claim that the lack of this special review rendered the state's death penalty law invalid under the Constitution. Harris then shifted his appeal to the federal court system. The court of appeals subsequently held that the proportionality review was constitutionally required and directed the California Supreme Court to undertake such an analysis within 120 days. Otherwise, the appeals court would reverse Harris' sentence. State officials appealed the decision to the U.S. Supreme Court.

Legal Issues

Harris' lawyers cited the Supreme Court's ruling in *Furman v. Georgia* that an arbitrary and capricious administration of the death penalty constituted cruel and unusual punishment under the Eighth Amendment. Without a comparative review of sentences, it was impossible to determine whether capital punishment was being imposed in an evenhanded and rational manner as required by the constitution. They argued that the Court's decisions in 1976 reinstating the death penalty had implicitly placed proportionality review on the level of a constitutional requirement. California officials maintained that there were already sufficient safeguards in the state's procedures to ensure the death penalty was consistently and fairly applied.

Decision

The Supreme Court sided with California. In a ruling announced January 23, 1984, the Court found that a state could carry out a death sentence without first conducting a proportionality review. The majority decision, written by Justice Byron White, stated that such a review was not required either by the Court's own death penalty precedents or by the Constitution's ban on cruel and unusual punishment.

Justice White observed that "any capital sentence may occasionally produce aberrational outcomes" but such inconsistencies were substantially different from the "major systemic defects" that led the Court to invalidate all existing death penalty laws in *Furman*. It was possible for a state to design a law that adequately protected against arbitrary executions without recourse to proportionality review. The fact the Court in 1976 had upheld Florida and Georgia statutes that included such review did not mean the procedure was indispensable. At the same time, the Court found that the Texas law, which did not contain proportional review, was also constitutional.

Impact

Pulley v. Harris had little direct effect on the pace of executions in California, where most death row inmates were far from exhausting their appeals. The decision had a more immediate impact in Texas, the only other state without proportionality review that also had a sizeable death row population. The proportionality question was the only substantive basis of appeal remaining for a number of prisoners there.

In his opinion, Justice White was careful to distinguish between ensuring a sentence was proportionate to the crime committed and the concept of proportionality review. He made it clear that the Court in *Pulley* was not retreating from the precedent established in cases such as *Coker v. Georgia* (where the death penalty was ruled an excessive punishment for rape) that capital punishment was only appropriate when it fit the crime.

FORD V. WAINWRIGHT, 477 U.S. 399 (1986)

Background

In 1974 Alvin B. Ford killed a Florida police officer while robbing a restaurant. He was convicted of murder and sentenced to death the same year. There was no suggestion of mental incompetence at the time of the offense, during his trial, or at his sentencing hearing. After an extended period on Florida's death row, however, Ford began to show signs of serious mental disorder. His attorneys argued that he had gone insane and consequently should not be executed. At their request, the governor of Florida, following the procedures in state law for determining the competency of a condemned inmate, appointed a panel of three psychiatrists who interviewed Ford for approximately 30 minutes. When the panel reported, as required by state law, that Ford knew why he was to die, the governor signed a death warrant for his execution. After a series of unsuccessful appeals in state and lower federal courts, Ford's attorneys prevailed upon the Supreme Court to hear their claim that Florida's procedure for assessing the mental competency of convicted prisoners did not meet minimum due process standards.

Legal Issues

Ford's counsel argued that a 30-minute interview was insufficient to determine their client's sanity. State procedures, however, had stopped the attorneys from introducing additional information about his psychiatric condition. They contended that the fact Ford had not received an impartial hearing where all relevant evidence of his mental state could be considered was a violation of his due process rights under the Fourteenth Amendment. In a broader sense, *Ford v. Wainwright* raised the question of whether it was appropriate to inflict the death penalty on a person who was insane. Even if Ford were found to be mentally incompetent, there was no clear legal precedent that could preclude his execution.

Decision

On June 26, 1986, the Supreme Court blocked Ford's execution, at least until Florida implemented new procedures to evaluate his sanity. These procedures had to meet basic standards of due process. At a minimum, this meant designation of an impartial board or officer to consider all available evidence to include psychiatric presentations or legal arguments made on behalf of the prisoner.

The Court went on to rule that the Eighth Amendment prohibited the execution of death row inmates who had become so insane they no longer understood they were going to be put to death or the reason why. In his majority opinion Justice Thurgood Marshall wrote: "For centuries no jurisdiction has countenanced the execution of the insane, yet this Court has never decided whether the Constitution forbids the practice. Today, we keep faith with our common-law heritage by holding that it does." Marshall concluded that the basic meaning of a punishment was negated if a person no longer comprehended its purpose. Execution of the insane was closer to "mindless vengeance" than it was to retribution.

Impact

Ford's real significance was in the procedural safeguards it extended to prisoners who possibly suffered mental difficulties. Prior to the ruling, many states had essentially cursory procedures for testing for insanity. Interestingly, the Court also held that if a death row inmate who had been judged mentally incompetent was subsequently cured of the condition, then a state was free to go forward with the execution. While this was a logical consequence of the reasoning behind the decision, opponents of capital punishment pointed out the irony that an inmate who went insane had to remain insane to stay alive.

The decision was also important symbolically. The Court's statement that the Constitution did not allow the execution of the insane had no direct legal relevance because no state permitted such a proceeding. However, *Ford* represented a further incremental narrowing by the Court of the circumstances under which a person could be put to death.

McCLESKEY V. KEMP,
481 U.S. 279 (1987)

Background

In October 1978, Warren McCleskey, a black man, was convicted of killing a white Atlanta police officer during an armed robbery. At the penalty phase of his trial, the jury of 11 whites and one black sentenced him to die in Georgia's electric chair. After McCleskey lost two rounds of appeals in state and federal courts, the NAACP Legal Defense and Education Fund (LDF) took over his case.

LDF attorneys filed a new appeal in Federal District Court challenging the constitutionality of Georgia's death penalty law on the grounds that it was administered in a racially discriminatory manner. In support of this claim, they cited a study conducted by Professor David C. Baldus of the University of Iowa. The Baldus study was a detailed and sophisticated statistical analysis of more than 2,000 murder cases in Georgia in the 1970s. The research indicated that black defendants were substantially more likely to receive the death sentence than white defendants. The disparity was even greater when the study compared the rate at which the death penalty was applied for black defendants who killed white victims as against white defendants who killed black victims. After the appeal was denied by both the district court and a circuit court of appeals, the Supreme Court agreed to hear the case.

The Law of Capital Punishment

Legal Issues

Since the early 1960s, the NAACP LDF had been engaged in defending black persons accused of capital crimes. At first, this activity was an outgrowth of the organization's involvement in the civil rights movement. Most of the court cases took place in the South. However, by the mid-1960s the LDF had committed to a nationwide campaign to abolish capital punishment.

The issue of possible racial bias against the defendant had been raised in several cases. In *Ham v. South Carolina* (1973), the Court had found that the defendant's counsel had the right to ask potential jurors about their possible racial biases if the facts of the case suggested bias might be a problem. (Ham was a civil rights activist who claimed that the charges against him were a frame-up.) In *Ristaino v. Ross* (1976), the Court did not extend this principle to a right to inquire about bias any time the defendant and victim were of different races. In *Turner v. Murray* (1986), however, the Court followed its common practice of requiring greater protection of rights in capital cases than in cases where the death penalty was not an issue. Here the Court ruled that in an interracial murder the defendant has the right to ask prospective jurors about racial bias.

Many LDF lawyers had concluded from personal experiences that the death penalty was imposed in a discriminatory manner. But trying to deal with possible individual bias on a case-by-case basis is very difficult. An alternative approach is to look not at individual behavior, but at outcomes—are minorities treated differently on a statistical basis then non-minorities?

In 1965 the organization initiated an exhaustive study of racial discrimination in the use of the death penalty for rape. The study revealed that black men frequently were sentenced to death for raping a white woman while white men who raped black women almost invariably were not. This statistical information was incorporated into a number of LDF challenges to capital punishment in the late 1960s and early 1970s. Although the Supreme Court did not specifically refer to racial bias in its 1972 decision striking down the nation's death penalty statutes, many of the opinions in *Furman v. Georgia* mentioned racial minorities as disproportionately affected by the capricious and arbitrary way capital punishment was administered.

When the Supreme Court reinstated the death penalty in 1976, patterns of racial discrimination in capital sentencing again became an issue. LDF's legal argument on behalf of McCleskey had two parts. First, the fact that black defendants convicted of murder were treated differently than white defendants convicted of murder was a violation of the equal protection clause of the Fourteenth Amendment. This clause requires that the laws be applied equally and uniformly to all. There cannot be one system of justice for whites and another for blacks. The LDF also maintained that the Baldus study demonstrated that Georgia's death penalty was not being imposed in an evenhanded manner. Although the law had been ruled constitutional by the Court in 1976, the actual practice of capital punishment in Georgia still singled out blacks for the harshest penalties. The LDF argued that the new death penalty statutes in Georgia were being applied in a way that did not meet the requirements the Court had established in *Furman* for fair and objective standards to guide capital sentencing decisions. McCleskey's counsel concluded this use of the death penalty was unconstitutional under the Eighth Amendment's ban on cruel and unusual punishment.

Decision

On April 22, 1987, a closely divided Supreme Court ruled against McCleskey. The 5-4 majority accepted the validity of the Baldus study but held that it was not enough to prove actual discrimination against the individual defendant in the case at hand. Writing for the majority, Justice Lewis F. Powell, Jr., allowed that the discretion provided to prosecutors and juries in the U.S. criminal justice system would inevitably lead to occasional abuses and disparities. For a defendant to show unconstitutional racial bias in a given death sentence, though, it was necessary to "prove that the decision makers in his case acted with discriminatory purpose." This proof required evidence specific to the case. A generalized study documenting "a discrepancy that appears to correlate with race" was insufficient.

The Court rejected the basic argument that statistics revealing a seeming disparity in sentencing were grounds for overturning Georgia's death penalty statute under the Fourteenth Amendment's equal protection provisions. The statistical evidence was not clear and convincing enough to warrant a finding of racial discrimination affecting the entire Georgia capital sentencing process. (An earlier appeals court had pointed out that the Baldus study did not break down cases by aggravating and mitigating factors and therefore may not have been a valid comparison of truly similar cases.) Similarly, the Baldus study by itself was not proof that the state's capital punishment system was arbitrary and capricious in application and that McCleskey's death sentence consequently was excessive in violation of the Eighth Amendment.

In previous decisions, the Court had approved the use of statistics in demonstrating instances of discrimination in areas such as employment. The majority found, however, that drawing an inference of prejudice in a specific trial from broad statistics was substantively different from inferring discrimination in a wide range of employment practices.

Justice Powell characterized the claim that Georgia juries were more prone to sentence a black man to death as an attack on the fundamental role discretion played in the criminal justice system. He contended that the discretion afforded to a jury was, in fact, a criminal defendant's core "protection of life and liberty against race or color prejudice." To the extent racism still infected the criminal justice system, the answer was to surround the process by which guilt and punishment were determined with procedural safeguards.

In an unusual step, the Court revealed several associated concerns that had guided its finding. McCleskey's claim, taken to its logical conclusion, meant that not only death sentences but potentially all criminal penalties were tainted with racism. Similarly, the methodology used in the Baldus study could be employed to allege patterns of discrimination involving other minority groups, gender, or any other arbitrary variables such as physical attractiveness. Absent the most compelling evidence, the Court was reluctant to reach a conclusion in the *McCleskey* case that might undermine the basic workings of the criminal justice system.

Impact

McCleskey v. Kemp is considered the most important Supreme Court decision on capital punishment since the death penalty was restored in 1976. The ruling removed what abolitionists had called their last sweeping challenge to the constitutionality of the death penalty itself. Numerous potential court challenges to capital punishment remained, but none would be applicable to more than a fraction of the death row population. The immediate effect of *McCleskey* for the approximately 1,900 persons on death row nationally was unclear. Although it was expected that the pace of executions would eventually quicken, the majority of the death row inmates had not exhausted their appeals on other issues.

Many opponents of capital punishment bitterly criticized the decision. They accused the Court of distorting established legal principles in order to avoid overturning numerous death sentences and creating disarray in the judicial system. Civil rights leaders also condemned the ruling. Legal experts pointed out that the Court had made it extremely difficult, if not impossible, to prove racial discrimination in the use of the death penalty. While it was possible to accumulate statistics evidencing a pattern of bias across a wide number of cases, it was an entirely different proposition to establish discriminatory intent in actions of a particular prosecutor, judge, or jury.

BOOTH V. MARYLAND, 482 U.S. 496 (1987)

Background

A 1983 Maryland law provided for the use of "victim impact statements" in death sentencing hearings. John Booth was subsequently convicted of two counts of first-degree murder. Together with an accomplice, he had bound, gagged, and stabbed to death an elderly couple in their Baltimore home during a robbery. At the sentencing phase of his trial, the prosecutor introduced a victim impact statement that described the personal characteristics of the victims and the emotional impact of their murders upon their family.

The state trial court refused to exclude the victim impact statement, rejecting the defendant's claim that its use in a capital case violated the Eighth Amendment. Based at least in part on the statement, the jury sentenced Booth to death. The Maryland Court of Appeals upheld the sentence, and Booth successfully petitioned the Supreme Court for review.

Legal Issues

Booth contended the victim impact statement was irrelevant to an appropriate consideration of the circumstances of his crime. Because of its inherently inflammatory nature, the statement had unduly influenced the jury in its deliberations. As a consequence, emotion rather than objective standards had guided the imposition of the death sentence in his case. This kind of subjective and capricious capital sentencing process was unconstitutional under the Eighth Amendment's ban on cruel and unusual punishment. Maryland officials maintained that a jury was entitled to consider any evidence that had a bearing on the sentencing decision. The victim impact statement served to inform the jury, as sentencing authority, of the full extent of harm caused by the crime.

Decision

On June 11, 1987, the Supreme Court invalidated the Maryland law in question. The Court found that the introduction of a victim impact statement at the sentencing phase of a capital trial was unconstitutional.

A capital sentencing decision, Justice Lewis F. Powell, Jr., wrote in the majority opinion, should center on the "blameworthiness" of the defendant. The victim impact statement created an unacceptable risk that a jury might impose the death penalty in an arbitrary and capricious manner in violation of the Eighth Amendment. A statement containing descriptions of the family's grief and suffering had the potential to divert a jury from its proper focus on the moral culpability of the defendant. Decisions on the death penalty had to be "based on reason rather than caprice or emotion." Many of the factors in a victim impact statement were irrelevant to the question of blameworthiness because they were unknown to the killer at the time of the crime.

Justice Powell pointed out that victim impact statements could lead to a double standard of justice. "We are troubled by the implication that defendants whose victims were assets to their community are more deserving of punishment than those whose victims are perceived to be less worthy."

In dissent, Justice Antonin Scalia emphasized the growing concern for victims' rights. He noted this concern stemmed from the feeling many citizens had that the criminal justice system increasingly failed to balance mitigating factors on behalf of a defendant against the harm that person caused to innocent members of society. He disputed the idea that blameworthiness was the only relevant consideration in death sentencing, observing that criminal codes routinely attached "more severe penalties to crimes based on the consequences to victims."

Impact

Justice Scalia's dissent was echoed by groups advocating the rights of crime victims. These organizations, which had become increasingly active in recent years, denounced *Booth v. Maryland* as a setback to legitimate efforts to furnish victims a more important role in the criminal justice process. At the time of the *Booth* ruling, 36 states and the federal government provided for the inclusion of victim impact statements in a variety of criminal proceedings. *Booth* made it clear that laws permitting the use of these statements at capital trials were unconstitutional.

South Carolina v. Gathers (1989) extended this principle to forbidding the prosecution from making statements about characteristics of the victim (such as his religiosity) that were not relevant to understanding the circumstances of the crime but suggested that the crime was more heinous because of the worthiness of the victim. However, *Payne v. Tennessee* (discussed later) represents an abrupt change of course for the Court on this issue.

BURGER V. KEMP,
483 U.S. 107 (1987)

Background

Christopher Burger was convicted for murder in Wayne County, Georgia, and sentenced to death on January 25, 1978. He brought a habeas corpus petition that asserted that he had been denied his constitutional right to "effective assistance of counsel" because his attorney "failed to make an adequate investigation of the possibly mitigating circumstances of his offense." The district court and the court of appeals successively turned down his claim.

Capital Punishment

Legal Issues

The Supreme Court has interpreted the "right to assistance of counsel" in criminal cases as specified in the Sixth Amendment to mean a right to a reasonably *effective* counsel. A lawyer, for example, who sleeps through most of the trial or is drunk cannot effectively assist the defendant, and such a defendant thus does not have the protection intended by the Constitution.

In *Strickland v. Washington* (1984), the Supreme Court declared that to make a claim of ineffective counsel, the defendant had to show the counsel was deficient, making mistakes or omissions that a reasonably competent professional would not make. The defendant also has to show that any such errors were so serious that they prejudiced the outcome of the case, thus depriving the defendant of a fair trial. In general, courts have interpreted this standard quite strictly in an attempt to prevent a flood of frivolous appeals.

In this case, the specific claim was that Burger's counsel was ineffective because he made no effort to investigate or establish mitigating circumstances (specifically, the defendant's troubled childhood in a drug-infested home) in the penalty phase. He also failed to put the defendant, his mother, and another witness on the stand to give testimony about these circumstances. This failure may have resulted in the defendant receiving the death penalty rather than a life sentence.

Decision

In his majority opinion, Justice Stevens agreed that a capital sentencing phase was sufficiently like a trial as to require similar standards of effective assistance of counsel. On the other hand, he noted that the earlier *Strickland* decision had insisted that evaluation of an attorney's performance must be "deferential" and strive to avoid second-guessing or speaking from hindsight.

Speaking for a 5-4 majority, Justice Stevens found that Burger's attorney had acted reasonably in evaluating evidence of the defendant's "unhappy childhood" and in deciding not to put witnesses relevant to that claim on the stand during the penalty hearing, including the defendant himself, whose lack of remorse and tendency to brag may have made him a poor witness. The Court went on to say that while the defendant's counsel "could well have made a more thorough investigation then he did," the court must address "not what is prudent or appropriate, but what is constitutionally compelled." Defendant's counsel did interview the relevant witnesses, and his decision not to use them was a "reasonable professional judgment." The Court majority thus denied Burger's petition. The four dissenters, led by Justice Harry Blackmun, disagreed that the defendant's counsel had adequately sought mitigating evidence, and also pointed out that the counsel rejected the free assistance of a lawyer who had known the defendant because the lawyer was black.

Impact

This decision shows the considerable reluctance of appeals courts to accept appeals based on ineffective assistance of counsel if counsel's actions are at all within the parameters of normal professional procedure. The justices in the appeals court and Supreme Court are concerned about avoiding being placed in the potential position of having to perform what might be called "quality control" on every criminal defense in a capital case.

THOMPSON V. OKLAHOMA,
487 U.S. 815 (1988)

Background

William Wayne Thompson was 15 when he participated in the murder of his brother-in-law in January 1983. The prosecution obtained an order allowing Thompson to be tried as an adult under the provisions of an Oklahoma statute that permitted such a proceeding if the court found the circumstances of the crime warranted the action, and there were no reasonable prospects for rehabilitation of the defendant in the juvenile system. The young man was convicted of first-degree murder and sentenced to death. After the Oklahoma Court of Appeals rejected his contention that the execution of a minor constituted cruel and unusual punishment in violation of the Eighth Amendment, Thompson successfully petitioned the Supreme Court for review.

Legal Issues

The question before the Supreme Court was whether it was appropriate to execute a defendant for a capital offense committed while the person was a juvenile. The issue was not the age of the defendant at the time the execution would be carried out. Thompson was 21 when the Court considered his case. Rather, the challenge to the Court was to determine whether a person at age 15 could be held fully accountable for criminal actions. American jurisprudence had gradually evolved to the belief that minors were not responsible in the same way as adults for their behavior. However, there was no clear precedent for deciding at what age a juvenile could, or should, be treated as an adult.

Decision

The Supreme Court on June 29, 1988, held that the execution under Oklahoma law of a defendant who was 15 at the time of the capital offense was unconstitutional. The five justices in the majority were unable to agree on a common opinion. In a plurality opinion, Justice John Paul Stevens stated the view of four of the five members of the majority that the execution of any person who committed a capital crime under age 16 offended contemporary standards of decency. It was excessive under the Eighth Amendment to punish with death a young person who was not yet "capable of acting with the degree of culpability" that would justify the ultimate penalty.

Justice Sandra Day O'Connor became the decisive, or swing, vote in the decision. Her opinion consequently expressed the basic consensus of the Court. She stopped short of declaring that all executions of defendants under 16 were unconstitutional. There was no conclusive evidence that the sentiment of society in general was against all such executions. However, she ruled that states could not sentence to death persons aged 15 or younger under capital punishment statutes that specified no minimum age standard for when the crime was committed.

Impact

Thompson v. Oklahoma effectively ended the execution of persons who committed capital offenses before the age of 16. No state had a capital punishment law that expressly allowed the execution of minors at this age, and none was considered likely to enact such a measure. The *Thompson* case had attracted international attention. Many opponents of capital punishment and others felt that the Supreme Court had not gone far enough in its decision. They argued that 18 should be the minimum age at which a person involved in a capital crime should be liable for the death penalty. However in 1989 the Court declined to raise the minimum age when it upheld the death sentences of two defendants who committed their offenses at ages 16 and 17.

Penry v. Lynaugh,
492 U.S. 302 (1989)

Background

In late 1979 Johnny Paul Penry was arrested for the rape and murder of a Texas woman. At a competency hearing before his trial, a clinical psychologist testified that Penry was mentally retarded. He was evaluated as having the mental age of six and one-half. His social maturity, or ability to function in the world, was described as that of a nine- or 10-year-old child. However the jury at the hearing found Penry competent to stand trial.

At the guilt–innocence phase of his trial, Penry's lawyers presented an insanity defense. The defendant was said to suffer from an organic brain disorder that resulted in an inability to learn and a lack of self-control. At the time of his offense, he did not grasp the difference between right and wrong and could not conform his behavior to the law. The prosecution countered with expert testimony that Penry was legally sane but had an antisocial personality. The jury rejected the insanity defense and convicted Penry of capital murder. During the penalty phase of his trial, he was sentenced to death.

The Texas Court of Criminal Appeals rejected the contention that Penry's sentence violated the Eighth Amendment. Although it denied a similar petition, a federal court of appeals noted that Penry's claim raised important issues. The Supreme Court subsequently decided to review the case.

Legal Issues

Penry's counsel argued first that Texas' capital punishment law was worded in such a way that it did not allow the jury to properly take into account the mental retardation of their client as a mitigating factor. The sentencing jury was instructed to include the evidence introduced at the trial in its deliberations. However, the aggravating circumstances presented to the jury were defined in such a way that Penry's limited mental ability was made essentially irrelevant. At a more fundamental level, defense lawyers contended that the Eighth Amendment ban on cruel and unusual punishment prohibited the execution of the mentally retarded. Penry was not fully responsible, or culpable for his actions and should not be punished as if he were.

Decision

The Supreme Court agreed with Penry's lawyers on their procedural issue. On June 26, 1989, the Court reversed Penry's death sentence and instructed Texas officials to revise their sentencing procedures to ensure that full consideration was given to a defendant's mitigating evidence of mental retardation. The Court again stressed the point it first had made in *Lockett v. Ohio* that a state's capital sentencing process had to provide for inclusion of any mitigating factor relevant to a defendant's background, character, and crime.

By a 5-4 vote, however, the Court declined to state that the Eighth Amendment categorically barred the execution of the mentally retarded. Writing for the majority, Justice Sandra Day O'Connor observed that the broad consensus was against holding the severely retarded culpable for their actions. Retarded persons, though, were individuals whose abilities varied greatly. There was no basis to conclude that mentally retarded persons invariably lacked the capacity to act with the degree of responsibility that would justify use of the death penalty. Instead, the court must make an individualized determination as to whether the death sentence is appropriate in each instance where retardation is a possible factor.

Impact

The decision in *Penry v. Lynaugh* has raised a number of difficult questions. Criminal justice experts estimate that roughly 10 percent of the death row population nationwide is at least mildly retarded. However, many of the inmates have never been formally evaluated for mental ability, and the number is at best an approximation. It is unclear what impact *Penry* will have on their legal status.

In large part, this uncertainty is due to the problems involved in determining mental retardation and its effect on criminal behavior. There is no single way to define retardation. In her opinion, Justice O'Connor noted that the concept of "mental age" was too imprecise to serve as a hard and fast rule for deciding whether to hold retarded persons accountable for their actions. In the aftermath of *Penry*, state criminal justice systems are struggling to find workable answers to the question of how retardation affects a person's ability to distinguish right from wrong, to act accordingly, and even to participate in a criminal proceeding.

PAYNE V. TENNESSEE,
501 U.S. 808 (1991)

Background

Defendant Pervis Tyrone Payne was convicted by a jury of two counts of first-degree murder and one count of assault with intent to commit murder in the first degree. He was sentenced to death for each of the murders, plus 30 years for the assault. During the sentencing phase of his trial, Payne presented witnesses, including his parents, who testified to his good character, and a psychologist, who testified that Payne was "mentally handicapped" and had a low IQ score. The State in turn presented the mother of one of the victims, who testified to the severe effects of the crime on her two young grandchildren. In calling for the death penalty, the prosecutor referred graphically to the pain and suffering of the victims and the continuing effect of their death on their loved ones.

Following his conviction, the defendant appealed, arguing that the testimony of the victim's grandmother and the references to victim impact in the prosecutor's closing argument were "prejudicial" and violated the defendant's rights. The Supreme Court of Tennessee rejected the defendant's appeal, and the U.S. Supreme Court agreed to hear the case.

Legal Issues

The basic issue is whether the use of victim impact testimony violates the defendant's Eighth Amendment rights by prejudicing the factfinder through introducing emotional material that is not relevant to the defendant's culpability or "blameworthiness." In *Booth v. Maryland* and *South Carolina v. Gathers*, the Supreme Court had banned victim impact testimony in capital trials for this reason.

Decision

In *Payne*, however, the Court effectively reversed its earlier opinions. Speaking for the majority, Chief Justice Rehnquist said that victim impact can indeed serve as evidence of the amount of harm caused by the crime, and that the criminal law had long recognized that different degrees of harm merit different amounts of punishment. For example, if a bank robber shoots a gun and kills a guard, he may well receive the death penalty, while if a robber in another case tried to shoot a guard but his gun jammed, he may not get the death penalty. Even though both defendants had an equal intent to kill, their actions had different effects. Hearing victim impact evidence, therefore, can help a jury decide the seriousness of the crime and use discretion in determining the penalty. Further, Justice Rehnquist noted that the defense had introduced considerable mitigating evidence concerning the defendant's character, and that it was unfair to deny the prosecution the ability to rebut such evidence by presenting the gruesome facts of the crime as evidence of the defendant's bad character.

Justices Marshall and Blackmun dissented. They reiterated the reasoning behind the Court's earlier decisions, and saw no reason to overturn them. Any value of victim impact evidence is outweighed by its prejudicial effect on the factfinder.

Impact

This decision seems to acknowledge the growing strength of the victim's rights movement and the desire of many states to give the victim's survivors a stronger role in the criminal justice system. If victim impact evidence is regularly introduced, it will tend to offset character evidence offered by the defense, and thus perhaps make the imposition of death sentences more likely.

HERRERA V. COLLINS, 113 U.S. 1993

Background

The defendant, Leonel Torres Herrera, was convicted in 1982 for killing two police officers. At the trial, an eyewitness testified that he saw Herrera do the shooting, and one of the officers was able to corroborate this testimony before he died. In appealing the convictions, Herrera first claimed that these witnesses were unreliable. The Texas Court of Criminal Appeals rejected this appeal, and the U.S. Supreme Court refused to hear the case.

Herrera then raised a new appeal. This time he asserted that his brother, before his death in 1984, had admitted to his lawyer and his son that he, not Leonel, had killed the two officers. The state district court rejected the appeal, saying that no evidence of this claim was made in the original trial and that the appeals court would not consider facts not in evidence. The Texas Court of Criminal Appeals upheld the lower court's ruling, and the U.S. Supreme Court again refused to hear the case.

Finally, in 1992, Herrera raised a constitutional claim that because he was innocent of the crime and further, because police had covered up evidence of his innocence, his rights under the Eighth and Fourteenth Amendment had been violated. Although higher state and federal courts were skeptical of this argument, this time the case made it to the U.S. Supreme Court.

Legal Issues

The question here is whether the federal courts were obliged to consider a claim of actual innocence, even if it is presented many years (and appeals) after the offense had been committed.

Decision

By a 6-3 majority, the Court rejected Herrera's claim. Speaking for the majority, Chief Justice Rehnquist noted that Herrera's evidence consisted of affidavits from people no longer around to be cross-examined, and mainly consisted of hearsay. Even so, if the evidence had been offered at the original trial, it could have been legitimately weighed by the jury against other evidence that would lead to a verdict. But such evidence appearing years later "falls far short of that which would have to be made in order to trigger the sort of constitutional claim which we have assumed . . . to exist."

Speaking in dissent Justice Harry Blackmun said that "Nothing could be more contrary to contemporary standards of decency . . . or more shocking to the conscience . . . than to execute a person who is actually innocent." For

the dissenters, the possibility of such a miscarriage of justice clearly outweighed any interest in maintaining orderly or workable court procedures.

Impact

The Court's findings in *Herrera* provoked considerable outrage on the part
of death penalty opponents and the general public. The possibility of executing the innocent is a major argument frequently made by abolitionists,
and many observers said they were shocked that the Court did not see a
need to seriously consider a claim of actual innocence, even one presented
belatedly.

Death penalty supporters generally replied that if the Court had found
otherwise defendants could launch last-minute appeals, based on tenuous or
possibly fabricated evidence, and forestall their execution indefinitely.
Courts should have strict procedures to ensure fairness in the death penalty
process, but there has to be a closure somewhere.

CHAPTER 3

CHRONOLOGY

This chapter presents a chronology of significant developments in the history of capital punishment. Although some important earlier historical events are included, the main focus is on developments since the 1920s, when capital punishment in its modern form became a part of American life.

1700s B.C.

■ The Code of Hammurabi decrees the death penalty for a variety of offenses, including the fraudulent sale of beer.

600s B.C.

■ The legal code of Dracon of Athens has numerous death penalties for even the most petty crimes, thus inspiring the word "draconian" to refer to excessive punishment.

CA. 399 B.C.

■ The execution of Socrates for heresy and "corruption of the young" illustrates a common use of capital punishment against offenders who attack religion and its close ally, the state.

CA. A.D. 29

■ In the execution that most shaped Western civilization, Jesus Christ is crucified by Roman authorities for sedition against the state. Abolitionists would note that Jesus forgave the two thieves who were executed with him, while death penalty supporters note that Jesus did not say the thieves should not die for their crime.

Chronology

1500s

- In the evolving English legal system, only seven crimes are now officially punishable by death: treason, petty treason (murder of a husband by his wife), burglary, larceny, robbery, rape, and arson. Nevertheless, Henry VIII sets a new record for extrajudicial executions.

1612

- The draconian criminal code of the newly founded colony of Virginia extends the death penalty even to trading with American Indians or killing chickens. Later, colonies such as Massachusetts and New York will also use the death penalty for a variety of offenses, such as witchcraft, adultery, and blasphemy.

1682

- Countering the trend toward harsh laws in colonial America, Pennsylvania and New Jersey, settled mainly by pacifist Quakers, allow only treason and murder to be punishable by death. Later, however, more capital offenses are added.

1689

- The British Bill of Rights forbids cruel and unusual punishments, using language that will be adopted later in the Eighth Amendment to the U.S. Constitution.

1764

- Italian jurist Cesare Beccaria publishes his *Essay on Crimes and Punishment*. It is the first systematic look at deterrence and proportionality of punishment, and his ideas will influence early attempts to abolish capital punishment.

1785

- The Virginia legislature fails to abolish capital punishment by only one vote.

1789

- On the eve of the French Revolution, Dr. Joseph-Ignace Guillotin proposes a beheading machine that is eventually given his name. Like later methods of execution, the guillotine is touted as a humane alternative. It also expresses the Revolutionary ideal of treating people of all stations alike, rather than reserving some forms of execution for the nobility.

1791

- The first 10 amendments to the U.S. Constitution, or Bill of Rights, is adopted. Several of the amendments are concerned with the rights of criminal defendants to due process. The Eighth Amendment prohibits "cruel and unusual punishment." The Constitution elsewhere, however, assumes the legitimacy of capital punishment.

1794

- Pennsylvania institutes the process of distinguishing different degrees of murder. Capital punishment is reserved for first-degree murders.

1833

- Edward Livingston's "Introductory Report to the System of Penal Law Prepared for the State of Louisiana" calls for the abolition of capital punishment in that state. Livingston's proposals are rejected, but they greatly contribute to the growing debate over abolition.

1837

- New Jersey introduces the right of jurors to impose at their discretion a lesser penalty than death for a capital crime.

1845

- Death penalty opponents meet in Philadelphia to form the first national abolitionist organization, the American Society for the Abolition of Capital Punishment.

1846

- Michigan becomes the first state to abolish the death penalty, except for treason against the state. A few years later, Rhode Island and Wisconsin will also abolish capital punishment.

1868

- The Fourteenth Amendment is passed during the Reconstruction period following the Civil War. Its provisions for due process of the law and for equal protection of the laws will sometimes be used to challenge capital punishment.

1879

- The Supreme Court applies the Eighth Amendment to a capital case for the first time. In *Wilkerson v. Utah*, the Court decides that a public execution of a murderer does not violate the amendment's ban on cruel and unusual punishment.

1890

- The Supreme Court decision *In re Kemmler* finds that capital punishment is not inherently cruel and unusual and that the newly invented electric chair may be used.

1895

- The American Federation of Labor calls for the abolition of the "revolting practice" of capital punishment.

1897

- The number of federal capital offenses reaches a low of three: treason, murder, and rape.

1910

- In *Weems v. United States*, the Supreme Court says that what constitutes "cruel and unusual punishment" is subject to change due to the "enlightenment" of public opinion. This "evolving standard" will be called upon by later justices as a justification for banning aspects of capital punishment.

1924

- *February 8:* A gas chamber is used for the first time in the execution of Gee John, a convicted tong (gang) murderer, in Nevada. Although electrocution remains the predominant mode of execution for some time, five other states construct gas chambers in the next five years.
- *September 10:* In a case which gains nationwide attention, Richard A. Loeb and Nathan F. Leopold, Jr., are sentenced to life imprisonment in Chicago for the murder of a neighborhood child. Their attorney, Clarence Darrow, had argued the execution of the two young men would serve no useful purpose. The success of this argument encourages opponents of capital punishment across the country.

1925

- *January 31:* President Calvin Coolidge signs a measure substituting electrocution for hanging in federal death sentences.
- *July 20:* The American League to Abolish Capital Punishment is formed in New York City by Clarence Darrow, Lewis E. Lawes, and other leading opponents of the death penalty. In its first year, the league enrolls over 1,000 members nationwide and establishes affiliates in several states.
- *August 23:* Nicola Sacco and Bartolomeo Vanzetti are executed in Massachusetts for two murders that took place in 1920. The case, which commanded worldwide interest, had precipitated an unprecedented six-year legal battle over their guilt or innocence. Their executions contribute to an upsurge of abolitionist activity and lead to the formation of the Massachusetts Council for the Abolition of the Death Penalty.

1931

- *December 31:* The federal government begins to publish annual statistics on executions in the United States. It is reported 155 persons were executed in 1930.

1932

- *March 1:* The baby son of Charles A. Lindbergh is kidnapped from his home in Hopewell, New Jersey. The body of the infant is found in the nearby woods two months later. The incident leads Congress to pass a federal kidnapping statute, popularly known as the Lindbergh Act, that makes the crime a capital offense. Similar "Lindbergh laws" are enacted in more than 20 states by the end of the decade.
- *March 13:* Kansas reinstates the death penalty following a series of violent crimes by "Bonnie and Clyde" (Bonnie Parker and Clyde Barrow), Charles "Pretty Boy" Floyd, and others.
- *November 7:* In a decision related to the Scottsboro Boys case, the U.S. Supreme Court rules in *Powell v. Alabama* that failure to provide counsel to a defendant in a capital case violates constitutional due process protections.

1936

- *April 3:* After a sensational trial, Bruno Richard Hauptmann is executed in New Jersey for the kidnapping murder of the Lindbergh baby.
- *August 14:* In the last freely accessible public execution in the United States, a crowd of 20,000 watches as Rainey Bethea is hanged in Owensboro, Kentucky.

Chronology

1937

- *January 4:* The American League to Abolish Capital Punishment initiates a drive to seek state laws preventing the execution of minors.
- *May 21:* In Galena, Missouri, approximately 500 persons pay an admission fee to the gallows to view the execution of Roscoe Jackson. It is the last execution in America that general spectators are allowed to attend.

1939

- *October 11:* The National Association for the Advancement of Colored People (NAACP) forms the Legal Defense and Education Fund (LDF) to provide legal assistance to the poor and to challenge racial segregation in the courts. This will lead to involvement in defending blacks in capital cases and in challenging the death penalty.

1944

- *November 13:* Pope Pius XII justifies the use of capital punishment.

1945

- *January 31:* Private Eddie D. Slovik is executed by firing squad in the European theater of operations. He is the only U.S. soldier put to death for desertion during World War II.

1946

- *January 19:* President Harry S Truman and the War Department limit imposition of the death penalty by military courts-martial.
- *October 1:* An international military tribunal at Nuremberg, Germany, sentences 12 former Nazi leaders to death. In subsequent "Nuremberg trials," an additional 25 German war criminals receive the death penalty.

1947

- *January 13:* The U.S. Supreme Court, in *Louisiana ex rel Francis v. Resweber,* rules that a second attempt to execute an individual after a malfunctioning electric chair had halted the first try does not constitute cruel and unusual punishment under the Eighth Amendment.

1948

- *May 22:* Caryl Chessman is sentenced to death in California for a kidnapping crime he insists he did not commit. Chessman later becomes a famous death row author and symbol of resistance to capital punishment.

- *July 14:* The U.S. Army ends mandatory death sentences for murder and rape.
- *October 19:* The United Nations Human Rights Commission rejects an amendment proposed by the Soviet Union to the International Bill of Rights that would ban the death penalty during peacetime.

1950

- *May 24:* Austria abolishes the death penalty.

1952

- *November:* The November issue of the *Annals of the American Academy of Political and Social Science* is dedicated to research on the issue of capital punishment. The conclusion in all of the articles and reports is that the death penalty is ineffective and unwise.

1953

- *June 19:* Julius and Ethel Rosenberg are put to death for furnishing information about the atomic bomb to the Soviet Union. They are the first U.S. civilians executed for espionage.

1957

- *June 6:* Hawaii, which had not executed anyone in more than 25 years, abolishes the death penalty for all crimes.
- *June 30:* Arthur Koestler's *Reflections on Hanging*, a highly critical study of the death penalty, is published in the United States.

1958

- *April 2:* Delaware governor J. Caldo Boggs signs into law a bill that abolishes capital punishment. The state is the first to eliminate the death penalty in 40 years.

1959

- *January 4:* The New York Committee to Abolish Capital Punishment is established.

1960

- *February 18:* California governor Edmund G. Brown announces he will call a special session of the state legislature to consider elimination of the death penalty. Brown links the issue of capital punishment to the case of death row inmate Caryl Chessman.

- *March 10:* The California legislature rejects Governor Edmund G. Brown's abolition bill and adjourns from special session.
- *April 6:* The UN Economic and Social Council calls on Secretary General Dag Hammarskjold to study the effect of the death penalty on crime.
- *April 9:* The death penalty is backed by Vice President Richard M. Nixon and opposed by Senator Hubert H. Humphrey in responses to a questionnaire sent to major presidential contenders by the Union of American Hebrew Congregations.
- *May 2:* After a protracted 12-year legal struggle, the internationally renowned death row author Caryl Chessman is executed at San Quentin, California.

1961

- *January 28:* In a study conducted at the request of the Governors Board of the American Bar Association (ABA), the American Bar Foundation finds that long delays in carrying out death sentences weaken public confidence in the law. The study urges uniform post conviction procedures.
- *April 1:* A pioneering law article, "Testing the Death Penalty," by Los Angeles attorney Gerald Gottlieb is published in the spring issue of the *Southern California Law Review.* In the article, Gottlieb suggests the traditional abolitionist tactic of persuading state legislatures to end capital punishment has met with only limited success. He argues that the death penalty should be attacked through the court system on the grounds that it violates the Eighth Amendment's prohibition of cruel and unusual punishment.
- *December 18:* Delaware legislators override a veto by Governor Elbert N. Carvel to reinstate the death penalty.

1963

- *March 14:* Georgia raises the minimum age for execution from 10 to 17.
- *March 15:* Victor Feuger is hanged in Iowa for kidnapping. He is the last federal prisoner executed in the United States.
- *October 21:* In a dissent to a U.S. Supreme Court decision to refuse to hear the case of *Rudolph v. Alabama,* Justice Arthur J. Goldberg, joined by Justices William O. Douglas and William J. Brennan, Jr., contends there are substantive reasons to consider whether the Eighth and Fourteenth Amendments to the Constitution permit the death penalty for a convicted rapist who neither took nor endangered human life.

1964

- *May 2:* Attorney Melvin Belli charges that of 23 verdicts by Dallas juries entailing death sentences, seven were given after only four to seven minutes of deliberation.
- *November 4:* In a statewide referendum, Oregon voters approve abolition of the death penalty by a margin of 455,000 to 302,000.

1965

- *March 5:* Vermont ends the death penalty except for a second conviction for murder.
- *March 12:* West Virginia legislators vote to eliminate the death penalty for all crimes.
- *March 17:* The National District Attorney's Association urges the abolition of capital punishment.
- *June 1:* New York governor Nelson Rockefeller signs into law an abolition bill. However, the measure retains the death penalty for killing a law enforcement officer in the line of duty.
- *June 20:* The American Civil Liberties Union (ACLU) announces a nationwide drive to end capital punishment.
- *November 8:* The United Kingdom abolishes the death penalty for a trial period of five years.

1966

- *April 24:* The NAACP Legal Defense and Education Fund (LDF) announces an extensive survey on the use of the death penalty for rape convictions in the South.
- *June 29:* The Lutheran Church in America urges the abolition of capital punishment.
- *November 9:* Colorado voters reject a proposal to end capital punishment in the state.

1967

- *April 12:* California carries out its first execution in four years.
- *April 13:* The NAACP LDF and the ACLU challenge the constitutionality of Florida's death penalty laws in federal court. The court temporarily halts executions in the state pending its review of the class action suit.
- *June 2:* Luis Jose Monge dies in Colorado's gas chamber. Soon after, mounting legal challenges to the constitutionality of the death penalty bring about a moratorium on its use. Monge becomes the last person executed in the United States until 1977.

Chronology

- *June 27:* Charging there is a disproportionate number of blacks on San Quentin's death row, the NAACP LDF files a class action suit in federal court in San Francisco to block executions in the state.
- *July 5:* A federal district court stays all California executions while it considers the NAACP LDF claim that the state's death penalty law is unconstitutional.
- *August 10:* The NAACP LDF, contending that attorneys often stop representing death row inmates when a case has gone beyond state court appeals, urges a federal district court in California to order hearings on the contention that the legal rights of the inmates have been violated.
- *August 25:* A federal court in San Francisco cancels the blanket stay of executions in California and rules that appeals for each inmate must be considered separately.
- *November 27:* In response to a suit brought by the ACLU, a California superior court rules that the state's death penalty does not constitute cruel and unusual punishment even in cases where murder has not been committed.

1968

- *May 3:* NAACP LDF director Jack Greenberg releases statistics showing 90% of persons executed in the South for rape since 1930 were black.
- *June 3:* The U.S. Supreme Court, in *Witherspoon v. Illinois*, holds that persons who oppose the death penalty cannot automatically be excluded from juries in capital cases.
- *July 2:* The Johnson administration asks Congress to abolish the death penalty for all federal crimes and to reduce to life imprisonment the sentences of federal prisoners on death row. Attorney General Ramsey Clark urges the United States to join over 70 other nations that have abandoned capital punishment.
- *September 13:* The National Council of Churches issues a policy statement calling for the abolition of capital punishment.
- *October 30:* Novelist and journalist Truman Capote, at odds with ABC-TV over the scheduling of his documentary *Death Row, USA*, demands that the program be aired prior to a pending U.S. Supreme Court decision on whether protracted delays in capital cases constitute cruel and unusual punishment. ABC ultimately decides not to broadcast the film.
- *November 18:* The California Supreme Court rules that the state's death penalty is constitutional, rejecting arguments that the law does not provide sufficient standards by which judges and juries should decide who receives a death sentence.
- *November 26:* A U.S. appeals court rules that North Carolina's provisions for imposing the death penalty are unconstitutional.

- *December 31:* The Federal Prisons Bureau reports that 1968 marks the first year without an execution since statistics were first collected in 1930. NAACP LDF director Jack Greenberg describes the current legal moratorium on capital punishment as a "de facto national abolition of the death penalty."

1969

- *February 15:* A Gallup Poll survey finds growing support among whites for the death penalty for murder and opposition by a majority of blacks.
- *March 3:* The National Urban League urges abolition of the death penalty throughout the United States.
- *March 31:* New Mexico becomes the 13th state to abolish or severely limit capital punishment. The death penalty is retained only for killing a police officer or jail guard.
- *April 4:* The U.S. Supreme Court hears arguments in the case of William L. Maxwell, a black man sentenced to death for rape in Arkansas in 1962. The case is expected to produce a landmark decision on the constitutionality of the death penalty.
- *December 18:* Great Britain makes permanent its ban on capital punishment for all crimes except treason.

1970

- *January 31:* The American Psychiatric Association, in a brief to the U.S. Supreme Court, claims the threat of the death penalty may incite certain persons to crime rather than deter them.
- *March 25:* President Richard M. Nixon calls for the death penalty to curb the rise of bombings in cities.
- *June 2:* The U.S. Supreme Court sends the case of *Maxwell v. Bishop* back to a lower court for procedural review, in effect postponing a decision on the constitutionality of the death penalty. The action leaves intact a judicial freeze that has halted all executions in the United States for the past three years.
- *October 8:* Congress enacts legislation that makes it a capital offense to cause a fatality by a bombing.
- *October 15:* The Justice Department, in a friend-of-the-court brief, notifies the Supreme Court it does not support pending constitutional challenges to capital punishment.
- *December 11:* Setting an important precedent, a federal appeals court in Virginia holds that the death penalty for rape when the victim's life is neither taken nor endangered is unconstitutional.

- *December 29:* Arkansas governor Winthrop Rockefeller commutes the death sentence of all 15 death row inmates in the state to life imprisonment.

1971

- *January 7:* The U.S. National Commission on Reform of Federal Criminal Laws, headed by former California governor Edmund G. Brown, issues a series of recommendations, including abolition of capital punishment.
- *January 20:* The World Council of Churches Central Committee, meeting in Addis Ababa, Ethiopia, urges the nations of the world to eliminate capital punishment as a violation of the "sanctity of life."
- *May 3:* The Supreme Court rejects two major constitutional challenges to the death penalty. Neither an absence of clear standards to guide the imposition of the death sentence nor the common practice of allowing a single jury to determine both guilt and penalty are found to be unconstitutional. The court does not address the basic constitutional question of whether the death penalty constitutes cruel and unusual punishment, thus the nationwide moratorium on executions remains in effect.
- *May 25:* The Connecticut legislature defeats a measure to abolish capital punishment.
- *June 28:* The U.S. Supreme Court, setting aside the death sentences of 39 persons, including mass murderer Richard Speck, announces it will hear several cases during its next term on the constitutionality of capital punishment, but absences from the Court will lead to a delay.
- *September 24:* Faced with the likelihood that only seven justices will be on the bench when its new term begins in early October, the Supreme Court postpones scheduled hearings on capital punishment.
- *October 9:* Pennsylvania governor Milton Shapp and eight former governors from around the country file a friend-of-the-court brief with the U.S. Supreme Court that argues the death penalty does not deter murder.

1972

- *January 17:* The New Jersey Supreme Court in a 6-1 vote rules that the state's capital punishment statute as currently written is unconstitutional.
- *January 26:* A bill calling for the death penalty for drug pushers is defeated in the Georgia legislature.
- *February 18:* The California Supreme Court, in *People v. Anderson*, rules that the state's death penalty is unconstitutional. Among those whose

Capital Punishment

sentences are changed to life imprisonment by the decision are Sirhan Sirhan, convicted assassin of Senator Robert F. Kennedy, and mass murderer Charles Manson. California governor Ronald Reagan charges that the court has set itself "above the people and the legislature."

- *February 23:* A California superior court judge releases black militant Angela Davis on bail, holding that the statutory ban on bail in capital cases had been invalidated by the California Supreme Court decision.
- *April 2:* A UN inquiry into the death penalty indicates that many governments are reluctant to abolish capital punishment. Replies from 69 countries reveal that 75 percent still employ the death penalty, although few people are actually sentenced to death and even fewer executed.
- *April 26:* The United Methodist Church, at a convention in Atlanta, Georgia,adopts a doctrine of social principles that includes opposition to capital punishment.
- *June 25:* Governor Ronald Reagan leads a successful drive to place on the November ballot a proposed amendment to the California constitution that would restore capital punishment.
- *June 29:* In a landmark decision in *Furman v. Georgia,* the U.S. Supreme Court rules that the death penalty, as imposed under current statutes, is unconstitutional. The court finds that the arbitrary and capricious manner in which the death penalty is applied constitutes cruel and unusual punishment. The decision spares more than 600 persons on death row. In his dissent, Chief Justice Warren Burger notes that states could retain capital punishment by altering their laws to conform to the court's ruling. At a news conference, President Richard Nixon criticizes the Supreme Court decision and urges retention of the death penalty.
- *November 7:* A referendum to restore the death penalty is approved by a large margin of California voters.
- *November 22:* A Gallup Poll finds that public support for capital punishment is at its highest point in nearly two decades. Fifty-one percent of the persons questioned favored the death penalty for persons convicted of murder.
- *December 6:* The National Association of Attorneys General approves a resolution recommending the death penalty for violent crimes. The association notes that while the Supreme Court outlawed the death penalty in its present form, it did not rule that it is inherently cruel and unusual punishment.
- *December 8:* Governor Reuben Askew signs into law a measure making Florida the first state to reinstate capital punishment since the Supreme Court decision in *Furman v. Georgia.* The bill authorizes the death penalty for premeditated murder and the raping of a child under the age of 11.

Chronology

1973

- *February 12:* The American Bar Association (ABA) votes to recommend a one-year delay on actions to reinstate death penalty statutes on the grounds the issue remains unsettled in the wake of the Supreme Court decision in *Furman v. Georgia.*
- *March 14:* President Richard Nixon in his State of the Union message advocates the imposition of the death penalty for a number of violent crimes.
- *July 26:* The Florida Supreme Court upholds the state's new capital punishment statute. The law provides for a separate sentencing procedure for capital crimes and automatic appeal of all death sentences.
- *December 31:* By the end of 1973, 23 states have enacted new death penalty statutes since the Supreme Court struck down capital punishment laws in June 1972. A total of 44 prisoners await execution across the nation.

1974

- *March 13:* The U.S. Senate approves legislation to reinstate capital punishment for a variety of serious crimes, but the legislation fails to emerge from the House Judiciary Committee.
- *November 21:* The National Conference of Catholic Bishops speaks out against capital punishment in a reversal of the traditional Roman Catholic Church position supporting the death penalty as a legitimate means of self-protection for the state.
- *December 31:* An additional six states by year's end have approved new capital punishment laws.

1976

- *April 28:* A Gallup Poll shows that 65 percent of Americans favor the death penalty for convicted murderers, 28 percent are opposed, and seven percent are undecided.
- *July 2:* The Supreme Court rules that the death penalty is not inherently cruel or unusual. In its landmark decision in *Gregg v. Georgia* and two related cases, the Court upholds the constitutionality of the new statutes in Georgia, Florida, and Texas. However, in *Woodson v. North Carolina* the Court rules that mandatory death penalty laws that do not allow for differences in defendants and circumstances are unconstitutional.
- *July 6:* Canada abolishes capital punishment for all but traitorous military crimes.
- *August 14:* The Southern Christian Leadership Conference passes a strongly worded resolution against capital punishment.

- *November 2:* Convicted murderer Gary Mark Gilmore, denied a new trial in Utah, says he will not want to appeal and wants to be executed by firing squad as scheduled on November 15.
- *November 15:* Gary M. Gilmore's execution is delayed by legal maneuvers and two unsuccessful attempts at suicide.
- *November 28:* The Law Enforcement Assistance Administration reports that 285 persons were sentenced to death in 1975, bringing the death row population at the end of the year to 479.

1977

- *January 12:* The U.S. Supreme Court rejects motions filed by abolitionist groups seeking to oppose the execution of Gary M. Gilmore scheduled for January 17.
- *January 17:* Gary M. Gilmore is executed by firing squad in Utah State Prison. It is the first execution in the United States since 1967. In what is to become a common practice, opponents of the death penalty conduct a vigil outside the prison.
- *February 15:* The ABA rejects a proposal calling for an end to capital punishment.
- *June 6:* The Supreme Court rules that states may not make the death penalty mandatory for the murder of a police officer. Citing its decisions in July 1976, the Court holds that judges and juries must be allowed to consider mitigating circumstances.
- *June 29:* In *Coker v. Georgia*, the Supreme Court finds that the death penalty for rape is unconstitutional. Citing the *Coker* decision in a summary opinion, the Court holds that the death sentence for nonhomicidal kidnapping is also unconstitutional.
- *August 3:* A federal appeals court in New Orleans reverses a Texas court ruling that TV camerapersons can film executions of condemned prisoners.
- *December 8:* Amnesty International announces a campaign for abolition of the death penalty.

1978

- *January 2:* Results of a study conducted by the Center for Applied Social Research show that murderers of whites are far more likely to be sentenced to death than murderers of blacks.
- *April 22:* The National Legal Aid and Defender Association announces it will not hold future conventions in states that have adopted the death penalty.

- *July 3:* The Supreme Court, in *Lockett v. Ohio*, requires that every person convicted of a capital offense be permitted to offer a broad range of extenuating evidence prior to sentencing.
- *December 31:* Opponents of capital punishment hail the absence of executions in 1978 but note there are 475 persons on death row.

1979

- *February 13:* The American Bar Association calls on the Supreme Court to require that free counsel be provided to persons who are appealing their state death sentences in federal court.
- *May 25:* Convicted murderer John A. Spenkelink is electrocuted in Florida. He is the first person executed in two years and only the second since the Supreme Court restored the death penalty in 1976.

1980

- *February 12:* Serial killer Theodore R. Bundy is sentenced to death for the kidnapping and murder of a 12-year old girl.
- *April 14:* Norman Mailer wins the Pulitzer Prize for *The Executioner's Song*, a fictionalized account of the last nine months of Gary M. Gilmore, the first person executed in the United States after a 10-year moratorium in 1977.
- *May 19:* In *Godfrey v. Georgia*, the Supreme Court sets aside death penalty statutes that are excessively broad or vague.
- *May 26:* Amnesty International calls for the creation of a presidential commission on capital punishment.
- *July 22:* Delegates to the annual meeting of the American Medical Association (AMA) proclaim that physicians should not participate in the execution of prisoners.
- *November 13:* The Roman Catholic bishops of the United States object to the fact that the death penalty is more likely to be exercised unjustly against the poor who cannot afford adequate defense but uphold the principle of the state's right to impose capital punishment.

1981

- *March 15:* A Gallup Poll reveals that two-thirds of all Americans, the highest percentage in 28 years, favor the death penalty for murder. Reflecting the level of support, 35 states have enacted new death penalty statutes since the Supreme Court invalidated current capital punishment laws in 1972.

- *May 4:* The U.S. Supreme Court for the first time extends constitutional protection against double jeopardy beyond the question of guilt to the sentence itself, ruling in *Bullington v. Missouri* that a defendant who had received a life sentence at a first trial could not be sentenced to death on retrial.
- *August 9:* Justice Department statistics show that more than half the prison inmates awaiting execution in 1980 were in Georgia, Florida, and Texas.
- *August 28:* The Food and Drug Administration (FDA) rejects a request by five condemned prisoners to use federal drug regulations to block their execution by lethal injection because the chemicals used are not federally approved.
- *September 28–October 2:* The World Medical Association issues a resolution condemning physician participation in capital punishment.
- *September 30:* France abolishes capital punishment.

1982

- *July 2:* The Supreme Court determines, in *Enmund v. Florida*, that death is an excessive and disproportionate punishment for a defendant who aided and abetted in the commission of murder but who had not killed, attempted to kill, or intended to kill the victim.
- *August 22:* The number of prisoners under death sentence in the United States exceeds 1,000.
- *December 7:* Charlie Brooks is executed by a combination of sedatives and drugs in Texas. He is the first person put to death by lethal injection.

1983

- *January 15:* In the first instance of a pontiff speaking out against capital punishment, Pope John Paul II condemns the death penalty in an address to the Vatican diplomatic corps.
- *May 9:* Associate Supreme Court Justice Lewis F. Powell, Jr., in a speech delivered in Georgia, says that unless Congress and the courts can find a speedier way to handle death penalty appeals, states should abolish capital punishment.
- *July 6:* In *Barefoot v. Estelle*, the Supreme Court holds that petitions for review in capital cases must raise issues that are at least "debatable among jurists of reason" and establishes guidelines for lower federal courts handling death penalty appeals.
- *October 11:* The Court of Military Appeals, the nation's highest military court, strikes down procedures used for sentencing members of the armed forces to death. The court notes the president can remedy the constitutional defects without new legislation.

Chronology

- *October 15:* A federal appeals court panel orders the FDA to weigh evidence that drugs used for execution by lethal injection can cause "torturous pain."

1984

- *January 23:* The Supreme Court, in *Pulley v. Harris,* rules that a state may carry out the death penalty without first conducting a "proportionality" review to ensure the sentence is in line with other sentences imposed in the state for similar crimes.
- *January 31:* President Ronald Reagan signs an executive order during the month designed to correct defects in the administration of the death penalty under the Uniform Code of Military Justice.
- *November 1:* Margie Velma Barfield, who was convicted of killing her fiancé and who confessed to killing three other people by poisoning, is executed by lethal injection in North Carolina. She is the first woman put to death in the United States in 22 years.

1985

- *March 20:* The Supreme Court rules that the FDA is not required to approve the drugs used to execute prisoners by lethal injection.
- *July 26:* Reflecting concern over a string of recent spying cases involving Navy personnel, Congress approves a measure that would permit execution of military personnel for peacetime espionage.
- *September 11:* Charles Rumbaugh, convicted of committing robbery and murder when he was 17, is executed by lethal injection in Texas. The execution is the first in more than two decades for a crime committed by someone under age 18.
- *November 13:* A study conducted by the ACLU asserts that since 1900, 343 persons were wrongfully sentenced to death in America, 25 of whom were actually executed.
- *November 28:* A Gallup Poll shows that American support of capital punishment for a variety of serious crimes has increased sharply over the last seven years. Seventy-five percent of Americans now favor the death penalty for murder.

1986

- *January 10:* James Terry Roach, who was 17 when he took part in the murder of a teenage couple, dies in South Carolina's electric chair despite international protests against the execution of offenders for crimes they committed while juveniles. Mother Teresa and UN Secretary General Javier Perez de Cuellar are among those pleading for mercy.

- *February 23:* President Ronald Reagan signs a measure under which members of the armed forces convicted of espionage during peacetime could be executed.
- *April 15:* Amnesty International reports that there were more than 1,125 documented executions worldwide in 1985.
- *May 5:* The Supreme Court holds that dedicated opponents of capital punishment may be barred from juries in capital cases regardless of whether the move increases the likelihood of conviction.
- *June 26:* In *Ford v. Wainwright*, the Supreme Court rules that the Eighth Amendment bars the execution of persons presently insane. The Court requires states to establish procedures for determining sanity that meet minimum due process standards.
- *November 4:* A conservative backlash results in California Supreme Court Chief Justice Rose Bird and other liberal justices who had voted against capital punishment being voted out of office.
- *November 26:* New Mexico governor Toney Anaya, who leaves office in a few weeks, commutes the death sentences of all five persons awaiting execution in the state.

1987

- *February 18:* Amnesty International announces it is opening a worldwide campaign against the death penalty in the United States.
- *April 23:* In a controversial decision, the Supreme Court finds that Georgia's capital punishment law is constitutionally applied despite a wide statistical disparity between whites and blacks in the imposition of death sentences. The ruling in *McClesky v. Kemp* ends what opponents had called their last sweeping constitutional challenge to capital punishment.
- *June 15:* The Supreme Court annuls a Maryland law that provided for the use of "victim impact statements" at death sentence hearings. The decision in *Booth v. Maryland* is denounced by victims rights groups.
- *June 23:* The Supreme Court strikes down the last vestiges of the mandatory death penalty in the United States, holding that state laws making executions compulsory for murders committed by prisoners serving life terms without parole are unconstitutional.
- *September 26:* Pope John Paul II appeals for clemency in the case of Paula R. Cooper, an 18-year-old Indiana woman facing execution for a murder she committed when she was 15.
- *November 1:* A study published in the *Stanford Law Review* by professors Hugo Adam Bedau and Michael L. Radelet finds that 349 innocent persons were convicted and 23 put to death in 20th-century America.

Chronology

1988

- **March 15:** Willie Jasper Darden, a convicted murderer whose case attracted worldwide attention, is executed in Florida.
- **June 29:** Addressing the issue of juvenile executions, the Supreme Court rules in *Thompson v. Oklahoma* that a state may not impose the death sentence for crimes committed by persons when they were less than 16 years old unless the state has specifically legislated the death penalty for minors.
- **July 31:** The Justice Department reports that of every 30 persons sentenced to death since capital punishment was reinstated in 1976, 10 left death row and one was executed.
- **August 1:** The movie *The Thin Blue Line* by filmmaker Errol Morris is released. The documentary film examines the possible innocence of Randall Dale Adams, on death row in Texas for murder of a police officer. The movie brings national attention to the case, and Adams is subsequently released.
- **September 25:** Republican candidate George Bush favors capital punishment and Democratic candidate Michael S. Dukakis opposes it in their first presidential election debate.
- **October 12:** In the second presidential election debate, CNN newsperson Bernard Shaw asks Democratic candidate Michael S. Dukakis if he would still oppose the death penalty if Dukakis' wife were raped and murdered. Dukakis answers he would still oppose the death penalty. The appropriateness of the question, as well as Dukakis' response, generates considerable controversy.
- **November 22:** Congress adjourns after passing a comprehensive drug bill that includes the death penalty for homicides connected to drug-related crimes.

1989

- **January 24:** After numerous appeals and delays, serial killer Ted Bundy is electrocuted in Florida.
- **February 6:** In his annual message before the midyear convention of the American Bar Association, Supreme Court Justice William H. Rehnquist urges reform of the system by which death sentences are reviewed in federal courts. Calling for changes to speed up the appeals process, he notes that the elapsed time between the commission of a capital crime and the date of execution averages eight years nationally.
- **February 28:** The Supreme Court, in its decision in *Dugger v. Adams*, turns down an appeal that argued that the trial judge had improperly instructed the jury about its role in sentencing.

- *May:* The United Nations Economic and Social Council passes a resolution calling for a ban on execution of mentally retarded or mentally incompetent people.
- *June 12:* In *South Carolina v. Gathers* the Supreme Court declares that it is unconstitutional to present "victim impact" evidence in the penalty phase of a capital trial.
- *June 23:* The Supreme Court rules that indigent inmates on death row do not have a constitutional right to a lawyer to assist them in a second round of appeals.
- *June 26:* In *Penry v. Lynaugh*, the Supreme Court rules that execution of the mentally retarded is not precluded by the Eighth Amendment, but the Court requires states to establish clear standards for considering mental retardation as a mitigating factor. In two other decisions (*Stanford v. Kentucky* and *Wilkins v. Missouri*), the court holds that the execution of defendants who committed a capital offense at age 16 or 17 is not unconstitutional "cruel and unusual" punishment.
- *July 13:* The Indiana Supreme Court bars the execution of Paula R. Cooper for a murder she committed when she was 15 years old. Her death sentence had drawn appeals for leniency from a number of groups around the world.

1990

- *August 16:* Louisiana governor Buddy Roemer commutes to life imprisonment the death sentence of Ronald Monroe. The case had attracted national attention because of the possibility that it was an estranged husband, not Monroe, who had killed a woman in 1977.
- *September 21:* A special committee of federal judges established by Supreme Court Chief Justice William H. Rehnquist submits its findings on the judicial system's handling of death penalty cases. The panel, headed by retired Supreme Court Justice Lewis F. Powell, Jr., recommends imposing strict limits on the multiple appeals filed by death row inmates. Chief Justice Rehnquist formally transmits the panel's proposal to the Senate Judiciary Committee for consideration.
- *October 5:* Fourteen of the nation's most senior federal judges forward an unusual letter to the Senate and House Judiciary Committees. The letter notes that the proposal submitted by Supreme Court Chief Justice William H. Rehnquist for reform of the appeals process in death penalty cases does not reflect the views of the entire federal judiciary on the issue.
- *December 15:* The UN General Assembly adopts the Second Optional Protocol to the International Covenant on Civil and Political Rights. It

calls on all member nations to work to abolish capital punishment. The vote is 59 nations for, 26 against, and 48 abstaining.

1991

- *April 16:* In its decision *McCleskey v. Zant,* the Supreme Court strictly limits the ability of death row prisoners to use habeas corpus petitions to challenge their death sentences in federal court. The Court states that a petitioner will get only one petition and generally cannot raise additional issues later.
- *May:* Ray Copeland, 76, becomes the oldest person to receive a death sentence, for a murder he committed when he was 71 years old.
- *June 24:* The Supreme Court refuses to consider the appeal of convicted murderer Roger Keith Coleman because he had been a day late in filing an appeal in Virginia state court. In *Coleman v. Thompson,* the Court rules that failure to properly use the state appeal system precludes a petitioner from taking the appeal to federal court. This decision becomes part of a broad trend to reduce the appeals rights of death row inmates.
- *June 27:* In *Payne v. Tennessee,* the Supreme Court, reversing its earlier trend, says that juries can take the character of the victim and the impact on his family into account when deciding a capital sentence.
- *June 30:* The parliament of Canada votes 148 to 127 to defeat a proposal to reintroduce capital punishment, which had been abolished in Canada in 1976.
- *October:* The Supreme Court of Canada, in a narrow 4-3 vote, allows accused murderer, rapist, and kidnapper Charles Ng and convicted murderer Joseph Kindler to be extradited to the United States. Previously, Canada, which had abolished capital punishment, had refused to extradite people to countries where they might be subjected to the death penalty. Lawyers for the accused had argued that Canada should demand assurances that the United States would not impose the death penalty before allowing extradition.
- *October 25:* Jerome Allen is sentenced to death in Florida for a murder committed during a robbery when he was 15 years old. Generally, courts had not permitted execution of persons under 16 years of age.
- *December:* The Comprehensive Violent Crime Control Act of 1991 fails to become law when it is vetoed by President George Bush. The bill would have added many new federal capital crimes and restricted a condemned prisoner to a single habeas corpus appeal to the federal courts—something the Court seemed to be doing anyway. Bush vetoed the law in part because he wanted to completely eliminate the habeas corpus appeal.

1992

- *April 21:* Robert Alton Harris is led to the gas chamber at San Quentin prison, California. Harris had fought a tenacious appeals battle. At the last minute, he received a stay of execution from the Ninth District Court of Appeals, but the U.S. Supreme Court, apparently angry at the lower court's continuing to follow a more liberal policy, swiftly overturns the stay and prohibits lower courts from entering any further stays. Harris becomes the first person to be executed in California in 25 years.
- *May 20:* Roger Keith Coleman, who had been the subject of many appeals for mercy from around the world, is executed in Virginia for a murder many believe he did not commit.
- *June 22:* In *Sawyer v. Whittley* the Supreme Court seems to back off somewhat from its restrictions on federal appeals, ruling that certain issues could be raised even if they hadn't been raised earlier at the state level. The issues, however, are limited to procedural violations that prevented defendants from proving innocence of the crime, not mitigation of the sentence.
- *November 3:* Voters in Washington, D.C., overwhelmingly reject a referendum that would have introduced the death penalty into the District of Columbia.

1993

- *January 3:* Westley Allan Dodd, a three-time child killer, is hung in Washington State prison. This is the first hanging in the United States since 1965. Dodd had demanded to be executed, saying that if he were allowed to live he would try to escape and kill again. Offered a choice of hanging or lethal injection, he chose hanging as a more fitting death because he had strangled his youngest victim. Despite his wishes, death penalty opponents tried to block the hanging as cruel and unusual punishment and held a midnight vigil (facing death penalty supporters).
- *January 23:* In *Herrera v. Collins* the Supreme Court refuses to allow Leonel Herrera to introduce new evidence that he said proved that his brother, not he, had killed a Texas policeman in 1981. The court ruled 6-3 that the deadline had long since passed for reexamining the factual part of the case. Justices Blackmun, Stevens, and Souter vigorously dissent, arguing that evidence of actual innocence must always be considered.
- *March 2:* Walter McMillen, a black man convicted in 1988 of killing a white teenager, is released after spending six years on death row. Evidence had emerged that key witnesses against McMillen had lied, possibly with the prosecution's knowledge or encouragement. The outcome is used by abolitionists to argue that an irrevocable penalty of death should not be

imposed because some innocent persons will inevitably be executed. Death penalty supporters point out, however, that McMillen was after all exonerated.

1994

- *February 22:* In his dissent in the case of *Callins v. Collins,* Supreme Court Justice Harry Blackmun declares that the constitutional requirements for individual consideration of defendants and the avoidance of "arbitrary and capricious" sentencing decisions cannot be reconciled, and that he will "no longer tinker with the machinery of death."
- *September 13:* A federal crime bill adds dozens of new federal capital offenses. Congressional Black Caucus members had tried to amend the bill by including the Racial Justice Act, which would have allowed defendants to use statistical evidence of racial disparities in death sentencing in their court appeals, but the amendment was defeated.

1995

- *March 7:* New York governor George Pataki signs a bill restoring capital punishment in the state. Pataki's predecessor Mario Cuomo had regularly vetoed each year's death penalty bill.
- *March 25:* Pope John Paul II issues the encyclical *Evangelium Vitae.* The document takes a tougher stand against capital punishment, saying that it is justified only in extreme cases where the criminal's guilt is certain and he or she poses an exceptional danger to society. Most Catholic observers believe that few if any executions in modern countries can meet this standard.
- *July 28:* A jury decides to give Susan Smith a life sentence rather than the death penalty. Smith was convicted of murdering her two young children, and her life was revealed to be a tangled web of molestation, manipulation, and compulsion that fascinated tabloid audiences. The jury's leniency is in sharp contrast to the results of a *Newsweek* poll that found 63 percent in favor of the death penalty for Smith.

1997

- *February 3:* The House of Delegates of the American Bar Association calls for a moratorium on all execution in the United States. The A.B.A. declares that the capital punishment system is "a haphazard maze of unfair practices with no internal consistency," and also points to racial bias in capital sentencing.
- *March 25:* Observers at the execution of Pedro Medina in Florida's electric chair are horrified when sparks and flames erupt from his head.

Capital Punishment

Florida governor Lawton Chiles refuses to suspend pending executions but appoints a special medical examiner to investigate the mishap.

- *April:* The tally of prisoners awaiting execution on America's death rows now stands at almost 3,000 (50 of them women). Since the restoration of capital punishment in 1976, 372 men and one woman have been executed in the United States.
- *April:* The United Nations Commission on Human Rights votes to call upon member nations to abolish capital punishment. The United States joins China, Indonesia, and eight other nations in opposing the resolution.
- *June 13:* Timothy McVeigh is sentenced to death for the Oklahoma City bombing, the worst domestic terrorist act in American history. His case challenges abolitionists to remain consistent in their opposition to the death penalty.
- *October:* Mexico claims that the United States is in violation of international law for sentencing a Mexican national to death in Texas without allowing him to seek the help of the Mexican Consulate.

1998

- The Pennsylvania Supreme Court refuses to overturn the conviction of Mumia Abu-Jamal for the murder of police officer Daniel Faulkner in 1981. Abu-Jamal's case had been brought to public attention by a vocal group of supporters.
- *February 3:* Despite pleas from many religious leaders, Karla Faye Tucker, a murderer who had become a born-again Christian, is executed in Texas.
- *April 2:* A Racial Justice Act is signed into law in Kentucky. It allows courts to consider statistical evidence of racial disparities in death sentencing and allows the defense to try to prove that a prosecutor's decision to seek the death penalty was motivated by racial factors.

1999

- *January 27:* Pope John Paul II, during his visit to St. Louis, Missouri, preaches a homily in which he calls the death penalty "cruel and unnecessary." The pope also asks Missouri governor Mel Carnahan, a supporter of the death penalty, to commute the death sentence of prisoner Darrell J. Mease. The governor first postpones the execution, but then commutes the sentence to life imprisonment.
- *February 5:* Anthony Porter is released from prison in Illinois. He had nearly been executed in September 1998, but his lawyers won a stay of execution to evaluate his mental competency. Using the time thus gained, investigators (including Northwestern University journalism students) turned up evidence that proved his innocence.

- *February 25:* White supremacist John William King is given the death penalty by a jury for taking part in the brutal murder-by-dragging of James Byrd, Jr., an African American, in June 1998. Many death penalty opponents have mixed feelings because the sentence is one of the rare instances in which a white man is condemned to death for murdering a black man. Many people consider it to be a just retribution for a terrible hate crime.
- *May 26:* Nebraska governor Mike Johans vetoes a bill that would have imposed a two-year moratorium on executions during which time the fairness of the death penalty would be studied. At the time it was passed, the bill was hailed as a sign of the strength of an emerging national death penalty moratorium movement.

2000

- *January 24:* The Supreme Court drops consideration of a challenge to Florida's electric chair as being cruel and unusual punishment (*Bryan v. Moore*, 99-6723) because the state has passed legislation offering inmates lethal injection as an alternative.
- *January 31:* Illinois governor George Ryan announces that there will be a moratorium on executions in the state until an inquiry into the operation of the death penalty has been completed. Since 1977, more death row inmates in the state have been exonerated than have been executed.
- *February 16:* At a press conference, President Clinton, who supports the death penalty, praises Illinois for its moratorium on executions. He says that the Justice Department is conducting a study to determine whether death sentences have been disproportionately given to blacks. Clinton also backs legislation that would give death row inmates access to DNA testing in cases where it might prove their innocence.
- *February 22:* The Supreme Court declines to hear the appeal of an Alabama death row inmate. Robert Lee Tarver had contended that the state's "antiquated" electric chair would expose him to an unacceptable risk of "excessive burning, disfigurement and . . . pain and suffering."
- *February 28:* Several hundred protesters block the Supreme Court building in Washington, D.C., demanding a new trial for death row inmate Mumia Abu-Jamal. A similar demonstration takes place in San Francisco at a federal courthouse, and protesters are arrested at both locations for blocking sidewalks.
- *April 18:* The Supreme Court overturns the death sentence of Michael Williams, ruling that the 1996 Death Penalty Act's ban on appeals by defendants who "fail to develop the factual basis of a claim in state court proceedings" cannot be applied in a case where the defendants made a "reasonable effort" based on their knowledge at the time.

- *May 19:* New Hampshire governor Jeanne Shaheen vetoes legislation that would have abolished the state's death penalty.
- *June 1:* Texas governor (and Republican presidential candidate) George W. Bush, having announced support for DNA testing in some death penalty cases, gives death row inmate Ricky Nolen McGinn a 30-day reprieve to allow for a DNA test.
- *June 12:* A study of 23 years of death sentences by Columbia University law professor James S. Liebman reveals only 5 percent of death row inmates were executed, while two out of three convictions were overturned on appeal, usually leading to reduced sentences after retrial or plea bargaining. In 7 percent of retried cases, however, the defendant was acquitted.

CHAPTER 4

Biographical Listing

This chapter contains brief biographical sketches of selected persons who are important in the history of capital punishment in the United States. They include scholars, advocates, judicial and political figures, as well as inmates whose cases raised important issues or public controversy. The entries focus on the person's relationship to the issue of capital punishment, and do not attempt to recount other areas of significance.

Anthony G. Amsterdam, prominent law professor and constitutional expert. Amsterdam directed the NAACP Legal Defense and Education Fund's campaign to have the death penalty declared unconstitutional. He is a leading figure in the legal struggle over capital punishment. Amsterdam has argued numerous capital cases before the Supreme Court.

Cesare Beccaria, 18th-century Italian jurist and legal reformer. Beccaria was the first modern writer to urge complete abolition of the death penalty. His book *Essay on Crimes and Punishment*, published in 1764, is considered the single most influential work on criminal justice reform. Beccaria argued that the certainty of punishment was more effective as a deterrent than the severity and that penalties should be proportionate to the crime. His ideas strongly influenced early American abolitionists.

Hugo Adam Bedau, chairman of the philosophy department of Tufts University since 1966. Bedau has been a leading opponent of capital punishment for the past 40 years. His anthology *The Death Penalty in America*, first published in 1964 and revised periodically since, is considered the authoritative work on the subject.

Jeremy Bentham, British social philosopher and economist. Bentham's principle achievement was his attempt to create a systematic approach to social policy that became known as utilitarianism. According to this approach, social policies (including punishments for crime) should be based on the goal of creating the greatest amount of happiness for the greatest number of people. He suggested that the use of capital punishment should be limited if not totally eliminated because it did not serve the overall needs of society well.

Walter Berns, political scientist and supporter of capital punishment. Berns has served on the faculties of leading universities including Yale, Cornell, and Georgetown. From 1979 to 1986 he was a resident scholar at the American Enterprise Institute, a leading conservative think tank. His 1979 book *For Capital Punishment: Crime and the Morality of the Death Penalty* is a comprehensive defense of capital punishment. Berns insists that capital punishment is not "cruel and unusual," and is in fact a legitimate punitive (or retributive) response by society to persons who wantonly disregard the lives of others.

Rose Elizabeth Bird, chief justice of the California Supreme Court, 1977–86. A reform-minded liberal jurist, Bird was a stalwart opponent of California's capital punishment statutes, contending that the death penalty was disproportionately applied to blacks and other minorities. She and fellow liberal justices were targeted by a conservative campaign and voted out of office in 1986.

Harry Andrew Blackmun, associate justice of the U.S. Supreme Court, 1970–94. Blackmun generally supported capital punishment until the end of his judicial career. In *Furman v. Georgia* (1972), he sided with the minority in finding capital punishment as currently practiced to be constitutional. In *Gregg v. Georgia* (1976), he agreed with the majority in accepting the validity of revisions the states had made in their capital punishment laws in response to *Furman*. In the case of *Spaziano v. Florida* (1984), he sided with the majority in allowing a judge to override a jury's sentencing recommendation of a life sentence and impose the death penalty. However, in 1993 he told interviewers that he now believed the death penalty "comes close to violating the Equal Protection Clause of the Constitution," referring to evidence of racial bias in the imposition of the sanction. Finally, in his dissent in *Callins v. Collins* (1994), Blackmun said that there was no way to reconcile the constitutional requirements of individualized discretion and the need to avoid "arbitrary and capricious" decisions. He vowed that "from this day forward I will no longer tinker with the machinery of death."

SueZann Bosler, advocate for nonviolent reconciliation and abolition of the death penalty. In 1982 she testified on behalf of leniency for the man who had attacked her and killed her father. She is a board member of the organization Journey of Hope.

Marvin H. Bovee, politician and prominent 19th-century crusader against capital punishment. As a state senator, he lead the successful fight to repeal the death penalty in Wisconsin in 1853. He subsequently dedicated himself over the next 30 years to ending capital punishment nationwide. At a time when the country was absorbed by the issues of the Civil War, his efforts generated little support. Nonetheless, his perseverance kept the question of capital punishment an object of public debate.

William J. Brennan, Jr., Supreme Court justice, 1956–90. Brennan is considered by most observers to be part of the liberal core of the "Warren Court." In numerous opinions, Brennan argued that the death penalty constitutes cruel and unusual punishment under the Constitution and should be prohibited. Further, he believed that the killing of a human being by the State was "an absolute denial of the executed person's humanity," and agreed with his compatriot Harry Blackmun that the death penalty must be completely abolished.

Stephen B. Bright, director of the Southern Center for Human Rights in Atlanta and a director of the National Association of Criminal Defense Lawyers. He has handled numerous capital cases and appeals and has taught courses on capital punishment, criminal procedure, and international human rights at Yale, Harvard, and other universities. In 1998 he received the American Bar Association's Thurgood Marshall Award.

Edmund G. Brown, governor of California, 1959–67. Brown opposed the continuance of capital punishment in the state and sought without success to have the death penalty repealed. Brown subsequently headed the National Commission on Reform of Federal Criminal Laws, which issued a report in 1971 critical of capital punishment. In 1989, in his book *Public Justice, Private Mercy: A Governor's Education on Death Row*, he recounted how his involvement as governor with death penalty cases had shown him that capital punishment was both barbaric and ineffective.

Theodore R. Bundy, notorious serial killer. The subject of numerous books and a television miniseries, *The Deliberate Stranger*, the case of Ted Bundy fascinated and horrified America. An intelligent and attractive young man, he was also one of the most infamous serial killers in the nation's history. Sentenced to death in Florida in 1980 for the murder of a 12-year old girl, Bundy was executed on January 24, 1989, after many appeals and delays. In his final days he reportedly confessed to killing at least 20 young women in five states. Bundy was frequently cited by advocates of capital punishment as an example of the kind of criminal who richly merited the death penalty.

Warren E. Burger, chief justice of the U.S. Supreme Court, 1969–86. Burger presided over several landmark rulings on capital punishment. He was in the minority when the Court declared the nation's death penalty laws unconstitutional in 1972. Four years later, Burger was part of the majority that authorized a resumption of executions.

George H. W. Bush, president of the United States, 1988–92. Considered a moderate Republican earlier in his political career, Bush moved toward the conservative wing of his party during his tenure as vice president in

Capital Punishment

the Reagan administration. In the 1988 presidential campaign, he stressed his support for the death penalty in contrast to Democratic candidate Michael Dukakis' opposition to the measure. As president, Bush continued to call for wider use of capital punishment.

Albert Camus, French intellectual and author who won the Nobel Prize in literature. Camus wrote a powerful critique of the death penalty in 1957. His essay "Reflections on the Guillotine" contributed to the growing debate over capital punishment in the United States in the late 1950s. Camus' ideas and the responses they provoked became part of an ultimately successful effort to repeal the death penalty in France.

Truman Capote, American author. Capote was the best-known writer of his generation to oppose capital punishment. His controversial 1968 TV documentary *Death Row, USA* strongly criticized the practice.

George Cheever, 19th-century clergyman and a prolific writer on social issues. Cheever advocated the end of slavery but also vigorously defended capital punishment on biblical and moral grounds. His 1846 *Defense of Capital Punishment* is probably the leading defense of the death penalty in the 19th century from a Christian viewpoint.

Caryl Chessman, convicted murderer and successful death row author. In trouble with the law since his youth, Chessman was convicted in 1948 of kidnapping with bodily injury, a crime he insisted he did not commit, and was sentenced to death. While on death row in California, Chessman authored three books against capital punishment that won him an international audience. His case provoked the largest public outcry against the death penalty since the Sacco and Vanzetti trial 30 years earlier. After 12 years of legal maneuvering, Chessman was executed on May 2, 1960.

William Ramsey Clark, attorney general in the Johnson administration who became an outspoken social reformer. Clark was the first and only head of the Justice Department to call for the end of the death penalty. In testimony before Congress, he urged elimination of the federal death sentence. Since leaving office, Clark has remained a prominent and active opponent of capital punishment.

Lande Cohen, Canadian writer and supporter of capital punishment. His book *Law without Order: Capital Punishment and the Liberals* (1970) argues that while there should be strict procedural safeguards and execution should be humanely administered, the state may sometimes have to resort to capital punishment to protect itself from extreme violence or anarchy.

Mario M. Cuomo, governor of New York, 1983–94. Cuomo earned a national reputation for his forceful and outspoken opposition to capital punishment. During his years in office he successfully resisted efforts to reimpose the death penalty in his state, vetoing reinstatement measures each year. (New York enacted a death penalty law in 1995 under Republican governor George Pataki.)

Newton M. Curtis, U.S. representative from New York, elected in 1890 and an active proponent of prison reform and the humane treatment of the mentally ill. Although Congress did not approve his abolitionist proposals, in 1897 it enacted his bill to greatly reduce the number of federal capital offenses.

George Mifflin Dallas, politician and prominent 19th-century activist against the death penalty. He was chosen to be the first president of the American Society for the Abolition of Capital Punishment.

Clarence S. Darrow, renowned defense attorney and advocate for controversial causes. Darrow was an ardent opponent of the death penalty. In a famous trial in 1924, he persuaded the judge to sentence Nathan Leopold and Richard Loeb, young men convicted of kidnapping and murder, to life imprisonment rather than death. The verdict infused new energy into the abolitionist movement nationwide. The following year he helped found the American League to Abolish Capital Punishment. Darrow continued to attack capital punishment in various lectures and in his autobiography in 1935.

Michael S. Dukakis, governor of Massachusetts and Democratic presidential candidate in 1988. His opponent, Vice President George Bush, sought to make their differences over capital punishment a major issue in the campaign. In a presidential debate, Dukakis fumbled when asked whether he would support the death penalty for someone who raped and killed his wife. Political analysts believe Dukakis' candidacy was seriously weakened by his opposition to the death penalty.

Herbert B. Ehrmann, defense attorney in the Sacco and Vanzetti case. As a result of his experience, he and his wife Sara became active in the movement to abolish capital punishment. He published two books critical of the Sacco-Vanzetti verdict, as well as articles on the death penalty and the criminal justice system.

Gary M. Gilmore, first person put to death following the Supreme Court's 1976 decision reinstating the death penalty. His case attracted worldwide attention and eventually became the subject of a Pulitzer Prize–winning book, *The Executioner's Song,* by Norman Mailer. Gilmore refused to contest his pending death sentence and twice attempted to commit suicide when appeals filed by various legal groups opposed to capital punishment threatened to block his execution. He was shot by a Utah firing squad on January 17, 1977.

Horace Greeley, prominent 19th-century newspaper editor and founder of the *New York Tribune* in 1841. He used the influential newspaper as a nationwide platform to campaign for a number of reform causes including the abolition of capital punishment. A frequent lecturer across the country, Greeley provided many rural Americans their first exposure to arguments against the death penalty.

Jack Greenberg, legal crusader against capital punishment. As director of the NAACP Legal Defense and Education Fund from 1961 to 1984, Greenberg coordinated the legal campaign against capital punishment that resulted in the Supreme Court striking down the nation's death penalty laws in 1972. He participated in several of the most important cases argued before the Court. Following the reinstatement of capital punishment in 1976, Greenberg maintained his organization's leading role in the legal fight against the death penalty.

Joseph-Ignace Guillotin, French doctor and inventor of the beheading machine that would later be named the guillotine. Interestingly, he developed his machine because he believed it would provide a uniform method of execution that could be applied to all classes of offenders, upholding the ideal of equality that fueled the French Revolution. In later years he was said to be uncomfortable with the fact the machine had been given his name.

Victor Hugo, noted 19th-century French author. His novels and other stories often exposed and attacked social injustices, and he had a particular interest in the harsh treatment of prisoners. Several of his works included negative portrayals of the death penalty, including *Last Days of a Condemned Man* and *The Death Penalty*, as well as his most famous work, *Les Misérables.*

Joe Ingle, minister and prison reformer. A minister of the United Church of Christ, the Reverend Ingle served as director of the Southern Coalition on Jails and Prisons since the 1970s. As part of this work he ministered to hundreds of prisoners on southern death rows and helped organize legal challenges to their sentences. Ingle was nominated for the Nobel Peace Prize in 1988 and 1989.

Arthur Koestler, renowned Hungarian-born author who became a British subject. Koestler was deeply involved in the successful campaign to abolish the death penalty in his adopted country. His 1955 book *Reflections on Hanging*, a critical study of the death penalty in Great Britain and an indictment of the practice in general, is considered among the classic works on the subject. Published in the United States in 1957, the book has had a major impact on abolitionist activity.

Lewis E. Lawes, warden of New York's Sing Sing prison for 20 years during the early 20th century. Lawes took part in hundreds of electrocutions. His firsthand experience with criminals and his study of death sentence statistics led him to conclude that capital punishment was misguided and wrong. A founder and later chairman of the American League to Abolish Capital Punishment, he presented his views in six books and numerous articles and speeches.

Nathan Leopold and **Richard Loeb,** infamous kidnappers and murderers of the 1920s. Leopold and Loeb were young men who considered themselves to be clever and superior persons, and decided to prove their superiority by committing the perfect crime. The result was the kidnapping and murder of a 14-year-old boy, for which they were soon arrested. With the facts of the crime in little dispute, famed attorney Clarence Darrow entered guilty pleas for both men but appealed to the judge to spare their lives. They received sentences of life plus 99 years. Loeb was stabbed to death in a prison dispute in 1936, but Leopold was paroled in 1958, the same year he published *Life Plus 99 Years,* in which he wrote about his rehabilitation.

Edward Livingston, Louisiana legislator and later secretary of state under President Andrew Jackson. As a member of the Louisiana Assembly in the early 1820s, Livingston introduced several new arguments against capital punishment: the risk of executing the innocent, the ineffectiveness of the death penalty as a deterrent, and the problems the sanction posed in the administration of justice. Livingston's writings had a major impact across the nation and in Europe. Considered by many the preeminent American abolitionist of his time, he raised issues that continue to shape the terms of the debate over capital punishment today.

Thurgood Marshall, associate justice of the U.S. Supreme Court, 1967–90. Although his proudest achievement was his successful argument against segregation in *Brown v. Board of Education* (1954), Marshall was also director of the NAACP Legal Defense and Education Fund from 1940 until 1961, where he led the organization's efforts to overturn capital punishment statutes. While on the Court, he consistently voted against capital punishment and dissented vigorously when the court majority reinstated capital punishment in the *Gregg* decision of 1976. Marshall frequently stated his belief that the death penalty is unconstitutional in all circumstances.

Edwin Meese, III, attorney general during the Reagan administration. As an assistant to the then-governor of California Ronald Reagan, Meese helped coordinate the successful referendum drive to restore the death penalty in the state. Meese has been an outspoken advocate of capital punishment.

John L. O'Sullivan, 19th-century American legislator and champion of American expansionism (he coined the term "Manifest Destiny"). O'Sullivan advocated repeal of the death penalty. He believed that capital punishment was incompatible with the "democratic genius" of the United States. O'Sullivan's 1841 report to the New York Assembly, written while he was a member, became one of the most influential abolitionist appeals of the time.

Albert Pierrepoint, British executioner who dispatched 450 people by the time of his retirement in 1956. After his retirement, he became an opponent of capital punishment and described his experiences in *Executioner: Pierrepoint*, published in 1974.

Lewis F. Powell, Jr., associate Supreme Court justice, 1972–87, who was nominated by President Richard Nixon. Considered the swing vote on many issues during his years on the Court, he cast the decisive vote in many important capital punishment decisions. Since the mid-1980s, Powell suggested that if a solution could not be found to the protracted appeals process in capital cases, then the death penalty should be abandoned as unworkable.

Helen Prejean, American nun who ministers to inmates on death row, particularly in the Louisiana State Penitentiary at Angola. Her book *Dead Man Walking* (later made into an Academy Award–winning movie), describes these painful and moving encounters. Prejean now serves as the national chairperson for the National Coalition to Abolish the Death Penalty.

Robert Rantoul, Jr., 19th-century death penalty abolitionist. The leading American opponent of capital punishment in the 1830s and 1840s, Rantoul served as president of the Massachusetts Society for the Abolition of Capital Punishment and assisted in reform efforts nationwide. In his writings, he strongly contested the inherent right of society to inflict the death penalty.

Ronald W. Reagan, governor of California (1967–74) and president of the United States, 1980–88. As governor of California, Reagan responded to the California Supreme Court's overturning of capital punishment in 1972 by leading a successful referendum to amend the constitution to restore the death penalty. As president, Reagan spoke out frequently in defense of the death penalty. He vigorously supported Congressional legislation in 1988 that made drug-related murders a federal capital offense.

William H. Rehnquist, associate justice of the Supreme Court (1971–86) and chief justice (1987–   ). Throughout his tenure on the Court, he has maintained that the issue of capital punishment should be settled in the legislative branch of government. He has criticized the lengthy appeals process involved in capital cases. (In 1992 he and his colleagues quashed a last-minute stay of execution of Robert Alton Harris and ordered the lower court not to issue any further stays.) As chief justice, Rehnquist has attempted to find ways to reduce the number of appeals. He has resisted making decisions that broaden protections for death row inmates retroactively and has refused to entertain appeals that should have been made in state courts.

Biographical Listing

Samuel Romilly, 18th- and early 19th-century British member of parliament and legal reformer. Influenced by the writings of French Enlightenment thinkers such as Jacques Rousseau as well as the pioneering criminological and legal work of Cesare Beccaria, Romilly became interested in comprehensive legal reform. He set out to eliminate the more than 200 capital offenses in the British law of the time, many of which would be only misdemeanors by modern standards. While only modestly successful, his work gave impetus to a reform movement that would have a significant impact on British use of the death penalty later in the 19th century.

Julius and **Ethel Rosenberg,** American communists who were tried and convicted in 1951 as part of a spy ring accused of providing secret information about the atomic bomb to the Soviets. The couple vigorously maintained their innocence but also appealed their conviction on the grounds they had been sentenced under a statute that had been enacted in 1946 although the acts they were accused of committing had taken place earlier, during World War II. While Supreme Court Justice William O. Douglas wanted to give them a stay of execution on that basis, the majority of the court disagreed and the Rosenbergs were executed on June 19, 1953.

Benjamin Rush, prominent Pennsylvania physician and a signer of the Declaration of Independence. Rush was the first prominent American to publicly oppose capital punishment. In 1787 he published *An Enquiry into the Effects of Public Punishments upon Criminals and upon Society*, the first of several essays calling for the complete abolition of the death penalty. Rush is credited with building support for the elimination of many death penalty statutes in the early 19th century.

Nicola Sacco and **Bartolomeo Vanzetti,** Italian-born anarchists who became the central figures in one of the most controversial trials of the 20th century. Maintaining their innocence to the end, the two men were executed on August 23, 1927, for the 1920 murder of a shoe factory paymaster and guard in South Braintree, Massachusetts. Their supporters claimed that guilt had been established on inconclusive evidence and that the two men were convicted at least in part because of their radical political beliefs. Defense attorneys filed numerous unsuccessful motions and appeals in state and federal court in what was the first instance of a now-common protracted legal struggle over a death sentence.

Antonin Scalia, associate justice of the U.S. Supreme Court since 1986. Scalia generally forms the core of the conservative wing of the Court, joined later in many decisions by Clarence Thomas. Scalia has been a consistent supporter of capital punishment and has voted against the appellant in most death penalty cases. In his dissent in *Booth v. Maryland* Scalia defended the role of victim impact statements in trials and sentencing procedures, arguing that without them jurors heard witnesses offering mitigating explanations for heinous crimes without a counterbalancing sense of the full suffering of the victims.

Henry Schwarzchild, prominent anti–death penalty activist. In the 1960s he was active in the civil rights struggle in the South. He was director of the American Civil Liberties Union Capital Punishment Project from 1975 to 1990. In 1976 he also founded and became first executive director of the National Coalition to Abolish the Death Penalty.

Thorsten Sellin, one of the leading criminologists of the 20th century; affiliated with the University of Pennsylvania. He based his opposition to the death penalty on a detailed study of the subject. He wrote numerous scholarly books and articles. Sellin's expertise led to frequent invitations to testify before legislative hearings on capital punishment.

Edward Donald Slovik, American soldier executed for desertion in France during World War II. This was the first execution for desertion since 1864. Military officers reviewing Slovik's death sentence argued that it was necessary to execute Slovik because of his lengthy criminal record and manifest cowardice, fearing that if they did not do so it could cause increased desertion just as the war effort was reaching its climax.

John A. Spenkelink, the second person to be executed after the Supreme Court reinstated the death penalty in 1976. Unlike Gary Gilmore, he fought his death sentence to the last moment. For this reason, many viewed his case as signaling a full resumption of executions in America. Numerous abolitionist individuals and groups joined in efforts to halt his execution. Spenkelink was electrocuted on May 25, 1979.

Potter Stewart, associate justice of the United States Supreme Court, 1958–81. Stewart was known for his pragmatic approach to jurisprudence, and coined the famous observation that while he might not be able to define pornography, "I know it when I see it." Because of his practicality and moderation, he was often responsible for carving out the middle ground on death penalty issues. In *Furman,* for example, he agreed that the death penalty was being administered in an unconstitutionally arbitrary and capricious way, but did not believe the sanction was inherently unconstitutional.

Ernest van den Haag, a leading conservative intellectual who has written extensively about capital punishment since the late 1960s. Van den Haag is widely viewed as the most influential advocate of the death penalty today. He has consistently maintained that the sanction is morally justified for some crimes and that it does, in fact, serve as a deterrent.

CHAPTER 5

GLOSSARY

This chapter presents a short glossary of terms that have particular application to the practice of capital punishment. It does not attempt to be an exhaustive treatment of legal terms in general.

abolitionist   A person, in the context of the death penalty debate, who opposes capital punishment and seeks to have it abolished.

actual innocence   A claim, usually made in postconviction appeals, that the defendant did not commit the crime. Such a claim is based on facts rather than procedural considerations.

affirm   A higher (appeal) court's finding that a lower court's decision was justified.

aggravating circumstance (or factor)   In a capital case, something that makes a murder more serious such that the death penalty can be asked for by the prosecutor or imposed by the jury. States often specify aggravating circumstances by statute. Examples include felonies such as arson, rape, or robbery committed in conjunction with the murder; crimes against certain types of victims (such as children or police officers), or crimes with particularly venal motives (such as monetary gain).

arbitrary and capricious   The claim that a punishment or procedure is administered without regard to the facts of individual cases, inconsistently or irrationally.

bifurcated trial   Division of the legal process in a capital case into a regular trial to determine factual guilt and a special sentencing phase hearing to determine whether to impose the death penalty. Bifurcation was deemed necessary to comply with the ruling in *Furman v. Georgia*.

brutalization   The hypothesis that frequent executions may increase violent crime by demonstrating the use of violence as a way to solve problems.

capital offense   A crime subject to the death penalty.

127

capital punishment jurisdiction   One of the 38 states and two federal jurisdictions that impose capital punishment.

certiorari   A writ from the Supreme Court or another higher court to a lower court, ordering that the record of a case be turned over for review. The Supreme Court must "grant cert" before a prisoner's appeal will be heard.

clemency   An act by an executive (state governor or the president) that reduces or eliminates a defendant's punishment.

commutation   Reducing the length or severity of a sentence. Death sentences, if commuted, are usually reduced to sentences of life imprisonment.

concurring opinion   An opinion in the Supreme Court that agrees with what the majority has decided to do, but gives different reasons or justifications.

court-appointed counsel   Attorney appointed by the trial court to represent a defendant who cannot afford a private attorney.

court of appeals   A state or federal court whose primary purpose is to review the appropriateness of verdicts or decisions made by lower courts.

cruel and unusual punishment   According to the Supreme Court, this phrase from the Eighth Amendment to the Constitution should be interpreted as banning punishment that, according to the "evolving standards of decency," is no longer acceptable to society. Abolitionists argue that capital punishment is inherently cruel and unusual, but the Supreme Court has yet to agree.

death qualified jury   A jury whose members have all said they are willing to impose a capital sentence if the facts warrant it.

deterrence   The ability to discourage criminal activity because of the potential consequences to the criminal. While punishment is generally considered to be a deterrent, death penalty supporters and opponents disagree about whether the possibility of execution is an effective deterrent.

diminished capacity   Mental impairment due to disease, defect, retardation, or intoxication that makes a defendant unable to properly appreciate the wrongness of an action or unable to comply with the demands of the law. Diminished capacity can be used as a mitigating factor in capital sentencing in some states.

dissent   An opinion in the Supreme Court that disagrees with the majority's findings. While having no legal effect, a dissent sometimes influences later decisions.

due process   The right, guaranteed by the Fifth and Fourteenth Amendments, to fair consideration of one's arguments and evidence before a criminal penalty can be imposed.

effective assistance of counsel   The right, as interpreted by the Supreme Court, to have an attorney who is competent enough to represent the defendant effectively.

Glossary

Eighth Amendment   Amendment to the U.S. Constitution, part of the Bill of Rights. Its prohibition on "cruel and unusual punishment" has become a key contention of opponents of the death penalty.

equal protection   A right, guaranteed by the Fourteenth Amendment, for all persons to be treated equally by the law and to have equal recourse to its protections.

error   A mistake made (or alleged to be made) in a criminal proceeding. Error is the basic element of an appeal to higher courts.

extrajudicial execution   A killing that is committed by someone other than the duly constituted authorities, such as a dictator's "death squad," vigilante group, or lynch mob.

factfinder   The jury or judge who hears evidence and determines whether the facts amount to a crime for which the defendant is to be held accountable.

federal courts   The nationwide system of courts that includes district (trial) courts, circuit courts of appeals, and the U.S. Supreme Court.

felony   A serious crime punishable by a prison sentence.

felony-murder   A murder committed in the course of committing another felony. Such a murder is often treated as a capital offense.

first-degree murder   Generally, murder that involves a deliberate intent to kill, though precise definitions vary by state. Normally only first-degree murders can be subject to the death penalty.

habeas corpus   Latin for "you have the body"; a request for an order from a court to the authorities to "bring forth" the case of a person who claims to be punished unjustly and to justify that person's conviction.

"harmless error"   A mistake made during a judicial proceeding that did not affect the outcome of the case.

homicide   One person killing another. Homicides can be accidental, justifiable (as in self-defense), or criminal (murder).

individualized consideration   The requirement by the Supreme Court that juries or judges considering whether to sentence a defendant to death must take the particular circumstances of the defendant and the crime into account. Sometimes seen to be in conflict with the requirement not to be "arbitrary and capricious" in sentencing.

irrevocability   The fact that an executed person, unlike someone sentenced to a lesser penalty, cannot be compensated in any way if the conviction turns out to be wrongful. Combined with the possibility of execution of the innocent, irrevocability makes a powerful argument on behalf of abolitionists.

jury override   In capital sentencing, the right in some states for a reviewing judge to reverse the verdict given by the sentencing jury.

life without possibility of parole   A "true" life sentence from which the prisoner will not be released except perhaps through a pardon or a finding of actual innocence.

majority opinion   An opinion in the Supreme Court that is agreed to by more than half of the nine justices. Generally, one justice takes responsibility for writing the opinion.

mandatory death statutes   Laws that require a death penalty when certain criminal circumstances are found. Such laws were barred by the Supreme Court.

mitigating circumstance (or factor)   Something that the jury can consider in favor of the defendant in deciding whether to impose death or a lesser sentence. Mitigating circumstances are often specified by state statute. Examples include extreme emotional disturbance, mental impairment, or the lack of a previous criminal record.

murder   The unlawful and deliberate killing of a human being, with malice aforethought. There are generally different degrees of murder. An unlawful killing that lacks one of the elements of murder can be considered manslaughter.

penalty phase   A separate hearing held after conviction on a capital charge to determine whether to impose the death penalty. This phase is required by Supreme Court decisions.

plurality opinion   An opinion of the Supreme Court that is agreed to by more justices than any other. If the plurality and any concurring opinions make up a majority, the plurality opinion takes legal effect.

proportionality review   The requirement in some jurisdictions that before a capital sentence is given, similar cases must be reviewed to see whether they also resulted in capital punishment.

recidivist   A criminal who commits a crime again after being released from custody.

remand   To send a case back to a lower court for reconsideration.

reprieve   Temporary halt to enforcement of a sentence, such as a stay of execution.

retentionist   A person who seeks to retain capital punishment.

retribution   The infliction of punishment that is merited or deserved because of the offender's action.

reversible error   A mistake made during a criminal proceeding that is serious enough to require that the conviction or sentence be overturned.

sanction   A particular penalty, such as death or life in prison.

sentencing phase   As required by the Supreme Court, a separate hearing held to determine the sentence to be imposed on a convicted defendant. The sentencing phase in a capital case is like a "mini trial" with witnesses and opening and closing arguments.

three-tier system   A court system that has a lower level (trial court or court of general jurisdiction), an intermediate appeal court, and a final appeal court.

PART II

GUIDE TO FURTHER RESEARCH

CHAPTER 6

HOW TO RESEARCH CAPITAL PUNISHMENT

Since the first edition of this book was published in 1991, the tools and methods available to the researcher have undergone considerable evolution. In particular, the World Wide Web now provides a way for advocacy groups, government agencies, and academics to make the results of their work available virtually instantly. Given the wealth of material available online, mastery of a few basic online techniques enables today's researcher to accomplish in a few minutes what used to require long, tedious hours in the library. Therefore, it makes sense to begin our exploration of resources relating to capital punishment by looking at some of the sources available on the Internet.

As valuable as the Internet is for the student and professional researcher alike, it is important to keep its limitations in mind. What's on the Net represents only a subset of the universe of materials. While some older papers or articles have been scanned or transcribed onto web pages, most material found on the Net will date from the mid-1980s or later—about the time that computer-readable academic publications and full-text databases of popular periodicals became available.

Most online documents will be short works: the full text of books is usually not available online, except for some historical and older works that are no longer under copyright. Therefore the library remains a very important tool for the researcher. Fortunately, the nearly universal use of online (and often, remotely accessible) library catalogs has also made libraries easier to use.

Web pages, like all intellectual products, reflect the agenda and possible biases of their creator. Many of the most useful web sites on capital punishment have been created by abolitionists, although some sites by supporters of the death penalty can also be found. In using sites built by advocates, it is necessary to be aware of possible bias in the selection and annotation of materials.

In traditional publishing, various "gatekeepers" controlled what was disseminated. General publishers evaluated the quality of writing in a manuscript and considered its likely reception by the public, while academic and scientific publishers applied standards of peer review in which scholars had to defend their methodology. Some material on the web, such as scientific papers and law school journal articles, have passed through such scrutiny or are backed by other official credentials from government or other agencies. But far more online material represents the efforts of individuals who simply have something to say and now have the means to say it. This is good in that it enables freedom of expression to a degree unprecedented in history. But it does mean that the researcher must carefully inquire into the background of the author, the sources used, and the methodology used to arrive at a given conclusion, particularly in studies that involve statistical evidence.

CAPITAL PUNISHMENT ON THE WEB

There are a number of web sites that offer extensive information and links relating to all aspects of capital punishment and the debate over the death penalty. Most can be divided into two categories: sites hosted by advocates of abolition or retention of the death penalty and sites provided by government or other agencies that do not take a position on the issue.

ADVOCACY SITES

Most advocacy sites on the web take an abolitionist stance. Since the death penalty is the status quo in America, organizations seeking to reform or abolish the sanction are strongly motivated to challenge it through education and advocacy efforts.

Abolitionists

The Death Penalty Information Center web site (http://www.essential.org/dpic/) has made many "best of the web" lists in recent years. (Despite the neutral-sounding name, the organization is strongly abolitionist.) The site includes "What's New," an extensive collection of recent news and opinion, and "Information Topics," which provides links to both statistical information on use of the use of the death penalty and links to the major issues raised in the capital punishment debate, including race, execution of the innocent, and deterrence. There is also coverage of special topics such as women and juveniles on death row.

Another abolitionist organization that offers an extensive web site is the National Coalition to Abolish the Death Penalty. Its site at http://www.

ncadp.org/ offers news, statistics, and a featured campaign such as the release of a juvenile on death row whom the organization believes to be innocent. Researchers and advocates will particularly appreciate the extensive Abolitionist Directory, which provides contact information for both national and state anti–death penalty organizations.

The American Civil Liberties Union (ACLU) has a Capital Punishment Project dedicated to research and advocacy toward abolition of the death penalty. Its issue page for capital punishment is at http://www.aclu.org/issues/death/hmdp.html. It includes news, press releases and statements, various resource links, and the computer-readable version of its newsletter called *The ACLU Abolitionist.*

The international human rights organization Amnesty International has made a major effort in recent years to abolish the death penalty in those countries that still employ the sanction. This effort has particularly focused on the United States. The Amnesty International USA Program to Abolish the Death Penalty site at http://www.amnestyusa.org/abolish/index.html offers news, fact sheets, press releases, and a "weekly death penalty action" focusing on a particular death row case.

Lawrence M. Hinman's "Ethics Update" site has a useful page on "Punishment and the Death Penalty" at http://ethics.acusd.edu/death_penalty.html. Among other things, it offers an overview of the ethics of the death penalty in the form of a web-based Powerpoint slide presentation.

Pro–Death Penalty Sites

While defenders of capital punishment certainly have a presence on the web, they don't seem to have extensive sites comparable to those of the abolitionists. However, the site "Pro-death penalty.com" at http://www.prodeathpenalty.com/ does offer news and informational links similar to those provided by the abolitionist sites, as well as essays and articles by death penalty supporters, such as those opposing the efforts on behalf of Mumia Abu-Jamal. The host of this site also maintains a sister site on behalf of murder victims at http://www.murdervictims.com/. The site "Justice for All" at http://www.jfa.net/ also advocates on behalf of families of victims of murder and other serious crimes and links to the preceding site for death penalty information.

GOVERNMENT AGENCIES AND STATISTICS

Much of the debate over capital punishment involves statistics. These range from polling and survey data to crime statistics to demographics of death row inmates. There are several important government agency sites that provide such statistics.

The U.S. Department of Justice Bureau of Justice Statistics offers complete and up-to-date statistics on every aspect of the criminal justice system. These include crime rates, statistics about criminal offenders, and statistics about every aspect of criminal procedure from arrests to sentencing to prison life. Statistics specifically related to capital punishment are found under "Corrections," at http://www.ojp.usdoj.gov/bjs/cp.htm. This page includes a summary of executions from the previous year broken down by state, by demographics, including race, and by method used. Reports are also available for prior years. Some statistics are also available in spreadsheet and tabular form.

Another important publication with Bureau of Justice Statistics information is the *Sourcebook of Criminal Justice Statistics*, which is available online at http://www.albany.edu/sourcebook/index.html. This annual publication gathers statistics from more than 100 sources and compiles them into more than 600 tables grouped into a number of files in Adobe™ Acrobat™ format. If your computer is not already equipped to read these files, you can download a free reader at http://www.adobe.com/products/acrobat/readstep.html.

The *Sourcebook* is divided into six main sections, each with a detailed table of contents. For example, Section 2, Public Attitudes Toward Crime and Criminal Justice-Related Topics, includes a subsection, Death Penalty, which in turn offers a number of files containing survey data, such as Attitudes toward the death penalty, by demographic characteristics, United States, 1999 (Table 2.54). Section 6, Persons Under Correctional Supervision, includes the subcategory State and Federal Prisoners Executed, which includes three tables with data from 1930 to 1996 or 1997, with breakdowns by jurisdiction, offense, and race. The subcategory Persons Removed from Death Row is particularly interesting in view of the controversy over possible execution of innocent people.

Advanced researchers who are familiar with statistical data sets and software such as SPSS can find a treasure trove of data at The National Archive of Criminal Justice Data at http://www.icpsr.umich.edu/NACJD/. The site also offers the Uniform Crime Reports, compiled by the Federal Bureau of Investigation. This is the largest and most complete source of standard crime data and is widely cited in scholarly papers.

The National Archive of Criminal Justice Data also offers data from the Inter-University Consortium for Political and Social Research (ICPSR), which has its own site at http://www.icpsr.umich.edu/index.html that provides a broad range of social science data.

Researchers on capital punishment issues will need to become familiar with penal systems. The Federal Bureau of Prisons site at http://www.bop.gov/ offers useful summaries under "Public Information." They include "Quick Facts and Statistics" on federal prison inmates. For state prison statistics, some information is available from the Bureau of Justice Statistics (under "Corrections."). Individual state prison systems can usually be found via a web search using the state name followed by "department of corrections," such as "California department of corrections." (For other statistics on capital punishment, also see Appendix A of this book.)

BIBLIOGRAPHIC RESOURCES

As useful as the web is for quickly finding information and the latest news, in-depth research still requires trips to the library or bookstore. Getting the most out of the library requires the use of bibliographic tools and resources. Bibliographic resources is a general term for catalogs, indexes, bibliographies, and other guides that identify the books, periodical articles, and other printed resources that deal with a particular subject. They are essential tools for the researcher.

LIBRARY CATALOGS

Access to the largest library catalog, that of the Library of Congress, is available at http://lcweb.loc.gov/catalog/. This page explains the different kinds of catalogs and searching techniques available.

Yahoo offers a categorized listing of libraries at http://dir.yahoo.com/Reference/Libraries/. Of course for materials available at one's local public or university library, that institution will be the most convenient source.

Online catalogs can be searched not only by the traditional author, title, and subject headings, but also by matching keywords in the title. Thus a title search for "capital punishment" will retrieve all books that have those words somewhere in their title. (Of course a book about capital punishment may well not have that phrase in the title and perhaps instead refer to "death penalty" so it is still necessary to use subject headings to get the most comprehensive results.)

The most important LC subject heading is, of course "Capital Punishment." Its entry in the Library of Congress subject headings guide is as follows:

CAPITAL PUNISHMENT
Used for:
  Abolition of *CAPITAL PUNISHMENT*
  Death penalty
Narrower terms:
  Crucifixion
  Death row

Discrimination in *CAPITAL PUNISHMENT*
Electrocution
Garrote
Hanging
Last meal before execution
Stoning
Related terms:
  Executions and executioners
Broader terms:
  Criminal law

Note that there's no separate heading here for abolition of capital punishment. "Death Penalty" is not a valid LC subject heading but instead cross references to "Capital Punishment."

Once the record for a book or other item is found, it is a good idea to see what additional subject and name headings have been assigned. These in turn can be used for further searching.

BIBLIOGRAPHIES, INDEXES, AND DATABASES

Bibliographies in various forms provide a convenient way to find books, periodical articles, and other materials. Most book-length bibliographies published before the 1970s are not very useful except for finding historical and philosophical works since the shape of capital punishment in America was so radically changed by the Supreme Court decisions of the 1970s and early 1980s. More useful are the bibliographies or bibliographical notes found at the end of the recent overview or reference works found in the first section of Chapter 7 of this book.

Popular and scholarly articles can be accessed through periodical indexes that provide citations and abstracts. Abstracts are brief summaries of articles or papers. They are usually compiled and indexed—originally in bound volumes, but increasingly, available online. Some examples of printed indexes where you might retrieve literature related to capital punishment include:

- ATLA Religion Database—for religious works dealing with capital punishment
- Criminal Justice Abstracts
- Criminal Justice Periodical Index
- Index to Legal Periodicals and Books
- Social Sciences Citation Index

- Social Sciences Index
- Sociological Abstracts

Some of these indexes are available online (at least for recent years). Generally, however, you can access them only through a library where you hold a card, and they cannot be accessed over the Internet (unless you are on a college campus). Consult with a university reference librarian for more help.

There are two good indexes that have unrestricted search access, however. UnCover Web (http://uncweb.carl.org/) contains brief descriptions of about 8.8 million documents from about 18,000 journals in just about every subject area. Copies of complete documents can be ordered with a credit card, or they may be obtainable for free at a local library.

Perhaps the most valuable index for topics related to criminal justice is the National Criminal Justice Reference Service Justice Information Center, at http://www.ncjrs.org/. It offers a searchable abstract database containing 150,000 criminal justice publications, and it can be a real gold mine for the more advanced researcher.

FREE PERIODICAL INDEXES

Most public libraries subscribe to database services such as InfoTrac that index articles from hundreds of general-interest periodicals (and some moderately specialized ones). The database can be searched by author or by words in the title, subject headings, and sometimes words found anywhere in the article text. Depending on the database used, "hits" in the database can result in just a bibliographical description (author, title, pages, periodical name, issue date), a description plus an abstract (a paragraph summarizing the contents of the article), or the full text of the article itself. Before using such an index, it is a good idea to view the list of newspapers and magazines covered and determine the years of coverage.

Many libraries provide dial-in, Internet, or telnet access to their periodical databases as an option in their catalog menu. However, licensing restrictions usually mean that only researchers who have a library card for that particular library can access the database (by typing in their name and card number). Check with local public or school libraries to see what databases are available.

For periodicals not indexed by Infotrac or another index (or for which only abstracts rather than complete text is available), check to see whether the publication has its own web site (many now do). Some scholarly publications are putting all or most of their articles online. Popular publications tend to offer only a limited selection. Some publications of both types offer archives of several years' back issues that can be searched by author or keyword.

BOOKSTORE CATALOGS

Many people have discovered that online bookstores such as Amazon.com at (http://www.amazon.com) and barnesandnoble.com (http://www.bn.com) are convenient ways to shop for books. A lesser-known benefit of online bookstore catalogs is that they often include publisher's information, book reviews, and reader's comments about a given title. They can thus serve as a form of annotated bibliography.

On the other hand, a visit to one's local bookstore also has its benefits. While the selection of titles available is likely to be smaller than that of an online bookstore, the ability to physically browse through books before buying them can be very useful.

KEEPING UP WITH THE NEWS

It is important for the researcher to be aware of currently breaking news. In addition to watching TV news and subscribing to local or national newspapers and magazines, there are a number of ways to use the Internet to find additional news sources.

NEWSPAPERS AND NETNEWS

Like periodicals, most large newspapers now have web sites that offer headlines and a searchable database of recent articles. The URL is usually given somewhere in one's local newspaper. Yahoo! is also a good place to find newspaper links: see http://dir.yahoo.com/News_and_Media/Newspapers/Web_Directories/.

Netnews is a decentralized system of thousands of "newsgroups," or forums organized by topic. Most web browsers have an option for subscribing to, reading, and posting messages in newsgroups. The Dejanews site (http://www.deja.com/usenet) also provides free access and an easy-to-use interface to newsgroups. The general newsgroup for discussing capital punishment issues is alt.activism.death-penalty.

Mail Lists offer another way to keep up with (and discuss) recent developments. The best way to find them is through the activist groups that sponsor them. They will also have instructions on how to subscribe to the list. A good list to start with is ABOLISH, which features death penalty news and discussion from an abolitionist viewpoint. The list can be joined by sending email to listserv@maelstrom.stjohns.edu with the text "subscribe abolish" (no quotes) followed by the user name. There is also an Amnesty International mailing list that supplies news releases relating to death penalty campaigns. It can be joined by sending email to majordomo@oil.ca with the text "subscribe amnesty-deathpenalty".

SEARCHING THE WEB

A researcher can explore an ever-expanding web of information by starting with a few web sites and following the links they offer to other sites, which in turn have links to still other sites. But since this is something of a hit-and-miss proposition, some important sites may be missed if the researcher only "web surfs" in this fashion. There are two more focused techniques that can fill in the information gaps.

WEB GUIDES AND INDEXES

A web guide or index is a site that offers what amounts to a structured, hierarchical outline of subject areas. This enables the researcher to zero in on a particular aspect of a subject and find links to web sites for further exploration.

The best known (and largest) web index is Yahoo! at http://www.yahoo.com. The home page gives the top-level list of topics, and the researcher simply clicks to follow them down to more specific areas.

In addition to following Yahoo!'s outline-like structure, there is also a search box into which the researcher can type one or more keywords and receive a list of matching categories and sites.

Web indexes such as Yahoo! have two major advantages over undirected surfing. First, the structured hierarchy of topics makes it easy to find a particular topic or subtopic and then explore its links. Second, Yahoo! does not make an attempt to compile every possible link on the Internet (a task that is virtually impossible, given the size of the web). Rather, sites are evaluated for usefulness and quality by Yahoo!'s indexers. This means that the researcher has a better chance of finding more substantial and accurate information. The disadvantage of web indexes is the flip side of their selectivity: the researcher is dependent on the indexer's judgment for determining what sites are worth exploring.

To explore capital punishment via Yahoo!, the researcher should browse "Society and Culture," then "Crime," "Correction and Rehabilitation," and finally "Death Penalty." At the time of writing, subtopics available under that heading include:

Death Row Inmates *(40)*
Execution Methods *(10)*
Opposing Views *(26)*
Supporting Views *(6)*
Web Directories *(5)*

(The number in parentheses is the number of links available when the topic is clicked on.)

A number of individual links are listed following the subtopics:

- **Capital Punishment: Life or Death?**—school project covering both sides of the issue.
- **Capital Punishment: the Death Penalty**—information from different religious perspectives.
- **Death Penalty News & Updates**—with a list of pending executions.
- **Death Row**—published annually by Bobit Publishing Company and *Police Magazine*. Includes complete listing of inmates living on death row.
- **Execution of Caleb Adams**—a true story of crime and punishment in early 1800s New England.
- **Focus on the Death Penalty**—comprehensive resource which includes history, U.S. Supreme Court cases, statistics, death row, the international context, and both sides of the death penalty debate.
- **Frontline: The Execution**—an examination of capital punishment through the life and crimes of self-confessed double murderer Clifford Boggess, who was executed in Texas in June 1998 after spending almost 10 years on death row.
- **Jericho Road, The**—Michael Sharp posted this shortly before being executed in Texas on November 19, 1997.
- **Last Word, The**—collection of final statements of condemmed prisoners.
- **Usenet**—alt.activism.death-penalty

The Mining Company's About.com (http://www.about.com) is rather similar to Yahoo!, but gives a greater emphasis to overviews or guides prepared by experts in various topics. To find information on capital punishment on About.com, browse to "Society/Culture," "Crime/Punishment," "Death Row" or enter a direct keyword search such as "capital punishment." (Remember with guide sites it is often a good idea to supplement browsing with a direct search to ensure the most comprehensive results.)

How to Research Capital Punishment

Among other web indexes are LookSmart, at http://www.looksmart.com. To find links relating to capital punishment, the researcher should browse to "Society," "Crime and Justice," "Prisons & Sentencing," and then "Capital Punishment."

New guide and index sites are constantly being developed, and capabilities are improving as the web matures. One example is Ask Jeeves, at http://askjeeves.com. This site attempts to answer a researcher's plain-English question, such as "How many prisoners were executed in the United States in 1997?" It doesn't, alas, actually answer the question, but it does return a number of possibly useful links that it obtains by querying a whole series of search engines. (For the example question, the first link it found was "Bureau of Justice Capital Punishment Statistics," which would indeed have the desired information.)

There are also an increasing number of specialized online research guides that are similar to traditional bibliographical essays but with the added bonus of having many of the materials discussed already linked so they are just a click away. The Boston University Library has a research guide to capital punishment at http://www.bu.edu/library/research-guides/cappun.html.

SEARCH ENGINES

Search engines take a very different approach to finding materials on the web. Instead of organizing topically in a "top down" fashion, search engines work their way "from the bottom up" scanning through web documents and indexing them. There are hundreds of search engines, but some of the most widely used include:

- AltaVista (http://www.altavista.com)
- Excite (http://www.excite.com)
- Go (http://www.go.com)
- Google (http://www.google.com)
- Hotbot (http://www.hotbot.lycos.com)
- Lycos (http://www.lycos.com)
- Magellan (http://www.magellan.excite.com)
- Northern Light (http://www.northernlight.com)
- WebCrawler (http://www.WebCrawler.com)

Search engines are generally easy to use by employing the same sorts of keywords that work in library catalogs. There are a variety of web search tutorials available online. (Try "web search tutorial" in a search engine to find some.) One good one is published by The Web Tools Company at http://www.thewebtools.com/tutorial/tutorial.htm.

Here are a few basic rules for using search engines:

- When looking for something specific, use the most specific term or phrase. For example, when looking for information about habeas corpus appeals, use the specific term "habeas corpus," since this is the standard term. (Note that phrases should be put in quotes if you want them to be matched as phrases rather than as individual words. We show all search terms in quotes to separate them from the rest of the sentence, but that doesn't mean quotes should be used in actual searches other than for phrases.)
- When looking for a general topic that might be expressed using several different words or phrases, use several descriptive words (nouns are more reliable than verbs). For example, "death row statistics." (Most engines will automatically put pages that match all three terms first on the results list.)
- Use "wildcards" when a desired word may have more than one ending. For example, prison* matches "prison," "prisoner," and "prisoners" (but not, for example, "inmate").
- Most search engines support Boolean (*and, or, not*) operators that can be used to broaden or narrow a search.
- Use AND to narrow a search. For example, "juvenile AND capital" will match only pages that have both terms.
- Use OR to broaden a search: "'capital punishment' OR 'death penalty'" will match any page that has *either* term, and since these terms are often used interchangeably, this type of search is necessary to retrieve the widest range of results.
- Use NOT to exclude unwanted results: "'death row' NOT Texas" finds articles about death row except for those that also mention Texas.

Since each search engine indexes somewhat differently and offers somewhat different ways of searching, it is a good idea to use several different search engines, especially for a general query. Several "metasearch" programs automate the process of submitting a query to multiple search engines. These include:

- Metacrawler (http://www.metacrawler.com)
- Inference FIND (http://www.ifind.com)
- SavvySearch (http://www.savvysearch.com)

There are also search utilities that can be run from the researcher's own PC rather than through a web site. A good example is Mata Hari, a "shareware" (try before you buy) program available for download at http://thewebtools.com/.

FINDING ORGANIZATIONS AND PEOPLE

Chapter 8 of this book provides an extensive list of organizations that are involved with the capital punishment issue, but new groups are emerging all the time. A good place to look for information and links to advocacy organizations is the major resource sites such as the Death Penalty Information Center and others mentioned at the beginning of this chapter. Web indexes such as Yahoo! also have a subtopic for organizations under "Capital Punishment" or "Death Penalty." If such sites do not yield the name of a specific organization, the name can be given to a search engine. Generally the best approach is to put the name of the organization in quote marks such as "Murder Victims for Reconciliation."

Another approach is to take a guess at the organization's likely web address. For example, the American Civil Liberties Union is commonly known by its acronym ACLU, so it is not a surprise that the organization's web site is at www.aclu.org. Note that noncommercial organization sites normally use the .org suffix, government agencies use .gov, educational institutions have .edu, and businesses use .com. This technique can save time, but doesn't always work.

There are several ways to find a person on the Internet:

- Put the person's name (in quotes) in a search engine and possibly find that person's home page on the Internet.
- Contact the person's employer (such as a university for an academic, or a corporation for a technical professional). Most such organizations have web pages that include a searchable faculty or employee directory.
- Try one of the people-finder services such as Yahoo! People Search at http://people.yahoo.com or BigFoot at http://www.bigfoot.com. This may yield contact information such as e-mail address, regular address, and/or phone number.

LEGAL RESEARCH

While capital punishment is also a moral and ethical issue, the most decisive battles are generally those carried out in the legislative and legal arenas. Because of the specialized terminology of the law, legal research can be more difficult to master than bibliographical or general research tools. Fortunately, the Internet has also come to the rescue in this area, offering a variety of ways to look up laws and court cases without having to pore through huge bound volumes in law libraries (which may not be easily accessible to the general public, anyway).

Capital Punishment

FINDING LAWS

Since the vast majority of death sentences are passed under state laws, access to the relevant portions of state penal codes is a must for the legal research. The Cornell Law School Death Penalty Project provides a very useful set of links at http://www.lawschool.cornell.edu/lawlibrary/death/ dstate.html. These links include the state's constitution, laws, court opinions, and death penalty advocacy organizations. For example, the links for California are:

Statutes
  http://www.leginfo.ca.gov/calaw.html
Constitution
  http://www.leginfo.ca.gov/const.html
Supreme Court and Courts of Appeal Opinions
  http://www.courtinfo.ca.gov/ Information and Organizations
California Coalition for Alternatives to the Death Penalty
  http://www.abolition-now.com/ccadp/
Prisons and Prison Law
  http://www.wco.com/~aerick/prison.html

This same site also provides links to recent federal legislation. While few federal prisoners have been executed, numerous federal death penalty offenses have been added in recent years. When federal legislation passes, it eventually becomes part of the United States Code, a massive legal compendium. Title 18 of the U.S. Code deals with Crimes and Criminal Procedure. Part I of this Title defines crimes and penalties and can be used together with the summary in Chapter 2 of this book, The Law of Capital Punishment, to look up specific sections that include the provision of the death penalty. (The Cornell Law School Death Penalty resource site at http://www.law.cornell.edu/topics/death_penalty.html provides a direct link to the sections of the U.S. Code Title 18 that involve the death penalty.)

The U.S. Code can be searched online in several locations, but the easiest site to use is probably the Cornell Law School at http://www4.law. cornell.edu/uscode/. The fastest way to retrieve a law is by its title and section citation, but phrases and keywords can also be used.

KEEPING UP WITH LEGISLATIVE DEVELOPMENTS

Pending legislation is often tracked by advocacy groups, both national and those based in particular states. See Chapter 8, Organizations and Agencies, for contact information. The Cornell Law School Death Penalty Project site mentioned earlier also lists state organizations that provide information on legislation currently under consideration.

Proposed federal death penalty legislation normally turns up as part of a large bill often called an "omnibus crime bill," although there are other possible legislative vehicles, such as the Antiterrorism and Effective Death Penalty Act of 1996.

The Library of Congress catalog site (telnet to locis.loc.gov) includes files summarizing legislation by the number of the session of Congress (each two year session of Congress has a consecutive number: for example, the 105th Congress was in session in 1997 and 1998 and the 106th will be in session in 1999 and 2000). Legislation can be searched for by the name of its sponsor(s), the bill number, or by topical keywords.

For example, selecting the 105th Congress and typing in the command **retrieve "death penalty"** yields the first of several pages of results:

1. *H.R.22: SPON=Rep McHugh, (Cosp=2); OFFICIAL TITLE: A bill to reform the postal laws of the United States.*

2. *H.R.41: SPON=Rep Gingrich, (Cosp=37); OFFICIAL TITLE: A bill to provide a sentence of death for certain importations of significant quantities of controlled substances.*

3. *H.R.91: SPON=Rep Solomon, (Cosp=1); OFFICIAL TITLE: A bill to amend the Omnibus Crime Control and Safe Streets Act of 1968 to reduce funding if States do not enact legislation that requires the death penalty in certain cases.*

Note that the sponsor and title of the bill are given, along with a brief description. Typing "chrn" (for "chronology") for one of the numbered bills would then display any "floor actions" that have happened to the bill, such as it's being referred to committee or signed into law by the president.

The Library of Congress THOMAS site (http://thomas.loc.gov/), provides a web-based interface that may be easier to use for many purposes. Under the Legislation section of the page, existing laws can be looked up by Public Law number or summaries of legislation considered by each Congress can be searched by keyword or bill number. For example, if one has read something about a bill being debated in Congress that would impose a death penalty but can't remember the details, he/she can type in the keywords "death penalty" and see listings of bills like the following:

*Listing of **43** bills containing your phrase **exactly as entered**.*

1. *Federal Death Penalty Abolition Act of 1999 (Introduced in the Senate)*
[S.1917.IS]

2. *Accuracy in Judicial Administration Act of 2000 (Introduced in the House)[H.R.3623.IH]*

3. *Fairness for Permanent Residents Act of 1999 (Introduced in the House)*
[H.R.2999.IH]

4. *Correctional Officer Protection Act (Introduced in the House)*
[H.R.282.IH]

Clicking on one of the highlighted bill numbers (such as S.1917) gives a page with links to the text of the bill, references to the *Congressional Record*, and status information about the bill. If one then clicks on the link to "Bill Summary & Status," he/she will find a detailed listing that begins with the last major action taken with regard to the bill:

S.1917
Sponsor: Sen Feingold, Russell D. (introduced 11/10/1999)
Latest Major Action: 11/10/1999 Referred to Senate committee
Title: A bill to abolish the death penalty under Federal law.

FINDING COURT DECISIONS

If legislation is the front end of the criminal justice process, the courts are the back. The Supreme Court and state courts make important decisions every year that shape the administration of the death penalty. Like laws, legal decisions are organized using a system of citations. The general form is: *Party1 v. Party2 volume reporter,* [optional start page] *(court, year)*.

Here are some examples:

Gregg v. Georgia, 428 U.S. 153 (1976)

Here the parties are Gregg (a condemned prisoner) and the state of Georgia. The case is in volume 428 of the U.S. *Supreme Court Reports*, beginning at page 153, and the case was decided in 1976. (For the Supreme Court, the name of the court is omitted.)

Fierro v. Gomez, 77 F.3d 301 (9th Cir. 1996)

Here the case is in the 9th U.S. Circuit Court of Appeals, decided in 1996.

A state court decision can generally be identified because it includes the state's name. For example, in *State v. Torrance*, 473 S.E.2d. 703, S.C. 1996, the S.E.2d refers to the appeals district, and the S.C. to South Carolina.

Once the jurisdiction for the case has been determined, the researcher can then go to a number of places on the Internet to find cases by citation and sometimes by the names of the parties or by subject keywords. A couple of the most useful sites are:

- **The Legal Information Institute** (http://supct.law.cornell.edu/supct/) has all Supreme Court decisions since 1990 plus 610 of "the most important historic" decisions.
- **Washlaw Web** (http://www.washlaw.edu/) has a variety of courts (including states) and legal topics listed, making it a good jumping-off place for many sorts of legal research. However, the actual accessibility of state court opinions (and the formats they are provided in) varies widely.

LEXIS AND WESTLAW

Lexis and Westlaw are commercial legal databases that have extensive information including an elaborate system of notes, legal subject headings, and ways to show relationships between cases. Unfortunately, these services are too expensive for use by most individual researchers unless they are available through a university or corporate library.

MORE HELP ON LEGAL RESEARCH

For more information on conducting legal research, see the "Legal Research FAQ" at http://www.cis.ohio-state.edu/hypertext/faq/usenet/law/research/top.html. For complex research projects, the researcher who lacks formal legal training may also want to consult with or rely on the efforts of professional researchers or academics in the field.

PUTTING IT ALL TOGETHER

It can be hard to know where to begin when there are so many kinds of information sources available. Unless one is researching a very specific topic, it is probably best to gain an overview and working knowledge of the topic by using some of the resource sites and web indexes and guides and then pursue specific interests by using bibliographical tools (library and bookstore catalogs and periodical indexes) to obtain appropriate books, news articles, and scholarly papers. When legal research is required, having the general knowledge, context, and citations in hand will save time and frustration.

CHAPTER 7

ANNOTATED BIBLIOGRAPHY

This chapter presents a representative selection of books, articles, Internet documents, and multimedia products on the subject of capital punishment. These sources selected followed this criteria:

- Generally, sources were chosen for interest and accessibility to students and general readers. More technical legal and statistical materials, however, are included as a starting point for more advanced researchers.
- More recent publications are favored over older ones, particularly with articles that discuss news, controversial cases, and legal developments. Earlier works, however, are included when they are of enduring intellectual or historical interest.
- An attempt is made to include every significant aspect of the topic and a variety of points of view. (The relative preponderance of anti–capital punishment material reflects the available literature, not an editorial judgment on the part of the compiler.)

In order to organize this many-faceted topic, the bibliographies are presented under twelve topics as follows:

- Reference Works
- Introductions, Overviews, and Collections
- General Advocacy Works
- Punishment and Deterrence
- Race and the Death Penalty
- Special Cases: Gender, Youth, and Disability
- Execution of the Innocent
- Other Legal and Procedural Issues
- Religious, Moral Ethical, and Cultural Approaches

- Political and Legislative Developments
- Death Row Accounts and Particular Cases
- International and Historical Works

Within each of these categories, the works are grouped according to type:

- Books
- Articles and Papers
- Web Documents (specific articles or documents available primarily on the Internet. See Chapter 6, How to Research Capital Punishment, for additional Internet resources and Chapter 8, Organizations and Agencies, for additional web sites and addresses.)
- Audiovisual Materials (for some topics only)

Note that many newspaper and periodical items listed under "Articles and Papers" are also available from the publication's web site. For example, the *New York Times* (http://www.nytimes.com), *Los Angeles Times* (http://www.latimes.com), and *Washington Post* (http://www.washingtonpost.com) have online archives of staff-written articles that go back for at least five years. Generally, newspapers offer articles from the past few weeks free, but charge a fee of a dollar or two per article for the full text of older articles. Many of these articles may be available for free at a local library. Some magazines and scholarly publications offer a selection of articles at no charge.

REFERENCE WORKS

This section includes reference books, articles from general encyclopedias, and bibliographies.

BOOKS

Abbott, Geoffrey. *The Book of Execution: An Encyclopedia of Methods of Judicial Execution*. London: Headline, 1995. A graphically illustrated presentation of the many methods of judicial execution that have been devised in the course of human history.

Archer, Dane, and Rosemary Gartner. *Violence and Crime in Cross-National Perspective*. New Haven, Conn.: Yale University Press, 1984. Provides information on major crimes for 100 countries, exploring such trends as an increase or decrease in homicide rates if the death penalty is abolished.

Beyleveld, Deryck. *A Bibliography of General Deterrence Research.* Westmead, England: Saxon House, 1980. Covers English-language deterrence research published between 1946 and 1978.

Cook, Earleen H. *Death Penalty Since Witherspoon and Furman.* Monticello, Ill.: Vance Bibliographies, 1979. An unannotated bibliography to articles and books, 1968–79.

Grossman, Mark. *Encyclopedia of Capital Punishment.* Santa Barbara, Calif.: ABC-CLIO, 1998. An A to Z encyclopedia of topics, persons, court decisions, statistics, and other items relating to capital punishment. The book includes a bibliography and timeline.

Hall, Kermit. *The Oxford Companion to the Supreme Court of the United States.* New York: Oxford University Press, 1992. Contains an overview of capital punishment jurisprudence but is most useful for learning how the Court works and for looking up general concepts that arise in reading decisions.

Hearn, Daniel Allen. *Legal Executions in New York State: A Comprehensive Reference, 1639–1963.* Jefferson, N.C.: McFarland, 1997. A comprehensive reference to all cases of capital punishment in New York over a period of more than 300 years. Entries are arranged chronologically and include the facts of each case and the method of execution.

Kronenwetter, Michael. *Capital Punishment: A Reference Handbook.* Santa Barbara, Calif.: ABC-CLIO, 1993. A comprehensive guide to capital punishment issues. The book includes history, summary of issues, chronology, biographies, facts and documents, organizations, and a list of selected print and nonprint resources.

Latzer, Barry. *Death Penalty Cases: Leading U.S. Supreme Court Cases on Capital Punishment.* Boston: Butterworth-Heinemann, 1998. A collection of extensive excerpts from the decisions in 22 Supreme Court cases involving capital punishment, with a brief editorial introduction to each case. Each case is a separate chapter with a descriptive title that identifies the main issue involved.

Miller, Alan V. *Capital Punishment as a Deterrent: A Bibliography.* Monticello, Ill.: Vance Bibliographies, 1980. Ten-page list of works on capital punishment from the 1970s and earlier.

Radelet, Michael L., and Margaret Vandiver. *Capital Punishment in America: An Annotated Bibliography.* New York: Garland Publishing, 1988. An annotated listing of more than 950 books and articles on capital punishment. The book includes citations to relevant congressional publications and brief synopses of major Supreme Court decisions.

Triche, Charles W., III. *The Capital Punishment Dilemma: 1950–1977: A Subject Bibliography.* Troy, N.Y.: Whitston, 1979. An extensive topical (but not annotated) bibliography of works dealing with the death penalty debate in the 1950s through the mid-1970s

United Nations Social Defense Research Institute. *Death Penalty: A Bibliographic Research*. Monsey, N.Y.: Criminal Justice Press, 1988. A bibliographical survey and review of international research on capital punishment, covering the period 1979–86.

ARTICLES AND PAPERS

Allen, Francis A. "Capital Punishment" in *International Encyclopedia of the Social Sciences*, vol. 2. New York: Macmillan, 1968, pp. 290–294. Overview of capital punishment's history, the 18th-century abolition movement, trends in the United States and worldwide, and the sanction's effectiveness.

Bedau, Hugo Adam. "Capital Punishment" in *Academic American Encyclopedia*, vol. 4. Danbury, Conn.: Grolier, 1997, pp. 123–124. Synopsis of the topic and its current status by a foremost expert.

Caldwell, Robert G. "Capital Punishment" in *Encyclopedia Americana*, vol. 5. Danbury, Conn.: Grolier, 1987, pp. 596–599. Brief summary of the history of capital punishment from ancient times. Caldwell reviews the effects of the Enlightenment on the treatment of criminals and discusses issues surrounding capital punishment today.

Campion, D. R. "Capital Punishment" in *The New Catholic Encyclopedia*, vol. 3. Palatine, Ill.: Jack Heraty and Associates, 1981, pp. 79–81. Covers ancient history of capital punishment, the Catholic Church's limited recognition of the practice, and the Church's role in the death penalty debate.

Papke, David Ray. "Crime and Punishment" in *Encyclopedia of American Social History*, vol. 3. New York: Scribner's, 1993, pp. 2,073–2,087. A historical overview and bibliography that includes material on capital punishment.

Weisberg, Robert. "Capital Punishment" in *Encyclopedia of the American Constitution*, vol. 1. New York: Macmillan, 1986, pp. 201–206. A detailed review of the Supreme Court's constitutional regulation of the death penalty, followed by brief articles on the key Supreme Court cases of 1972 and 1976. Weisberg's article was updated in the 1992 Supplement on pp. 64–68.

Zimring, Franklin E. "Capital Punishment" in *The World Book Encyclopedia*, vol. 3. Chicago: World Book, 1990, p. 193. A leading criminological researcher describes the status of the death penalty in the United States as of the beginning of the 1990s.

WEB DOCUMENTS

"1000+ Death Penalty Links." Available online. URL: http://www.clarkprosecutor.org/html/links/dplinks.htm. Posted March 6, 2000. This site, maintained by the office of the Clark County, Indiana prosecuting attorney, has one of the largest collection of death penalty–related links available on the Internet. Links are grouped into categories such as pro–death penalty, anti–death penalty, general reference, articles and essays, history, statistics, as well as specific issues such as race and the death penalty, deterrence and incapacitation, and cost. Some links are annotated.

Bedau, Hugo. "Capital Punishment" in *Grolier Multimedia Encyclopedia Online*. Available online (requires subscription). URL: http://go.grolier.com. Brief overview with links and bibliography.

"Capital Punishment" in *Catholic Encyclopedia Online*. Available online. URL: http://www.newadvent.org/cathen/.

"Capital Punishment" in *Encyclopedia Britannica Online*. Available online. URL: http://www.Britannica.com. Brief article with general and law-related Internet links.

Death Penalty Information Center. "The Death Penalty in 1996: Year End Report." Available online. URL: http://www.essential.org/dpic/dpic96rpt.html. Posted on December 1996. Summarizes executions and other events. The page focuses on election year–related events and a 20-year retrospective since 1976 (when the Supreme Court reapproved the death penalty).

———. "The Death Penalty in 1997: Year End Report." Available online. URL: http://www.essential.org/dpic/yrendrpt.html. Downloaded on November 27, 1999. Summary of death penalty–related statistics and news events of 1997. The page summarizes progress in raising issues against capital punishment and describes persons executed during the year.

———. "The Death Penalty in 1998: Year End Report." Available online. URL: http://www.essential.org/dpic/yrendrpt98.html. Posted on December 1998. This report by the Death Penalty Information Center covers significant events regarding capital punishment in 1998, including renewed focus on the possibility of the execution of innocent people. The report also covers execution statistics, the death penalty and race, the Karla Faye Tucker case, other executions and events, and international developments.

INTRODUCTIONS, OVERVIEWS, AND COLLECTIONS

This section consists of introductions and overviews that offer broad treatment of the historical background and current issues of capital punishment.

Annotated Bibliography

These works attempt a balanced presentation without a strong advocacy slant. There are also collections of articles and papers covering a range of issues. Because they often contain well-rounded introductions and source materials, some juvenile nonfiction works are also included.

BOOKS

Acker, James R., Robert M. Bohm, and Charles S. Lanier. *America's Experiment with Capital Punishment: Reflections on the Past, Present, and Future of the Ultimate Penal Sanction*. Durham, N.C.: Carolina Academic Press, 1998. An extensive collection of essays that comprehensively covers the development of capital punishment in America—and the thinking about the death penalty in legal opinions and social analysis. Areas covered in this text include legal and legislative developments; the justice and utility of capital punishment; research on deterrence and incapacitation; the execution of children, the mentally impaired, and the innocent; the jury deliberation and sentencing process; and racial aspects of the death sentence process.

Baird, Robert M., and Stuart E. Rosenbaum. *Punishment and the Death Penalty: The Current Debate*. New York: Prometheus Books, 1995. A collection of essays in two parts. Part one deals with the justification for punishment in general in various frameworks of social philosophy. The second part focuses on capital punishment, in particular, its history, the movement to abolish the death penalty, deterrence, execution of the innocent, the confrontation between capital punishment and contemporary social values, and the debate between Justices Blackmun and Scalia.

Bedau, Hugo Adam. *The Death Penalty in America*. New York: Oxford University Press, 1997. An extensive collection including overviews, facts and statistics, and a variety of papers. Areas covered include: the death penalty vs. life imprisonment, deterrence and incapacitation, constitutionality (including "cruel and unusual punishment"), the part played by race and class in capital sentencing, and religious and moral arguments. Bedau includes a bibliography and case citations.

Bohm, Robert M. *The Death Penalty in America: Current Research*. Cincinnati, Ohio: Anderson Publishing Company, 1991. A collection of studies by various researchers. Topics include statistical analysis of executions, deterrence, decision making by jurors in capital cases, recidivism by death row inmates paroled after the *Furman* decision, and public opinion on capital punishment. Some material is somewhat dated.

———. *Deathquest: An Introduction to the Theory and Practice of Capital Punishment in the United States*. Cincinnati, Ohio: Anderson Publishing Company, 1999. A comprehensive legal textbook giving the history, issues, and court opinions relating to capital punishment.

Draper, Thomas. *Capital Punishment.* New York: H. W. Wilson, 1985. An anthology of articles, largely popular, examining capital punishment from different perspectives.

Gottfried, Ted. *Capital Punishment: The Death Penalty Debate.* Springfield, N.J.: Enslow, 1997. For young adult readers. A fairly balanced presentation of the pro and con arguments regarding the death penalty, with good citations of cases and examples. Gottfried includes historical background, facts, and statistics, as well as a chronology, glossary, and bibliography.

Grabowski, John F. *The Death Penalty.* San Diego: Lucent Books, 1999. For junior high and older readers. An overview presenting issues relating to the death penalty, with pro and con arguments.

Guernsey, JoAnn Bren. *Should We Have Capital Punishment?* Minneapolis: Lerner Publications, 1993. An introduction to the death penalty debate for young adult readers. The book includes a bibliography and glossary.

Harries, Keith, and Derral Cheatwood. *The Geography of Execution: The Capital Punishment Quagmire in America.* Lanham, Md.: Rowman & Littlefield, 1996. Begins with an overview and introduction to methodology. The authors give a historical, differential view of how particular constellations of practical and political considerations result in differences in the pace and methods of execution. They also present studies of race and gender in capital punishment and studies showing no discernable deterrent effect for the death penalty. The book also discusses the effectiveness and problems of life without parole.

Hook, Donald D., and Lothar Kahn. *Death in the Balance: The Debate Over Capital Punishment.* Lexington, Mass.: Lexington Books, 1989. Explores the moral complexities of capital punishment, focusing on recent cases in which the death penalty was implemented or requested.

Koosed, Margery B. *Capital Punishment: The Philosophical, Moral, and Penological Debate Over Capital Punishment.* New York: Garland Publishing Company, 1996. An overview of capital punishment issues from a variety of perspectives.

Lester, David. *The Death Penalty: Issues and Answers.* Springfield, Ill.: Charles C. Thomas, 1998. An overview of death penalty issues. Lester begins with an introduction to the operation of capital punishment, then discusses the results of research on topics such as public attitude, discrimination, juror behavior, and studies of deterrence. The book includes appendices summarizing surveys and studies.

Loeb, Robert H. *Crime and Capital Punishment,* 2d ed. New York: Franklin Watts, 1986. A basic introduction.

McGehee, Edward G., and William H. Hildebrand. *The Death Penalty: A Literary and Historical Approach.* Boston: D. C. Heath, 1964. Fifty opinions on capital punishment, covering several centuries.

Annotated Bibliography

Miller, Larry S., and John T. Whitehead. *Introduction to Criminal Justice Research and Statistics.* Cincinnati, Ohio: Anderson Publishing Company, 1996. A good introduction to the use of statistics, including methodology, data analysis, and decision making. The book is useful for evaluating the many statistical and survey studies relating to capital punishment.

Palmer, Louis J. *The Death Penalty: An American Citizen's Guide to Understanding Federal and State Laws.* Jefferson, N.C.: McFarland, 1998. An overview and summary of how capital punishment is implemented in federal and state law. A brief overview of common law is followed by sections on prosecutorial discretion and the charging mechanism, the capital penalty phase, aggravating and mitigating circumstances, appellate review, and laws relating to the execution process itself. Includes tables of death penalty provisions.

Pojman, Louis P., and Reiman Jeffrey. *The Death Penalty: For and Against.* Lanham, Md.: Rowman & Littlefield, 1998. The two authors debate each other over the philosophical proposition that the death penalty should be abolished in America. Each author then replies to the other's statement.

Randa, Laura E. *Society's Final Solution: A History and Discussion of the Death Penalty.* Lanham, Md.: University Press of America, 1997. Begins with a history of capital punishment and then presents all of the major issues through selections written by a variety of people who must confront them. Writers include lawyers, teachers, lobbyists, and legislators.

Rein, Mei Ling, Nancy R. Jacobs, and Mark A. Siegel, eds. *Capital Punishment: Cruel and Usual?,* 1998 ed. Wylie, Tex.: Information Plus, 1998. A compact, fact-filled guide to capital punishment issues, including history, court rulings, legal issues, statutes and legislation, statistics, public attitudes, and international aspects. The book also includes a brief pro/con debate and listings of resources and organizations.

Schonebaum, Stephen E. *Does Capital Punishment Deter Crime?* San Diego: Greenhaven Press, 1998. A collection of essays taking opposing viewpoints on capital punishment issues. The book is suitable for junior high or older readers.

Sellin, Thorsten, ed. *Capital Punishment.* New York: Harper and Row, 1967. A collection of influential essays on the death penalty.

Spear, Charles. *Essays on the Punishment of Death.* Littleton, Colo.: Fred B. Rothman, 1994. A collection of essays first published in 1845. The collection covers diverse aspects of capital punishment including the effects of public executions on the prisoner and spectators as well as the impact on domestic life and comparison to other countries. It also includes discussion of Bible passages relating to capital punishment.

157

Steins, Richard. *The Death Penalty: Is It Justice?* New York: Twenty-first Century Books, 1993. For junior high readers or older. Overview of the history and issues surrounding capital punishment.

Streib, Victor L. *A Capital Punishment Anthology.* Cincinnati, Ohio: Anderson Printing Company, 1997. An anthology of critical writings on capital punishment. The book includes general contributions by noted writers in the field and Supreme Court justices, followed by sets of selections focusing on issues such as racial disparities, execution of the innocent, and various aspects of judicial procedure.

Van den Haag, Ernest, and John P. Conrad. *The Death Penalty: A Debate.* New York: Plenum, 1983. A lay introduction to the major issues put together by authors with opposing viewpoints.

Vila, Bryan, and Cynthia Morris. *Capital Punishment in the United States: A Documentary History.* Westport, Conn.: Greenwood Press, 1997. An extensive collection of primary sources relating to capital punishment. Areas included are the Bible and colonial America, the 19th-century death penalty abolition movement, the mid-20th-century, court cases of the 1960s and 1970s, the revival of both capital punishment and the death penalty debate starting in the late 1970s, and contemporary issues. Documents include court opinions, articles, and essays.

White, Welsh S. *The Death Penalty in the Nineties: An Examination of the Modern System of Capital Punishment.* Ann Arbor: University of Michigan Press, 1994. Examines the modern capital punishment system, focusing on recent Supreme Court rulings.

Winters, Paul A. *The Death Penalty: Opposing Viewpoints.* 3d ed. revised. San Diego: Greenhaven Press, 1997. A collection of readings from a variety of writers, arranged into a series of pro and con pairings. Topics include early consideration of the death penalty in England and America; justice, morality, and the execution of the innocent; the effectiveness of the death penalty as a deterrent; and fairness in the application of the death penalty to minority groups and the handicapped. Each reading includes an introduction and discussion questions. The book was written for junior and senior high school students, but valuable for researchers at all levels.

Wolf, Robert V., and Austin Sarat, ed. *Capital Punishment: Crime, Justice, and Punishment.* Philadelphia: Chelsea House, 1997. For young adult readers. Provides a basic overview of capital punishment issues, introducing cases and arguments on each of the major topics.

Zimring, Franklin E., and Gordon Hawkings. *Capital Punishment and the American Agenda.* New York: Cambridge University Press, 1986. A view of capital punishment issues as they emerged during the 1980s.

Annotated Bibliography

WEB DOCUMENTS

"Focus on the Death Penalty." Available online. URL: http://www.uaa. alaska.edu/just/death/history.html. Posted March 3, 2000. This site, sponsored by the Justice Center at the University of Alaska, Anchorage, focuses primarily on legal issues, with background material, statistics, and discussion relating to key death penalty cases. However, access to current news updates and reports as well as some historical information is also provided.

"Issues and Controversies: Death Penalty." Issue overview from "Issues and Controversies On File." Facts On File. News Digest. Available online. URL: http://www.facts.com/cd/i00015.htm#I00015_b. Downloaded December 7, 1999. A well-organized introductory overview of the major legal issues relating to capital punishment, excerpted from the printed publication. The On File includes statistics and a bibliography.

Vanderhoof, J. W. "Prof. David's Death Penalty Resources." Available online. URL: http://www.uncp.edu/home/vanderhoof/death.html. Downloaded March 6, 2000. Prepared for a class syllabus, this is a well-organized guide to links and resources for the death penalty debate. It includes recorded lectures, archives relating to high-profile cases (such as the Jasper hate crime trial and the Timothy McVeigh trial), excerpts and supplemental materials for PBS and NPR programs, newspaper articles, and other material.

AUDIOVISUAL MATERIALS

"Death Penalty." A&E Network. VHS video of an episode of the *American Justice* documentary series. [n.d.] Available for ordering online at http://store.aetv.com/. Presents a pro-and-con overview of capital punishment issues. Includes an in-depth look at the case of Caryl Chessman, who was executed in 1960.

"The Death Penalty." Discussion on National Public Radio's program *Talk of the Nation* with Neal Conan and guests Susan Boleyn, Senior Assistant Attorney General, State of Georgia, Section Leader of the state's capital litigation section and Richard Deiter, Executive Director, Death Penalty Information Center. RealAudio file available online at http://www.npr. org/ramfiles/980113.totn.01.ram.Originally broadcast January 13, 1998. Discusses prosecutorial discretion, attempts to speed up the appeals process, racial bias in death sentencing, the politics of the death penalty, and the Karla Faye Tucker case.

GENERAL ADVOCACY WORKS

This section consists of advocacy works that include a variety of issues or arguments relating to the death penalty. The majority of these works have an abolitionist point of view. Discussions of abolition movements are also included. (For historical works, see the section International and Historical Works.)

BOOKS

Abu-Jamal, Mumia, and Cornel West. *Death Blossoms: Reflections From a Prisoner of Conscience.* Farmington, Penn.: Plough Publishing House, 1997. A collection of short essays in which Abu-Jamal explores the deeper implications of imprisonment and justice, moving beyond the particulars of his own case found in his book *Live from Death Row.*

Annual Chief Justice Earl Warren Conference on Advocacy in the United States. *The Death Penalty: Final Report.* Washington, D.C.: The Roscoe Pound–American Trial Lawyers Foundation, 1980. A collection of three papers advocating the abolition of the death penalty.

Bedau, Hugo Adam. *Death Is Different: Studies in the Morality, Law, and Politics of Capital Punishment.* Boston: Northeastern University Press, 1987. Ten essays explaining and refuting arguments in favor of the death penalty. Topics include retribution, deterrence, whether the convicted retains a right to life, and whether the death penalty is needed to buttress the social order. The book includes a bibliography, a list of court cases, and extensive notes.

Berns, Walter. *For Capital Punishment: Crime and the Morality of the Death Penalty.* Lanham, Md.: University Press of America, 1991. Advocates the continuance of capital punishment, based on the concept of justice as retribution.

Bigel, Alan I. *Justices William J. Brennan, Jr. and Thurgood Marshall on Capital Punishment: Its Constitutionality, Morality, Deterrent Effect, and Interpretation by the Court.* Lanham, Md.: University Press of America, 1997. A detailed study of the philosophical and legal evolution of the position that justices Brennan and Marshall took against the death penalty during their tenure on the court. Their opinions and arguments are placed within the context of the traditional arguments about fairness and cruelty.

Block, Eugene B. *When Men Play God: The Fallacy of Capital Punishment.* San Francisco: Cragmont Publishers, 1983. A general overview of the abolitionist movement in several contexts, including historical and international.

Annotated Bibliography

Brown, Edmund Gerald. *Public Justice, Private Mercy: A Governor's Education on Death Row.* New York: Knightsbridge Publishing Co., 1990. A former governor of California tells why he came to oppose capital punishment.

Carrington, Frank G. *Neither Cruel Nor Unusual.* New Rochelle, N.Y.: Arlington House, 1978. Defends the death penalty, refuting abolitionist reasoning step by step.

Cohen, Bernard L. *Law Without Order: Capital Punishment and the Liberals.* New Rochelle, N.Y.: Arlington House, 1970. Maintains that capital punishment is the cornerstone of any credible law enforcement system.

Costanzo, Mark. *Just Revenge: Costs and Consequences of the Death Penalty.* New York: St. Martin's Press, 1997. A comprehensive case for abolition of the death penalty. Costanzo begins by describing how the system actually works from trial to execution. He then addresses and refutes each pro–death penalty argument on the issues of cruelty, cost, fairness, deterrence, public support, and moral justification.

Davis, Michael. *Justice in the Shadow of Death: Rethinking Capital & Lesser Punishments.* Lanham, Md.: Rowman & Littlefield, 1996. Systematically looks at the major arguments for and against capital punishment, including deterrence, inhumaneness, considerations of medical ethics, proportional punishment, irrevocability, the purpose of punishment, and treatment of the insane. Davis comes to the conclusion that the United States should join most other developed nations in abolishing capital punishment.

Endres, Michael E. *The Morality of Capital Punishment: Equal Justice Under Law?* Mystic, Conn.: Twenty-Third Publications, 1985. Opposes capital punishment due to its unfair application and lack of valid usefulness.

Gorecki, Jan. *Capital Punishment: Criminal Law and Social Evolution.* New York: Columbia University Press, 1983. Argues that state use of violence declines as a society evolves, so that capital punishment becomes unnecessary.

Gray, Ian, ed., and Moira Stanley, ed. *A Punishment in Search of a Crime: Americans Speak Out Against the Death Penalty.* New York: Avon Books, 1989. Contemporary writings and statements against capital punishment.

Haas, Kenneth C., and James A. Inciardi. *Challenging Capital Punishment: Legal and Social Science Approaches.* Newbury Park, Calif.: Sage, 1988. A collection of essays marshalling legal and sociological critiques of capital punishment.

Haines, Herbert H. *Against Capital Punishment: The Anti-Death Penalty Movement in America, 1972–1994.* New York: Oxford University Press, 1996. A detailed discussion of the rise of the modern anti–death penalty movement and the ongoing strategic debates within the movement over such issues as whether to promote LWOP (life without parole) as an alter-

161

native, whether to form coalitions with groups such as pro-life activists, and the advantages and disadvantages of death penalty opponents also becoming involved in issues such as gun control and drug policy reform.

Hibbert, Christopher. *The Roots of Evil.* Boston: Little, Brown, 1963. Discusses the historical evolution of punishment and attitudes toward criminals. A chapter on capital punishment, with a British focus, argues for abolition of the death penalty.

Koestler, Arthur, and C. J. Rolph. *Hanged by the Neck: An Exposure of Capital Punishment in England.* London: Penguin, 1961. An expansion of Koestler's *Reflections on Hanging.*

Lawes, Lewis. *Man's Judgment of Death: An Analysis of Capital Punishment Based on Facts, Not Sentiment.* New York: Putnam, 1924. A Sing Sing warden's opposition to capital punishment. Lawes became a leading abolitionist of his time.

Mackey, Philip English, ed. *Voices Against Death: American Opposition to Capital Punishment, 1787–1975.* New York: Burt Franklin, 1976. A collection of 26 statements by leading abolitionists throughout the nation's history.

Meador, Roy. *Capital Revenge: 54 Votes Against Life.* Philadelphia: Dorrance and Co., 1975. Essays directed specifically to the 54 U.S. Senators who voted in 1974 to reinstate the death penalty.

Playfair, Giles, and Derrick Singleton. *The Offenders: The Case Against Legal Vengeance.* New York: Simon and Schuster, 1957. Presents six capital cases as examples of the ineffectiveness of legal vengeance.

Prejean, Helen. *Dead Man Walking: An Eyewitness Account of the Death Penalty in the United States.* New York: Vintage Books, 1994. The passionate account of Sister Prejean's friendship with two death row inmates and her involvement in the crusade to end capital punishment. While her arguments against the death penalty are the conventional ones, readers quickly become involved with her depiction of the gritty reality of life on death row and the grim details of the far-from-painless execution process. The book inspired a successful Academy Award–winning movie.

Radelet, Michael L. *Facing the Death Penalty: Essays on a Cruel and Unusual Punishment.* Philadelphia: Temple University Press, 1989. A collection of essays that describe how condemned inmates and their families face impending execution and how lawyers and other professionals struggle to assist them. Writers include anthropologists, criminologists, a minister, a philosopher, and three condemned prisoners. The collection is generally abolitionist in attitude.

Sarat, Austin. *The Killing State: Capital Punishment in Law, Politics, and Culture.* New York: Oxford University Press, 1999. A collection of essays by scholars from various fields that seeks to explain the social and political function served by the death penalty, bringing out perversities and contradictions with cherished American values. The book generally has an abolitionist point of view. It is divided into parts dealing with political, legal, and cultural issues.

Schwed, Roger E. *Abolition and Capital Punishment: The United States' Judicial, Political, and Moral Barometer.* New York: AMS Press, 1983. A concise overview of capital punishment and the movement to abolish it.

Stassen, Glen Harold. *Capital Punishment: A Reader.* Cleveland: Pilgrim Press, 1998. A varied collection of readings on capital punishment, mainly from the abolitionist point of view. It is grouped into the following areas: justice as retribution or restoration; deterrence; fairness and equal treatment before the law; scriptural background to capital punishment; capital punishment from the point of view of a consistent ethic of the sacredness of human life; the need for restoring a just social order, and the role of religion and people of faith in transforming the capital punishment debate.

Whitman, Claudia, and Julie Zimmerman. *Frontiers of Justice: Death Penalty.* Brunswick, Me.: Biddle Publishing Co., 1997. A large collection of essays and articles by a variety of persons involved in working with death row inmates, relatives of murder victims, and other persons involved with capital punishment. The selections reflect a generally abolitionist point of view.

ARTICLES AND PAPERS

Amsterdam, Anthony G. "Capital Punishment" in H. A. Bedau, ed., *The Death Penalty in America*, pp. 346–358. New York: Oxford University Press, 1982. A concise and forceful call for abolition of the death penalty by a leading abolitionist.

Anderson, George M. "Opposing the Death Penalty: an Interview with Helen Prejean." in *America*, vol. 175, November 9, 1996, pp. 8ff. Interview with the nun whose experiences with Louisiana death row inmates were described in the book (and movie) *Dead Man Walking.*

Barzun, Jacques. "In Favor of Capital Punishment" in *Crime and Delinquency*, vol. 15, 1969, pp. 21–28. A critique of arguments for abolishing the death penalty. The author stresses the value of human life.

Cauthen, Kenneth. "Capital Punishment" in Kenneth Cauthen, *The New Modernism*, pp. 151–165. Lanham, Md.: University Press of America, 1997. Also available online. URL: http://www.frontiernet.com/~kenc/cappun.htm. Argues that while two valid moral principles (love and justice) can lead to opposing conclusions about the validity of capital punishment, the moral arguments against capital punishment as actually practiced in the real world are overwhelming.

Clark, Ramsey. "The Death Penalty and Reverence for Life" in Ramsey Clark, *Crime in America*. New York: Simon and Schuster, 1970, pp. 308–315. The former U.S. Attorney General and human rights activist discusses his opposition to the death penalty.

"Conduct Unbecoming: Civilised Societies Don't Need the Death Penalty" in *The Economist*, vol. 311, May 6, 1989, pp. 10–11. Assesses the need for capital punishment in an advanced society and concludes that relevant social objectives can be achieved by other means.

Davis, David Brion. "The Movement to Abolish Capital Punishment in America, 1787–1861" in *American Historical Review*, vol. 63, 1957, pp. 23–46. An account of the movement to abolish capital punishment between the Revolution and the Civil War.

"Down with the Death Penalty" in *The Economist* (U.S.), vol. 351, May 15, 1999, p. 20. Argues that the United States should join the majority of developed nations that have abandoned the death penalty. Of the three main arguments for capital punishment (deterrence, incapacitation, and retribution), the death penalty is ineffective or unnecessary for the first two and incapable of truly satisfying the third.

Duff, Audrey. "Never Say Die: the Texas Resource Center's Aggressive Defense of Death Row Inmates" in *Texas Monthly*, vol. 21, October 1993, pp. 50ff. Describes a federally funded legal clinic that has succeeded in winning stays of execution for Texas death row inmates such as Gary Graham. Death penalty supporters have questioned the Resource Center's tactics and use of funds.

Ervin, Mike. "Leonard Weinglass" in *The Progressive*, vol. 60, May 1996, pp. 34ff. Interview with the activist attorney who defended the Chicago Eight during the 1960s and now works to change the legal system. His latest client is black journalist and death row prisoner Mumia Abu-Jamal.

Landsburg, Steven E. "Just Do It" in *Forbes*, vol. 154, November 21, 1994, p. 166. Argues that the death penalty is justified. Poverty is no more an excuse for robbery or murder than lack of a sexual outlet is an excuse for rape. The legal system should use scarce resources more efficiently by confining and punishing violent criminals and not using prison space for lesser offenders. Authorities should be held responsible by the public for their choices and priorities.

Mead, Margaret. "A Life for a Life: What That Means Today" in *Redbook*, June 1978, pp. 56–60. The noted anthropologist expresses her opposition to capital punishment.

Pallone, N. J. "Advocacy Scholarship on the Death Penalty" in *Society*, vol. 26, November/December 1988, pp. 84–87. Reviews research advocating capital punishment.

Prejean, Helen, Marcia Cohen, and Barbara Bartocci. "Should Killers Live? Or Die?" in *Good Housekeeping*, vol. 217, August 1993, pp. 94ff. Nun and death penalty activist Sister Helen Prejean discusses her experiences with inmates on death row and with two mothers of murdered children. One of the mothers wants the killer of her child to die, but Prejean believes killing by the state is unjustified and unnecessary.

Reiman, Jeffrey H. "Justice, Civilization, and the Death Penalty: Answering van den Haag" in *Philosophy and Public Affairs*, vol. 14, 1985, pp. 115–148. Advocates the abolition of the death penalty and refutes pro–capital punishment arguments advanced by Ernest van den Haag.

Schwarzschild, Henry. "A Social and Moral Atrocity" in *ABA Journal*, vol. 71, April 1985, pp. 38–42. A debate about capital punishment with proponent Ernest van den Haag.

Theis, David. "The Convict and the CPA" in *Lear's*, vol. 7, March 1994, pp. 50ff. Interview with anti–death penalty activist Susan Dillow, an accountant whose determination to fight capital punishment led her to defend Texas death row prisoner Gary Graham, who is also interviewed.

Valentine, Victoria. "In Defense of Life" in *Emerge*, vol. 7, November 1995, pp. 26ff. Interview with Steven W. Hawkins, executive director of the National Coalition to Abolish the Death Penalty. He describes the objectives of the organization in mobilizing public attention around pending executions and the issue of racial bias in death sentencing.

WEB DOCUMENTS

American Civil Liberties Union. "The Death Penalty (ACLU Briefing Paper)." Available online. URL: http://www.aclu.org/library/pbp8.html. Downloaded on November 28, 1999. States the ACLU's comprehensive anti–death penalty position. Issues summarized include unfairness based on race, class, and geography; irreversibility; and cruelty/barbarism.

Amnesty International. "The United States of America: 'A Macabre Assembly Line of Death': Death Penalty Developments in 1997." Available online. URL: http://www.amnesty.org/ailib/aipub/1998/AMR/25102098.htm. Posted April 1998. Summarizes executions, legal battles, and other events of 1997 from an abolitionist point of view.

———. "United States of America: Speaking Out: Voices Against Death." Available online. URL: http://www.amnesty.org/ailib/aipub/1999/AMR/25112899.htm. Posted October 1999. A collection of statements by Americans who are confronting the death penalty in various ways. The page includes contributions by an activist, the parent of a murder victim, and several death row inmates.

Bedau, Hugo Adam. "The Case Against the Death Penalty." Available on-line. URL: http://www.aclu.org/library/case_against_death.html. Downloaded on November 28, 1999. A comprehensive statement of op-position to the death penalty, covering the standard arguments that capi-tal punishment is not a deterrent, that it is unfair, irreversible, and barbarous, and that there are superior alternatives.

"Groups Joining the Call for a Moratorium on Executions." Available on-line. URL: http://www.quixote.org/ej/tally999.html. Posted on December 2, 1999. A regularly updated list of organizations that have joined the nationwide call for a moratorium on executions.

Justice for All. "Death Penalty and Sentencing Information in the United States." Available online. URL: http://www.prodeathpenalty.com/DP. html. Posted on October 1, 1997. A lengthy article defending capital punishment against its critics. Topics include deterrence, the risk of exe-cuting the innocent, racism and the death penalty, the cost of capital pun-ishment, procedural issues, and religious views on the death penalty.

"Justice for Police Officer Daniel Faulkner." Available online. URL: http://www.danielfaulkner.com/splash.htm. Downloaded on December 8, 1999. A site dedicated to countering what the author considers to be the myths and misinformation spread by advocates of Mumia Abdu-Jamal, who was convicted for Faulkner's murder but has protested his innocence. The site includes trial transcripts and a summary of developments.

"Organizations Jointly Oppose Death Penalty." Available online. URL: http://www.ngltf.org/press/deathpenalty.html. Downloaded March 6, 2000. This is a statement against capital punishment by eleven worldwide groups representing lesbian, gay, bisexual, and transgender people, in-cluding the Lambda Legal Defense and Education Fund and the National Gay and Lesbian Task Force. The page includes quotes from group lead-ers and contact information for the groups.

"Pro-Death Penalty Resources" Available online. URL: http://www. prodeathpenalty.com. Posted March 6, 2000. This site offers extensive news and resources from a pro–death penalty point of view. Includes up-dates on pending cases, articles, and advocacy papers.

PUNISHMENT AND DETERRENCE

This section consists of works that discuss theories of punishment, the issue of whether the death penalty deters criminal activity, and the concepts of retribution, revenge, vigilantism, and social cost and protection. (For lynch-ing or judicial execution related to racial issues, see the section Race and the Death Penalty.)

Annotated Bibliography

BOOKS

Andenaes, Johannes. *Punishment and Deterrence.* Ann Arbor, Mich.: University of Michigan Press, 1974. A collection of essays on methods of deterrence and their effectiveness.

Beccaria, Cesare, and Jane Grigson (translator). *Of Crimes and Punishments: The Groundbreaking Work That Began the Debate About Capital Punishment.* New York: Marsilio Publishers, 1996. Translation of an essay by an 18th-century Italian philosopher. In his systematic analysis of criminal justice, Beccaria raised most of the issues that would define the modern debate, including crime prevention, prompt punishment, and deterrence (which he believed was not contributed to by capital punishment). Beccaria's ideas influenced Benjamin Franklin and Thomas Jefferson in America and Jeremy Bentham and Voltaire in Europe.

Cederblom, J. B., and William L. Blizek. *Justice and Punishment.* Cambridge, Mass.: Ballinger, 1977. Essays originally presented at a University of Nebraska-Omaha symposium on "Criminal Justice and Punishment." The book focuses on the issue of retribution.

Gibbs, Jack P. *Crime, Punishment and Deterrence.* New York: Elsevier, 1975. Discusses theories of deterrence and presents research findings.

Jacoby, Susan. *Wild Justice: The Evolution of Revenge.* New York: Harper and Row, 1983. Discusses the meaning of justice and the corollary issue of revenge. Jacoby finds that revenge is legitimate but capital punishment is excessive and damaging to social morality.

Moberly, Walter. *The Ethics of Punishment.* London: Faber and Faber, 1968. An in-depth examination of penal theory, including a section on the morality of capital punishment.

Montague, Philip. *Punishment as Societal Defense.* Lanham, Md.: Rowman & Littlefield, 1995. Develops a theory of punishment that is based on an extension of the individual right of self-defense to society's collective defense. Montague argues that this theory is superior to conceptions of punishment as deterrence or retribution and that it would justify the imposition of capital punishment in some circumstances.

Murphy, Jeffrie G., ed. *Punishment and Rehabilitation.* 3rd ed. Belmont, Calif.: Wadsworth, 1994. Updated version of an anthology of articles outlining the major theories of punishment, including capital punishment. The anthology is useful for placing capital punishment within the general context of punishment and the social dynamics of justice.

Raper, Arthur F. *The Tragedy of Lynching.* Chapel Hill, University of North Carolina Press, 1933. A study of the causes, supposed and actual, of more than 3,000 lynchings that took place between 1889 and 1930. The book was prepared for the Southern Commission on the Study of Lynching.

167

Sheleff, Leon Shaskolsky. *Ultimate Penalties: Capital Punishment, Life Imprisonment, Physical Torture.* Columbus: Ohio State University Press, 1987. Considers the justification for extreme penalties for heinous crimes.

Shin, Kilman. *Death Penalty and Crime: Empirical Studies.* Fairfax, Va.: George Mason University Press, 1978. Surveys studies on the impact that capital punishment has on crime rates in America and worldwide.

Steffen, Lloyd. *Executing Justice: The Moral Meaning of the Death Penalty.* Cleveland: Pilgrim Press, 1999. Explores the moral theories that underlie support for the death penalty, including the right of society to defend itself from murder, the promotion of the greater good, just retribution, and a theory of "just execution" tested against actual practice.

van den Haag, Ernest. *Punishing Criminals: Concerning a Very Old and Painful Question.* New York: Basic Books, 1975. General discussion of the concept of punishment and the appropriateness of the death penalty.

Wilson, James Q. *Thinking About Crime.* New York: Basic Books, 1983. Argues that criminal behavior is rational and can be deterred.

ARTICLES AND PAPERS

Archer, Dane, Rosemary Gartner, and Marc Beittel. "Homicide and the Death Penalty: A Cross-National Test of a Deterrence Hypothesis" in *Journal of Criminal Law and Criminology,* vol. 74, 1983, pp. 991–1,013. Using data from 14 countries, the authors determined that homicide rates may actually decrease after the death penalty is abolished.

———. "Deterrence, Brutalization, and the Death Penalty: Another Examination of Oklahoma's Return to Capital Punishment" in *Criminology,* vol. 36, November, 1998, pp. 711–733. Study examines the immediate and possible delayed deterrent and brutalization effects of executions accompanying Oklahoma's return to capital punishment in 1990. The authors claim that there is a strong brutalization effect and possibly a delayed (lagging) deterrent effect.

Bailey, William C. "Capital Punishment and Lethal Assaults Against Police" in *Criminology,* vol. 19, 1982, pp. 608–625. An analysis of state data nationwide, 1961–71, found little evidence to link the rate of murders of police officers and the presence of the death sentence. Sociodemographic factors had greater effect on the rate of lethal assaults on police.

———. "Murder and Capital Punishment in the Nation's Capital" in *Justice Quarterly,* vol. 1, 1984, pp. 211–233. Examines the correlation between the homicide rate and the possibility of execution in Washington, D.C., between 1890 and 1970. The homicide rate increased slightly after executions.

Bailey, W. C., and R. D. Peterson. "Capital Punishment and Non-Capital Crimes: A Test of Deterrence, General Prevention, and System-Overload

Arguments" in *Albany Law Review*, vol. 54, 1990, pp. 681–707. Tests the theory that capital punishment may deter noncapital crimes by "educating" criminals about the general consequences of crime, by deterring felonies that might result in felony murder (and the death penalty), and by allowing reallocation of law enforcement resources due to reduced homicides. The authors' results find a "significant inverse relationship" between executions (and their publicity) and crime rates, lending support to this theory.

Bedau, Hugo Adam. "Bentham's Utilitarian Critique of the Death Penalty" in *Journal of Criminal Law and Criminology*, vol. 74, 1983, pp. 1,033–1,066. Examines the work of political and economic philosopher Jeremy Bentham and his opposition to the death penalty.

———. "Justice in Punishment and Assumption of Risks: Some Comments in Response to van den Haag" in *Wayne Law Review*, vol. 33, 1987, pp. 1,423–1,433. Criticizes an essay by death penalty advocate Ernest van den Haag on deterrence and retribution as justifications of punishment. A response by van den Haag follows the article.

Bosarge, B. B. "Police Chiefs', Sheriffs' Associations Reaffirm Support for Death Penalty" in *Crime Control Digest*, vol. 29, March 3, 1995, pp. 1–4. The president of the International Association of Chiefs of Police takes issue with a survey published by the Death Penalty Information Center that says the majority of police chiefs and sheriffs do not think the death penalty is a useful or cost-effective tool for controlling crime. He notes that both his organization and the National Sheriffs' Association have repeatedly adopted resolutions supporting the death penalty.

Brownlee, Shannon, Dan McGraw, and Jason Vest. "The Place for Vengeance: Many Grieving Families Seek Comfort in the Execution of a Murderer. Do They Find It?" in *U.S. News & World Report*, vol. 122, June 16, 1997, pp. 24ff. With public support for capital punishment holding steady, an examination of opinion suggests that the desire for vengeance and closure on the part of victims' families is more important to death penalty supporters than the need for deterrence and social protection. The disregard of the legal system for victims and survivors fuels this impulse. The execution, however, does not always bring the peace they sought.

Bull, Chris. "A Matter of Life and Death" in *The Advocate*, March 16, 1999, p. 38. Reports that gay and lesbian organizations and advocates were struggling over the question of seeking the death penalty for the killer of Matthew Shepherd, a gay man who was brutally murdered. Some activists believe a death sentence would send a strong message that such hate crimes will not be tolerated by society, but others are unwilling to make an exception to their opposition to capital punishment on human rights grounds.

Callahan, Sidney. "The Thirst for Revenge: Trying to Understand Capital Punishment" in *Commonweal*, vol. 122, June 16, 1995, pp. 8ff. The columnist suggests that when the pragmatic arguments on both sides in the death penalty debate are stripped away, the core issue is whether society needs a symbolic, ritual blood sacrifice to express its rejection of murder. This impulse should be rejected; life imprisonment offers sufficient moral sanction and social protection.

Davies, Christie. "Safely Executed" in *National Review*, vol. 43, August 12, 1991, pp. 44ff. Argues that the death penalty for persons who commit murder after a string of other violent offenses would provide both deterrence and a sense of fit retribution. Since the person is a career criminal, the chance of executing a truly innocent person would be minimized.

Finckenauer, J. O. "Public Support for the Death Penalty: Retribution as Just Desserts or Retribution as Revenge?" in *Justice Quarterly* 5, 1988, pp. 81–100. Reviews literature suggesting that public support for capital punishment is motivated largely by a desire for revenge.

Gelertner, David. "What Do Murderers Deserve?" in *Commentary*, vol. 105, April 1998, pp. 21ff. Gelertner, who was wounded by the Unabomber, Theodore Kaczynski, sees confusion about capital punishment as part of our society's larger loss of moral moorings. He argues that the ultimate purpose of capital punishment is neither deterrence nor vengeance, but the affirmation of society's moral rejection of murder. Gelertner includes discussion of the cases of Kaczynski and Karla Faye Tucker and the moral conclusions that might be drawn from them.

Goldberg, Steven. "So What If the Death Penalty Deters?" in *National Review*, vol. 41, June 30, 1989, pp. 42ff. Argues that while conclusively showing the deterrent effect of capital punishment is very difficult, common sense suggests that the death penalty follows our general experience that greater punishments do have greater deterrent effect. From a utilitarian viewpoint, imposing capital punishment will save more innocent lives than will be lost through mistaken convictions.

Kleinman, M. A. R. "Dead Wrong: Capital Punishment for Murders by Drug Dealers" in *The New Republic*, vol. 199, September 26, 1988, pp. 14ff. Argues that executing drug traffickers would have virtually no effect on the drug trade.

Lempert, Richard O. "Desert and Deterrence: An Assessment of the Moral Bases of the Case for Capital Punishment" in *Michigan Law Review*, vol. 79, 1981, pp. 1,177–1,231. Assesses the validity of arguments for capital punishment on the basis of desert (retribution) and deterrence.

———. "The Effect of Executions on Homicides: A New Look in an Old Light" in *Crime and Delinquency*, vol. 29, 1983, pp. 88–115. A state-by-state comparison of execution and homicide rates finds no evidence of - deterrence.

Lowenstein, L. F. "Licence to Kill: Is There a Case for the Death Penalty?" in *Contemporary Review*, vol. 252, January 1988, pp. 32–36. A study that concludes that capital punishment may be the only means of providing the victim's relatives with a sense of retribution.

Paredes, J. A. "Some Anthropological Observations on Capital Punishment in the U.S.A." in *International Journal of Comparative and Applied Criminal Justice*, vol. 17, Spring/Fall 1993, pp. 219–227. Suggests that the persistence of capital punishment in the United States reflects Americans' need to reassure themselves that they can cope with the nation's murder rate, which is much higher than that of other industrialized countries. The authors argues that belief in the deterrent value of executions represents magical thinking.

Spence, K. "Crime and Punishment" in *National Review*, vol. 35, September 16, 1983, pp. 18ff. Argues that society must accept the duty of exacting retribution until or unless research conclusively proves that capital punishment is not a deterrent.

Stack, S. "Impact of Publicized Executions on Homicide" in *Criminal Justice and Behavior*, vol. 22, June 1995, pp. 172–186. Study that tested the hypothesis that blacks would be less receptive to the deterrent effect of publicized executions because they experienced themselves as "outsiders" to society and had little stake in conformity. The study results seemed to confirm this hypothesis, finding that publicized executions had significant deterrent effect on whites but not on blacks.

van den Haag, Ernest. "Can Any Legal Punishment of the Guilty Be Unjust to Them?" in *Wayne Law Review*, vol. 33, 1987, pp. 1,413–1,421. Argues that punishments should be set according to the differing needs of society for deterrence and retribution for a given crime, without reference to any claim of injustice on the part of the offender, who committed the act knowingly.

———. "Death and Deterrence" in *National Review*, vol. 38, March 14, 1986, pp. 44ff. Offers new evidence to support the author's claim that the death penalty acts as a deterrent to murder.

Van Wormer, Katherine. "Those Who Seek Executions: Capital Punishment as a Form of Suicide" in *USA Today*, vol. 123, March 1995, pp. 92ff. In an interesting and little-known argument against capital punishment, the author suggests that some criminals with suicidal feelings, such as Gary Gilmore, may commit murders in order to be given the death penalty. Capital punishment may thus put the public at greater risk.

"Wild Justice: The Death Penalty" in *The Economist* (U.S.), vol. 334, March 11, 1995, pp. A27ff. Describes the New York law signed by Governor George Pataki that restored capital punishment for a variety of murders. While the law incorporates numerous procedural safeguards, there are doubts about its effectiveness in fighting crime.

Wilkes, John. "Murder in Mind" in *Psychology Today*, vol. 21, June 1987, pp. 27–32. Profiles homicide expert Dale Archer. Archer argues that when a society inflicts violence on humans, via war or capital punishment, it incites people to increased violence.

Zobel, Hiller B. "The Undying Problem of the Death Penalty" in *American Heritage*, vol. 48, December 1997, pp. 64ff. Uses the 1901 case of Luigi Storti, the first person to die in the Massachusetts electric chair, to illustrate the ethical and legal problems involved in balancing the rights of the convicted and the desire for retribution—problems that persist to this day.

WEB DOCUMENTS

Dieter, Richard C. "Millions Misspent: What Politicians Don't Say About the High Costs of the Death Penalty." (Issued by the Death Penalty Information Center.) Available online. URL: http://www.essential.org/dpic/dpic.r08.html. Posted October 1992 and revised Fall 1994. Argues that the very high cost of capital punishment is actually making people less safe by diverting money from effective law enforcement activities. Because of its utility for political rhetoric, the death penalty is often not subjected to cost-benefit analyses.

———. "On the Front Line: Law Enforcement Views on the Death Penalty." Available online. URL: http://www.essential.org/dpic/dpic.r03.html. (Issued by the Death Penalty Information Center.) Posted February 1995. Describes a poll of police chiefs conducted in 1995. The chiefs ranked the death penalty as the least cost effective method for controlling crime and said that several other measures (including strengthening neighborhoods, fighting drugs, and gun control) were more important than the death penalty.

RACE AND THE DEATH PENALTY

This section consists of writings and studies that attempt to show or disprove racial bias in the administration of capital punishment or that explore the implications of such bias on the legal system or society as a whole.

Annotated Bibliography

BOOKS

Baldus, David C., Charles A. Pulaski, and George Woodworth. *Equal Justice and the Death Penalty: A Logical and Empirical Analysis*. Boston: North-eastern University Press, 1990. Using an analysis of cases from 1972 to 1987, the author tests the proposition that the strengthened legal safe-guards called for by the Supreme Court in 1972 and reaffirmed in 1976 can remove the arbitrariness and potential for discrimination from the death penalty process. Appendices contain further statistical information.

Carter, Dan T. *Scottsboro: A Tragedy of the American South*. Baton Rouge: Louisiana State University Press, 1969. An account of an Alabama case in which nine black men were wrongfully convicted of raping two white women.

Dance, Daryl Cumber. *Long Gone: The Mecklenburg Six and the Theme of Escape in Black Folklore*. Knoxville: University of Tennessee Press, 1987. In the context of themes in black folklore, describes the escape and recapture of six condemned men in Virginia in 1984 and the subsequent execution of two of them.

Gross, Samuel R., and Robert Mauro. *Death and Discrimination: Racial Disparities in Capital Sentencing*. Boston: Northeastern University Press, 1989. Traces the history of racial differences in sentencing for capital crimes.

Henson, Burt M., and Ross R. Olney. *Furman v. Georgia: The Death Penalty and the Constitution*. New York: Franklin Watts, 1996. An account for young readers of the historic Supreme Court decision that led to the de-claration that capital punishment as practiced in the 1960s was unconsti-tutionally biased against blacks. The issues and appeals over the years since then are explained.

Jackson, Jesse. *Legal Lynching: Racism, Injustice & the Death Penalty*. New York: Marlowe, 1996. A general brief for the abolition of capital punish-ment. Jackson describes the history of capital punishment, rebuts argu-ments by death penalty supporters, and highlights the problem of execution of the innocent and the inevitable expression of racism in the imposition of capital punishment. He concludes with a plea based on the dignity of life as expressed in the biblical tradition.

Kytle, Calvin, and David Z. H. Pollitt. *Unjust in the Much: The Death Penalty in North Carolina: A Symposium to Advance the Case for a Moratorium as Proposed by the American Bar Association*. Chapel Hill, N.C.: Chestnut Tree Press, 1999. Edited transcript of a symposium sponsored by North Carolinians Against the Death Penalty. Topics covered include race and class as factors in convictions, the demographics of capital punishment, and constitutional issues. In his contributions, author Pollitt draws on his

experience teaching constitutional law and serving as a volunteer defense
attorney representing poor and disabled clients in capital cases.

Marquart, James W., et al. *The Rope, the Chair, and the Needle: Capital Punishment in Texas, 1923–1990.* Austin: University of Texas Press, 1998. An analysis of data from original records that suggests that attitudes from the time of slavery and lynching drove the institutionalization of capital punishment and created a system with race, class, and gender bias.

McFeely, William S. *Proximity to Death.* New York: W. W. Norton, 1999. The author, a Civil War historian, tells the story of a group of blacks who were sentenced to death for killing a white man. Although they were probably guilty, a group of lawyers headed by Stephen Bright of the Southern Center for Human Rights argued that they should not have received a capital sentence because of the inflammatory racism that they had been exposed to, and because the death penalty was itself unfair and racist in its application.

Rise, Eric W. *The Martinsville Seven: Race, Rape and Capital Punishment.* Charlottesville: University Press of Virginia, 1998. Explores a case in Martinsville, Virginia, where seven black men were convicted of rape and executed in 1951. The author, a professor of criminology and social justice, describes how community concern about crime impinged on due process, with the ever-present factor of race creating a disturbing equation. Rise also describes the battle of the NAACP and other groups against discriminatory application of capital punishment to blacks.

Russell, Gregory D. *The Death Penalty and Racial Bias: Overturning Supreme Court Assumptions.* Westport, Conn.: Greenwood Press, 1994. Uses statistical evidence to argue that the Supreme Court is wrong in its assumption that the process of selecting a "death qualified" jury does not bias the jury against the defendant. Russell's study results suggest that death qualification leads to a concentration of biased racial attitudes in particular.

Smead, Howard. *Blood Justice: The Lynching of Mack Charles Parker.* New York: Oxford University Press, 1986. Recounts a 1959 lynching in Mississippi.

Walker, S., C. Spohn, and M. DeLone. *Color of Justice: Race, Ethnicity, and Crime in America.* Belmont, Calif.: Wadsworth Publishing Co., 1996. Discusses the experience of African Americans, Hispanic Americans, and Asian Americans, and Native Americans in the criminal justice system. The book covers a variety of topics in detail, including politics and the use of ethnic categories, geographical factors, myths about criminals and victims, and how race influences law enforcement, the courts, and the corrections system.

Weinglass, Leonard. *Race for Justice: Mumia Abu-Jamal's Fight Against the Death Penalty.* Monroe, Me.: Common Courage Press, 1995. The author, chief counsel for Abu-Jamal's defense, describes an alternative theory of the crime and recounts discrepancies in the prosecution's case. He argues that the trial was essentially political, and that Abu-Jamal is a victim of a deeply flawed justice system. The book includes court documents and contacts for advocacy.

ARTICLES AND PAPERS

Arkin, Steven D. "Discrimination and Arbitrariness in Capital Punishment: An Analysis of Post-*Furman* Murder Cases in Dade County, Florida, 1973–1976" in *Stanford Law Review*, vol. 33, 1980, pp. 75–101. A study of 350 homicide cases in Miami during the time capital punishment had been effectively halted by the Supreme Court. No conclusive evidence of racial discrimination is found.

Chapman, Frank. "The Death Penalty, U.S.A.: Racist and Class Violence" in *Political Affairs*, vol. 66, July 1987, pp. 17–19. Discusses class and racial bias in death penalty sentencing from a Marxist viewpoint.

Diamond, S. A., and J. D. Casper. "Empirical Evidence and the Death Penalty: Past and Future" in *Journal of Social Issues*, vol. 50, Summer 1994, pp. 177–197. Describes the utilization of social science data by the Supreme Court. The Court has largely ignored or discounted such evidence. The author suggests other areas of research (such as jury decision making) that might command the attention of courts.

Dugger, Ronnie. "The Numbers on Death Row Prove that Blacks Who Kill Whites Receive the Harshest Judgment" in *Life*, vol. 11, Spring 1988, pp. 88–92. A look at racial bias in death sentencing based on the racial identities of offender and victim.

Gest, Ted. "Crime's Bias Problem" in *U.S. News & World Report*, vol. 117, June 25, 1994, pp. 31ff. Gives background to the congressional debate over the Racial Justice Act, a proposed amendment to the 1994 omnibus crime bill that would allow defendants to cite statistics in court arguments in an attempt to prove racial bias in death sentencing. Gest discusses the political calculations on the part of congressional Democrats, Republicans, and the Clinton administration. He also discusses the difficulties in proving bias and the author's belief that racial differences in justice outcomes are caused not so much by direct bias as by the lack of quality legal representation for poor defendants and the effects of the excessive war on drugs.

Grant, Meg. "Bryan Stevenson: Alabama Lawyer Fights to Overturn Death Penalty" in *People Weekly*, vol. 44, November 27, 1995, pp. 71ff. Describes the work of lawyer and activist Bryan Stevenson, who has represented many death row inmates in Alabama and has dedicated himself to abolishing the death penalty in that state. Stevenson is the founder of the Equal Justice Initiative.

"He Shot the Sheriff" in *The New Republic*, vol. 213, September 4, 1995, p. 9. Editorial arguing that trial irregularities and discrepancies in testimony are not sufficient to cast reasonable doubt that Mumia Abu-Jamal was guilty of murdering a police officer. Writers who defend Abu-Jamal as a fellow journalist are misguided.

Hitchens, Christopher. "Death and the Maidens" in *The Nation*, vol. 264, April 14, 1997, p. 8. Summarizes the debate over the guilt of Mumia Abu-Jamal, whose growing legion of supporters demand a new trial for the African-American journalist who was convicted of the murder of a police officer in 1981 and has been on death row since 1982. Hitchens suggests that discrepancies in the physical evidence, doubt about his alleged confession, two witnesses against him who have now recanted, and a hasty, shoddy trial all lend credence to the demands of Abu-Jamal's supporters.

McFeely, William S. "A Legacy of Slavery and Lynching: The Death Penalty as Tool of Social Control" in National Association of Criminal Defense Lawyers. *The Champion.* November 1997, np. Available online. URL: http://www.nacdl.org/CHAMPION/ARTICLES/97nov03.htm. Posted in November 1997. Describes the use of the death penalty against African Americans during the slavery period and later during Reconstruction and the era of lynchings. McFeely suggests that many of the motives for using the death penalty for social control persist in the legal process even today.

"More Blacks Favor Death Penalty, Studies Say" *Jet*, vol. 93, May 11, 1998, p. 5. Reports that support for the death penalty among African Americans has risen from only 40 percent in 1974 to 57 percent in 1996. Fear and outrage and high crime in many black communities may be outweighing concern about discriminatory imposition of the death sentence.

Rabe, G. A. "Supreme Court and Evidence of Discrimination: A Comparison of Death Penalty and Employment Discrimination Cases" in *Criminal Justice Policy Review*, vol. 9, 1998, pp. 209–231. Concludes that the Supreme Court has been willing to rely considerably on social science findings about discrimination when reviewing employment cases, but has been very reluctant to accept similar findings in death penalty cases. The most likely reason is the Court's fear of the consequences of overturning the capital punishment system.

"Rep. Jackson, Ex-Sen. Simon Back Moratorium on Death Penalty" in *Jet*, vol. 91, May 12, 1997, pp. 37ff. Reports that Representative Jesse Jackson, Jr., and former Senator Paul Simon have joined the Death Penalty Moratorium Campaign, which seeks to halt and investigate the practice of capital punishment, based on evidence of racial bias.

Annotated Bibliography

Roman, Nancy E. "Researchers Debunk Idea of Racial Bias: Some Researchers Now Say that Racial Bias in Death Sentences Doesn't Exist—Contrary to the Conventional Wisdom Behind the Proposed Racial Justice Act" in *Insight on the News*, vol. 10, June 13, 1994, p. 17. Reports on a study of California murderers by Stephen Klein of the Rand Corporation. Once he controlled for the circumstances of the offense, any apparent disparity based on race of offender or victim disappeared.

Seligman, Daniel. "Uh Oh! More Stats" in *Fortune*, vol. 130, September 5, 1994, pp. 114ff. Argues that studies of possible racial bias in death sentencing are at best inconclusive. Controlling for the specific circumstances of the crime eliminates much of the apparent discrepancy between white and black capital conviction rates.

Wayne, Jim. "Racial Bias in Capital Sentencing" in *America*, vol. 180, January 2, 1999, p. 11. Reports on Kentucky's passage of a Racial Justice Act that allows judges to consider statistical evidence of racial bias in capital prosecution and allows defense attorneys to try to prove that bias motivated the seeking of the death penalty.

WEB DOCUMENTS

Amnesty International. "United States of America: Rights for All—Killing with Prejudice: Race and the Death Penalty." Available online. URL: http://www.amnesty.org/ailib/aipub/1999/AMR/25105299.htm. Posted May 20, 1999. A detailed report on racial bias in the administration of the death penalty in the United States, with statistics and footnotes.

Death Penalty Information Center. "The Death Penalty in Black & White: Who Lives, Who Dies, Who Decides." Available online. URL: http://www.essential.org/dpic/racerpt.html. Posted June 1998. Reports two studies that show pervasive racial bias continues in the administration of the death penalty. The fact that the overwhelming majority of district attorneys responsible for bringing capital charges are white is identified as a key contributing factor.

AUDIOVISUAL MATERIALS

American Civil Liberties Union. *Double Justice*. VHS Video. [n.d.] Available from ACLU online store at http://www.aclu.org. Described as "a documentary about race and the death penalty with accompanying written materials and promotional poster."

Mumia Abu-Jamal: A Case for Reasonable Doubt? New York: Fox Lorber, 1996. Video documentary that details new evidence that it suggests makes a strong case for the innocence of Abu-Jamal.

SPECIAL CASES: GENDER, YOUTH, AND DISABILITY

This section presents writings that discuss the application of capital punishment to particular classes of persons, such as women, youth, and the physically or mentally disabled.

BOOKS

Barfield, Velma. *Woman on Death Row*. Nashville: Oliver-Nelson, 1985. The author's account of her conviction for quadruple murder and her subsequent religious conviction before her execution in 1984.

Death Row U.S.A. Reporter: 1975–1988 and 1989–1997 Supplements. NAACP Legal Defense Educational Fund. Buffalo, N.Y.: William S. Hein, 1990. Describes cases and legal actions undertaken on behalf of minority inmates on death row.

Dicks, Shirley, ed. *Young Blood: Juvenile Justice and the Death Penalty*. Amherst, N.Y.: Prometheus Books, 1995. Presents a variety of essays that discuss the question of whether juveniles should face capital charges. Many of the writings describe particular cases and the experiences of young people facing the death penalty. A number of groups seeking to reform the juvenile justice system are profiled.

Gillespie, L. Kay. *Dancehall Ladies: The Crimes and Executions of America's Condemned Women*. Lanham, Md.: University Press of America, 1997. Interesting (albeit rather lurid) accounts of American women who were condemned to die. Gillespie describes their crimes, personalities, and attitudes. Generally the book is arranged one chapter per case, each chapter titled using the words of the condemned.

Hale, Robert L. *A Review of Juvenile Executions in America*. Lewiston, N.Y.: Edwin Mellen, 1997. A study that examines the execution of juveniles in America starting in 1642. Hale identifies five periods characterized by the religious, legal, and political influences that determined which juveniles would be subject to the ultimate penalty. The book includes tables, notes, references, and case citations.

Huie, William Bradford. *Ruby McCollum: Woman in the Suwanee Jail*. New York: Signet Books, 1957. An account of the case of Ruby McCollum, who received the death sentence in 1952 in Florida but was transferred to an asylum instead of being executed.

Jones, Ann. *Women Who Kill*. New York: Holt, Rinehart and Winston, 1980. Studies women and homicide from several viewpoints, focusing on notable cases of female murderers.

Miller, Kent S., and Michael L. Radelet. *Executing the Mentally Ill: The Criminal Justice System and the Case of Alvin Ford.* Newbury Park, Calif.: Sage Publications, 1993. Discusses the question of whether a person who should be executed even after becoming so mentally ill that he or she cannot comprehend the process. The centerpiece is the case of Alvin Ford, convicted of murder and then becoming psychotic while imprisoned on death row. Miller's psychological expertise is combined with Radelet's work on death penalty issues.

Naish, Camille. *Death Comes to the Maiden: Sex and Execution, 1431–1933.* New York: Routledge, 1991. The history of execution of women as illustrated by specific cases such as Joan of Arc and Anne Boleyn, with a focus on the Middle Ages, the Renaissance, and the French Revolution. Naish also discusses the work of writers such as Jean Genet, Marguerite Yourcenar, and Bertolt Brecht in exploring the links between death and the erotic in the execution of prominent females.

O'Shea, Kathleen A. *Women and the Death Penalty in the United States, 1900–1998.* Westport, Conn.: Praeger, 1999. Presents the history of execution of women in America as well as the personal stories of women who have been executed or are awaiting execution on death row. O'Shea includes state by state summaries of the legal process and status of female death row inmates and statistical appendices.

Pucci, Idanna. *The Trials of Maria Barbella: The True Story of a 19th Century Crime of Passion.* Translated by Stefania Fumo. New York: Vintage Books, 1997. The account of the first woman to be sentenced to die in the newly invented electric chair in America. She was convicted of killing the man who seduced her and then refused to marry her. This 1895 case became a cause célèbre that raised issues of capital punishment and women's rights, and her appeal was ultimately successful.

Reed, E. F. *The Penry Penalty: Capital Punishment and Offenders with Mental Retardation.* Lanham, Md.: University Press of America, 1993. Begins with the implications of the Supreme Court's *Penry* decision allowing execution of the mentally retarded. Reed offers arguments against the practice, drawing on case studies of both executed and pardoned retarded offenders.

ARTICLES AND PAPERS

Anders, James. "Should Juvenile Murderers Be Sentenced to Death? Punish the Guilty" in *American Bar Association Journal*, vol. 72, June 1, 1986, pp. 32–33. A debate with Richard Brody. Anders believes that death sentences should not have a minimum age limitation.

Curtis, Gregory. "Seven Women" in *Texas Monthly*, vol. 25, October 1997, pp. 7ff. Describes the cases of three of the seven women on Texas' death row. Their appeals are running out, and the chance of a woman being executed for the first time in the state since 1863 is increasing.

Farley, Christopher John, and James Willwerth. "Dead Teen Walking" in *Time*, vol. 151, January 19, 1998, pp. 50ff. An in-depth look at the case of condemned juvenile murderer Shareef Cousin. Cousin, convicted at the age of 16, denies his guilt. The authors, describe the situation of other juveniles on death row and debate the issue of whether juveniles should be executed. They also report possible exonerating evidence and problems with the trial procedure.

George, Whitney. "Women on Death Row" in *off our backs*, vol. 28, January 1998, pp. 16ff. Argues that the 47 women on death row are often ignored in debates over the death penalty because the vast majority of condemned prisoners are men. Women on death row are often denied privileges routinely given to men in the same situation.

Hitchens, Christopher. "Old Enough to Die" in *Vanity Fair*, June 1999, pp. 76ff. Describes and argues against the practice of executing juveniles, a practice the United States shares only with a handful of countries such as Iran, Yemen, Pakistan, Saudi Arabia, and Nigeria.

Reed, Julia. "Capital Crime" in *Vogue*, vol. 188, March 1998, pp. 338ff. Discusses issues raised by the case of Karla Faye Tucker (who was later executed). Issues include the role of gender in capital sentencing and the factor of possible brain damage.

Ross, Michael B. "Don't Execute Mentally Disturbed Killers" in *The Humanist*, vol. 59, January 1999, p. 43. Argues that if as absolute a punishment as the death penalty is to be given, it must never be given to persons who lack the mental capability to understand their actions or the consequences. Ross describes the difficulty of convincing judges and juries that someone is truly mentally ill and suggests that new verdict types of "guilty but mentally ill" or "guilty but mentally retarded" together with life sentences without possibility of parole might satisfy the need for public protection and closure while preventing execution of the mentally incompetent.

Streib, V. L. "Death Penalty for Female Offenders" in *Cincinnati Law Review*, vol. 58, 1990, pp. 845–880. Presents demographic and offense-related statistics for females who have received the death penalty. Streib discusses the sources of gender bias in death sentencing.

———. "Juvenile Death Penalty Today: Present Death Row Inmates Under Juvenile Death Sentences and Death Sentences and Executions for Juvenile Crimes, January 1, 1973, to June 30, 1997." Ohio Northern University Law School, 1997. [Research paper available through Rockville,

Md.: National Institute of Justice/NCJRS Paper Reproduction Sales.] Presents statistics on juveniles on death row and those who have been executed, including offender and crime characteristics. Streib discusses the constitutionality of the juvenile death penalty in light of the findings.

WEB DOCUMENTS

Amnesty International. "United States of America: Shame in the 21st Century: Three Child Offenders Scheduled for Execution in January 2000." Available online. URL: http://www.amnesty.org/ailib/aipub/1999/AMR/25118999.htm. Posted in December 1999. Reports on the possible execution of three juvenile offenders in the context of the failure of the United States to live up to international agreements that would ban such executions. For example, under the Geneva Convention the United States agreed not to perform such executions, even during wartime.

Baroff, George S. "Why Mental Retardation is 'Mitigating'" in *The Champion*, August 1998. On the National Association of Criminal Lawyers web page. Available online. URL: http://www.nacdl.org/CHAMPION/ARTICLES/98aug02.htm. Posted in August 1998. Explains mental retardation and differentiates it from mental illness. Baroff describes signs that attorneys should look for. He also discusses issues of competency and diminished capacity and their impact on sentencing decisions.

Bauschard, Stephen. "Death Penalty: Annotated Bibliography." Available online. URL: http://www.umich.edu/~debate/mndi/supp/death.html. Downloaded March 6, 2000. Despite its generic title, this lightly annotated bibliography, prepared for a debate team, focuses on works dealing with the controversy over application of the death penalty to juveniles.

Stetler, Russell. "Mental Disabilities and Mitigation" in *The Champion*, April 1999. On the National Association of Criminal Defense Lawyers web page. Available online. URL: http://209.70.38.3/public.nsf/championarticles/99apr10. Posted in April 1999. Introduces issues involving mentally disabled clients. Mental disabilities can be a powerful factor in avoiding conviction or mitigating sentences, but they can also make it difficult for counsel to work with clients or cause jurors to fear them and respond with harsher sentences. Stetler discusses the selection of mental health experts and the many roles they can play in investigation, in helping the client behave appropriately, and in testifying at trial. He also discusses appropriate use of physical and psychological tests and examinations.

———. "Mitigation Evidence in Capital Cases" in *The Champion*, April 1999. On the National Association of Criminal Defense Lawyers, web page. Available online. URL: http://www.nacdl.org/public.nsf/

championarticles/99jan04. Posted in April 1999. Introduces the types and purposes of mitigating evidence, starting with an overview of court decisions. Stetler discusses the many mitigating circumstances (including family background and mental illnesses and impairments) that can apply to clients facing capital punishment. He gives suggestions for approaching and interviewing witnesses who offer potential mitigating evidence.

Whatever Design. Women Speak Out from Prison and Death Row web site. Available online. URL: http://www.whateverdesign.com/speakout/html/death_row.htm. Downloaded on January 10, 2000. Site dealing with the situation of women prisoners, particularly those on death row. The site provides news updates and stories about particular women.

AUDIOVISUAL MATERIALS

Flynn, T., and E. Shapiro. *Juveniles and the Death Penalty*. CBS Films for the Humanities. VHS [n.d.] video. Video of a CBS *48 Hours* program that presents interviews with a variety of opinions on the issue of execution of juveniles. Interviewees include victims' families and friends and prosecutors, both of when are strongly in favor of the death penalty. Offenders and their attorneys oppose execution on grounds of abusive background, mental disorders, and youth.

EXECUTION OF THE INNOCENT

Works in this section discuss the question of whether (or to what extent) innocent persons are being sentenced to death or executed, and the implications for the morality or workability of capital punishment.

BOOKS

Black, Charles L., Jr. *Capital Punishment: The Inevitability of Caprice and Mistake*. 2nd ed. New York: W. W. Norton, 1981. Strong advocacy for abolition of capital punishment on the grounds that discrimination and errors in the administration of the death penalty are inevitable.

Kennedy, Ludovic. *The Airman and the Carpenter: The Lindbergh Kidnapping and the Framing of Richard Hauptmann*. New York: Viking, 1985. The 1932 Lindbergh kidnapping case; presents the theory that Hauptmann's execution in 1936 was a mistake.

Parloff, Roger. *Triple Jeopardy: A Story of Law and Its Best—and Worst*. Boston: Little, Brown, 1996. The story of John Henry Knapp, accused of killing his two young daughters. The author covered the case as a reporter and found it to be riddled with prosecutorial misconduct, bogus testimony, and disappearing evidence. Eventually a team of lawyers used forensic evidence to prove that Knapp could not have started the fire that killed his children.

Radelet, Michael L., Hugo Adam Bedau, and Constance E. Putnam. *In Spite of Innocence: Erroneous Convictions in Capital Cases.* Boston: Northeastern University Press, 1992. Compiles the stories of more than 400 innocent Americans who were convicted of capital crimes—some of whom were executed. The authors suggest that the safeguards intended to prevent wrongful convictions are weak and unreliable, leaving the innocent to fight against forbidding odds in the hope they can eventually prove their innocence. The conclusion is that since there is no realistic way to prevent a significant number of miscarriages of justice, the death penalty should be abolished.

Strauss, Frances. *Where Did the Justice Go? The Story of the Giles-Johnson Case.* Boston: Gambit, Inc., 1970. Recounts the wrongful capital sentencing of three men in a Maryland case in 1961.

Tucker, John C. *May God Have Mercy: A True Story of Crime and Punishment.* New York: Norton, 1997. Tells the story of Roger Coleman, convicted and executed for the brutal murder of his sister-in-law Wanda Fay McCoy. The author describes how the police quickly concluded that Coleman was guilty and how, despite the emergence of contrary evidence, the legal process moved swiftly and inexorably toward execution. The complex maze of legal maneuvering is explained for the lay reader, revealing the complex yet arbitrary nature of the legal process.

ARTICLES AND PAPERS

Allen, Jenny, and Lori Grinker. "Stolen Lives" in *Life*, vol. 17, October 1994, pp. 64ff. Profiles seven of the 53 people who have been released from death row since 1976 after it was concluded that they were wrongfully convicted. Such incidents point out serious flaws in the administration of justice and strengthen the case against capital punishment.

Alter, Jonathan. "How Sure Is Sure Enough?" in *Newsweek*, vol. 133, March 22, 1999, p. 37. Reports misgivings about the case of Roy Roberts, who was executed in Missouri for murder despite having passed a lie detector test. Some observers suggest Missouri governor Mel Carnahan may have taken a hard line on the Roberts case to counter criticism from death penalty supporters after he gave clemency to Albert Mease after pressure from the visiting Pope John Paul II.

Belluck, Pam. "Class of Sleuths to Rescue on Death Row" in *New York Times*, February 5, 1999, p. A16. Reports the activities of a Northwestern

University journalism class that was given the assignment to reinvestigate cases where persons on death row may be innocent. A surprise stay of execution gives the class enough time to discover a new witness—who said that Illinois death row inmate Anthony Porter did not fire the fatal shots—and a possible alternative suspect as well.

Carroll, Ginny, and Aric Press. "Only Two Weeks to Live: As an Execution Nears, Troubling Questions Are Raised about a Murder Case" in *Newsweek*, vol. 114, August 21, 1989, pp. 62ff. Discusses the controversial Louisiana case of Ronald Monroe, who some observers feel may be innocent.

"Change of Heart: The Death Penalty" in *The Economist*, vol. 335, June 24, 1995, pp. 28ff. Describes how the fate of Joseph Spaziano, sentenced to die for murder, was changed by investigations by *Miami Herald* reporters that led eventually to the key prosecution witness admitting that he had made up his damning testimony.

Davis, Michael. "Is the Death Penalty Irrevocable?" in *Social Theory and Practice*, vol. 10, 1984, pp. 143–156. Argues that the risk of a mistaken execution is not a strong abolitionist argument, since prison time mistakenly imposed can also not be given back.

Fein, Bruce. "Death Penalty Isn't Claiming Innocent Men" in *Insight on the News*, vol. 9, March 1, 1993, pp. 23ff. Discusses how the Supreme Court's decision not to grant death row inmate Leonel T. Herrera a new hearing demonstrates that the courts can prevent execution of the innocent while also preventing inmates using last-minute frivolous claims to endlessly delay their execution.

Fulwood, Sam, III. "Death Penalty Foes Demand New DNA Test for Executed Man" in *Los Angeles Times*, August 31, 1999, p. A5. Despite the fact Joseph O'Dell III had been executed in 1997 for a rape-murder, a team of activists is seeking to perform a DNA test that may exonerate him. He was tested in 1986, but today's tests are more sophisticated and precise.

Gwynne, S. C. "Guilty, Innocent, Guilty: Despite Having Argued that the Prisoner Didn't Commit the Crime, Texas Carries Out His Execution" in *Time*, vol. 145, January 16, 1995, p. 38. Describes the case of Jesse DeWayne Jacobs, who was convicted of being the sole killer of Etta Ann Urdailes. Later, however, his sister is tried for the same murder, and the prosecution introduces evidence that she, not he, had pulled the trigger. Despite this new conviction, Mr. Jacobs' final appeal is dismissed by the Supreme Court. The case raises the issue of whether someone should receive the death penalty for a murder in which he or she was not the "trigger person."

"Innocent on Death Row" (Editorial) in *America*, vol. 174, January 13, 1996, p. 3. Editorial objects to the political backlash against death row prisoners, resulting in Congress cutting off funding to Death Penalty

184

Resource Centers, depriving defendants of adequate representation and increasing the likelihood of execution of some innocent people.

"Innocents on Death Row" (Editorial) in *New York Times*, May 23, 1999, p. 16. Suggests that just as the magnitude of the problem of potential innocent persons on death row is starting to become apparent, New York governor George Pataki is seeking to expand use of the death penalty.

"It's Still Not Easy: Reprieved from Execution" in *The Economist* (U.S.), vol. 344, September 27, 1997, pp. 30ff. Describes the cases of Dennis Williams and other inmates who have been released from death row after their innocence had been established. The number of such cases suggests that the justice system may be rushing toward final judgment too quickly.

Markman, Stephen. "Innocents on Death Row? Blackmun Is Convinced that Innocent People are Likely to be Executed. Where Is the Evidence?" in *National Review*, vol. 46, September 12, 1994, pp. 72ff. Argues that the Stanford University study, which concluded that in 350 cases innocent people received death sentences, is flawed. Only 23 of the people in the study were actually executed and some of these were clearly guilty. What the study actually reveals is the rarity of execution of the innocent.

McCarthy, Colman. "Things Some People Do If They're Not Executed" in *National Catholic Reporter*, vol. 29, February 12, 1993, p. 12. Describes how Joseph Giarratano, after his death sentence was commuted by Virginia governor Douglas Wilder, joined 40 other inmates in completing a college course on nonviolence.

Shapiro, Joseph P. "The Wrong Men on Death Row" in *U.S. News & World Report*, November 9, 1998, p. 22. Reports that one death row prisoner for every seven executed has been found innocent. Shapiro describes many causes of wrongful convictions, including hasty investigations, false confessions, and inadequate representation for defendants. Social "outsiders" tend to get railroaded to conviction.

WEB DOCUMENTS

"The Case for Innocence." PBS *Frontline* episode, broadcast January 11, 2000. Web site with supplementary materials including background and interviews. Discusses cases where DNA tests exonerate persons who had been convicted of serious crimes such as murder and rape, but the legal system often refuses to consider such new evidence. Available online. URL: http://www.pbs.org/wgbh/pages/frontline/shows/case/.

Dieter, Richard C. "Innocence and the Death Penalty: The Increasing Danger of Executing the Innocent." On the Death Penalty Information Center web site. Available online. URL: http://www.essential.org/dpic/inn. html. Posted in June 1997. Since 1973, a total of 63 people have been released from death row after evidence of their innocence emerged. The pace has picked up, with 21 released between 1993 and 1997. But the cut in federal funding for death penalty information services and the narrowing of the right of appeal is increasing the danger that inmates will be executed before they can prove their innocence.

National Association of Criminal Defense Lawyers. "Criminal Defense Lawyers Call for Illinois Death Penalty Reform." Press release on the National Association of Criminal Defense Lawyers web site. Available online. URL: http://209.70.38.3/public.nsf/newsreleases/99mn022. Posted November 4, 1999. States that evidence about wrongful convictions exposes the "sacred cows" or mistaken beliefs that underlie the justice system. Reforms proposed include eliminating the death penalty in cases where there is only a single witness to the crime, requiring "reliability hearings" for government informants prior to any testimony and requiring videotaping of all police interrogations.

OTHER LEGAL AND PROCEDURAL ISSUES

This section discusses legal issues involved in sentencing and appeals in capital cases. Such issues include errors in sentencing phase proceedings, the lack of adequate legal representation, discovery of new evidence, habeas corpus appeals, and possible streamlining of the appeals process. Materials in this section necessarily tend to be more technical in nature.

BOOKS

Bentele, Ursula. *Capital Case Sentencing: How to Protect Your Client.* Washington, D.C.: American Bar Association, 1988. Systematic approach to developing a case against the death penalty, including "humanizing" the client for the jury, clarifying legal issues for the judge, and building a record for appeal.

Berkson, Larry Charles. *The Concept of Cruel and Unusual Punishment.* Lexington, Mass.: D. C. Heath, 1975. A review of the Eighth Amendment's origins and its importance in the concept of punishment.

Coyne, Randall, and Lyn Entzeroth. *Capital Punishment and the Judicial Process.* Durham, N.C.: Carolina Academic Press, 1994. A detailed legal casebook that brings out the inconsistencies and arbitrary and unfair applications in administration of the death penalty. Coyne, a professor of law, was a member of the team that defended Oklahoma City bomber Tim McVeigh.

Darrow, Clarence. *Clarence Darrow on Capital Punishment.* Chicago: Chicago Historical Bookworks, 1991. Writings on capital punishment by the famous advocate.

Annotated Bibliography

Epstein, Lee, and Joseph Fiske Kobylka. *The Supreme Court and Legal Change: Abortion and the Death Penalty.* Chapel Hill: University of North Carolina Press, 1992. Looks at capital punishment and abortion as case studies in abrupt legal change. In both cases the Supreme Court intervened decisively to change the operation of society. The authors conclude that the structure and tactics of legal argumentation is at least as important as judicial temperament and political or social pressures in determing radical legal changes.

Lazarus, Edward. *Closed Chambers: the First Eyewitness Account of the Epic Struggles Inside the Supreme Court.* New York: Random House Times Books, 1998. A former Supreme Court clerk reveals the culture, personalities, and struggles within the Court. Because of their urgency and complexity, death penalty cases play an important role in his account.

Loh, Wallace D. *Social Research in the Judicial Process: Cases, Readings, and Text.* New York: Russell Sage Foundation, 1984. A collection of legal studies. Chapter 5 covers capital punishment.

Mello, Michael. *Against the Death Penalty: The Relentless Dissents of Justices Brennan and Marshall.* Boston: Northeastern University Press, 1996. A detailed study of the dissents written by Supreme Court Justices Brennan and Marshall in more than 2,500 capital cases. Drawing upon personal papers and biographical materials, the author shows how they developed their opinions, based both upon the Constitution (Eighth and Fourteenth amendments) and factors in individual cases.

Mello, Michael, and David Von Drehle. *Dead Wrong: A Death Row Lawyer Speaks Out Against Capital Punishment.* Madison: University of Wisconsin Press, 1998. The author, who worked as a counsel to convicted capital offenders, takes the reader inside the world of death row appeals and last minute stays of execution. He argues that the lack of adequate legal resources for death row inmates coupled with the indifference of many people in "the system" to constitutional rights has made the legal process a travesty.

Meltsner, Michael. *Cruel and Unusual: The Supreme Court and Capital Punishment.* New York: Random House, 1973. Recounts the legal campaign against capital punishment leading to the *Furman* decision.

Nakell, Barry, and Kenneth A. Hardy. *The Arbitrariness of the Death Penalty.* Philadelphia: Temple University Press, 1987. A study that contrasts the death penalty process as described in law with the actual practice in North Carolina following the Supreme Court's upholding of reformed procedures in 1976. The authors conclude that disparate results in cases could not be explained by legal procedures alone, but sometimes correlated with the identity of the prosecutor or the race of the defendant or the victim.

Philipson, Coleman. *Three Criminal Law Reformers: Beccaria, Bentham, Romilly.* Montclair, N.J.: Patterson Smith, 1970. Examines the backgrounds, thought, and achievements of three thinkers who helped inaugurate the modern debate about crime, punishment, and public policy.

Robbins, Ira P. *Rationalizing Federal Habeas Corpus Review of State Court Criminal Convictions in Capital Cases: Background and Issues Paper.* Chicago: American Bar Association, 1989. An overview of issues involved in federal review of habeas corpus petitions arising from state death penalty convictions. Robbins suggests the use of a comprehensive approach to the criminal justice process as a way to provide consistent, workable standards.

———. *Toward a More Just and Effective System of Review in State Death Penalty Cases.* Chicago: American Bar Association, 1990. A report from the American Bar Association Criminal Justice Section Project to Study Habeas Corpus Review of State Death Penalty Convictions. Robbins discusses the status of five issues relating to habeas corpus appeals: competency of counsel, procedural default, exhaustion of state judicial remedies, stays of execution, and obtaining of certificates of probable cause. The book includes a bibliography.

White, Welsh S. *Life in the Balance: Procedural Safeguards in Capital Cases.* Ann Arbor: University of Michigan Press, 1984. A collection of essays evaluating the success of legal procedures designed to ensure fairness and prevent ultimate errors.

Woodward, Bob, and Scott Armstrong. *The Brethren: Inside the Supreme Court.* New York: Simon and Schuster, 1979. Looks at the workings of the Supreme Court from 1969 to 1975, including background on the *Furman* ruling.

ARTICLES AND PAPERS

"After a Respite, Death Makes a Comeback" in *U.S. News & World Report*, vol. 127, Nov. 15, 1999, p. 16. Reports that the federal government, which has not executed anyone since 1963, is getting ready to resume executions. The first person to be executed may be Juan Raul Garza, convicted in 1993 of three murders. As of the time the article was released, 21 federal prisoners awaited execution, including Timothy McVeigh, the convicted Oklahoma City bomber.

Amsterdam, Anthony G. "The Supreme Court and Capital Punishment" in *Human Rights*, vol. 14, Winter 1987, pp. 14–17ff. A critique of the Supreme Court's review of, or refusal to review, execution appeals.

Anderson, George M. "Capital Punishment in Perspective: An Interview with Kevin Doyle" in *America*, vol. 174, April 20, 1996, pp. 16ff. Interviews Kevin Doyle, manager of the New York Capital Defender office.

Annotated Bibliography

Doyle describes his previous experience in the South, where defendants, usually poor and sometimes mentally retarded or emotionally disturbed, usually received inadequate legal representation. Doyle argues that the situation is little better in New York, and that loss of public funding for capital defense is making the situation worse.

Bedau, Hugo Adam. "Thinking of the Death Penalty as Cruel and Unusual Punishment" in *University of California-Davis Law Review*, vol. 18, 1985, pp. 873–925. Considers ways to determine whether punishment in general and the death penalty in particular are being administered in a way that makes them unacceptably severe.

Belluck, Pam. "In Nebraska, Amendment for Equal Rights Keeps Condemned Killer Alive" in *New York Times*, February 20, 1999, p. A9. The case of Randolph Reeves takes a new twist when his lawyers use an equal rights provision recently added to the state constitution to argue that Reeves, a Native American, may have been a victim of discrimination. They also argue that the jury should have been offered the alternative of a lesser charge.

Clark, Ramsey. "Rush to Death: Spenkelink's Last Appeal" in *The Nation*, vol. 229, October 27, 1979, pp. 385, 400–404. Former U.S. attorney general and human rights advocate describes the last 48 hours of appeals made in an unsuccessful attempt to prevent the execution of John Spenkelink in Florida in 1979.

"The Death March" in *The Progressive*, vol. 61, August 1997, pp. 8ff. Argues that the trial of Oklahoma City bomber Timothy McVeigh typifies Americans' growing turn toward the death penalty. Victims' relatives were not allowed to testify on behalf of a lesser penalty. In recent years courts have limited the avenues of appeal for death row inmates.

Dispoldo, Nick. "Capital Punishment and the Poor" in *America*, vol. 172, February 11, 1995, pp. 18ff. Argues that the death penalty pervasively discriminates against the poor, who cannot afford adequate counsel to deal with complex legal issues. Dispoldo also discusses the conflicting trends in recent Supreme Court decisions.

Dworkin, Ronald. "The Court's Impatience to Execute" in *Los Angeles Times*, July 11, 1999, p. M1. Reports on recent cases that suggest that the Supreme Court, while having said that death requires a special level of scrutiny, has in practice been refusing to overturn death sentences even when juries receive misleading instructions or important evidence is withheld. Even if capital punishment is "right in principle," it may prove to be intolerable due to its strain on a legal system that seeks to balance efficiency and protection of rights.

Fein, Bruce. "Death Penalty Polemic Scorns Rule of Law" in *Insight on the News*, vol. 10, April 4, 1994, p. 30. Argues that Supreme Court Justice Harry Blackmun's renunciation of the death penalty and refusal to "tinker with the machinery of death" may be emotionally moving, but lacks any reasoned argument.

Galati, Frank T. "Killer's Sentence Followed Law" in *Arizona Republic*, September 28, 1999, p. B7. The judge who sentenced murderer Bobby Purcell to life without parole rather than death replies to critics who had insisted on the death penalty. He explains that his duty required that only the law guided him in his deliberations, and the law required that he give substantial weight to the offender's young age of 16.

Gest, Ted. "A House Without a Blueprint: After 20 Years, the Death Penalty Is Still Being Meted Out Unevenly" in *U.S. News & World Report*, vol. 121, July 8, 1996, pp. 41ff. A retrospective on the 20 years since the restoration of capital punishment in 1976. Torn between advocates' demand for fairness and the public's continuing demand for the death penalty, the courts preside over a system that is tangled, inefficient, and still unfair.

Jolly, Robert W., Jr., and Deward Sagarin. "The First Eight Years after *Furman:* Who Was Executed with the Return of the Death Penalty?" in *Crime and Delinquency*, vol. 30, 1984, pp. 610–623. Describes the resumption of executions following the *Gregg* decision in 1976, with analysis of accounts of the first eight persons to be executed.

"A Lawyer Without Precedent" in *Harpers Magazine*, vol. 294, June 1997, pp. 24ff. An excerpt from a court transcript from a hearing to determine whether death row prisoner Wallace Fugate had been adequately represented by his attorney Leo Browne. Browne appears to have little knowledge of the key Supreme Court rulings that determine the modern practice of capital punishment, such as *Furman* and *Gregg*, and has seldom if ever used investigators or called upon the help of expert witnesses.

Lazarus, Edward. "Mortal Combat: How the Death Penalty Polarized the Supreme Court" in *Washington Monthly*, vol. 30, June 1998, pp. 32ff. Excerpt of the author's book *Closed Chambers*, describing how conflict and tension over capital punishment between liberal and conservative blocs in the Court boiled over during the 1985–86 decisions, with Justice Powell providing the swing vote.

Ragavan, Chitra. "The Toll in Texas" in *U.S. News & World Report*, vol. 127, August 16, 1999, p. 29. Reports that it is "rush hour" on the Texas death row, with the state on its way to set a new record in executions. The biggest factor in the pace of executions in Texas is the lack of a statewide public defender system, resulting in the mostly poor defendants receiving inadequate representation.

Savage, David G. "Justices Reject Cases on Execution Delay" in *Los Angeles Times*, November 9, 1999, p. A14. Reports that the Supreme Court has turned down two unusual death penalty appeals. Two inmates had argued that long delays of more than 20 years on death row constitute cruel and unusual punishment. Justice Clarence Thomas called the claim "bizarre," noting that the delays were the results of the inmates own incessant efforts.

Simon, Jonathan, and Christina Spaulding. "Tokens of Our Esteem: Aggravating Factors in the Era of Deregulated Death Penalties" in Austin Sarat, ed. *The Killing State: Capital Punishment in Law, Politics, and Culture.* New York: Oxford University Press, 1999, pp. 81–113. Explores the significance of the "capital aggravating factors" specified by state legislators to be used in determining whether to sentence a person to death. The authors argue that such factors have a complex political as well as judicial significance and are used by legislators to gain favor with constituencies.

Sloan, Clifford. "Death Row Clerk, in the Court of Last Resort" in *The New Republic*, vol. 196, February 16, 1987, pp. 18ff. The author recounts his experience as one of the clerks who evaluate requests for stays of execution sent to the Supreme Court. He describes how his work involved him emotionally in grappling with the horrifying facts of crimes, the procedural complexity, and the stress that the capital punishment process puts on all who participate.

Stevenson, Bryan. "The Hanging Judges: Once the Court Said, 'Death Is Different.' Now It Says: 'Let's Get On with It'" in *The Nation*, vol. 263, October 14, 1996, pp. 16ff. Reports how the Supreme Court, which had once agonized over the constitutionality of the death penalty, now seems inclined to streamline the appeals process, denying the continuing challenges to capital punishment on grounds of discrimination, inadequate representation for defendants, or prosecutorial or police misconduct.

Stout, David G. "The Lawyers of Death Row: Long Hours and Low Pay in the Battle Against Capital Punishment" in *The New York Times Magazine*, vol. 137, February 14, 1988, pp. 46ff. Examines lawyers who have dedicated themselves to representing death row inmates.

Thomas, Andrew Peyton. "Penalty Box: A Much-Needed Reform Seemed Poised to Hasten Executions—Until Federal Judges Got Their Hands on It" in *National Review*, vol. 50, May 4, 1998, pp. 40ff. Reports that federal judges have blocked state application of the 1996 Congressional "effective death penalty" legislation, which had sought to speed up the appeals process, in part by requiring that the judges resolve appeals quickly. Thomas suggests that Congress should make minor changes to end the discretion being used by liberal judges who oppose capital punishment and resent infringement of their prerogatives.

Traub, James. "The Executioner's Songs" in *The New Yorker*, vol. 72, November 25, 1996, pp. 48ff. Reports that despite New York's reintroduction of capital punishment, the death penalty is being sought in relatively few cases. One reason is the strict criteria the law has for capital crimes.

Willing, Richard, and Gary Fields. "Geography of the Death Penalty" in *USA Today*, December 20, 1999, n.p. Describes how the chance of someone being given the death penalty for the same sort of murder varies widely according to where the crime is committed. Thirty-eight states have the death penalty, but even among these states there is wide variation in charging and sentencing practices.

Zimring, Franklin E. "The Executioner's Dissonant Song: On Capital Punishment and American Legal Values" in Austin Sarat, ed. *The Killing State: Capital Punishment in Law, Politics, and Culture.* New York: Oxford University Press, 1999, pp. 137–147. Argues that capital punishment is in conflict with principles of human dignity, compromises the integrity of the judicial system, and reduces respect for due process.

WEB DOCUMENTS

American Civil Liberties Union. "The Impact of Habeas Reform on Innocent People Sentenced to Death." On the ACLU web site. Available online. URL: http://www.aclu.org/issues/death/death3.html. Downloaded on November 28, 1999. Describes the consequences on Supreme Court cases through April 1995 that have restricted the ability to file habeas petitions to get a new trial when there is evidence of innocence. Nine cases are discussed in detail.

Bright, Stephen B. "Death in Texas" in *The Champion,* July 1999. On the National Association of Criminal Defense Lawyers web site. Available online. URL: http://www.nacdl.org/public.nsf/championarticles/99jul01. Posted in July 1999. The director of the Southern Center for Human Rights blasts Texas courts for allowing the appointing of incompetent counsel for death penalty appeals and then punishing the clients for the results of the incompetence. Bright gives as an example the refusal of an appeals court to overturn a conviction after the defense attorney slept through much of the trial.

———. "Does the Bill of Rights Apply Here Any More? Evisceration of Habeas Corpus and Denial of Counsel to Those Under Sentence of Death in *The Champion,* November 1996." On the National Association of Criminal Defense Lawyers website. Available online. URL: http://www.criminaljustice.org/Champion/articles/96nov02.htm. Posted in November 1996. Argues that the historic "great writ" of habeas corpus that was meant to ensure due process for the powerless has been eviscerated by court decisions that limit additional appeals and actions of the 104th Congress such as cutting funds for death penalty resource centers.

Dieter, Richard C. "Twenty Years of Capital Punishment: A Re-evaluation." Dealth Penalty Information Center. Available online. URL: http://www.essential.org/dpic/dpic.r01.html. Posted in June 1996. Discusses and summarizes events relating to capital punishment in the 20 years since the

Supreme Court reinstated capital punishment in the case of *Gregg v. Georgia* in 1976. The book includes a chronology and covers the issues of racial discrimination, other inequities, arbitrary decisions to bring capital charges, the cost of capital punishment, politicization of the death penalty, the risk of executing the innocent, and international developments.

———. "With Justice for Few: The Growing Crisis in Death Penalty Representation." Available online. URL: http://www.essential.org/dpic/dpic.r02.html. Death Penalty Information Center. Posted in October 1995. Argues that as the number of executions in the United States continues to grow, most capital defendants receive poor legal representation from incompetent or inexperienced attorneys. States provide inadequate resources, discouraging involvement by better lawyers. A variety of illustrative cases are discussed, including Aden Harrison, Jr., a black man whose court-appointed counsel was 83-year-old James Venable, an Imperial Wizard of the Ku Klux Klan.

Doyle, Kevin M. "Capital Cases: Heart of the Deal: Ten Suggestions for Plea Bargaining" in *The Champion*, November 1999. On the National Association of Criminal Defense Lawyers web site. Available online. URL: http://www.nacdl.org/public.nsf/championarticles/99nov08. Posted in November 1999. Suggests a strategy for giving clients facing the death penalty a realistic understanding of what they can expect.

Kreitzberg, Ellen. "How Much *Payne* Will the Courts Allow?" in *The Champion*. Jan./Feb. 1998. On the National Association of Criminal Defense Lawyers web site. Available online. URL: http://www.nacdl.org/CHAMPION/ARTICLES/98jan04.htm. Posted in February 1998. Discusses the decision in *Payne v. Tennessee*, which partly reversed earlier decisions in holding victim impact statements to not be in conflict with the Eighth Amendment. Kreitzberg describes kinds of victim testimony that still aren't permitted (such as expressing an opinion of the crime or possible punishment) and suggests a strategy for challenging or excluding victim impact testimony.

Stetler, Russell. "Post-Conviction Investigation in Death Penalty Cases" in *The Champion*, August 1999. On the National Association of Criminal Defense Lawyers web site. Available online. URL: http://www.nacdl.org/public.nsf/championarticles/99aug06. Posted in August 1999. Gives suggestions for defense counsel seeking to overturn death sentences. Stetler emphasizes the need to find new facts that challenge the facts that led to the sentencing decision and the need to create empathy in judges so they will see legal errors as demanding relief. With the speeded-up death sentence appeals process in most jurisdictions, investigations must be conducted quickly yet thoroughly.

———. "Working with the Victim's Survivors in Death Penalty Cases" in *The Champion*, June 1999. On the National Association of Criminal

Defense Lawyers web site. Available online. URL: http://www.nacdl. org/public.nsf/championarticles/99jun06. Posted in June 1999. Approaches the sensitive topic of how defense attorneys can interview survivors at various phases of the trial process. Stetler emphasizes the need to understand the experiences and feelings of survivors and their complex and sometimes conflicting feelings. It is important for defense attorneys to develop good contacts because of the significant role survivors often have in determining whether the death penalty is sought, whether the jury returns a death verdict, and sometimes whether a later appeal for clemency succeeds.

Wheelan, Dick. "Significance of *Simmons* and Future Dangerousness" in *The Champion*, May 1996. On the National Association of Criminal Defense Lawyers web site. Available online. URL: http://www.criminaljustice.org/CHAMPION/ARTICLES/96may01.htm. Posted in May 1996. Discusses the decision in *Simmons v. South Carolina*, where the Supreme Court ruled that if the prosecution argues that the defendant should receive the death penalty because of his or her future dangerousness, the court must allow the defense to inform the jury that the defendant is ineligible for parole. Wheelan describes strategic considerations determining whether to seek to inform the jury about life (or lengthy non-life) sentences.

AUDIOVISUAL MATERIALS

Born Killers: Leopold and Loeb. A&E Network. VHS video of an episode of *In Search of History.* [n.d.] Available for ordering online at http://store.aetv. com/. Tells the story of the two cold-blooded killers whose trial pitted a public prosecutor demanding the death penalty against famed advocate Clarence Darrow, who won them a life sentence.

The Death Penalty. Taped discussion on National Public Radio's program *Talk of the Nation* with host Ray Suarez. Real Audio file available online at http://www.npr.org/ramarchives/ne7f1101-6.ram. First broadcast February 11, 1997. Guests: Alex Kozinski, Judge, United States Court of Appeals for the Ninth Circuit, 1985–present; Steve Reinhart, Judge, United States Court of Appeals for the Ninth Circuit, 1980–present; and others. Discussion covers a number of legal issues and concerns with administration of capital punishment.

Life or Death: A Battle Over Capital Punishment. A&E Network. VHS video of an episode of *20th Century with Mike Wallace.* [n.d.] Available for ordering online at http://store.aetv.com/. Traces the story of the legal challenges against capital punishment during the past 30 years, including interviews with advocates on both sides.

RELIGIOUS, MORAL, ETHICAL, AND CULTURAL APPROACHES

This section includes a variety of writings reflecting evaluation of capital punishment from a variety of perspectives, consideration of the cultural impact of the death penalty, and advocacy by religious groups.

BOOKS

Arendt, Hannah. *Eichmann in Jerusalem: A Report on the Banality of Evil.* New York: Viking Press, 1963. Describes the trial and execution of Adolph Eichmann in Israel for crimes he committed as a Nazi official.

Bockle, Franz, and Jacques Pohiers. *The Death Penalty and Torture.* New York: Seabury Press, 1979. Essays on the death penalty and torture, from a range of religious viewpoints.

Devine, Philip E. *The Ethics of Homicide.* Ithaca, N.Y.: Cornell University Press, 1978. Considers the moral issues of homicide and possible exceptions. Discusses homicide in the context of abortion, capital punishment, war, suicide, and euthanasia.

Erdahl, Lowell O. *Pro-Life/Pro-Peace: Life-Affirming Alternatives to Abortion, War, Mercy-Killing and the Death Penalty.* Minneapolis, Minn.: Augsburg Publishing House, 1986. A Lutheran bishop's call for a consistent, Christian and pro-life stance on a number of issues including capital punishment.

Eshelman, Byron, and Frank Riley. *Death Row Chaplain.* Englewood Cliffs, N.J.: Prentice-Hall, 1962. A former chaplain at San Quentin recounts his experiences and criticizes the death penalty.

Glover, Jonathan. *Causing Death and Saving Lives.* New York: Penguin, 1977. Considers various moral approaches to such life-or-death issues as suicide, euthanasia, capital punishment, and abortion.

Guest, David. *Sentenced to Death: The American Novel and Capital Punishment.* Jackson: University Press of Mississippi, 1997. A study of the social context of five novels in which the operation of capital punishment plays an important part: *McTeague, An American Tragedy, Native Son, In Cold Blood,* and *The Executioner's Song.*

Hanks, Gardner C. *Against the Death Penalty: Christian and Secular Arguments Against Capital Punishment.* Scottsdale, Penn.: Herald Press, 1997. A concise, accessible presentation of arguments against capital punishment from a Christian perspective. Hanks places the Old Testament background in perspective and argues that the understanding of God and humankind developed in the New Testament compels the rejection of capital punishment. Hanks also rebuts secular justifications for capital punishment.

Ingram, T. Robert. *Essays on the Death Penalty*. Houston: St. Thomas Press, 1963. Essays on capital punishment from several Christian perspectives.

Kaminer, Wendy. *It's All the Rage: Crime and Culture*. Reading, Mass.: Addison-Wesley, 1995. A witty commentary on the capital punishment debate and its historical, social, legal, and ethical aspects. The author points out numerous examples of what she considers to be the irrationality of capital punishment: the media hype surrounding recent cases, the public's embrace of draconian measures such as the "three strikes" laws, and contradictions such as that between peoples' desire to blame others for their difficulties while holding others to the ultimate standard of responsibility.

Megivern, James J. *The Death Penalty: An Historical and Theological Survey*. New York: Paulist Press, 1997. A history of the theological, philosophical, and legal debate about capital punishment since ancient times, including teachings of the early Christian fathers, St. Thomas Aquinas, and later works. The author, a religious scholar, is abolitionist but maintains an even-handed approach.

Nathanson, Stephen. *An Eye for an Eye? The Morality of Punishing by Death*. Totawa, N.J.: Rowman and Littlefield, 1987. An evaluation and rejection of arguments supporting capital punishment.

Otterbein, Keith F. *The Ultimate Coercive Sanction: A Cross-Cultural Study of Capital Punishment*. New Haven, Conn.: HRAF Press, 1986. Studies the death penalty from an anthropological viewpoint; examination of 53 tribal societies suggests that capital punishment is universal.

ARTICLES AND PAPERS

Allen, John L., Jr. "Pa. Youth Rally Against Death Penalty" in *National Catholic Reporter*, vol. 33, August 29, 1997, p. 8. Describes a demonstration at a Pennsylvania prison by young people belonging to the Bruderhof religious community.

Anderson, David E. "Bombing Tests Death Penalty Theory" in *National Catholic Reporter*, vol. 31, May 12, 1995, p. 3. Discusses whether the Oklahoma City bombing might require an exception to Pope John Paul II's general condemnation of capital punishment. Some theologians believe that while the heinousness of the crime should not provoke an execution, a death sentence may be justified if necessary to defend society to deter against the threat of extreme terrorism.

Anderson, George M. "Organizing Against the Death Penalty" in *America*, vol. 178, January 3, 1998, pp. 10ff. Describes a gathering of religious and lay people under the title "Envisioning a World Without Violence."

Annotated Bibliography

Sister Helen Prejean (of *Dead Man Walking* fame) was keynote speaker at the conference, which was sponsored by the Quaker group American Friends Service Committee.

Bernardin, Joseph Cardinal. "The Consistent Ethic after 'Webster': Opportunities and Dangers" in *Commonweal*, vol. 117, April 20, 1990, pp. 242ff. Following the Supreme Court's developments in abortion decisions, a Roman Catholic leader examines the need for a consistent pro-life ethic that can address issues such as abortion, capital punishment, and war.

Block, Richard A. "Death, Thou Shalt Die: Reform Judaism and Capital Punishment" in *Journal of Reform Judaism*, vol. 30, Spring 1983, pp. 1–10. A survey of Jewish doctrine and writings opposing capital punishment.

Boyd, George N. "Capital Punishment: Deserved and Wrong" in *The Christian Century*, vol. 105, February 17, 1988, pp. 162–165. Examines several aspects of the morality of capital punishment.

Camus, Albert. "Reflections on the Guillotine" in *Resistance, Rebellion and Death*. New York: Knopf, 1966, pp. 173–234. A classic abolitionist essay, by the existentialist author, opposing capital punishment for moral and philosophical reasons.

"Capital Punishment 'Cruel and Unnecessary'" in *America*, vol. 180, March 20, 1999, p. 3. Discusses the commutation of the death sentence of Darrell J. Mease after intervention by Pope John Paul II and the application of the emerging Catholic opposition to the death penalty as part of a consistent pro-life ethic. The article also discusses the death sentence for white supremacist John William King for a brutal dragging murder of an African American and the necessity to oppose capital punishment even in such egregious cases.

"Catechism Takes Harder Line on Death Penalty" in *National Catholic Reporter*, vol. 33, September 19, 1997, p. 12. Reports that the latest Latin edition of the Catholic catechism has taken a stronger position against capital punishment, reflecting Pope John Paul II's 1995 encyclical *Evangelium Vitae*. The Church now accepts use of the death penalty only when there is no question of the guilt of the accused and the State has no other way to suppress the offender. This is a situation that is expected to arise seldom if ever in developed nations.

Cohen, Daniel A. "In Defense of the Gallows: Justifications of Capital Punishment in New England Execution Sermons, 1674–1825" in *American Quarterly*, vol. 40, June 1988, pp. 147ff. A historical look at religious justification for the death penalty.

"Colosseum Used by Death Penalty Foes" in *Los Angeles Times*, December 18, 1999, Religious News Service section, n.p. Reports on Pope John Paul II's inauguration of a year-long project in which the Colosseum of Rome, where Christians were sacrificed to lions and gladiators fought to the death, will be illuminated for 48 hours each time a death sentence is suspended or commuted, or a country abolishes the death penalty.

Dear, John. "Mother Teresa and the Death Penalty" in *America*, vol. 180, June 19, 1999, p. 20. The author, executive director of the Fellowship of Reconciliation, recounts his contacting Mother Teresa, who agreed to intervene with various state governors to stop executions. Her simple appeal, "What would Jesus do if he were in your position?" worked in some cases but not others.

Doyle, Kevin. "No Defense" in *U.S. Catholic*, vol. 64, August 1999, p. 18. A Catholic lawyer recounts his encounters with death row inmates, and sums up his opposition to the death penalty in three statements: "1. Human beings are fallible. 2. Racism is mortally sinful. 3. Human life is sacred."

Drinan, Robert F. "Lay Group Adds Muscle to Death-Penalty Fight" in *National Catholic Reporter*, vol. 29, May 28, 1993, p. 15. Describes the group Catholics Against Capital Punishment, which seeks to apply a "consistent pro-life ethic." Among other things, Drinan challenges anti-abortion groups to also oppose the death penalty.

Elshtain, Jean Bethke. "Sacrilege" in *The New Republic*, vol. 216, June 16, 1997, p. 27. Argues that capital punishment represents the prideful usurpation of ultimate power over life and death by a secular society.

"Encyclical Condemns 'Culture of Death'" in *National Catholic Reporter*, vol. 31, April 7, 1995, p. 3. Summarizes the encyclical *Evangelium Vitae* issued by Pope John Paul II. It condemns capital punishment, together with abortion and euthanasia, as part of an immoral, destructive, and dehumanizing "culture of death."

Erez, Edna. "Thou Shalt Not Execute: Hebrew Law Perspective on Capital Punishment" in *Criminology*, vol. 19, 1981, pp. 25–43. Examines the Hebraic historical and legal context for capital punishment.

Frame, Randy. "A Matter of Life and Death: As the Number of Executions Surges, Christians Remain Divided on the Death Penalty's Morality and Purpose" in *Christianity Today*, vol. 39, August 14, 1995, pp. 50ff. The growing number of executions keeps the issue of capital punishment in the spotlight, but Christian groups are deeply divided over the sanction. Some groups such as Murder Victims' Families for Reconciliation oppose the death penalty and seek alternative ways to prevent crime. Most major Christian denominations officially oppose the death penalty. However, 77 percent of the population supports capital punishment in recent polling. Frame also reviews biblical and theological positions as well as the standard issues of deterrence and racial bias.

Frankel, Bruce. "Fighting for Life: Death Penalty Foe SueZann Bosler Helps Save Her Father's Killer" in *People Weekly*, vol. 48, August 18, 1997, pp. 93ff. Although SueZann Bosler was attacked and her father killed by James Campbell in December 1986, she told the sentencing court that Campbell's life should be spared. She believes the death penalty only creates additional victims and is now a spokesperson for the group Murder Victims' Families for Reconciliation.

Gardner, Martin R. "Mormonism and Capital Punishment, a Doctrinal Perspective, Past and Present" in *Dialogue: A Journal of Mormon Thought*, vol. 12, 1979, pp. 9–26. Explores the historical context for Mormon support of the death penalty. There appears to be little evidence of doctrinal basis for that support.

Kennedy, Eugene. "Inner Peace Restored for Victims' Families when Murderer Is Executed" in *National Catholic Reporter*, vol. 35, July 2, 1999, p. 21. Catholic writer challenges the Church's condemnation of capital punishment. The capital punishment debate has focused mainly on the moral situation of the State and the experience of the condemned murderer, ignoring the moral stature of the crime's survivors. The author suggests that only execution of the murderer can make the victim's survivors feel whole again and that securing such restitution is a legitimate objective of government.

Kroll, Michael. "Pro-life Parents: Their Children Were Murdered. Still, They Oppose the Death Penalty" in *Mother Jones*, vol. 15, February–March 1990, p. 13. Recounts parents whose pro-life beliefs lead them to eschew the vengeance of capital punishment.

"The Lesson of Karla Faye Tucker: Evangelical Instincts against Her Execution Were Right, But Not Because She Was a Christian" in *Christianity Today*, vol. 42, April 6, 1998, pp. 15ff. Argues that Christians who first became opposed to capital punishment in the case of born-again Christian Karla Faye Tucker need to broaden their perspective and realize that it is inappropriate to execute anyone, both because the capital punishment system is unfair and discriminatory and because vengeance is not a Christian answer to the problem of crime.

Malcolm, Teresa. "Activists Share Strategies for Ending Death Penalty" in *National Catholic Reporter*, vol. 35, April 23, 1999, p. 3. Describes a meeting of a group called Religious Organizing Against the Death Penalty. Representatives of many faiths discuss how to better communicate their opposition to capital punishment to a public (including many of their own congregants) that strongly supports the death penalty.

———. "Tucker's Death Affected Robertson Views" in *National Catholic Reporter*, vol. 35, April 23, 1999, p. 4. Describes how the involvement of Pat Robertson (formerly a death penalty supporter) and Christian Coalition activists in the struggle to spare Karla Faye Tucker from execution may have made many conservative Christians a potent new force for abolition of capital punishment.

Pennington, Judy. "Helen Prejean" in *The Progressive*, vol. 60, January 1996, pp. 32ff. Interview with Sister Helen Prejean whose Pulitzer

Prize–nominated book *Dead Man Walking* became a successful movie in 1995. Prejean recounts how she became involved in social justice work and the struggle against capital punishment.

Prejean, Helen. "A Way Out of No Way" in *America*, vol. 179, August 29, 1998, p. 7. A letter from Sister Helen Prejean to her congregation describing her ministering to death row inmate Dobbie Williams on the day he was scheduled to be executed. Human touches add poignancy to the account, in which a last minute stay of execution is granted.

Riga, Peter J. "The Death Chamber" in *America*, vol. 172, February 18, 1995, pp. 20ff. A former prison chaplain recounts his close relationship with a decorated Vietnam veteran who had been sent to death row for the killing of two policemen, how he accompanied him to the gas chamber, remaining in eye contact with him as he died. The author believes that the "awesome and mysterious" nature of death is such that no human should have the moral power to kill another.

Rosin, Hanna. "Catholic, Jewish Leaders Target Death Penalty in National Effort; Group Aims to Abolish Practice by Raising Moral Awareness" in *Washington Post*, December 6, 1999, p. A02. Reports on a new joint campaign between Catholic and Jewish activists that seeks to revive the rather dormant religious movement against the death penalty.

"Speaking ex Soapbox" in *National Review*, vol. 47, December 11, 1995, pp. 22ff. Argues that the moral equivalency implied in recent U.S. Catholic Conference statements condemning abortion, capital punishment, welfare reform, and sanctions against illegal aliens is not justified. The culpability of these different classes of people is quite different.

Stafford, J. Francis. "Blackmun's 'Conversion' on Death Penalty Hailed" in *National Catholic Reporter*, vol. 30, April 22, 1994, p. 14. Archbishop Stafford notes Supreme Court Justice Harry Blackmun's dramatic decision to refuse to "tinker with the machinery of death" in capital punishment cases and urges him to reconsider his stand on abortion and support for *Roe v. Wade* in the same light.

Vanderpool, Tim. "Buddhists Protest Death Sentence" in *The Progressive*, vol. 58, March 1994, p. 14. Reports that the execution of Johnathan Doody for the 1991 slaying of nine Buddhist monks in their temple in Phoenix is being protested by Buddhists who oppose capital punishment. The Buddhists say they don't believe in revenge and have urged the prosecutor to show leniency.

WEB DOCUMENTS

"Karla Faye Tucker Home Page." LifeWay Services/FamilyLife Training Center. Available online. URL: http://www.straightway.org/karla/karla.

htm. Downloaded on January 11, 2000. Recounts the story of Karla Faye Tucker, a death row inmate who became a born-again Christian and aroused an unsuccessful movement to spare her from execution by the state of Texas. The page also provides a variety of links to death penalty–related news and resources.

AUDIOVISUAL MATERIALS

Marietta on Forgiveness. Mennonite Central Committee of Ontario, VHS Video, 1988. Interview with Marietta Jaeger, whose daughter was murdered after being kidnapped from a family outing. She describes her feelings during the year in which she did not know whether her daughter was alive or dead, and her eventual contact with the kidnapper, leading to his capture and her working toward forgiving him.

POLITICAL AND LEGISLATIVE DEVELOPMENTS

This section includes general consideration of the death penalty as a political issue, analysis of public opinion, particular cases that have had a political impact, and debates and developments surrounding state or federal legislation.

BOOKS

Bessler, John D. *Death in the Dark: Midnight Executions in America.* Boston: Northeastern University Press, 1997. The author, a law professor who has helped defend death row inmates, argues that executions are deliberately staged at midnight and out of the public eye so that the public will not see the gruesome process of execution or question the rhetoric of pro–death penalty politicians. He suggests that executions be televised. The book includes an overview of capital punishment and the media in American history, starting with public hangings in colonial days and ending with the manipulation of public opinion in the age of television.

Cabana, Donald A. *Death at Midnight: The Confession of an Executioner.* Boston: Northeastern University Press, 1996. Former prison warden and now a criminal justice professor, the author gives an account of his career and how he changed from a proponent of capital punishment to an abolitionist. As warden of the Parchman Penitentiary in Mississippi, he became friends with Connie Ray Evans, who was executed for murder. He became disillusioned when popular pressure led the state to step up the pace of executions. He argues that the death penalty discussion must move beyond the simplistic rhetoric usually used by politicians.

Cook, Kimberly J. *Divided Passions: Public Opinions on Abortion and the Death Penalty.* Boston: Northeastern University, 1998. Argues that for both capital punishment and abortion public opinions are passionate but contradictory, such as abortion opponents who support the death penalty. Through a series of in-depth interviews the author seeks to identify the cultural forces that shape opinion. She concludes that both groups share an ethic of "punitiveness."

Ehrmann, Herbert B. *The Case That Will Not Die: Commonwealth vs. Sacco and Vanzetti.* Boston: Little, Brown, 1969. The account of an attorney for the defense in this famous and controversial case from the 1920s in which two immigrant anarchists were executed.

Frankfurter, Marion Denman, and Gardner Jackson, eds. *The Letters of Sacco and Vanzetti.* New York: Octagon Books, 1971. A collection of the letters and court speeches of two famous anarchists executed in Massachusetts in 1927. The case provoked widespread controversy.

ARTICLES AND PAPERS

Anderson, David C. "Expressive Justice Is All the Rage" in *The New York Times Magazine,* January 15, 1995, pp. 36ff. Written as crime rates were peaking, this article suggests that both capital punishment and denial of parole for lesser offenses is reflective of the fear and anger of a public that believes crime is out of control.

Bohm, R. "American Death Penalty Attitudes: A Critical Examination of Recent Evidence" in *Criminal Justice and Behavior,* vol. 4, 1987, pp. 380–396. Considers the factors that most frequently lead people to support the death penalty.

Bohm, R. M., and R. E. Vogel. "Comparison of Factors Associated with Uninformed and Informed Death Penalty Opinions" in *Journal of Criminal Justice,* vol. 22, 1994, pp. 125–143. Study of college undergraduates' attitudes to the death penalty. The degree of support for the death penalty was correlated with being white and accepting arguments based on deterrence, incapacitation, and revenge. Providing information about the death penalty seems to have little effect on core attitudes.

———. "Educational Experiences and Death Penalty Opinions: Stimuli that Produce Changes" in *Journal of Criminal Justice Education,* vol. 2, Spring 1991, pp. 69–80. Reports the results of a study in which various stimuli were presented to college students and the effects on their opinions of capital punishment measured. The authors discuss how the last days of Earl Johnson, a black man executed in Mississippi, had a significant effect in shifting black students' opinions against the death penalty but had only a small effect on white students.

Annotated Bibliography

Boyarsky, Bill. "Don't Bar the Public Eye at Executions" in *Los Angeles Times*, December 28, 1997, p. B1. Argues that the public that authorizes the death penalty should have the right—and the duty—to see what it has wrought. Claims by authorities on behalf of prisoner's privacy are hypocritical.

Buckley, William F. "Dark Night for George W." in *National Review*, v. 50, January 26, 1998, p. 59. Buckley describes the contradictions that have created a dilemma for Texas governor George W. Bush, Jr., in deciding whether to commute the death sentence of Karla Faye Tucker. Buckley describes how her life of promiscuity and drug abuse caused many conservatives to view her unsympathetically and how the idea of executing a woman, and a born-again Christian woman at that, is troubling to many religious conservatives. However, favoring people for their gender or religious beliefs contradicts liberal ideology as well.

DeVries, Brian, and Lawrence J. Walker. "Moral Reasoning and Attitudes Toward Capital Punishment" in *Developmental Psychology*, vol. 22, 1986, pp. 509–513. Using Kohlberg's moral development theory, the authors find that university students at higher stages of moral development oppose capital punishment.

Dionne, E. J., Jr. "Karla Tucker's Legacy: The Death Penalty Debate Takes a Turn" in *Commonweal*, vol. 125, February 27, 1998, pp. 9ff. Suggests that the execution of Karla Faye Tucker and the troubling emotions raised by her show of remorse may mark a turning point in public support for the death penalty.

Drinan, Robert F. "Catholic Politicians and the Death Penalty" in *America*, May 1, 1999, p. 19. Points out the contradiction between Catholic teachings against capital punishment and the views of the 15 Catholic state governors in the United States, most of whom are in states that have the death penalty and most of whom have expressed support for the sanction. Political realities put governors who want to follow their church's teachings in a very difficult position.

———. "Catholics and the Death Penalty" in *America*, vol. 170, June 18, 1994. Father Drinan begins by acknowledging that 70 percent of Catholic laypersons support the death penalty, in keeping with the attitudes of the general public. He then explains the church's position that the sanction is unnecessary and recounts facts that suggest that the death penalty is imposed in an unfair and discriminatory way, particularly with regards to racial minorities.

Ellsworth, P. C., and S. R. Gross. "Hardening of the Attitudes: Americans' Views on the Death Penalty" in *Journal of Social Issues*, vol. 50, Summer 1994, pp. 19–52. Reports the steady increase in American support for the death penalty since 1966. The authors suggest that such support is based on emotion, with people having little desire to consider new facts. They suggest other areas of research such as considering the death penalty in relation to racial issues and to alternative forms of punishment.

Gelman, David. "The Bundy Carnival: A Thirst for Revenge Provokes a Raucous Send-off" in *Newsweek*, vol. 113, February 6, 1989, p. 66. Describes the circus-like atmosphere and public reaction surrounding the execution of mass murderer Ted Bundy.

Gest, Ted. "The Law That Grief Built" in *U.S. News & World Report*, vol. 120, April 29, 1996, p. 58. Describes how Oklahoma attorney general Drew Edmondson mobilized the outrage following the Oklahoma City bombing to pass a bill in Congress that curtailed the appeal rights of death-row prisoners. Families of Oklahoma City bombing victims played a crucial role in this effort.

Harvey, O. J. "Belief Systems and Attitudes Toward the Death Penalty and Other Punishments" in *Journal of Personality*, vol. 54, December 1986, pp. 659–675. Explores the values and attitudes from which opinions of punishment stem.

Kaplan, David A. "Anger and Ambivalence" in *Newsweek*, vol. 126, August 7, 1995, pp. 24ff. A detailed look at the status of the death penalty in the United States and American attitudes toward it. Kaplan describes a sort of stalemate where the populace demands capital punishment but there are few actual executions as death rows fill up and court procedures drag on. Sidebar articles look at four specific cases.

———. "Life and Death Decisions" in *Newsweek*, vol. 129, June 16, 1997, pp. 28ff. Describes the nation's ambivalence with the death penalty; despite strong public support for capital punishment as measured in polls, the relatively small number of executions reflects the public's lack of willingness to put their beliefs into practice. On the other side, the heinous nature of the Timothy McVeigh case caused many death penalty opponents to keep silent. The article also summarizes the situation on federal death row: the federal government executes people only rarely, and there are only 12 federal prisoners awaiting execution.

Kohlberg, Lawrence, and Donald Elfenbein. "Capital Punishment, Moral Development, and the Constitution" in Lawrence Kohlberg, *Essays on Moral Development*, vol. 1, pp. 243–293. New York: Harper and Row, 1981. Draws on a 20-year study of American males' development of moral judgment. The results suggest that men in the most mature stages of moral development reject the concept of capital punishment. Such an "evolving standard" offers a basis for rejecting capital punishment under the Supreme Court's interpretation of the Eighth Amendment.

Linebaugh, Peter. "The Farce of the Death Penalty" in *The Nation*, vol. 261, August 14, 1995, pp. 165ff. Describes the political and cultural history of capital punishment since ancient times as a farcical social ritual. Today, in a supposedly enlightened time, the farce goes on, unabated and even growing.

Morganthau, Tom. "Condemned to Life" in *Newsweek*, vol. 126, August 7, 1995, pp. 18ff. Describes the case of Susan Smith as a good example of the ambivalence with which many Americans face the decision of whether a person actually deserves death. While the majority of Americans support the death penalty, testimony about Smith's background of molestation, compulsive promiscuity, and possible mental illness led a jury to give her life rather than death for the drowning of her two young children. Sidebar articles include a chronology, a *Newsweek* poll on attitudes toward the death penalty under various circumstances, and an account of how the trial was conducted.

Morganthau, Tom, and Peter Annin. "Should McVeigh Die?" in *Newsweek*, vol. 129, June 16, 1997, pp. 20ff. Reports how the trial of the Oklahoma City bomber brings the debate over the death penalty into sharper focus. Americans broadly but shallowly support capital punishment, but are often reluctant to call for death in specific cases.

Pataki, George E. "Death Penalty Is a Deterrent" in *USA Today*, vol. 125, March 1997, pp. 52ff. New York governor Pataki, who defeated former governor Mario Cuomo, a death penalty opponent, says he is a strong supporter of capital punishment, which he says is an essential part of a strategy for reclaiming society from the most violent and inhuman criminals.

Payne, B. K., and V. Coogle. "Examining Attitudes About the Death Penalty" in *Corrections Compendium*, vol. 23, April 1998, pp. 1ff. Study examining college students' attitudes about capital punishment in order to measure possible changes as the students pursued their academic studies. Results showed that race and political affiliation correlated with attitudes toward the death penalty, while gender, academic major, and community size did not.

Rosen, Jeffrey. "Shell Game" in *The New Republic*, May 13, 1996, p. 6. Attacks the Effective Death Penalty and Public Safety Act of 1996 for its crass political motivations and assault on both states' rights and the independence of the judiciary.

Rosenberg, Tina. "The Deadliest D.A." in *The New York Times Magazine*, July 16, 1995, p. 20. Describes the career of Lynne Abraham, the Philadelphia district attorney who firmly believes in the death penalty and zealously seeks it whenever possible. Rosenberg also examines the workings of Philadelphia's justice system.

Serrano, Richard A. "Federal Death Cases Often End with Life" in *Los Angeles Times*. August 3, 1998, p. A5. Despite the increase in federal crimes for which the death penalty may be imposed, in practice the federal government sentences very few defendants to death. Although tough talk is used for political purposes, many people in the administration and career prosecutors oppose the death penalty and are reluctant to seek it.

Terry, Don. "Term Just Begun, Governor Faces Life-or-Death Choice" in *New York Times*, February 4, 1999, p. A18. Reports that newly elected California governor Gray Davis must decide whether to stop the execution of Jaturun Siripongs, who committed two brutal murders 18 years ago but has been a model prisoner since then. (In the event, Gray Davis, who had campaigned as a supporter of capital punishment, denied clemency.)

Worsnop, Richard L. "Death Penalty Debate: Will Support for Executions Continue to Grow?" in *CQ Researcher*, vol. 5, March 10, 1995, pp. 195ff. An extensive article that assesses the future of the death penalty in the latter part of the 1990s. Public attitudes are strongly in favor of capital punishment, probably because of a continuing high crime rate. Death penalty opponents are well-organized and vocal, however. Includes sidebars on interesting historical and current cases.

WEB DOCUMENTS

Dieter, Richard C. "Killing for Votes: The Dangers of Politicizing the Death Penalty Process." Death Penalty Information Center. Available online. URL: http://www.essential.org/dpic/dpicrkfv.html. Posted in October 1996. Discusses the use of the death penalty issue in election campaigns and how it leads to political pressure on judges and prosecutors to bring capital charges. A variety of campaigns and cases are discussed.

———. "Sentencing for Life: Americans Embrace Alternatives to the Death Penalty." Death Penalty Information Center. Available online. URL: http://www.essential.org/dpic/dpic.r07.html. Posted in April 1993. Reviews public opinion on the question of the death penalty versus life without parole. When respondents are given life without parole as an alternative, it is favored more than the death penalty. Jurors are often not informed that they have life without parole as an alternative.

DEATH ROW ACCOUNTS AND PARTICULAR CASES

This section presents a variety of interviews with death row inmates, lawyers, victims' families, and other persons involved with capital cases. It includes accounts of the appeals process and executions and discussion of particular methods of execution. (Cases primarily concerned with the question of innocence are included in the earlier section Execution of the Innocent.)

Annotated Bibliography

BOOKS

Arriens, Jan, ed. *Welcome to Hell: Letters & Writings from Death Row.* Boston: Northeastern University Press, 1997. A collection of letters from death row inmates to members of the pen friend group Lifelines. Alternately grotesque, tender, and surprising, the writings reveal the hidden face of capital punishment. A foreword by Sister Helen Prejean is included.

Bentley, Robert. *Dangerous Games: The True Story of a Convicted Murderer on Death Row Who Changed His Sex and Won Her Freedom.* Secaucus, N.J.: Carol Publishing Group, 1993. A flamboyant account by a screenwriter of the true story of Leslie Douglas Ashley. Ashley, a male transvestite, was involved with a cast of unsavory characters and a life of hustling, leading to a murder conviction, appeals, and retrials. Ashley's conviction was eventually overturned because the prosecutor had withheld evidence relating to his mental condition, and he was put in a mental institution following a new sanity hearing. After being pardoned, Ashley underwent a sex-change operation and later became an activist with ACT-UP.

Brandon, Craig. *The Electric Chair: An Unnatural American History.* Jefferson, N.C.: McFarland, 1999. A history of the electric chair, which has been used to execute more than 4,300 individuals in 23 states since 1890, though its use has sharply declined in recent years. Brandon discusses how the chair's introduction was seen as a "humane" alternative to hanging and in part was the result of a rivalry between Thomas Edison and George Westinghouse.

Brasfield, Philip, and Jeffrey M. Elliot. *Deathman Pass Me By: Two Years on Death Row.* San Bernadino, Calif.: Borgo Books, 1983. Account of the author's two years as an inmate on death row in Texas.

Brown, Larry K. *You Are Respectfully Invited to Attend My Execution: Untold Stories of Men Legally Executed in Wyoming Territory.* Glendo, Wyo.: High Plains Press, 1997. Stories of men executed in Wyoming during the days of the Old West. Brown does not discuss directly capital punishment issues, but his book is useful for exploring the role of capital punishment in the social and mythical world of the West.

Buchanan, William J. *Execution Eve.* Far Hills, N.J.: New Horizon Press, 1993. Describes the case in which golf star Marion Miley and her mother were murdered, and three men were convicted of the slaying and sentenced to death in Kentucky State Prison. The author's father, who was a warden responsible for overseeing the executions, had serious doubts about the guilt of one of them. Through a series of bizarre manipulations, the warden attempts to force out the truth as the execution night wore on.

Capote, Truman. *In Cold Blood: The True Account of a Multiple Murder and Its Consequences.* New York: Random House, 1965. An extensive account of a 1959 multiple murder in Kansas that became a nonfiction classic.

Chessman, Caryl. *Cell 2455, Death Row*. Englewood Cliffs, N.J.: Prentice-Hall, 1954. The first of three works by a California inmate whose case became famous. Chessman describes his life on death row.

———. *The Face of Justice*. Englewood Cliffs, N.J.: Prentice-Hall, 1957. The third and final book of the celebrated death row author who was executed in 1960.

———. *Trial by Ordeal*. Englewood Cliffs, N.J.: Prentice-Hall, 1955. Describes Chessman's ongoing legal battles and stays of execution and the emotional toll death row takes on prisoners, their families, and legal counsel.

Davis, Christopher. *Waiting For It*. New York: Harper and Row, 1980. A biography of Troy Gregg. In 1976 the Supreme Court denied his death sentence appeal, upholding Georgia's death penalty law.

Dicks, Shirley. *Congregation of the Condemned: Voices Against the Death Penalty*. Reprint edition. Amherst, N.Y.: Prometheus Books, 1995. A collection of essays edited by a person whose own son is on death row. The essays focus on the unfairness of the death penalty, arguing that it is imposed mostly on the poor, while wealthier persons convicted of similar crimes receive lighter penalties.

Dicks, Shirley, ed. *Death Row: Interviews with Inmates, Their Families and Opponents of Capital Punishment*. Jefferson, N.C.: McFarland, 1990. The author's first of several books on capital punishment, written after her son was executed after what she believes was a wrongful conviction. The author interviewed experts, inmates, and the relatives of murder victims.

Drimmer, Frederick. *Until You Are Dead: The Book of Executions in America*. Secaucus, N.J.: Carol Publishing Group, 1990. A survey of executions in America from colonial times to the execution of Ted Bundy. Drimmer describes the development of the five methods of execution (hanging, firing squad, electric chair, gas, and lethal injection).

Duffy, Clinton T., with Al Hirshberg. *88 Men and 2 Women*. New York: Doubleday, 1962. A San Quentin warden's account of 90 executions, with strong arguments for the abolition of the death penalty.

Eliot, Robert G. *Agent of Death: The Memoirs of an Executioner*. New York: Dutton, 1940. An executioner in several states during the first decades of the 20th century recounts his experiences and his opposition to the death penalty.

Engel, Howard. *Lord High Executioner: An Unashamed Look at Hangmen, Headsmen, and Their Kind*. London: Robson Books, 1997. A vivid, compelling social history of the executioner: the person who carries out the collective will of the people by killing criminals using any of a variety of different methods. Engel describes the personalities of executioners and their way of life and work. The book is abolitionist, but generally not preachy.

Annotated Bibliography

Gillespie, L. Kay. *The Unforgiven: Utah's Executed Men*. Salt Lake City: Signature Books, 1997. The author, a member of Utah's Board of Pardons, vividly describes his experiences interviewing most of Utah's death row inmates.

Hammer, Richard. *Between Life and Death*. New York: Macmillan, 1969. An account of the trial, incarceration, and appeal of John Brady, leading to the 1963 Supreme Court ruling *Brady v. Maryland*.

Jackson, Bruce, and Diane Christian. *Death Row*. Boston: Beacon Press, 1980. Interviews with 26 inmates on death row in Texas.

Johnson, Robert. *Condemned to Die: Life Under Sentence of Death*. New York: Elsevier, 1981. Examines the effect of the death sentence on death row inmates and their families.

———. *Death Work: A Study of the Modern Execution Process*. Second edition. Belmont, Calif.: Wadsworth, 1998. A detailed look at how capital punishment works today, and how it affects the various participants—guards, executioners, and prisoners. The author argues that the death penalty has a hidden cost in psychological damage and brutalization to all involved and should be replaced by other forms of effective punishment.

Jones, Lou, and Michael Radelet. *Final Exposure: Portraits from Death Row*. Boston: Northeastern University Press, 1996. Photographer Lou Jones presents powerful images from death row with interviews and commentary. The presentation seeks to humanize the lives and deaths of the condemned and to challenge popular preconceptions.

Kunstler, William M. *Beyond a Reasonable Doubt? The Original Trial of Caryl Chessman*. New York: William Morrow, 1961. An account by a prominent advocate of the famous case of Caryl Chessman, executed in 1960. Chessman became renowned for several books he wrote while on death row.

Leslie, Jack. *Decathlon of Death*. Mill Valley, Calif.: Tarquin Books, 1979. Discusses three California cases leading to executions in 1955.

Levine, Stephen. *Death Row*. San Francisco: Glide Publications, 1972. Essays, the majority of which were written by death row inmates.

Lezin, Katya. *Finding Life on Death Row: Profiles of Six Inmates*. Boston: Northeastern University Press, 1999. A compelling narrative of six cases of death row inmates represented by Stephen Bright, director of the Southern Center for Human Rights. According to the author, these cases show how people with mental conditions such as schizophrenia or with drug problems that call their competency into question were improperly charged and often represented by incompetent attorneys. Judges, driven by political ambition, often refuse to consider mitigating factors such as retardation or a battered woman being in imminent danger. The legal techniques used by the Center's attorneys to try to stop death sentences are explained.

Light, Ken (photographer), and Suzanne Donovan. *Texas Death Row*. Jackson: University Press of Mississippi, 1997. Uses striking photographs and a thoughtful essay to present the condemned prisoners, their jailers, and the social decisions represented by America's busiest death row.

Magee, Doug. *Slow Coming Dark: Interviews on Death Row*. New York: Pilgrim Press, 1980. Focuses on the lives of death row inmates before and after their death sentences.

———. *What Murder Leaves Behind: The Victim's Family*. New York: Dodd, Mead, 1983. Accounts of the impact of homicide on victims' families. The book is important for evaluating arguments in favor of capital punishment.

Mailer, Norman. *The Executioner's Song*. Boston: Little, Brown, 1979. A fictionalized account of the last months of convicted murderer Gary Gilmore, the first person executed following the reinstatement of capital punishment in 1976.

Malone, Dan, and Howard Swindle. *America's Condemned: Death Row Inmates in Their Own Words*. Kansas City: Andrews & McMeel, 1999. Presents the results of a 1995 survey of the nation's death row inmates by the *Dallas Morning News*. Seven hundred inmates responded to 75 questions about their crimes, experiences, and attitudes, resulting in a fascinating and comprehensive set of data.

Masters, Jarvis Jay, and Melody E. Chavis. *Finding Freedom: Writings from Death Row*. Junction City, Calif.: Padma Publishing, 1997. A collection of vivid, moving stories about life on death row, told by a convict who became a Tibetan Buddhist. The stories are told without polemics or an overt anti–capital punishment agenda.

Miller, Arthur S., and Jeffrey Brown. *Death by Installments: The Ordeal of Willie Francis*. Westport, Conn.: Greenwood Press, 1988. Study of the case of Willie Francis, who was executed in Louisiana in 1947 after a previous attempt to put him to death in the electric chair had failed.

Miller, Kent S., and Betty Davis Miller. *To Kill and Be Killed: Case Studies From Florida's Death Row*. Pasadena, Calif.: Hope Publishing House, 1991. A psychological and social profile of inmates on Florida's death row.

Reid, Don, and John Gurwell. *Eyewitness*. Houston: Cordovan Press, 1973. A journalist's eyewitness account of nearly 200 executions in Texas.

Smith, Edgar. *Brief Against Death*. New York: Knopf, 1968. An autobiographical account of trial for murder, conviction, and years on death row.

Teeters, Negley K. *Hang by the Neck: The Legal Use of Scaffold and Noose, Gibbet, Stake, and Firing Squad from Colonial Times to the Present*. Springfield, Ill.: Charles C. Thomas, 1967. An excellent history of executions and execution methods in the United States.

Trombley, Stephen. *The Execution Protocol: Inside America's Capital Punishment Industry*. New York: Crown Books, 1998. Combines history with interviews, including one with the designer of the lethal injection apparatus. Trombley focuses on the method of execution and the people involved in implementing it.

Annotated Bibliography

United States—Breach of Trust: Physician Participation in Executions in the United States. New York: Human Rights Watch, 1994. Statements prepared by the Physicians for Human Rights, Human Rights Watch, American College of Physicians, and National Coalition to Abolish the Death Penalty. These groups strongly oppose participation of doctors in any aspect of the capital punishment process, viewing it as a serious breach of a physician's duty to "do no harm" under the Hippocratic Oath.

ARTICLES AND PAPERS

Abu-Jamal, Mumia. "Live from Death Row" in *The Progressive*, vol. 59, May 1995, pp. 18ff. The African-American journalist and death row inmate whose battle against the death penalty has become a cause célèbre describes his day to day life in a Pennsylvania correctional facility. He recounts incidents that reflect the irony, human dimension, and small injustices that accumulate in prison life.

American Medical Association. Council on Ethical and Judicial Affairs. "Physician Participation in Capital Punishment" in *JAMA, Journal of the American Medical Association*, v. 270, 1993, pp. 365–368. Declares that medical ethics requires that physicians not participate in executions, such as by pronouncing death.

Anderson, George M. "Fourteen Years on Death Row: An Interview with Joseph Green Brown" in *America*, vol. 176, March 29, 1997, pp. 17ff. Interview with Joseph Green Brown (now known as Shabaka) who was imprisoned on death row since his conviction for murder in 1974 and nearly executed in 1987. His sentenced was reversed only 15 hours before his execution when the appeals court ruled that the prosecutor had knowingly allowed perjured testimony by the state's main witness. He describes his hasty trial and life in prison.

Bedau, Hugo Adam. "A Condemned Man's Last Wish: Organ Donation and a 'Meaningful' Death" in *Hastings Center Report* 9, February 1979, pp. 16–17. Debate with Michael Zeik over whether a condemned man should be allowed to choose the method by which he dies so that his organs can be donated. Bedau opposes the concept while Zeik endorses it.

Beichman, Arnold. "The First Electrocution" in *Commentary*, vol. 35, 1963, pp. 410–419. Recounts the history of the first electrocution in 1890. Beichman discusses the dispute between George Westinghouse and Thomas Edison. Edison argued that the person electrocuted would feel no pain.

Blaustein, Susan. "Witness to Another Execution: In Texas, Death Walks an Assembly Line" in *Harper's Magazine*, vol. 288, May 1994, pp. 53ff. Describes the prison complex at Huntsville, Texas, arguably the death capital of the United States with as many as two executions a week and the rituals that are carried out by guards, executioners, protesters, and supporters of the death penalty.

Brown, Edmund G., and Dick Adler. "Private Mercy: As Debate Over the Death Penalty Opens Again, a Former State Governor Reflects on the 36 People He Let Die" in *Common Cause Magazine* 15, July–August 1989, pp. 28ff. Former California governor Edmund G. Brown reflects on his experience of being the "court of last resort" for clemency appeals from death row prisoners. He describes how he changed from being an advocate of capital punishment to supporting its abolition.

Clarke, Kevin. "Waiting for Gacy" in *U.S. Catholic*, vol. 59, November 1994, pp. 33ff. Account that weaves together the author's experience of events surrounding the execution of mass killer John Wayne Gacy and the legal and moral issues surrounding capital punishment.

Corum, Michael. "The Art of Hanging" in *Wild West*, vol. 9, December 1996, p. 50. Describes techniques used in hanging during the 18th and 19th centuries. It is not easy to hang a person "cleanly," avoiding strangulation or decapitation.

Creque, Stuart A. "Killing with Kindness" in *National Review*, vol. 47, September 11, 1995, pp. 51ff. Advocates use of nitrogen asphyxiation (breathing pure nitrogen) as an alternative method of execution that would be painless and reliable, avoiding botched executions.

Dix, Tara K. "A Night Spent Waiting for Death to Come: College Students Join Vigil at Prison, Learn of Crime, Punishment" in *National Catholic Reporter*, vol. 34, May 1, 1998, pp. 3ff. Describes the experience of an execution vigil by Indiana college students, woven together with the personal and legal details of the case of Gary Burris that had brought them there. The effect of the crime on the victim's family is also discussed.

Dorius, Earl F. "Personal Recollections of the Gary Gilmore Case" in *Woodrow Wilson Journal of Law*, vol. 3, 1981, pp. 49–129. Diary account by a Utah assistant attorney general who was one of the state attorneys in the case that culminated in the execution of Gary Gilmore in 1977.

Egbert, Lawrence D. "Physicians and the Death Penalty" in *America*, vol. 178, March 7, 1998, pp. 15ff. An anesthesiologist describes his investigation into the practice of lethal injection and declares his opposition to capital punishment.

Grogan, David, and Barbara Sandler. "Looking for a Lifeline: With His Days Numbered, Convicted Killer Girvies Davis Takes to the Internet" in *People Weekly*, vol. 43, May 22, 1995, pp. 59ff. Describes the attempt by a death row inmate to use the Internet to arouse public support for his appeal for clemency. (Davis was executed at about the time the article was published.)

Annotated Bibliography

Hentoff, Nat. "Execution in Your Living Room" in *The Progressive*, vol. 55, November 1991, pp. 16ff. Argues that while opponents of the death penalty are uncomfortable with televising executions for fear the public will support their continuance, banning the camera violates the First Amendment and is dangerous to civil liberties.

Hitchens, Christopher. "Scenes from an Execution" in *Vanity Fair*, January 1998, pp. 30ff. A reporter witnesses, reacts to, and analyses the execution by lethal injection of a convicted murderer in Potosi, Missouri.

Kenworthy, Tom. "'I'm Going to Grant You Life'; Parents of Slain Gay Student Agree to Prison for His Killer" in *Washington Post*, November 5, 1999, p. A02. Reports the dramatic moment when the parents of Matthew Shepherd asked the court to spare the life of the convicted murderer of their son.

Kozinski, Alex. "Tinkering with Death: A Death-Penalty Judge Reflects: How Does It Feel to Send Another Man to Die?" in *The New Yorker*, vol. 72, February 10, 1997, pp. 48ff. A U.S. Appeals Court judge describes the experience of hearing last-minute appeals from condemned prisoners. While he supports the death penalty, he acknowledges the difficulty and anguish of the position he and his fellow judges are put in by the system.

Lehman, Susan. "A Matter of Engineering: Capital Punishment as a Technical Problem" in *The Atlantic*, vol. 265, February 1990, p. 26ff. Examines the technical aspects of electrocution.

Nesbitt, Charlotte A. "Managing Death Row" in *Corrections Today*, vol. 48, July 1986, pp. 90–94ff. Describes an American Correctional Association project to determine how death row inmates are managed.

"Letter from Death Row" in *America*, vol. 180, February 13, 1999, p. 24. New Year's letter from Sister Helen Prejean, author of *Dead Man Walking*. She recounts her weeks spent with death row inmate Dobie Williams as he prepared for his execution.

"The Long Goodbye" in *The New Republic*, vol. 210, June 6, 1994, p. 8. Editorial describes botched executions such as that of John Wayne Gacy, which showed that even the "humane" method of lethal injection could be botched. Such executions are cruel and unusual punishment that violates the Eighth Amendment and calls the entire institution of capital punishment into question.

Owens, Virginia Stem. "Karla Faye's Final Stop" in *Christianity Today*, vol. 42, July 13, 198, pp. 45ff. Account of the execution of Karla Faye Tucker, the convicted murderer who became a born-again Christian and the focus for appeals for clemency by religious groups.

"Physician Participation in Capital Punishment" in *JAMA, The Journal of the American Medical Association*, vol. 270, July 21, 1993, pp. 365ff.

Statement and guidelines on medical participation in executions, from the AMA's Committee on Ethical and Judicial Affairs. Definitions are provided to clarify the AMA's 1980 denunciation of the practice.

Ponessa, Jeanne. "Have We Seen Our Last Execution by Hanging?" in *Governing*, vol. 6, June 1993, pp. 14ff. Suggests that the hanging of Wesley Dodd in Washington State is likely to be the last hanging in the United States. (After the hanging, legislation abolishing hanging was introduced into the Washington legislature.)

Radelet, Michael L. "Poorly Executed" in *Harper's Magazine*, vol. 290, June 1995, pp. 21ff. Describes six failed or botched executions using lethal injection, lethal gas, and the electric chair.

Radelet, Michael L., Margaret Vandiver, and Felix Bernardo. "Families, Prisons, and Men with Death Sentences: The Human Impact of Structured Uncertainty" in *Journal of Family Issues*, vol. 4, 1983, pp. 593–612. Discusses the psychological impact of the death sentence and appeals process on death row inmates and their families.

Schneider, Alison. "Through an Executioner's Eyes" in *The Chronicle of Higher Education*, vol. 42, May 17, 1996, p. A6. Interviews Donald Cubana, author of *Death at Midnight: The Confession of an Executioner*. Cabana describes how he became an opponent of the death penalty while serving as warden of the Mississippi State Penitentiary. A young inmate he had befriended was executed, and what he saw as a senseless act led him to leave the corrections field.

Seligman, Daniel. "Doctors Confront the Death Penalty" in *Fortune*, vol. 129, June 27, 1994, p. 136. Criticizes the recent declaration by the American Medical Association against physician participation in executions. Seligman argues that the AMA should have left the matter up to the conscience of individual doctors.

Shapiro, Andrew L. "End of the Rope?" in *The Nation*, vol. 258, June 6, 1994, pp. 772ff. Reports that an appeals court in the state of Washington has refused to prevent the hanging of convicted murderer Charles Campbell, declaring that this method of execution is not "unnecessarily painful." The author disagrees and believes that given the risk of very painful botched hangings, they can no longer be justified in a civilized society.

Smith, A. LaMont, and Robert M. Carter. "Count Down for Death" in *Crime and Delinquency*, vol. 15, 1969, pp. 77–93. A detailed chronicle of the life of an inmate in California during the week before his execution.

Smykla, John Ortiz. "The Human Impact of Capital Punishment: Interviews with Families of Persons on Death Row" in *Journal of Criminal Justice*, vol. 15, 1987, pp. 331–347. Explores the impact of capital punishment on those who work with or are related to death row inmates.

Stumbo, Bella. "Executing the Murderer: The Victims' Families Speak Out" in *Redbook*, vol. 186, November 1995, pp. 58ff. Recounts the responses of relatives of murder victims in five different cases. The emotions expressed differ greatly from case to case: some experience a degree of satisfaction, while others are disappointed or repelled by the process.

Sullivan, Robert A. "Waiting to Die: A Prisoner's Diary from Florida's Death Row" in *Rolling Stone*, March 6, 1980, pp. 48–49ff. Excerpts from a diary account of experiences on death row. Sullivan was executed four years later.

Truog, Robert D., and Troyen A. Brennan. "Participation of Physicians in Capital Punishment" in *The New England Journal of Medicine*, vol. 329, October 28, 1993, pp. 1346ff. Argues that participation of medical professionals in executions is a violation of fundamental principles of medical ethics. It is different from mercy killing, which is done on behalf of (and with the agreement of) the patient, rather than on behalf of the state. Medical societies should revoke the licenses of doctors who participate in capital punishment.

"U.S. Physicians and the Death Penalty" in *The Lancet*, vol. 343, March 26, 1994, p. 743. Summarizes the statements made by American medical organizations with regard to physician participation in capital punishment.

Weisberg, Jacob. "This Is Your Death; Capital Punishment, What Really Happens" in *The New Republic*, vol. 205, July 1, 1991, pp. 23ff. Describes what people would see if they could actually view each of the five currently authorized methods of execution: hanging, the firing squad, the electric chair, the gas chamber, and lethal injection. All these methods of execution probably cause at least some pain, and any can be botched, leading to grotesque results.

WEB DOCUMENTS

American Medical Association. Council on Ethical and Judicial Affairs. "Physician Participation in Capital Punishment: Evaluating Competence of Condemned Prisoners; Treating Condemned Prisoners to Restore Competence." Texas Medical Association. Available online. URL: http://www.texmed.org/physician_advocacy/ethics/pa_texmedfeb97ethcp.htm. Posted on January 1997. Discusses the ethics of doctors' participation in various parts of the capital sentencing process. The page states that physicians may testify at pretrial, sentencing, and post-conviction hearings, but should not be required to do so if they conscientiously oppose participation in the capital punishment system. Treating incompetent prisoners so they can become competent to be executed is a serious ethical dilemma, and states should instead automatically commute the sentence of an incompetent condemned prisoner to life imprisonment.

"Angel on Death Row: The Real Life Case in 'Dead Man Walking.'" PBS. Available online. URL: http://www.pbs.org/wgbh/pages/frontline/angel/. Downloaded on December 17, 1999. Web page with transcripts of interviews, links, and resources relating to a *Frontline* episode originally broadcast April 9, 1996. The page discusses the cases that made up the material for Sister Helen Prejean's book and the subsequent movie.

Bobit, Bonnie. "Death Row." Bobit Publishing Company. Available online. URL: http://www.editionnine.deathrowbook.com/noflash/nf_home.htm. Downloaded on December 20, 1999. Web site of "death row trivia" excerpted from the book *Death Row*, which contains detailed profiles of each and every inmate on death row.

"The Execution." PBS. Available online. URL: http://www.pbs.org/wgbh/pages/frontline/shows/execution/. Downloaded on December 17, 1999. Web page with transcripts, video, interviews, links, and resources relating to a *Frontline* episode originally broadcast on February 9, 1999.

Physicians Committee for Responsible Medicine. Medicine and Society Curriculum. "Physician-Assisted Suicide and Capital Punishment: What Role Should Physicians Play?" Available online. URL: http://www.pcrm.org/issues/Medicine_and_Society_Curriculum/med_soc_curr_4.html. Downloaded on December 8, 1999. Offers a pro-and-con look at physician participation in causing death through euthanasia, assisted suicide, and capital punishment. The page offers hypothetical cases for discussion.

AUDIOVISUAL MATERIALS

Dead Man Walking. MGM/UA Contemporary Classics, 1995, 122 minutes. Available on VHS and DVD. Video of the award-winning movie in which Susan Sarandon plays Sister Helen Prejean, the nun who went to death row to minister to inmates and confront the capital punishment system.

Execution at Midnight: Death Row/Last Hours. A&E Network. VHS video of an episode of *Investigative Reports* produced by Jim Thebault, [n.d.]. Available for ordering online at http://store.aetv.com/. Follows several Missouri death row inmates through their last day, as they talk about their lives, crimes, and impending death. The video shows both the ritual of execution proceeding within the prison walls and the vigils of death penalty opponents and supporters outside.

Gary Gilmore: A Fight to Die. A&E Network. VHS video of an episode of *Biography,* [n.d.]. Available for ordering online at http://store.aetv.com/.

Explores the bizarre case of Gary Gilmore, which had a number of unusual features. Gilmore's execution was the first after the restoration of capital punishment by the Supreme Court, the method used (firing squad) is virtually extinct in America, and Gilmore, far from fighting to postpone his execution, sought to die as soon as possible.

The History of Executioners. A&E Network. VHS video of an episode of *Investigative Reports*, [n.d.]. Available for ordering online at http://store. aetv.com/. Explores the history of capital punishment and the methods of execution from ancient Sumeria to today's "humane" lethal injections. The video includes interviews with judges, executioners, and families of murder victims.

I Want to Live. MGM/UA Vintage Classics, 1998. Available on VHS. Video of the 1958 classic movie in which Susan Hayward won an Oscar for her portrayal of death row inmate Barbara Graham, who some journalists became convinced had been framed.

Mr. Death: The Rise and Fall of Fred A. Leuchter, Jr. Directed by Errol Morris. Lions Gate Films, 1999. The sardonic, funny, yet disturbing story of a man who "reinvented" the electric chair and other modern execution devices. The second half of the film explores Leuchter's transformation into a neo-Nazi and Holocaust denier.

The Thin Blue Line. Directed and written by Errol Morris. J.G. Films, 1988. [Out of print in video and laserdisc.] Uses innovative cinematic techniques that go beyond the traditional documentary form to portray the story of drifter Randall Dale Adams and his fateful involvement with young David Harris that resulted in what Morris believes to be a wrongful conviction and death sentence. A compelling and evocative score by Philip Glass sets the mood.

INTERNATIONAL AND HISTORICAL WORKS

This final section presents works on the administration of the death penalty outside the United States, international movements to abolish capital punishment, and works dealing with the history of capital punishment (generally in the 19th century and earlier).

BOOKS

Atholl, Justin. *Shadow of the Gallows.* London: John Long, 1954. A history of capital punishment in England.

Capital Punishment

Bowers, William J., Glenn L. Pierce, and John F. McDevitt. *Legal Homicide: Death As Punishment in America, 1864–1892.* Boston: Northeastern University Press, 1984. An important source providing extensive information on executions during the second half of the nineteenth century. Portions of this work were previously published in *Executions in America.*

Chandler, David B. *Capital Punishment in Canada: A Sociological Study of Repressive Law.* Toronto: McClelland and Stewart, 1976. Discusses capital punishment and the social background to the debate over the death penalty in Canada.

Cooper, David D. *The Lesson of the Scaffold: The Public Execution Controversy in Victorian England.* Athens: Ohio University Press, 1974. Discusses social attitudes surrounding efforts to abolish capital punishment in Victorian England.

Evans, E. P. *The Criminal Prosecution and Capital Punishment of Animals.* Union, N.J.: Lawbook Exchange, 1998. Recounts amazing and bizarre court cases from the early history of English law where animals such as chickens, rats, bees, and pigs were tried, convicted, and executed for various offenses.Evans uses these cases as a mirror to explore the often contradictory attitudes people have about justice and responsibility.

Evans, Richard J. *Rituals of Retribution: Capital Punishment in German Politics and Society Since the Seventeenth Century.* New York: Oxford University Press, 1996. Describes the role of capital punishment in German customary law, and then examines how the system broke down under the impact of social change during the early 19th century. Discusses the brief liberal triumph of 1848 in which the death penalty was abolished, its reinstatement by Bismarck in the 1880s, and the role of social Darwinism in harsh treatment of criminals in the early 20th century, leading to Hitler's use of large scale executions. Evans also discusses these events in the light of modern theories by Norbert Elias, Michel Foucault, and others.

Fogelson, Robert M. *Capital Punishment: Nineteenth Century Arguments.* New York: Arno Press, 1974. Describes arguments in the Massachusetts legislature during the 19th century on capital punishment.

Gatrell, V. A. C. *The Hanging Tree: Execution and the English People, 1770–1868.* New York: Oxford University Press, 1996. A history of public executions in England during the later 18th and early 19th centuries. Describes the reactions of crowds and literary observers such as James Boswell, Lord Byron, William Makepeace Thackeray, and Charles Dickens.

Gowers, Sir Ernest. *A Life for a Life? The Problem of Capital Punishment.* London: Chatto and Windus, 1956. A discussion of capital punishment issues in England by the chairman of the 1953 Royal Commission on Capital Punishment. He argues strongly for abolition of the death penalty.

Annotated Bibliography

Great Britain Royal Commission on Capital Punishment. *Report of the Royal Commission on Capital Punishment: Presented to Parliament by Command of Her Majesty, Sept. 1953.* Westport, Conn.: Greenwood Publishing Group, 1980. Report of a commission charged with considering whether Britain's capital punishment system should be modified. The report is in three parts: I. Limitation or modification of the liability to suffer capital punishment; II. The alternative to capital punishment; III. Methods of execution. The report includes extensive appendices.

Hood, R. *Death Penalty: A World-Wide Perspective.* New York: Oxford University Press, 1989. Analyzes worldwide data to determine the extent to which countries around the world administer their death penalty laws in compliance with international standards of fairness and human rights.

Jayewardene, C. H. S. *The Penalty of Death: The Canadian Experience.* Lexington, Mass.: D. C. Heath, 1977. Considers Canada's moratorium on and subsequent abolition of the death penalty.

Koestler, Arthur. *Dialogue with Death.* New York: Macmillan, 1966. An account of Koestler's capture, incarceration, and death sentence during the Spanish Civil War.

Levy, Barbara. *Legacy of Death.* Englewood Cliffs, N.J.: Prentice-Hall, 1973. History of the Sanson family, the official executioners of France for seven generations.

Linebaugh, Peter. *The London Hanged: Crime & Civil Society in the Eighteenth Century.* New York: Cambridge University Press, 1993. This historical study of capital punishment in 18th century London concludes that the criminal law and capital punishment were tools used by the upper class to keep the lower classes in line. Many capital crimes reflected the generalized outrage of the poor about their miserable conditions. The upper class enacted new laws to protect their status as property owners and employers.

Mackey, Philip English. *Hanging in the Balance: The Anti-Capital Punishment Movement in New York State, 1776–1861.* New York: Garland Books, 1982. Recounts the history of New York State's death penalty law and attempts to reform it, from the American Revolution to the Civil War.

Masur, Louis P. *Rites of Execution: Capital Punishment and the Transformation of American Culture, 1776–1865.* New York: Oxford University Press, 1991. A history that shows the institutionalization of capital punishment as reflecting major changes in American society from the nation's beginnings through the Civil War.

McManners, John. *Death and the Enlightenment: Changing Attitudes to Death Among Christians and Unbelievers in Eighteenth-Century France.* New York: Oxford University Press, 1981. Includes information on public executions and changing attitudes toward death.

Mikhlin, Aleksandr Solomonovich. *The Death Penalty in Russia.* Boston: Kluwer Law International, 1999. A survey and statistical study of the operation of capital punishment in Russia, including theories and regimes of punishment, the appeal and pardon process, and methods of execution.

Pierrepoint, Albert. *Executioner: Pierrepoint.* Sevenoaks, Kent, England: Hodder and Stoughton, 1974. The autobiography of a British executioner whose father and uncle had preceded him in the trade; the author now opposes capital punishment.

Ramcharan, B. G. *The Right to Life in International Law.* Dordrecht, Mass.: Martinus Nijhoff, 1985. Surveys international human rights law, including capital punishment.

Schabas, William A. *The Abolition of the Death Penalty in International Law.* 2d edition. New York: Cambridge University Press, 1997. Describes the development of standards in international law that have effectively abolished the death penalty in many countries. Topics covered include the Universal Declaration of Human Rights, the International Convenant on Civil and Political Rights, and the death penalty in international humanitarian law, European human rights law, and Inter-American human rights law.

————. *The Death Penalty As Cruel Treatment and Torture: Capital Punishment Challenged in the World's Courts.* Boston: Northeastern University Press, 1996. The author argues on the basis of universal declarations of human rights and principles of international law that both sentencing procedures and methods of execution used throughout the world violate legal norms, and that capital punishment should be abolished worldwide. Schabas includes both historical background and detailed analysis of recent decisions.

Schabas, William A., Hugo Adam Bedau, and Peter Hodgkinson. *The International Sourcebook on Capital Punishment, 1997.* Boston: Northeastern University Press, 1997. A compendium of recent articles, book reviews, documents, and statistics dealing with capital punishment. The book is useful for comparative studies and reference.

Spierenburg, Pieter. *The Spectacle of Suffering: Executions and the Evolution of Repression: From a Preindustrial Metropolis to the European Experience.* New York: Cambridge University Press, 1984. Explores the evolution of capital punishment debates in an international historical context.

Taylor, D. *Crime, Policing and Punishment in England, 1750–1914.* New York: St. Martin's Press, 1998. History of the development and operation of the criminal justice system in Great Britain, 1750–1914, including the role of capital punishment.

Thesing, William B. *Executions and the British Experience from the 17th to the 20th Century: A Collection of Essays.* Jefferson, N.C.: McFarland & Co., 1990. A collection of 10 essays examining the responses of various writers to the issue of capital punishment over a span of three centuries of British history. Writers discussed include Henry Fielding and Samuel Johnson as well as authors who use psychological or sociological insights.

Woffinden, Bob. *Miscarriages of Justice*. London: Hodder and Stoughton, 1987. Discusses several cases of mistaken conviction in the British Isles after World War II.

ARTICLES AND PAPERS

Carro, Jorge L. "Capital Punishment from a Global Perspective: The Death Penalty: Right or Wrong?" in *Vital Speeches*, vol. 62, August 1, 1996, pp. 629ff. Text of an address by a University of Cincinnati law professor who argues that the judiciary must resist public pressure for swift resolution of death penalty cases. Carro places the American legal issues in the context of the broad international movement to abolish capital punishment and recounts his experience practicing law in Cuba, where executions often followed sentencing by days or even hours.

"China's Arbitrary State" in *The Economist* (U.S.), vol. 338, March 23, 1996, pp. 31ff. Reports that despite China's considerable economic process, the nation's legal system has changed little. Indeed, the number of different capital offenses has risen to 68 from 21 in 1980. There are still public mass executions. The prospects for success of criminal procedure reform recently enacted by the National People's Congress are uncertain.

"The Cruel and Ever More Unusual Punishment" in *The Economist* (U.S.), vol. 351, May 15, 1999, p. 95. Describes the growing international movement to abolish the death penalty, especially the efforts of the European Union. Only the United States, together with some Asian and Islamic countries, continue to hold out. The U.S. public may support the death penalty, but it is unlikely that they would support the level of executions needed to achieve any possible benefit in deterrence.

"Death and the American" in *The Economist* (U.S.), vol. 343, June 21, 1997, p. 32. Contrasts American and European attitudes toward the death penalty. Although popular sentiment in Europe is actually fairly strongly pro–death penalty, European politicians tend to put a damper on such attitudes while American politicians amplify and exploit them. The concept of "just retribution" seems to have a particular resonance in American culture.

Drinan, Robert F. "Even South Africa Drops Death Penalty" in *National Catholic Reporter*, vol. 31, July 28, 1995, p. 20. Reports that South Africa, despite its history of bloody repression, has now banned capital punishment.

Evans, Kathy. "Beheaded for Brewing Beer" in *World Press Review*, vol. 42, July 1995, p. 38. Describes a recent increase in executions in Saudi Arabia that have aroused the concern of human rights activists. Saudi officials blame a crime wave including drug trafficking by immigrant workers.

Evans, Richard. "Justice Seen, Justice Done? Abolishing Public Executions in 19th-century Germany" in *History Today*, vol. 46, April 1996, pp. 20ff. Detailed study of reforms in Germany and throughout much of Europe that resulted in the abolition of public executions. Evans discusses conflicting opinions over whether the change was due to humanitarian impulses or fear by authorities that crowds would get out of hand or would sympathize too much with the offender.

French, Howard. "Japan Carries Out Executions in Near-Secrecy" in *New York Times*. December 20, 1999, n.p. Reports on the extremely secretive procedure for capital punishment in Japan. The only public news is a single terse sentence naming the condemned. The death penalty is popular in Japan, and the secrecy helps preserve the status quo by preventing activists and the media from developing a cause célèbre.

Goshko, John M. "Helms Calls Death Row Probe 'Absurd U.N. Charade'" in *Washington Post*, October 8, 1997, p. A07. Reports on Senator Jesse Helms, chairman of the Senate Foreign Relations Committee, denouncing Senegal's Bacre Waly Ndiaye of the UN Human Rights Commission for his interviews with death row prisoners as part of a UN human rights investigation.

Grupp, Stanley. "Some Historical Aspects of the Pardon in England" in *The American Journal of Legal History*, vol. 7, 1963, pp. 51–62. Provides historical background on the power of pardon and its affect on capital punishment in England before the 18th century.

Kay, Marvin L. Michael, and Loren Lee Cary. "'The Planters Suffer Little or Nothing': North Carolina Compensations for Executed Slaves, 1748–1772" in *Science and Society*, vol. 40, 1976, pp. 288–306. Describes the rather curious practice by which southern colonies compensated slave owners when their slaves were executed.

Kikuta, K. "Death Penalty in Japan: Why Hasn't It Been Abolished?" in *International Journal of Comparative and Applied Criminal Justice*, vol. 17, Spring/Fall 1993, pp. 57–75. Gives reasons for Japan's insistence on retaining the death penalty. Kikuta suggests that strong public support for the sanction may be self-perpetuating. The author also suggests strategies for gradual abolition, such as promoting life sentences as an alternative.

King, W. M. "The End of an Era: Denver's Last Legal Public Execution, July 27, 1886" in *Journal of Negro History*, vol. 68, 1983, pp. 37–53. Recounts how the execution of Andrew Green became the catalyst that pushed Colorado governor Job Cooper to sign legislation ending public hangings.

"Mandela Says 'No' to Reinstating the Death Penalty in South Africa" in *Jet*, vol. 90, October 14, 1996, p. 17. Quotes the South African president on his refusal to consider reinstating capital punishment, despite the support of 93 percent of the population for the death penalty, driven by fear of mounting violent crime.

Ndiaye, Bacre Waly. "Death Penalty Issue Addressed by Special Rapporteur" in *UN Chronicle*, vol. 35, Summer 1998, p. 72. Presents the comments by the special rapporteur on death penalty issues to the United Nations Commission on Human Rights on January 22, 1998. Ndiaye's observes that U.S. state authorities have virtually no knowledge of the requirements of international agreements in this area. He recommends that the U.S. adopt a moratorium on executions and permanently bar the execution of juveniles and the mentally disabled.

O'Sullivan, John. "O'Sullivan's First Law" in *National Review*, vol. 41, October 27, 1989, p. 14. Critique of Amnesty International's efforts against the death penalty.

Phillips, Andrew. "A Deathly Silence" in *Maclean's*, December 7, 1998, p. 24. Reports on the case of Stanley Faulder, a Canadian convicted of murder and awaiting execution in a Huntsville, Texas death row. The case raised international issues such as the defendant's right to consult with his nation's consulate, but neither Texas courts nor the public have shown much interest in his appeal.

Selin, Thorsten. "Two Myths in the History of Capital Punishment" in *Journal of Criminal Law, Criminology, and Police Science*, vol. 50, 1959. Argues that estimates of the number of executions in earlier historical eras are inflated.

"Singapore, World Execution Capital" in *The Economist* (U.S.), vol. 351, April 3, 1999, p. 35. Reports on the high number of hangings in Singapore, which leads the world in proportional numbers of executions.

Walker, J. "Homicides and the Death Penalty in Australia—1915–1975" in *Criminology Australia*, vol. 3, January–February 1992, pp. 19–25. Study of Australian homicide rates that finds little or no deterrence effect of the death penalty.

Weinstein, Henry. "Foreigners on Death Rows Denied Rights, U.S. Says" in *Los Angeles Times*, December 10, 1998, p. A1. Reports on the violations of the rights of as many as 70 foreign nationals on U.S. death rows who were never allowed their right to consult their nation's consul as required by international agreements. This issue is coming to a head with executions of foreigners in Texas and California.

Wyatt, Donald W. "Rhode Island's Last Execution" in *Yankee*, vol. 59, February 1995, pp. 122ff. Recounts the execution of a 22-year-old Irish immigrant for murder in 1845, after sentencing by an all-Protestant jury. Public outcry led to the abolition of capital punishment in the state in 1852.

Youkey, Bill. "Invitation to a Beheading: Fighting Crime in Saudi Arabia" in *Commonweal*, vol. 122, February 10, 1995, pp. 4ff. Reports on the growing use of public beheadings in Saudi Arabia. Describes the beheading of a convicted Pakistani drug dealer. Religion and the justice system are inextricably intertwined.

WEB DOCUMENTS

"Capital Punishment—UK: the Resource Site." Available online. URL: http://www.geocities.com/CapitolHill/6142/index.html. Downloaded March 6, 2000. This site provides an overview of capital punishment in the United Kingdom and worldwide, including historical chronology and statistics, and number and methods of execution.

"The Death Penalty: Abolitionist and Retentionist Countries." Available online. URL: http://worldpolicy.org/americas/dp/maps-dp.html. Posted October 1, 1999. This set of color-coded world maps shows the status of the world's nations with regard to capital punishment. Nations are divided into four categories: those currently retaining the death penalty, those who have the sanction on the books but haven't used it for at least 10 years, those who limit the death penalty to a few exceptional crimes (such as treason), and nations that have completely abolished capital punishment.

United Nations High Commissioner for Human Rights. "Special Rapporteur on Extrajudicial, Summary, or Arbitrary Executions." Available online. URL: http://www.unhchr.ch/html/menu2/7/b/execut/exe_main.htm. Downloaded March 6, 2000. This is the home page for the UN investigatory agency charged with reporting on executions carried out outside the legal process, but it also has broader concerns about the fair administration of the death penalty in judicial systems. The site explains the agency's purpose, methods, and scope, and provides guidelines for submitting information about possible abuses.

Potas, Ivan and John Walker. "Capital Punishment in Australia." Australian Institute of Criminology. *Trends and Issues in Crime and Criminal Justice*, no. 3 February 1987. Also available online in PDF format. URL: http://www.aic.gov.au/publications/tandi/tandiO3.html. Downloaded on March 6, 2000.

CHAPTER 8

ORGANIZATIONS AND AGENCIES

This chapter presents a selection of organizations and agencies concerned with capital punishment and related issues. The listings are broken down into four categories:

- Government and academic organizations that provide statistics and other resources. These usually do not take a position.
- National advocacy organizations, nearly all of which promote abolition of the death penalty.
- State and local organizations: these are mainly abolitionist in perspective.
- International organizations for the abolition of capital punishment.

Where available, web (URL) and e-mail addresses have been provided in addition to phone numbers and postal addresses. A brief description of the group's focus or activities is also given for government and academic organizations and for international organizations. (Phrases in quotes are taken from the organizations' web sites.)

It should be noted that contact information for the more local or obscure groups frequently changes, and such groups often become defunct or dormant. The major resource web sites discussed in Chapter 6 are a good place to look for up-to-date information and links to organizations.

GOVERNMENT AND ACADEMIC ORGANIZATIONS

Bureau of Justice Statistics
URL: http://www.ojp.usdoj.gov/ bjs/welcome.html
E-mail: askbjs@ojp.usdoj.gov
Phone: (800) 732-3277

633 Indiana Avenue, NW, #1142 Washington, DC 20531
Provides a wide range of statistics relating to the criminal justice system, including courts, sentencing,

and corrections (prisons). Produces annual summary report on capital punishment in the United States.

Cornell Law School Death Penalty Project
URL: http://www.lawschool. cornell.edu/lawlibrary/death/ index.html
E-mail: ds104@cornell.edu
Consists of a Capital Punishment Clinic offering law students the opportunity to learn about capital defense practice while helping capital defense attorneys; a program for continuing education for capital defense attorneys; and a research and data collection program.

Federal Bureau of Investigation
URL: http://www.fbi.gov
Phone: (202) 324-3691
935 Pennsylvania Avenue, NW
Washington, DC 20535-0001
Issues the uniform crime reports, a basic source for criminal justice research.

Federal Bureau of Prisons
URL: http://www.bop.gov
E-mail: webmaster@bop.gov
Phone: (202) 307-3198
320 1st Street, NW
Washington, DC 20534
Provides extensive information about the operation of prisons.

House Judiciary Committee
URL: http://www.house.gov/ judiciary
E-mail: Judiciary@mail.house.gov
Phone: (202) 225-3951

2138 Rayburn House Office Building
Washington, DC 20515
Important source for crime and justice-related legislative developments in the House of Representatives.

Justice Research and Statistics Association
URL: http://www.jrsainfo.org/
E-mail: webmaster@jrsa.org
Phone: (202) 842-9330
777 North Capital Street, NE, #801
Washington, DC 20002
Clearinghouse for state Statistical Analysis Centers (SACs); provides coordination and training for government statisticians and other researchers.

Legal Services Corporation
URL: http://www.lsc.gov/ index2.htm
E-mail: info@lsc.gov
Phone: (202) 336-8800
750 1st Street, NE, 10th Floor
Washington, DC 20002-4250
Nonprofit federally funded corporation that promotes "equal justice under the law for all Americans." The corporation funds local legal services agencies for representing the poor.

National Institute of Justice
URL: http://www.ojp.usdoj.gov/ nij/
E-mail: askncjrs@ncjrs.org
Phone: (202) 307-2942
810 7th Street, NW
Washington, DC 20531

Research and development arm of the Department of Justice. The institute provides the NCJRS (National Criminal Justice Reference Service) abstracts database, an important source of information on criminal justice–related publications.

Senate Judiciary Committee
**URL: http://www.senate.gov/
~judiciary/**
**E-mail: meryl_vlatas@judiciary.
senate.gov (webmaster)**
Phone: (202) 224-5225
Dirksen Senate Office Building
Room SD-224
Washington, DC 20510-6275
Important source for information on pending federal criminal justice legislation.

U.S. Commission on Civil Rights
**URL: http://www.usccr.gov/
index.html**
**E-mail: wwwadmin@usccr.gov
(webmaster)**
Phone: (202) 376-7700
624 9th Street, Northwest, #700
Washington, DC 20425
An "independent, bipartisan fact-finding agency" established to investigate civil rights violations and to collect information about civil rights problems.

U.S. Department of Justice
URL: http://www.usdoj.gov/
E-mail: web@usdoj.gov
Phone: (202) 514-2007
950 Pennsylvania Avenue, NW
Washington, DC 20530-0001

Parent organization of the Attorney General's Office, FBI, Federal Bureau of Prisons, Bureau of Justice Statistics, and other organizations.

U.S. Sentencing Commission
**URL: http://www.ussc.gov/
index.htm**
E-mail: pubaffairs@ussc.gov
Phone: (202) 273-4500
1 Columbus Circle, NE
Suite 2-500 South Lobby
Washington, DC 20002-8002
Government body charged with establishing and reviewing federal sentencing guidelines.

U.S. Supreme Court
**URL: http://supct.law.cornell.
edu/supct/**
Phone: (202) 479-3211
1 1st Street, NE
Washington, DC 20543
(Note that URL given is for the home page for the Legal Information Institute; not home page of the Court itself)

NATIONAL ADVOCACY GROUPS

Abolitionist Action Committee
**URL: http://abolition.org/www.
cuadp.org/aac.htm**
E-mail: aac@abolition.org
Phone: (800) 973-6548
c/o Citizens United for Alternatives to the Death Penalty

177 U.S. Highway #1 B-297
Tequesta, FL 33469
"An ad-hoc group of individuals committed to highly visible and effective public education for alternatives to the death penalty through nonviolent direct action." The group is a division of Citizens United for Alternatives to the Death Penalty (CUADP).

American Bar Association (ABA)
Criminal Justice Section
URL: http://www.abanet.org/
  crimjust/
E-mail: crimjustice@abanet.org
Phone: (202) 662-1500
740 15th Street, NW
Washington, DC 20005-1002
Division of America's largest lawyers' organization that is concerned with criminal procedure issues.

American Civil Liberties Union
  (ACLU)
Capital Punishment Project
  (CPP)
URL: http://www.aclu.org/
  issues/death/hmdp.html
E-mail: cappunaclu@aol.com
Phone: (202) 675-2319
122 Maryland Avenue, NE
Washington DC 20002
The ACLU is a consistent and vigorous opponent of capital punishment on constitutional, procedural, and philosophical grounds. The CPP files "friend of the court" briefs in capital punishment cases. Their web site includes an index to ACLU materials on capital punishment, congressional action, archives, and links to other resources. There is also a searchable news database.

American Friends Service
  Committee
URL: http://www.afsc.org/
E-mail: pclark@afsc.org
Phone: (215) 241-7130
1501 Cherry Street
Philadelphia, PA 19102
National Quaker Organization has a variety of local programs that work on anti–death penalty advocacy.

Amnesty International U.S.A.
Program to Abolish the Death
  Penalty
URL: http://www.amnesty-usa.
  org/abolish/index.html
E-mail: dpprogram@aiusa.org
Phone (800) AMNESTY
600 Pennsylvania Avenue,
  5th Floor
Washington, DC 20003
U.S. division of the worldwide human rights organization. The organization has a web page for its anti–death penalty campaign at http://www.amnesty-usa. org/abolish/index.html that provides information and a featured campaign.

Campaign to End the Death
  Penalty
URL: http://www.
  nodeathpenalty.org
To contact via e-mail, go to
URL: http://www.nodeathpenalty.
  org/contact.html
Phone: (312) 409-7145

P.O. Box 25730
Chicago, IL 60625
National organization with chapters in a number of cities. Its purpose is to publicize and campaign for death penalty issues. The campaign has a newsletter, *The New Abolitionist*, which is also available at the organization's web site.

Capital Punishment Research Project
Phone: (334) 693-5225
P.O. Drawer 277
Headland, AL 36345
Maintains a massive database of information about executions in America, with over 19,000 case files.

Catholics Against Capital Punishment
URL: http://www.igc.org/cacp/
E-mail: cacp@bellatlantic.net
Phone: (301) 652-1125
P.O. Box 3125
Arlington, VA 22203
National organization to promote abolition of capital punishment in accordance with the teachings of the Catholic Church.

Center for Constitutional Rights
E-mail: mratner@igc.org
Phone: (212) 614-6430
666 Broadway, 7th Floor
New York, NY 10012
A general organization dedicated to advance and to protect the rights guaranteed in the U.S. Constitution and the Universal Declaration of Human Rights.

Citizens United for Alternatives to the Death Penalty (CUADP)
URL: www.cuadp.org
E-mail: cuadp@cuadp.org
Phone: (800) 973-6548
177 U.S. Highway #1 B-297
Tequesta, FL 33469
Organization that coordinates and assists anti–death penalty campaigns, working toward an eventual goal of abolishing capital punishment in the United States. Their web site provides a variety of resources and action items.

Citizens United for Rehabilitation of Errants (CURE)
URL: http://www.curenational.org/index1.html
Phone: (202) 789-2126
P.O. Box 2310
Washington, DC 20013-2310
A criminal justice and prison reform organization that seeks effective alternatives for the reduction of crime and humane treatment of the incarcerated. CURE has a number of state and local affiliates.

Death Penalty Information Center (DPIC)
URL: http://www.essential.org/dpic
E-mail: dpic@essential.org
Phone: (202) 293-6970
1320 Eighteenth Street, NW, 5th Floor
Washington, DC 20036
Provides in-depth resources and briefing papers on death penalty–related issues for the media and the general public. DPIC is not

explicitly abolitionist but heavily emphasizes abolitionist materials.

Death Penalty Net
URL: http://www.deathpenalty.
net/
E-mail: (via web) http://www.
deathpenalty.net/Feedback.html
Web site maintained by a group of anti–death penalty organizations. Provides information on the basic issues such as execution of the innocent, execution and race, women, and juveniles.

Death Row Support Project
URL: http://www.scn.org/
activism/wcadp/write.html
E-mail: Bgross@igc.org (Rachel Gross)
Phone: (219) 982-7480
P.O. Box 600
Liberty Mills, IN 46946
Primarily engaged in providing support for death row inmates and facilitating correspondence ("pen pals") to keep them linked to the outside community.

Equal Justice USA
URL: http://www.igc.org/
quixote/ej/
E-mail: www.jusa@curixote.org
Phone: (301) 864-2182
Quixote Center
P.O. Box 5206
Hyattsville, MD 20782
A program of the Quixote Center, primarily working on a "Moratorium Now!" campaign to gather resolutions calling for an end to the death penalty.

Fellowship of Reconciliation
URL: http://www.nonviolence.
org/for/
E-mail: for@forusa.org
Phone: (914) 358-4601
P.O. Box 271
Nyack, NY 10960
An interfaith peace and justice organization with many local affiliates. Its areas of concern include criminal justice, prisons, and opposition to the death penalty.

Feminists for Life of America
URL: http://www.serve.com/
fem4life
E-mail: comackay@erols.com
(webmaster)
Phone: (202) 737-3352
733 15th Street, NW, Suite 1100
Washington, DC 20005
A pro-life feminist organization that opposes the death penalty, along with abortion and euthanasia.

Friends Committee on National Legislation
URL: http://www.fcnl.org/
E-mail: fcnl@fcnl.org
Phone: (202) 547-6000
245 Second Street, NE
Washington, DC 20002
A Quaker organization promoting social justice through legislation. It includes abolition of the death penalty as one of its issues.

Friends Committee to Abolish the Death Penalty
URL: http://www.quaker.org/
fcadp/
E-mail: fcadp@aol.com
Phone: (215) 951-0330

3721 Midvale Avenue
Philadelphia, PA 19129
Quaker group that advocates against the death penalty and promotes alternatives such as "restorative justice."

Jewish Peace Fellowship
URL: http://www.jewishpeacefellowship.org/
E-mail: jpf@forusa.org
Phone: (914) 358-4601
P.O. Box 271
Nyack, NY 10960
Organization that began as a counseling service for Jewish conscientious objectors but now serves a variety of social justice issues. The organization opposes capital punishment as a violation of Jewish tradition.

Journey of Hope . . . From Violence to Healing Inc.
URL: http://www.journeyofhope.org
E-mail: Kevin@journeyofhope.org
Phone: (918) 743-8119
P.O. Box 50293
Tulsa, OK 74150
An educational organization whose purpose is "to spotlight murder victims family members who do not seek revenge, and have chosen to promote compassion for all humanity."

Justice for All
URL: http://www.jfa.net
E-mail: jfanet@msn.com
Phone: (713) 935-9300
Pro–death penalty and victim's rights organization. The organization opposes appeals and paroles for murderers. Web site has news and case updates and offers a mail list.

Mennonite Central Committee USA
Office of Criminal Justice
URL: http://www.mcc.org/
E-mail: mccwash@mcc.org (Washington office)
Phone: (717) 859-1151
21 South 12th Street
P.O. Box 500
Akron, PA 17501-0500
Works on a variety of social issues including abolition of the death penalty.

Murder Victims Families for Reconciliation
URL: http://www.mvfr.org/
Phone: (617) 868-0007
2161 Massachusetts Avenue
Cambridge, MA 02140
Organization that unites families of murder victims with families of executed persons. The organization seeks to promote healing for victims as an alternative to the death penalty and the "cycle of violence."

NAACP Legal Defense and Educational Fund
URL: http://www.ldfla.org/framest.htm (Western Regional Office)
Phone: (212) 219-1900
99 Hudson Street, 16th Floor
New York, NY 10013-2897
One of the oldest and most effective civil rights litigation organizations. The organization played an important role in the legal assault on the

death penalty that culminated in the *Furman v. Georgia* case in 1972.

National Association of Criminal Defense Lawyers (NACDL)
URL: http://www.criminaljustice.org
E-mail: assist@nacdl.com
Phone: (202) 872-8600
1025 Connecticut Avenue, NW, Suite 901
Washington, DC 20036
Organization of defense attorneys promoting legal reforms and the rights of defendants. NACDL has a committee on death penalty issues.

National Bar Association
URL: http://www.nationalbar.org/
E-mail: nba@nationalbar.org
Phone: (202) 842-3900
1225 W Street, NW
Washington, DC 20001-4217
Organization of (primarily African-American) attorneys, dedicated to professional development and the protection of civil rights.

National Black Police Association
URL: http://www.blackpolice.org/
E-mail: NBPANATOFC@world.att.net
Phone: (202) 986-2070
3251 Mt. Pleasant Street, NW, 2nd Floor
Washington, DC 20010-2103
Promotes relations between police and the community and criminal justice reform.

National Coalition to Abolish the Death Penalty
URL: http://www.ncadp.org
E-mail: info@ncadp.org
Phone: (202) 387-3890
1436 U Street, NW
Suite 104
Washington, DC 20009
Educational coalition organization whose web site provides news, alerts and links, including a link to a comprehensive directory of abolitionist organizations.

National Conference of Black Lawyers
URL: http://www.geocities.com/CapitolHill/Lobby/9470/national.html
Phone: (212) 864-4000
2 West 125th Street
New York, NY 10027
Activist civil rights legal organization. The organization advocates against the death penalty.

National Council on Crime and Delinquency
URL: http://www.cascomm.com/users/nccd/
E-mail: nccd@hooked.net
Phone: (415) 896-6223
685 Market Street, #620
San Francisco, CA 94105
Conducts research to develop policies to reduce crime and delinquency, and to promote a fair, humane, and effective legal system. The organization opposes capital punishment as a violation of these principles.

National District Attorney's Association
URL: http://www.ndaa.org

Phone: (703) 549-4253
99 Canal Center Plaza, #510
Alexandria, VA 22314
Formed in 1950 (originally as the "National Association of County and Prosecuting Attorneys") in response to the growth of crime and the increasing demand for community protection.

National Lawyers Guild (NLG)
URL: http://www.nlg.org/
Phone: (212) 627-2656
126 University Place, 5th Floor
New York, NY 10003
Left-wing lawyers group that seeks to use the legal system to protect people from oppressive institutions. The NLG works on many issues including the death penalty.

National Legal Aid & Defender
    Association
URL: http://www.nlada.org
E-mail: info@nlada.org
Phone: (202) 452-0620
1625 K Street, NW,
    Suite 800
Washington, DC 20006
Provides training and support for lawyers who represent poor people, including death row inmates.

Parents of Murdered Children
URL: http://www.pomc.com/
E-mail: NatPOMC@aol.com
Phone: (888) 818-POMC
100 East Eighth Street, B-41
Cincinnati, OH 45202
Supports families of homicide victims, assists in solving murder cases and in opposing parole for convicted murderers, advocates tougher criminal justice policies, and helps victims cope with the criminal justice system.

Partisan Defense Committee
Phone: (510) 839-0852
P.O. Box 77462
San Francisco, CA 94107
Left-wing organization that fights for issues such as opposition to the death penalty on the basis of class struggle.

Presbyterian Church (USA)
Criminal Justice Program
URL: http://horeb.pcusa.org/
    crim_justice/
E-mail: kathy_lancaster@
    pcusa.org
Phone: (502) 569-5810
100 Witherspoon Street
Louisville, KY 40202
Part of the National Ministries Division, a ministry of the General Assembly Council, Presbyterian Church (USA). The organization examines the criminal justice system from a religious perspective.

Prison Radio Project
URL: http://www.quixote.org/
    prp/
E-mail: radioqc@sirius.com
Phone: (415) 648-4505
558 Capp Street
San Francisco, CA 94110
Helps set up opportunities for prisoners to communicate with the public via radio. Death row inmates and

death penalty issues are one of the organization's focuses.

Project Hope to Abolish the Death Penalty
URL: http://www.pip.dknet.dk/
~pip1019/dp/wings/ (Danish affiliate)
E-mail: vineyfig@mindspring.com
Phone: (334) 499-2380
11076 Country Road 267
Lanett, AL 36863
Originally founded in 1989 by Alabama death row inmates, this organization seeks to educate the public about death penalty issues and to support death row inmates and their families.

Religious Organizing Against the Death Penalty Project
URL: http://www.envisioning.
org/home.htm
Phone: (215) 241-7130
c/o Criminal Justice Program
American Friends Service Committee
1501 Cherry Street
Philadelphia, PA 19102
Organization dedicated to mobilizing and coordinating the efforts of the many churches that have come out against the death penalty. The organization promotes advocacy and helping faith communities minister to the needs of death row inmates, their families, and the families of crime victims.

The Sentencing Project
URL: http://www.
sentencingproject.org/
Phone: (202) 628-0871
918 F Street, NW #501
Washington, DC 20004
Independent criminal justice policy analysis, education, and research group. The project calls for a "rational debate on crime and punishment."

Southern Center for Human Rights (SCHR)
URL: http://www.schr.org/
center/index.html
E-mail: rights@schr.org
Phone: (404) 688-1202
83 Poplar Street, NW
Atlanta, GA 30303-2122
Organization that advocates for civil rights and criminal justice reform, including rights of capital defendants. SCHR also has a Death Penalty Resource Counsel provided by the National Association of Criminal Defense Lawyers.

Truth in Justice
URL: http://www.
truthinjustice.org/
E-mail: dberry@i2020.net
Organization dedicated to freeing persons believed to be wholly innocent and wrongly convicted. The organization critiques use of forensic evidence ("junk science"). Their web site offers links to books and other resources.

STATE AND LOCAL ADVOCACY ORGANIZATIONS

Note: States listed here represent those in which the debate of capital punishment is most active. For reasons of space, state affiliates of national organizations are not listed here. Contact the national organization (or see its web site) for information about local affiliates.

ARIZONA

Coalition of Arizonans to Abolish the Death Penalty
URL: http://www.azstarnet.com/~afscaz/caadp.html
E-mail: ann.nichols@asu.edu or norgard@azstarnet.com
Phone: (520) 325-6240
931 N 5th Avenue
Tucson, AZ 85705

Sanctity of Life, People Against Executions (SOLPAE)
E-mail: norguard@azstarnet.com
Phone: (520) 888-8522

ARKANSAS

Arkansas Coalition to Abolish the Death Penalty
Phone: (501) 374-2660
103 W. Capitol, Suite 1120
Little Rock, AR 72201

CALIFORNIA

California Appellate Project
Phone: (800) 779-0507
One Ecker Place, Suite 400
San Francisco, CA 94105

California Coalition for Alternatives to the Death Penalty
URL: http://www.igc.apc.org/sjpc/ccadp.htm
E-mail: sjpc@sjpeace.org
Phone: (408) 297-2299

Death Penalty Focus of California
URL: http://www.deathpenalty.org/
E-mail: dpfocus@aol.com
Phone: (415) 243-0143
74 New Montgomery, Suite 250
San Francisco, CA 94105

Northern California Coalition to Abolish the Death Penalty
Phone: (510) 836-3013
1611 Telegraph Avenue, Suite 1501
Oakland, CA 94612

COLORADO

Coloradans Against the Death Penalty
Phone: (303) 777-5482
P.O. Box 1745
Denver, CO 80201-1745

Colorado Students Against the Death Penalty
Phone: (303) 448-9517

Capital Punishment

735 Arapahoe Avenue, #103
Boulder, CO 80302

CONNECTICUT

Connecticut Network Against
the Death Penalty
Phone: (203) 860-5995
55 Van Dyke Avenue
Hartford, CT 06106

United Students Against the
Death Penalty
URL: http://members.tripod.
com/~deathpenalty/
E-mail: ahinds@wesleyan.edu
Phone: (860) 685-4734
Box 4592
222 Church St.
Middletown, CT 06459

DELAWARE

Delaware Citizens Opposed to
the Death Penalty
Phone: (302) 656-2721
833 Market Street Mall
Wilmington, DE 19801-3078

Pacem in Terris
Phone: (302) 656-2721
900 Washington Street
Wilmington, DE 19801

FLORIDA

Florida Coalition Against the
Death Penalty
Phone: (813) 332-3449
2363 Union Street
Fort Myers, FL 33901

Gainesville Citizens Against the
Death Penalty
Phone: (352) 373-7899
1215 Northwest 4th Street
Gainesville, FL 32601

GEORGIA

Georgia Resource Center
Phone: (404) 614-2014
101 Marrieta Tower, Suite 3300
Atlanta, GA 30303

Koinonia Prison and Jail Project
URL: http://www.ccda.org/g-l/
koinonia.html
E-mail: koinonia@habitat.org
Phone: (912) 924-0391
1324 Georgia Highway 49 South
Americus, GA 31709

New Hope House
Phone: (770) 358-1148
P.O. Box 1213
Griffin, GA 30224

Team Defense Project
Phone: (404) 688-8116
P.O. Box 1728
Atlanta, GA 30301

IDAHO

Capital Habeas Unit
Phone: (208) 883-1472
201 North Main Street
Moscow, ID 83843

ILLINOIS

Campaign to End the Death
Penalty

Phone: (312) 409-7145
P.O. Box 25730
Chicago, IL 60625

**Illinois Coalition Against the
  Death Penalty**
URL: http://www.keynet.net/
  ~icadp/index.html
E-mail: icadp@hotmail.com
Phone: (312) 849-2279
180 North Michigan Avenue,
  Suite 2300
Chicago, IL 60601

**Lutheran Social Services
Prisoner & Family Ministry**
Phone: (708) 635-4627
1001 Touhy Avenue
Des Plaines, IL 60018

INDIANA

**Hoosiers Opposing Executions
  (HOPE)**
Phone: (219) 533-0756
1325 Greencroft Drive, Apt. 350
Goshen, IN 46526

**Indiana Coalition to Abolish the
  Death Penalty**
Phone: (317) 924-1553
c/o Indianapolis Peace & Justice
  Center
500 East 42nd
Indianapolis, IN 46205

Indiana Public Defender Council
URL: http://www.ai.org/pdc/
  index.html
E-mail: ipdc@iquest.net
Phone: (317) 232-2490

309 West Washington Street,
  Suite 401
Indianapolis, IN 46204

L.O.V.(E), Inc.
Love Over Vengeance/Empathy
Phone: (219) 879-4146
P.O. Box 2151
Michigan City, IN 46361

IOWA

Criminal Justice Ministries
Phone: (515) 284-5047
P.O. Box 70033
Des Moines, IA 50311

**Iowans Against the Death
  Penalty Fund**
Phone: (515) 277-8096
P.O. Box 27120
West Des Moines, IA 50265

KANSAS

**Kansas Coalition Against the
  Death Penalty**
Phone: (913) 321-9400
636 Tauromee
Kansas City, KS 66101

**Kansas Religious Leaders
  Against the Death Penalty**
Phone: (913) 272-8921
4000 Drury Lane
Topeka, KS 66604

**Murder Victims Families
  Reconciliation**
Victim Services
Phone: (913) 232-5958
1176 SW Warren Avenue
Topeka, KS 66604

KENTUCKY

Kentucky Coalition Against
   Executions
Catholic Conference
   of Kentucky
E-mail: KYCONFL@aol.com
Phone: (302) 656-2721
1042 Burlington Lane
Frankfort, KY 40601

Kentucky Coalition to Abolish
   the Death Penalty
URL: http://www.kcadp.org/
E-mail: kcadp@earthlink.net
Phone: (502) 634-6005

LOUISIANA

Bienville House Center for
   Peace & Justice
Capital Trials Project
URL: http://www.igc.apc.org/
   bhcfpj/
Phone: (504) 344-0405
P.O. Box 4363
Baton Rouge, LA 70821

Louisiana Coalition to Abolish
   the Death Penalty
Pilgrimage for Life
Phone: (504) 344-LIVE
P.O. Box 64635
Baton Rouge, LA 70896

MAINE

Mainers Against the Death
   Penalty
Phone: (207) 774-5444
P.O. Box 8703
Portland, ME 04101

MARYLAND

Maryland CASE
URL: http://www.mdcase.org/
E-mail: info@mdcase.org
Phone: (410) 243-8020
P.O. Box 39205
Baltimore, MD 21212

MASSACHUSETTS

Massachusetts Citizens Against
   the Death Penalty
Phone: (617) 338-1040
P.O. Box 3404
Boston, MA 02101

MICHIGAN

AFSC Michigan Criminal Justice
   Program
Phone: (313) 761-8283
1414 Hill Street
Ann Arbor, MI 48104

Michigan Coalition Against the
   Death Penalty
Phone: (734) 487-9058
Box 31-5303
Detroit, MI 48231

Michigan Committee Against
   Capital Punishment
Phone: (517) 484-4165
Michigan National Tower, #1202
Lansing, MI 48933

MINNESOTA

Minnesota Advocates for Human
   Rights
Death Penalty Defense Project

Organizations and Agencies

URL: http://www.mnadvocates.
  org/
E-mail: hrights@mnadvocates.org
Phone: (612) 341-3302
310 4th Avenue South, Suite 1000
Minneapolis, MN 55415-1012

Minnesota Coalition to Abolish
  the Death Penalty
Phone: (612) 522-2423
1021 West Broadway
Minneapolis, MN 55411

MISSOURI

Criminal Justice Ministry
Phone: (314) 241-0862
1408 South Tenth Street
St. Louis, MO 63104

Eastern Missouri Coalition to
  Abolish the Death Penalty
E-mail: mphillips@igc.apc.org
  (Margaret Phillips)
Phone: (314) 241-8062
1408 South 10th Street
St. Louis, MO 63104

Missouri Association for Social
  Welfare (MASW)—Criminal
  Justice Task Force
Phone: (573) 634-2901
308 E. High St.
Jefferson City, MO 65101

Missouri Coalition Against the
  Death Penalty
Phone: (573) 635-7239
P.O. Box 1022
Jefferson City, MO 65102

Western Missouri Coalition to
  Abolish the Death Penalty
URL: http://qni.com/~billw/
  death/wmcadp.html
E-mail: cburnett@vax1.umkc.edu
  (Cathy Burnett)
Phone: (816) 235-1600
Department of Sociology
University of Missouri
5100 Rock Hill Road
Kansas City, MO 64110

MONTANA

Montana Ad Hoc Abolition
  Coalition
URL: http://www.helenamontana.
  com/abolition/

Montana Coalition to Abolish
  the Death Penalty
Phone: (406) 585-2408
9650 Hyalite Canyon Road
Bozeman, MT 59715

NEBRASKA

Nebraskans Against the Death
  Penalty
Phone: (402) 474-6575
c/o ACLU
941 O Street, Suite 1020
Lincoln, Northeast 68508

NEVADA

Rising Son Ministries, Inc.
Phone: (702) 454-6430
2686 Dulcinea Drive
Henderson, NV 89014

239

NEW HAMPSHIRE

New Hampshire Citizens
  Against the Death Penalty
41 A Court Street
Dover, NH 03820

NEW JERSEY

New Jersey Coalition to Abolish
  the Death Penalty
Phone: (201) 642-2086
c/o ACLU of New Jersey
2 Washington Place
Newark, NJ 07102

Trenton Colloquia Organizing
  Project
E-mail: kathy-s@k2nesoft.com
Phone: (609) 810-0543
810 South Cropwell Road
Marlton, NJ 08053-2052

NEW MEXICO

Coalition for Prisoners' Rights
Prison Project of Santa Fe
Services for Prisoners and Their
  Families
Phone: (505) 982-9520
P.O. Box 1911
Santa Fe, NM 87504

Committee to Stop Executions
Phone: (505) 827-3909
P.O. Box 1911
Santa Fe, NM 87504

NEW YORK

New York Civil Liberties Union
URL: http://www.nyclu.org/

E-mail: NYCLUnas@aol.com
Phone: (212) 344-3005
125 Broad Street
New York, NY 10004

New York Lawyers Against the
  Death Penalty
Phone: (212) 735-2226
019 Third Avenue, 35th Floor
New York, NY 10022-3897

New York State Coalition for
  Criminal Justice
Phone: (716) 773-1426
P.O. Box 207
Grand Island, NY 14072

New Yorkers Against the Death
  Penalty
Phone: (518) 453-6797
40 North Main Avenue
Albany, NY 12203

NORTH CAROLINA

Carolina Justice Policy Center
Phone: (919) 682-1149
P.O. Box 309
Durham, NC 27702

Center for Death Penalty
  Litigation
Phone: (919) 956-9545
123 W. Main Street, Suite 500
Durham, NC 27701

North Carolinians Against the
  Death Penalty
Phone: (919) 682-1149
P.O. Box 309
Durham, NC 27702-0309

People of Faith Against the Death Penalty
URL: http://www.netpath.net/~ucch/pfadp/
E-mail: SJDear@aol.com (Stephen J. Dear)
Phone: (919) 557-7567
157 1/2 E. Franklin St.
Chapel Hill NC 27514

Seamless Garment Network
URL: http://www.seamless-garment.org/
P.O. Box 792
Garner, NC 27529

Western Carolinians for Criminal Justice
Phone: (704) 252-2485
P.O. Box 7472
Asheville, NC 28802

OHIO

Ohioans to Stop Executions
URL: http://www.otse.org/
E-mail: otse_webmaster@yahoo.com
Phone: (614) 224-7147
9 E. Long Street, Suite 201
Columbus, OH 43215

Ohio Coalition to Abolish the Death Penalty
Phone: (614) 445-7670
612 American Boulevard
Columbus, OH 43223

Ohio Death Penalty Task Force
Phone: (216) 375-6793
University of Akron Law School
Akron, OH 44325

OKLAHOMA

Death Penalty Institute of Oklahoma
URL: http://www.dpio.org/
E-mail: Comments@dpio.org

Oklahoma Coalition to Abolish the Death Penalty
URL: http://www.ocadp.org
Phone: (405) 720-7441
P.O. Box 713
Oklahoma City, OK 73101

Oklahoma Indigent Defense System
Capital Post-Conviction Division
Legal Services
URL: http://www.state.ok.us/~oids/
E-mail: randy@appellate.oids.ou.edu
Phone: (405) 325-0802
1660 Cross Center Drive
Norman, OK 73019

OREGON

Oregon Coalition to Abolish the Death Penalty
URL: http://members.tripod.com/ocadp/
E-mail: ocadp@CompuServe.com
Phone: (503) 249-1556
P.O. Box 361
Portland, OR 97207

PENNSYLVANIA

Center Region Coalition to Abolish the Death Penalty
Phone: (814) 238-1983

P.O. Box 502
State College, PA 16804

Defender Association of
Philadelphia
Phone: (215) 568-3190
70 North 17th Street
Philadelphia, PA 19103

Northeast Pennsylvania Coalition Against the Death Penalty
Phone: (717) 342-4117
712 Linden Street
Scranton, PA 18503

Pennsylvania Abolitionists
United Against the Death
Penalty
Phone: (610) 891-8968
Jeffrey Garis, Director
P.O. Box 58128
Philadelphia, PA 19102

Pennsylvania Coalition to
Abolish the Death Penalty
Phone: (215) 564-6005 ext. 7919
c/o Pennsylvania Prison Society
2000 Spring Garden Street
Philadelphia, PA 19130

Pennsylvania Post-Conviction
Organization
Phone: (215) 451-6500
437 Chestnut Street, Suite 501
Philadelphia, PA 19106

Western Pennsylvania Coalition
Against the Death Penalty
Phone: (412) 761-4319
P.O. Box 9125
Pittsburgh, PA 15224

SOUTH CAROLINA

South Carolina Coalition Against
the Death Penalty
E-mail: blpears@scarolina.edu
Phone: (803) 776-7471
6248 Yorkshire Drive
Columbia, SC 29208

SOUTH DAKOTA

South Dakota Peace & Justice
Center
URL: http://www.dailypost.com/
~sdpjc/index.html
E-mail: sdpjc@dailypost.com
Phone: (605) 882-2822
P.O. Box 405
Watertown, SD 57201

TENNESSEE

Tennessee Association of
Criminal Defense Lawyers
URL: http://www.tncrimlaw.
com/tacdl
E-mail: tacdl@aol.com
Phone: (615) 726-1225
207 3rd Avenue North, 2nd Floor
Nashville, TN 37201-1610

Tennessee Coalition to Abolish
State Killing
URL: http://www.tcask.org/
E-mail: ssharpe@cdc.net
Phone: (615) 329-0048
Box 120552
Nashville, TN 37212

Tennessee Friends Outside
URL: http://members.xoom.
com/sjdicks/index.htm

Organizations and Agencies

E-mail: sdicks@bellsouth.net
  (Shirley Dicks)
Phone: (615) 893-9862
P.O. Box 321
Murfreesboro, TN 37130

TEXAS

Texas Coalition to Abolish the
  Death Penalty
URL: http://lonestar.texas.net/
  ~acohen/tcadp/
E-mail: tcadp@adelante.com
Phone: (713) 520-0300
3400 Montrose, Suite 312
Houston, TX 77006

Texas Resource Center
Phone: (512) 320-8300
P.O. Box 280
Austin, TX 78767

VERMONT

Vermont Coalition Against the
  Death Penalty
Phone: (802) 885-3327
c/o Unitarian Universalist Church
21 Fairground Road
Springfield, VT 05156

VIRGINIA

Virginia Capital Representation
Resource Center
Phone: (804) 643-6845
P.O. Box 506
Richmond, VA 23204

Virginians for Alternatives to the
  Death Penalty
URL: http://www.vadp.org/
E-mail: mail@vadp.org
Phone: (804) 263-8148
P.O. Box 4804
Charlottesville, VA 22905

WASHINGTON

Inland Northwest Death Penalty
  Abolition Group (INDPAG)
Phone: (509) 838-7870
224 S. Howard Street
Spokane, WA 99204

Washington Association of
  Criminal Defense Lawyers
Phone: (206) 623-1302
810 3rd Avenue, Suite #421
Seattle, WA 98104

Washington Coalition to Abolish
  the Death Penalty
URL: http://www.scn.org/
  activism/wcadp/index.html
E-mail: wcadp@scn.org
Phone: (206) 622-8952
705 Second Avenue, #300
Seattle, WA 98104

WEST VIRGINIA

West Virginians Against the
  Death Penalty
Phone: (304) 445-2980
Anderson Hospitality House
P.O. Box 579
Anderson, WV 24910-0579

INTERNATIONAL ADVOCACY ORGANIZATIONS

Amnesty International
URL: http://www.amnesty.org
E-mail: admin-us@aiusa.org
  (U.S. office)
Phone: (202) 544-0200
  (Washington, D.C. office)
600 Pennsylvania Avenue
  Southeast, 5th floor
Washington, D.C. 20003
Worldwide human rights organization that has adopted abolition of the death penalty as one of its ongoing campaigns. Web page for death penalty is at URL: http://www.amnesty.org/ailib/intcam/dp/index.html.

Canadian Coalition Against the Death Penalty
URL: http://members.tripod.com/ccadp/homepage.htm
E-mail: ccadp@home.com
Phone: (416) 686-1630
80 Lillington Avenue
Toronto, Ontario M1N-3K7
CANADA
Organization of Canadians working to abolish capital punishment in the United States. They are also active on behalf of Canadians facing the death penalty in the United States.

Hands Off Cain (Nessuno Tochi Caino)
URL: http://www.handsoffcain.org/english/home.html
Phone: (212) 813-1334
866 UN Plaza #408
New York, NY 10017
An Italian-based international "citizens' and parliamentarian's league" dedicated to the worldwide abolition of the death penalty. The organization provides statistics and reports on the status of the death penalty in various nations and in international law.

Human Rights Watch
URL: http://www.hrw.org
E-mail: hrwnyc@hrw.org
Phone: (212) 290-4700
350 Fifth Avenue, 34th Floor
New York, NY 10018-3299
Although not directed explicitly toward abolition of the death penalty, the organization has an active campaign against abusive prison conditions throughout the world.

International Bannister Foundation
URL: http://www.banfound.u-net.com/homepage.htm
E-mail: postmaster@banfound.u-net.com
Phone: +44 01383 823611
28 Craigdimas Grove
Dalgety Bay
Fife, KY11 9XR
Scotland
UNITED KINGDOM
International organization founded in memory of executed death row inmate Alan Jeffrey Bannister. De-

scribes itself as "an anti–capital punishment and pro–human rights action and support group." The organization has chapters in a number of U.S., European, and other world cities.

The Lamp of Hope
Texas Death Row Project
URL: http://www.lampofhope.
  org/index.html
P.O. Box 305
League City, TX 77574-0305
Organization in support of Texas death row prisoners. Has affiliates in Canada and several European nations.

Lifelines
URL: http://www.crynwr.com/
  lifelines/
E-mail: 101702.1425@
  compuserve.com
96 Fallowfield
Cambridge CB4 1PF
UNITED KINGDOM
British-based organization that offers correspondence and support to U.S. death row prisoners.

Lifespark
Swiss Organization Against the
  Death Penalty
URL: http://www.geocities.com/
  EnchantedForest/Glade/3216/
Phone: 0041 91 968 14 83
P.O. Box 4002
Basel
SWITZERLAND
Organization emphasizes correspondence with and support services for death row inmates, lobbying, and coordination with international human rights organizations.

Moratorium 2000 International
  Campaign
URL: http://www.santegidio.org/
  solid/pdm/pdm_eng.htm
E-mail: m2000@santegidio.org
International petition drive sponsored by the Communita di Sant Egidio. Its goal is for a worldwide moratorium on the death penalty and eventual abolition. Petition text is available online and the petition can be signed electronically.

PART III

APPENDICES

APPENDIX A

STATISTICS ON
CAPITAL PUNISHMENT

The following selection of tables and charts summarizes recent trends in death sentences and executions in the United States.

PERSONS SENTENCED TO DEATH

On the chart Persons Under Sentence of Death, 1953–1999, note the dip between 1972 and 1976. In 1972, the Supreme Court suspended imposition

PERSONS UNDER SENTENCE OF DEATH, 1953–1999

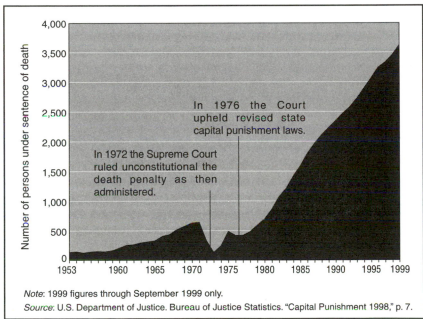

Note: 1999 figures through September 1999 only.

Source: U.S. Department of Justice. Bureau of Justice Statistics. "Capital Punishment 1998," p. 7.

249

of the death penalty, ruling that capital punishment as then practiced by the states was unconstitutional. In 1976 the Supreme Court approved revised state procedures and imposition of the death penalty resumed. Notice that the number of persons under sentence of death has climbed sharply—and steadily—since then.

The demographics of death row inmates are important to the death penalty debate because of legal and moral arguments that claim that the sanction falls disproportionately on the poor, on the uneducated, and on racial minorities. (See accompanying chart Persons Under Sentence of Death, by Race, 1968–1998 and table Demographic Characteristics of Prisoners Under Sentence of Death, 1998.)

PERSONS UNDER SENTENCE OF DEATH, BY RACE, 1968–1998

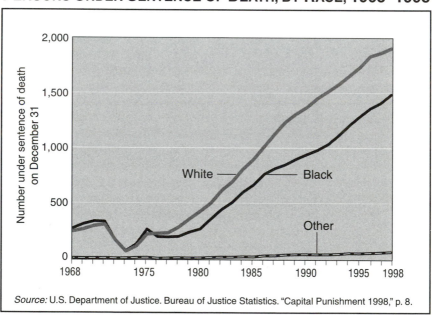

Source: U.S. Department of Justice. Bureau of Justice Statistics. "Capital Punishment 1998," p. 8.

Appendix A

DEMOGRAPHIC CHARACTERISTICS OF PRISONERS UNDER SENTENCE OF DEATH, 1998

Characteristic	Prisoners under sentence of death, 1998		
	Year-end	Admissions	Removals
Total number under sentence of death	3,452	285	161
Gender			
Male	98.6%	97.2%	97.5%
Female	1.4	2.8	2.5
Race			
White	55.2%	50.9%	64.0%
Black	43.0	46.3	33.5
Other*	1.7	2.8	2.5
Hispanic origin			
Hispanic	10.0%	15.4%	10.2%
Non-Hispanic	90.0	84.6	89.8
Education			
8th grade or less	14.3%	15.1%	17.1%
9th–11th grade	37.6	39.3	37.1
High school graduate/GED	38.0	36.8	37.1
Any College	10.1	8.8	8.6
Median	11th	11th	11th
Marital status			
Married	24.0%	17.1%	23.6%
Divorced/separated	20.8	16.0	22.3
Widowed	2.7	4.7	4.1
Never married	52.5	62.3	50.0

Note: Calculations are based on those cases for which data were reported. Missing data by category were as follows:

Characteristic	Year-end	Admissions	Removals
Hispanic origin	299	38	14
Education	501	46	21
Marital status	327	28	13

*At year-end 1997, "other" consisted of 28 American Indians, 17 Asians, and 11 self-identified Hispanics. During 1998, 3 American Indians, 2 Asians, and 3 self-identified Hispanics were admitted; 2 American Indians, 1 Asian, and 1 self-identified Hispanic were removed.

Source: U.S. Department of Justice. Bureau of Justice Statistics, "Capital Punishment 1998," p. 8.

PERSONS EXECUTED

The number of persons executed is a small proportion of the number receiving death sentences. It also varies more sharply from year to year than does the total number sentenced. (See the chart Persons Executed, 1930–1999 and the table Number of Executions by State, 1976–1999.) Note that the virtual absence of executions from the late 1960s to the early 1980s was the result of successful legal challenges to executions culminating in the suspension of capital punishment by the Supreme Court in 1972 and the court's approval of revised state procedures in 1976.

PERSONS EXECUTED, 1930–1999

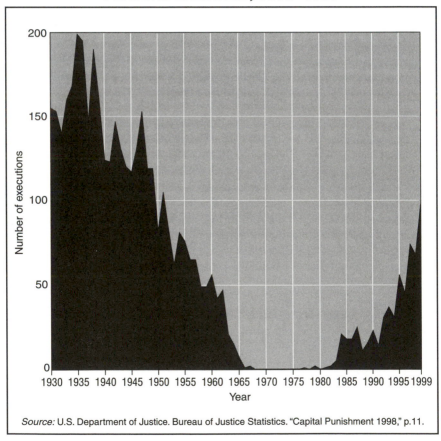

Source: U.S. Department of Justice. Bureau of Justice Statistics. "Capital Punishment 1998," p.11.

Appendix A

Among those states that have the death penalty, the number of executions varies widely. (Two states alone, Texas and Virginia, account for 45 percent of all executions in 1998 and 1999).

NUMBER OF EXECUTIONS BY STATE, 1976–1999

State	Total	1998	1999
Texas	199	20	35
Virginia	73	13	14
Florida	44	4	1
Missouri	41	3	9
Louisiana	25	0	1
Georgia	23	1	0
South Carolina	24	7	4
Arkansas	21	1	4
Alabama	19	1	2
Arizona	19	4	7
Oklahoma	19	4	6
Illinois	12	1	1
North Carolina	15	3	4
Delaware	10	0	2
Nevada	8	1	1
California	7	1	2
Indiana	7	1	1
Utah	6	0	1
Mississippi	4	0	0
Nebraska	3	0	0
Washington	3	1	0
Maryland	3	1	0
Pennsylvania	3	0	1
Oregon	2	0	0
Montana	2	1	0
Wyoming	1	0	0
Idaho	1	0	0
Kentucky	2	0	1
Colorado	1	0	0
Ohio	1	0	1
Total	**598**	**68**	**98**

Source: Death Penalty Information Center.

253

EXECUTIONS BY REGION, 1976–1999

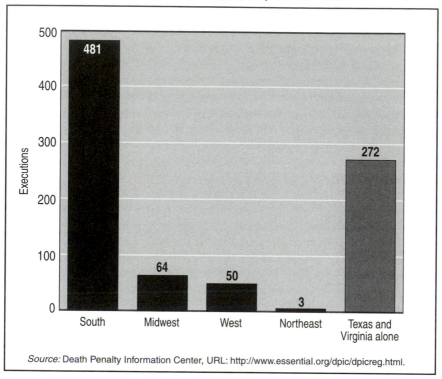

Source: Death Penalty Information Center, URL: http://www.essential.org/dpic/dpicreg.html.

Geographical disparities in the number of executions become even more striking when the totals are broken down by region. The South accounts for 80 percent of all executions since 1976.

APPENDIX B

POLLS AND SURVEYS

In general, support for capital punishment has generally been high in the United States as long as polls have been conducted. However, some interesting divergences and nuances become evident when the poll response is broken down demographically and when support for the death penalty is compared to support for alternative punishments.

OVERALL SUPPORT FOR THE DEATH PENALTY

The question "Are you in favor of the death penalty for a person convicted of murder?" has been asked by the Gallup Poll since 1953. In 1953, 68 percent of respondents supported the death penalty. Support fluctuated but generally fell

SUPPORT FOR THE DEATH PENALTY, 1953–1999

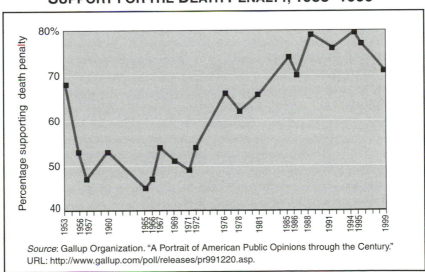

Source: Gallup Organization. "A Portrait of American Public Opinions through the Century." URL: http://www.gallup.com/poll/releases/pr991220.asp.

255

to its low point of 42 percent in 1966, when 47 percent opposed the death penalty. This time coincides with the beginning of a period of few executions as major court challenges to the death penalty were underway. By the late 1970s, with the Supreme Court giving the green light for executions, support for the death penalty was on the rise, reaching well over 60 percent. During the 1980s and early 1990s support for the death penalty soared, reaching 80 percent in 1994. It seems evident that this trend correlates with the growing crime rates and public concern about crime during the same period. In the late 1990s, however, both the crime rate and support for capital punishment dipped, with 71 percent supporting the death penalty in 1999.

SUPPORT FOR ALTERNATIVES TO THE DEATH PENALTY

When the alternative of life without parole (LWOP) is called to the attention of poll respondents, support for the death penalty drops. For example, in a Gallup Poll released on February 24, 1999, when the question asked is "Are you in favor of the death penalty for a person convicted of murder?"[1] the results were:

In favor	71%
Against	22%
No opinion	7%

When respondents were asked "In your opinion, is the death penalty imposed too often today or not enough?" The responses were:

Too often	25%
Not often enough	64%
About the right amount	4%
No opinion	7%

This might suggest that death penalty supporters are impatient with the reluctance of the legal system to actually proceed to execute people.

However, when respondents were asked "What do you think should be the penalty for murder—the death penalty, or life imprisonment with absolutely no possibility of parole?," the results were:

Death penalty	56%
Life imprisonment	38%
No opinion	6%

Clearly a significant minority of death penalty supporters are willing to consider life without parole as an option. The inclusion of a requirement that offenders provide restitution (that is, work to compensate the victims of the crime) also increases support for a life (or even long term) sentence as an alternative to the death penalty.[2]

---

[1] All poll results in this appendix are from Mar Gillespie. "Public Opinion Supports Death Penalty." Gallup Organization poll release, February 24, 1999. Available online, URL: http://www.gallup.com/poll/releases/pr990224.asp.

[2] Richard C. Dieter, "Sentencing for Life: Americans Embrace Alternatives to the Death Penalty." Death Penalty Information Center. Available online, URL: http://www.essential.org/dpic/dpic.r07.html#sxn4.

APPENDIX C

━━━━━━━━━━

OVERVIEW OF
RESEARCH STUDIES

There are four principal areas in the capital punishment debate that are amenable to quantitative analysis:

- The possible deterrent effect of the death penalty
- Racial and other demographic disparities in administration of capital punishment
- The cost of execution versus the cost of life imprisonment
- The number of innocent persons who have been sentenced to death or executed

DETERRENCE

One of the most pervasive arguments made in favor of the death penalty is that it deters murder. (Implicit in this assertion is that the death penalty provides a level of deterrence greater than that afforded by alternatives such as life imprisonment without parole.)

The argument for deterrence is often presented on an intuitive basis: if the penalty for doing something is increased, most people would be less likely to do it. Thus while many people in a hurry might risk a $20 parking fine, if the parking fine is raised to $250, fewer people are likely to take the risk. Since most people would consider death to be the worst thing that could happen to them, by that argument regular imposition of the death penalty for murder would result in fewer people committing murders.

Starting in the 1950s Thorsten Sellin[1] did a comparative analysis of pairs of neighboring states with similar demographics, with one state having the death penalty and the other not having the sanction. He also looked at murder rates in the same state before and after it either abolished or reinstated capital punishment. If the deterrence hypothesis is correct, one would expect death penalty states to have a lower murder rate than neighboring, similar non–death penalty states. A state that abolishes the death penalty should experience a rise in the murder rate, while a state that reinstates the sanction should benefit from a lower murder rate. However, none of these effects were seen by most researchers, even after the analysis was refined by comparing not the entirety of each state, but counties in neighboring states selected for similarity according to a variety of demographic and socioeconomic criteria.

Proponents of the deterrence hypothesis then argued that it was not the mere existence of a death penalty that had a deterrent effect, but rather the certainty that a murderer would actually receive the ultimate sanction. During the mid-1970s, Isaac Ehrlich[2] included several measures of the risk of execution in his analysis, along with considering other variables relating to law enforcement practices and demographics that he claimed had been inadequately treated by previous researchers. Ehrlich found a strong correlation between the number of executions and the murder rate, which he quantified by saying that each execution may have prevented seven or eight murders on the average. However, most researchers who attempted to replicate Ehrlich's results failed to do so and made a number of technical criticisms of his methodology. The overwhelming majority of studies conducted since the 1970s continue to find no significant deterrent effect for the death penalty as compared to life imprisonment.

Deterrence proponents have further argued that having executions occur speedily (within say a few years of the offense) rather than 10–20 years later would considerably improve the deterrence effect. Although this is also an intuitively plausible notion, the only major study in the literature, by William C. Bailey in 1980,[3] found no connection between the swiftness of punishment and deterrence.

Another possibility is that widespread publicity about executions would have an increased deterrent effect, at least in the short term. However, in 1990 Bailey[4] studied television coverage of executions between 1976 and 1987, and found no relationship between the amount of coverage and execution rates and no difference in impact between matter-of-fact reports and reports with graphic depictions.

It is possible that even without general deterrence effect, the death penalty may have a deterrent effect on certain kinds of murders. Most general deterrence studies have simply looked at the rate for all sorts of murders, not just "capital murders" subject to the death penalty. Available statistics generally don't differentiate capital murders from murders in general, making a more focused study difficult to carry out. Generally, however, the relatively few studies that have attempted to estimate the number of capital murders occurring around the time of an execution have failed to find a deterrent effect.

Since killing a police officer is virtually always a capital offense, studying the rate of such murders does offer an accessible test of the "specific deterrence hypothesis" with regard to capital murders. In 1994 William C. Bailey and Ruth D. Peterson[5] conducted such a study, comparing rates of killing police to the rate of executions for "cop killers." No deterrence effect was found.

A discussion of the possible relationship between executions and murder rates may also have to take into account the possibility that executions may actually encourage murder. Some theorists have suggested that the death penalty, particularly if well publicized, may have a "brutalization" effect. That is, by showing state-sanctioned killing, it may encourage would-be offenders to see murder as a natural way to accomplish their criminal objectives. Brutalization can be thought of as a sort of "reverse deterrence" and has been equally difficult to demonstrate. It is also possible that capital punishment may lead some persons to kill in order to commit suicide with the help of the state.[6]

Some writers have speculated on the possible cause for the disconnection between the intuitive perception that the death penalty *should* deter murder and the findings that it does not. One possibility is that many murderers simply do not make rational calculations about penalties before committing their crimes. And even with the kind of cold-blooded, non-impulsive murder that is more likely to receive the death penalty, it may mean that someone willing to risk life in prison is also willing to risk a relatively small chance of eventual execution.

To summarize, the majority of experts remain unconvinced that the death penalty has a significant deterrent effect. Proponents of capital punishment have argued that a strong deterrence effect would show up if execution for capital murder were swift and certain. But such a policy would inevitably increase the rate of execution of innocent persons as well, and it is not clear whether the general public would tolerate the routine executions of hundreds of persons every year.

THE DEATH PENALTY AND RACE

Unlike the case with deterrence, racial disparities in death sentencing have been extensively demonstrated. Most obviously, the demographics of death sentences (see Appendix A) reveal that as of the end of 1998, African Americans made up 43 percent of the death row population, even though they make up only 12 percent of the nation's population as a whole. This disparity can be at least partly accounted for by the fact that blacks are eight times as likely to commit homicide as whites.[7] However, in 1983, David Baldus, George Woodworth, and Charles Pulaski[8] released their study of 594 homicide cases in Georgia. The results were startling and disturbing: they found that blacks convicted of killing whites were sentenced to death in 22 percent of capital cases, compared to 3 percent of whites who were convicted of killing blacks and received the death penalty. (The study attempted to control more than 250 variables or characteristics of the crime in an attempt to compare truly similar crimes.) In 1990, the U.S. General Accounting Office reviewed 28 studies on racial disparities in death sentencing. They concluded that the race of the victim was a strong predictor of the likelihood of the offender receiving a death sentence, though the race of the offender had a less consistent effect.[9]

But while the existence of at least some racial bias in death penalty sentencing is accepted by the majority of researchers and even by the justices of the Supreme Court, the question of how the criminal justice system and society in general should respond to the situation remains contentious. In its decision in the case of *McCleskey v. Kemp* (1987), the Supreme Court majority accepted the validity of the findings of the Baldus Study but ruled that overturning the verdict of a jury in an actual, particular case required showing that jurors exercised "discriminatory purpose" in that particular case. While courts have accepted statistical evidence in other kinds of cases (such as employment discrimination suits), they seem unwilling to overturn jury verdicts on the basis of statistics, for fear that the criminal justice system would become totally unworkable.

Therefore, the argument that the death penalty is imposed disproportionately on minorities (and on the poor and uneducated in general, who often receive slipshod legal representation) has largely moved from the legal arena to the arena of public opinion, where it has become a major argument for abolition of the death penalty.

THE COST OF CAPITAL PUNISHMENT

The question of whether it costs more to sentence a person to death (and eventually execute him or her) than to sentence the person to life imprisonment is sometimes brought up by opponents of the death penalty. Many members of the public assume that execution must be cheaper, since it avoids the cost (roughly $20,000 per year[10]) of lifetime incarceration.

However, both the great seriousness given by most participants in the legal system to the question of life or death and the requirements imposed by the Supreme Court during the past 30 years have made the death penalty process excruciatingly complex. To start with there is the additional "mini trial" of the penalty phase, and then there is a series of postconviction state and federal appeals that despite recent efforts to streamline the process means that the average death row inmate will spend 10 years or more (at the same high cost of incarceration) before execution. The seriousness of the stakes means that both sides will seek to deploy their full resources in terms of investigators and expert witnesses. As inadequate as the taxpayer-paid representation for the average capital defendant may prove to be, the expense is not inconsiderable.

Estimates of the total cost of a capital case can be figured in several ways. If one takes the total amount spent on capital prosecutions and divides it by the number of people actually executed, the ratio for California between 1977 and 1996 is $1 billion or more divided by 5, resulting in a cost per execution of more than $200 million. (Of course if the defendants had been prosecuted and sentenced to life they would still incur substantial costs.)

Looking only at the amount spent on each case where a person is executed, the average cost is $3.2 million in Florida.[11] Even in Texas, where the relatively high execution rate may have achieved some economy of scale, the cost is $2.3 million per execution[12] This latter figure is about three times the cost of 40 years imprisonment at $20,000 per year.[13]

Some death penalty supporters argue that costs for capital cases could be substantially reduced by speeding up the process and reducing the number of grounds or opportunities for appeal. Doing so, however, leads to increased risk of executing persons who are in fact innocent. Death penalty opponents doubt that most people would want to make such a tradeoff if they knew what it entailed.

EXECUTION OF THE INNOCENT

Given that there were more than 3,500 persons on death row at the end of the 1990s, it seems intuitively plausible that there are some persons there who did not commit the crime for which they were convicted—and that of the hundreds of persons executed since 1972, at least a few were innocent. A number of studies have attempted to get a more precise estimate of the number of wrongfully convicted or executed persons.

In 1987 Hugo Adam Bedau and Michael Radelet[14] published a study that identified 350 people who had been wrongly convicted in capital (or potentially capital) cases in the United States between 1900 and 1985. While some of these wrongful convictions took place in states without the death penalty, and others were overturned, 23 of the persons were eventually executed.

Stephen J. Markman and Paul G. Cassell wrote a rebuttal to the Bedau-Radelet study attacking its methodology.[15] They noted that Bedau and Radelet, found only 23 "mistaken" cases out of 7,000 executions. Further, they concluded that in the 12 of the 23 cases in which there were enough facts to thoroughly check, Bedau and Radelet's "judgments of error are un-convincing," and that "their methodology makes their conclusion in the other eleven cases suspect as well." They argued that the strongest cases for error took place early in the century, where today's rigorous procedural safe-guards were lacking. Finally, they noted that even granting the alleged error rate, it is "minuscule." Bedau and Radelet in turn responded by asserting that their critics were politically inspired and bound to a rigid, inflexible de-fense of the "infallibility" of the death penalty system.

Another approach to the question is to look at how many death row in-mates are in fact being released because convincing evidence of their inno-cence has emerged. According to a report by Richard C. Dieter of the Death Penalty Information Center,[16] 69 persons have been released from death row since 1973, and 21 of them were released since 1993 (7 of them in Illinois). This would be about 2 percent of the current death row population, though of course this figure doesn't include persons who may be innocent but have been unable to gain a hearing or prove their innocence. Dieter points to the growing number of such releases and the accelerating rate of executions as indicating an increasing risk that innocent persons will be executed.

Expressed as a percentage, the number of persons wrongfully sent to death row is probably rather small, and the number wrongly executed smaller still. However, looked at in another way, about 600 people have been executed since 1973, and the 70 released since then is about 8.5 per-cent of that total. Many people, looking at such numbers in terms of human lives, find the risk of executing the innocent to be a strong argument against the death penalty.

CONCLUSION

The four factors discussed in this appendix (deterrence, race, cost, and in-nocence) cannot be viewed in isolation. If one concludes that deterrence or some other compelling factor makes the death penalty desirable, then one must ask how much of the other three factors can be tolerated. On the other hand, if one is convinced that neither deterrence nor any other argument carries much weight, then the rather strong evidence for racial disparities, the high marginal cost of execution as compared to life imprisonment, and the probability of wrongful executions is likely to strengthen the case against the death penalty.

[1] For an overview of deterrence research and findings, see William C. Bailey and Ruth D. Peterson, "Murder, Capital Punishment, and Deterrence: A Review of the Literature" in Hugo Adam Bedau, ed. *The Death Penalty in America: Current Controversies.* New York: Oxford University Press, 1997, pp. 135–161.

[2] Isaac Ehrlich, "The Deterrent Effect of Capital Punishment: A Question of Life or Death" in *American Economic Review*, vol. 65, 1975, pp. 397–417.

[3] William C. Bailey, "Deterrence and the Celebrity of the Death Penalty: A Neglected Question in Deterrence Research" in *Social Forces*, vol. 58, 1980, pp. 1,308–1,333.

[4] William C. Bailey, "Murder and Capital Punishment: An Analysis of Television Execution Publicity" in *American Sociological Review*, vol. 55, 1990, pp. 628–633.

[5] William C. Bailey and Ruth D. Peterson. "Murder, Capital Punishment and Deterrence: A Review of the Evidence and an Examination of Police Killings" in *Journal of Social Issues*, vol. 50, 1994, pp. 53–74.

[6] K. Van Wormer, "Execution-Inspired Murder: A Form of Suicide?" in *Journal of Offender Rehabilitation*, vol. 22, 1995, pp. 1–10.

[7] "Homicide Trends in the United States," Bureau of Justice Statistics. Available online, URL: http://www.ojp.usdoj.gov/bjs/homicide/race.htm.

[8] D. C. Baldus, C. L. Pulaski, and G. Woodworth, "Comparative Review of Death Sentences: An Empirical Study of the Georgia Experience" in *Journal of Criminal Law and Criminology*, vol. 74, 1983, pp. 661–753.

[9] U.S. General Accounting Office, "Death Penalty Sentencing: Research Indicates Pattern of Racial Disparities." GAO/GGD-90-57, February 1990. Also in Hugo Adam Bedau, ed. *The Death Penalty in America*, pp. 268–274.

[10] D. P. Cavanaugh and M. A. Kleiman, *A Cost-Benefit Analysis of Prison Cell Construction and Alternative Sanctions.* Cambridge, Mass.: Botec Analysis, 1990.

[11] D. Van Drehle, "Bottom Line: Life in Prison One-Sixth as Expensive" in *The Miami Herald*, July 10, 1988, p. 12a.

[12] C. Hoppe, "Executions Cost Texas Millions" in *The Dallas Morning News*, March 8, 1992, p. A1.

[13] Also see P. J. Cook and D. B. Slawson, "Costs of Processing Murder Cases in North Carolina." Duke University/State Justice Institute, 1993. This study found that each case in North Carolina where the defendant was executed cost $2.16 million more than if the defendant had received a non-capital trial and had been sentenced to life imprisonment.

[14] Hugo Adam Bedau and Michael L. Radelet, "Miscarriages of Justice in Potentially Capital Cases" in *Michigan Law Review*, vol. 40, November

1987, p. 85ff. See also M. L. Radelet, H. A. Bedau, and C. E. Putnam, *In Spite of Innocence*. Boston, Mass.: Northeastern University Press, 1992. This book 400 detailed case histories of persons mistakenly convicted for capital or potentially capital offenses between 1900 and 1991.

[15] Stephen J. Markman and Paul G. Cassell. "Protecting the Innocent: A Response to the Bedau-Radelet Study" in *Stanford Law Review*, vol. 41, November 1988, pp. 121–160.

[16] Richard C. Dieter, "Innocence and the Death Penalty: The Increasing Risk of Executing the Innocent." Washington, D.C.: Death Penalty Information Center, July 1997. Available online, URL: http://www.essential.org/dpic/inn.html.

APPENDIX D

EXTRACT FROM U.S. SUPREME COURT RULING: *FURMAN v. GEORGIA*, 1972

408 U.S. 238
FURMAN V. GEORGIA
CERTIORARI TO THE SUPREME
COURT OF GEORGIA
NO. 69-5003.

Argued January 17, 1972
Decided June 29, 1972

[Note: Selected excerpts follow, with footnotes and most references deleted.]

[PER CURIAM]
. . . Certiorari was granted limited to the following question: "Does the imposition and carrying out of the death penalty in [these cases] constitute cruel and unusual punishment in violation of the Eighth and Fourteenth Amendments?" . . . The Court holds that the imposition . . . and carrying out of the death penalty in these cases constitute cruel and unusual punishment in violation of the Eighth and Fourteenth Amendments. The judgment in each case is therefore reversed insofar as it leaves undisturbed the death sentence imposed, and the cases are remanded for further proceedings.

So ordered.

MR. JUSTICE DOUGLAS, MR. JUSTICE BRENNAN, MR. JUSTICE STEWART, MR. JUSTICE WHITE, and MR. JUSTICE MARSHALL have filed separate opinions in support of the judgments. THE CHIEF

Appendix D

JUSTICE, MR. JUSTICE BLACKMUN, MR. JUSTICE POWELL, and MR. JUSTICE REHNQUIST have filed separate dissenting opinions.

MR. JUSTICE DOUGLAS, concurring.

. . . The generality of a law inflicting capital punishment is one thing. What may be said of the validity of a law on the books and what may be done with the law in its application do, or may, lead to quite different conclusions. It would seem to be incontestable that the death penalty inflicted on one defendant is "unusual" if it discriminates against him by reason of his race, religion, wealth, social position, or class, or if it is imposed under a procedure that gives room for the play of such prejudices. . . .

The words "cruel and unusual" certainly include penalties that are barbaric. But the words, at least when read in light of the English proscription against selective and irregular use of penalties, suggest that it is "cruel and unusual" to apply the death penalty—or any other penalty—selectively to minorities whose numbers are few, who are outcasts of society, and who are unpopular, but whom society is willing to see suffer though it would not countenance general application of the same penalty across the board. . . .

There is increasing recognition of the fact that the basic theme of equal protection is implicit in "cruel and unusual" punishments. "A penalty . . . should be considered 'unusually' imposed if it is administered arbitrarily or discriminatorily." The same authors add that "[t]he extreme rarity with which applicable death penalty provisions are put to use raises a strong inference of arbitrariness." The President's Commission on Law Enforcement and Administration of Justice recently concluded:

> *Finally there is evidence that the imposition of the death sentence and the exercise of dispensing power by the courts and the executive follow discriminatory patterns. The death sentence is disproportionately imposed and carried out on the poor, the Negro, and the members of unpopular groups. . . .*

Former Attorney General Ramsey Clark has said, "It is the poor, the sick, the ignorant, the powerless and the hated who are executed." One searches our chronicles in vain for the execution of any member of the affluent strata of this society. The Leopolds and Loebs are given prison terms, not sentenced to death. . . .

We cannot say from facts disclosed in these records that these defendants were sentenced to death because they were black. Yet our task is not restricted to an effort to divine what motives impelled these death penalties. Rather, we deal with a system of law and of justice that leaves to the uncontrolled discretion of judges or juries the determination whether defendants committing these crimes should die or be imprisoned. Under these laws no standards govern the selection of the penalty. People live or die, dependent on the whim of one man or of 12. . . .

Those who wrote the Eighth Amendment knew what price their forebears had paid for a system based, not on equal justice, but on discrimination. In those days the target was not the blacks or the poor, but the dissenters, those who opposed absolutism in government, who struggled for a parliamentary regime, and who opposed governments' recurring efforts to foist a particular religion on the people. . . . But the tool of capital punishment was used with vengeance against the opposition and those unpopular with the regime. One cannot read this history without realizing that the desire for equality was reflected in the ban against "cruel and unusual punishments" contained in the Eighth Amendment. . . .

The high service rendered by the "cruel and unusual" punishment clause of the Eighth Amendment is to require legislatures to write penal laws that are evenhanded, nonselective, and nonarbitrary, and to require judges to see to it that general laws are not applied sparsely, selectively, and spottily to unpopular groups.

A law that stated that anyone making more than $50,000 would be exempt from the death penalty would plainly fall, as would a law that in terms said that blacks, those who never went beyond the fifth grade in school, those who made less than $3,000 a year, or those who were unpopular or unstable should be the only people executed. A law which in the overall view reaches that result in practice has no more sanctity than a law which in terms provides the same.

Thus, these discretionary statutes are unconstitutional in their operation. They are pregnant with discrimination and discrimination is an ingredient not compatible with the idea of equal protection of the laws that is implicit in the ban on "cruel and unusual" punishments. . . .

I concur in the judgments of the Court.

MR. JUSTICE BRENNAN, concurring.

The question presented in these cases is whether death is today a punishment for crime that is "cruel and unusual" and consequently, by virtue of the Eighth and Fourteenth Amendments, beyond the power of the State to inflict.

II

. . . There are, then, four principles by which we may determine whether a particular punishment is "cruel and unusual." The primary principle, which I believe supplies the essential predicate for the application of the others, is that a punishment must not by its severity be degrading to human dignity. The paradigm violation of this principle would be the infliction of a torturous punishment of the type that the Clause has always prohibited. Yet "[i]t is unlikely that any State at this moment in history," would pass a law providing for the infliction of such a punishment. Indeed, no such punishment has ever been before this Court. The same may be said of the other principles. It is unlikely that this Court will confront a severe punishment that is obviously inflicted in wholly arbitrary fashion; no State would engage in a reign of blind terror. . . .

. . . The function of these principles, after all, is simply to provide means by which a court can determine whether a challenged punishment comports with human dignity. They are, therefore, interrelated, and in most cases it will be their convergence that will justify the conclusion that a punishment is "cruel and unusual." The test, then, will ordinarily be a cumulative one: If a punishment is unusually severe, if there is a strong probability that it is inflicted arbitrarily, if it is substantially rejected by contemporary society, and if there is no reason to believe that it serves any penal purpose more effectively than some less severe punishment, then the continued infliction of that punishment violates the command of the Clause that the State may not inflict inhuman and uncivilized punishments upon those convicted of crimes.

III

The question, then, is whether the deliberate infliction of death is today consistent with the command of the Clause that the State may not inflict punishments that do not comport with human dignity. I will analyze the punishment of death in terms of the principles set out above and the cumulative test to which they lead: It is a denial of human dignity for the State arbitrarily to subject a person to an unusually severe punishment that society has indicated it does not regard as acceptable, and that cannot be shown to serve any penal purpose more effectively than a significantly less drastic punishment. Under these principles and this test, death is today a "cruel and unusual" punishment.

Capital Punishment

Death is a unique punishment in the United States. In a society that so strongly affirms the sanctity of life, not surprisingly the common view is that death is the ultimate sanction. This natural human feeling appears all about us. There has been no national debate about punishment, in general or by imprisonment, comparable to the debate about the punishment of death. No other punishment has been so continuously restricted, or has any State yet abolished prisons, as some have abolished this punishment. And those States that still inflict death reserve it for the most heinous crimes.

The only explanation for the uniqueness of death is its extreme severity. Death is today an unusually severe punishment, unusual in its pain, in its finality, and in its enormity. No other existing punishment is comparable to death in terms of physical and mental suffering. Although our information is not conclusive, it appears that there is no method available that guarantees an immediate and painless death. . . .

In comparison to all other punishments today, then, the deliberate extinguishment of human life by the State is uniquely degrading to human dignity. I would not hesitate to hold, on that ground alone, that death is today a "cruel and unusual" punishment, were it not that death is a punishment of longstanding usage and acceptance in this country. I therefore turn to the second principle—that the State may not arbitrarily inflict an unusually severe punishment.

The outstanding characteristic of our present practice of punishing criminals by death is the infrequency with which we resort to it. The evidence is conclusive that death is not the ordinary punishment for any crime.

There has been a steady decline in the infliction of this punishment in every decade since the 1930's, the earliest period for which accurate statistics are available. In the 1930's, executions averaged 167 per year; in the 1940's, the average was 128; in the 1950's, it was 72; and in the years 1960–1962, it was 48. There have been a total of 46 executions since then, 36 of them in 1963–1964. Yet our population and the number of capital crimes committed have increased greatly over the past four decades. The contemporary rarity of the infliction of this punishment is thus the end result of a long-continued decline. . . . When a country of over 200 million people inflicts an unusually severe punishment no more than 50 times a year, the inference is strong that the punishment is not being regularly and fairly applied. To dispel it would indeed require a clear showing of nonarbitrary infliction. . . .

Appendix D

When there is a strong probability that an unusually severe and degrading punishment is being inflicted arbitrarily, we may well expect that society will disapprove of its infliction. I turn, therefore, to the third principle. An examination of the history and present operation of the American practice of punishing criminals by death reveals that this punishment has been almost totally rejected by contemporary society. . . .

In the United States, as in other nations of the western world, "the struggle about this punishment has been one between ancient and deeply rooted beliefs in retribution, atonement or vengeance on the one hand, and, on the other, beliefs in the personal value and dignity of the common man that were born of the democratic movement of the eighteenth century, as well as beliefs in the scientific approach to an understanding of the motive forces of human conduct, which are the result of the growth of the sciences of behavior during the nineteenth and twentieth centuries." It is this essentially moral conflict that forms the backdrop for the past changes in and the present operation of our system of imposing death as a punishment for crime. Our practice of punishing criminals by death has changed greatly over the years. . . . Our concern for decency and human dignity, moreover, has compelled changes in the circumstances surrounding the execution itself. No longer does our society countenance the spectacle of public executions, once thought desirable as a deterrent to criminal behavior by others. Today we reject public executions as debasing and brutalizing to us all.

Also significant is the drastic decrease in the crimes for which the punishment of death is actually inflicted. While esoteric capital crimes remain on the books, since 1930 murder and rape have accounted for nearly 99% of the total executions, and murder alone for about 87%. In addition, the crime of capital murder has itself been limited. . . . In consequence, virtually all death sentences today are discretionarily imposed. Finally, it is significant that nine States no longer inflict the punishment of death under any circumstances, and five others have restricted it to extremely rare crimes.
Thus, although "the death penalty has been employed throughout our history," in fact the history of this punishment is one of successive restriction. What was once a common punishment has become, in the context of a continuing moral debate, increasingly rare. . . .

It is, of course, "We, the People" who are responsible for the rarity both of the imposition and the carrying out of this punishment. Juries, "express[ing] the conscience of the community on the ultimate question of life or death," been able to bring themselves to vote for death in a mere 100 or so cases among the thousands tried each year where the punishment is available. Governors, elected by and acting for us, have regularly commuted a substantial number of those sentences. And it is our society that insists upon due process of law to the end that no person will be unjustly put to death, thus ensuring that many more of those sentences will not be carried out. In sum, we have made death a rare punishment today. . . .

The final principle to be considered is that an unusually severe and degrading punishment may not be excessive in view of the purposes for which it is inflicted. This principle, too, is related to the others. When there is a strong probability that the State is arbitrarily inflicting an unusually severe punishment that is subject to grave societal doubts, it is likely also that the punishment cannot be shown to be serving any penal purpose that could not be served equally well by some less severe punishment.

The States' primary claim is that death is a necessary punishment because it prevents the commission of capital crimes more effectively than any less severe punishment. The first part of this claim is that the infliction of death is necessary to stop the individuals executed from committing further crimes. The sufficient answer to this is that if a criminal convicted of a capital crime poses a danger to society, effective administration of the State's pardon and parole laws can delay or deny his release from prison, and techniques of isolation can eliminate or minimize the danger while he remains confined.

The more significant argument is that the threat of death prevents the commission of capital crimes because it deters potential criminals who would not be deterred by the threat of imprisonment. The argument is not based upon evidence that the threat of death is a superior deterrent. Indeed, as my Brother MARSHALL establishes, the available evidence uniformly indicates, although it does not conclusively prove, that the threat of death has no greater deterrent effect than the threat of imprisonment. The States argue, however, that they are entitled to rely upon common human experience, and that experience, they say, supports the conclusion that death must be a more effective deterrent than any less severe punishment. Because people fear death the most, the argument runs, the threat of death must be the greatest deterrent. . . .

In any event, this argument cannot be appraised in the abstract. We are not presented with the theoretical question whether under any imaginable circumstances the threat of death might be a greater deterrent to the commission of capital crimes than the threat of imprisonment. We are concerned with the practice of punishing criminals by death as it exists in the United States today. Proponents of this argument necessarily admit that its validity depends upon the existence of a system in which the punishment of death is invariably and swiftly imposed. Our system, of course, satisfies neither condition. A rational person contemplating a murder or rape is confronted, not with the certainty of a speedy death, but with the slightest possibility that he will be executed in the distant future. The risk of death is remote and improbable; in contrast, the risk of long-term imprisonment is near and great. . . .

There is, however, another aspect to the argument that the punishment of death is necessary for the protection of society. The infliction of death, the States urge, serves to manifest the community's outrage at the commission of the crime. It is, they say, a concrete public expression of moral indignation that inculcates respect for the law and helps assure a more peaceful community. Moreover, we are told, not only does the punishment of death exert this widespread moralizing influence upon community values, it also satisfies the popular demand for grievous condemnation of abhorrent crimes and thus prevents disorder, lynching, and attempts by private citizens to take the law into their own hands.

The question, however, is not whether death serves these supposed purposes of punishment, but whether death serves them more effectively than imprisonment. There is no evidence whatever that utilization of imprisonment rather than death encourages private blood feuds and other disorders. Surely if there were such a danger, the execution of a handful of criminals each year would not prevent it. The assertion that death alone is a sufficiently emphatic denunciation for capital crimes suffers from the same defect. If capital crimes require the punishment of death in order to provide moral reinforcement for the basic values of the community, those values can only be undermined when death is so rarely inflicted upon the criminals who commit the crimes. Furthermore, it is certainly doubtful that the infliction of death by the State does in fact strengthen the community's moral code; if the deliberate extinguishment of human life has any effect at all, it more likely tends to lower our respect for life and brutalize our values. . . .

In sum, the punishment of death is inconsistent with all four principles: Death is an unusually severe and degrading punishment; there is a strong probability that it is inflicted arbitrarily; its rejection by contemporary society is virtually total; and there is no reason to believe that it serves any penal purpose more effectively than the less severe punishment of imprisonment.

The function of these principles is to enable a court to determine whether a punishment comports with human dignity. Death, quite simply, does not.

IV

. . . Since [the nation's founding] successive restrictions, imposed against the background of a continuing moral controversy, have drastically curtailed the use of this punishment. Today death is a uniquely and unusually severe punishment. When examined by the principles applicable under the Cruel and Unusual Punishments Clause, death stands condemned as fatally offensive to human dignity. The punishment of death is therefore "cruel and unusual," and the States may no longer inflict it as a punishment for crimes. . . .

I concur in the judgments of the Court.

MR. CHIEF JUSTICE BURGER, with whom MR. JUSTICE BLACKMUN, MR. JUSTICE POWELL, and MR. JUSTICE REHNQUIST join, dissenting.

I

If we were possessed of legislative power, I would either join with MR. JUSTICE BRENNAN and MR. JUSTICE MARSHALL or, at the very least, restrict the use of capital punishment to a small category of the most heinous crimes. Our constitutional inquiry, however, must be divorced from personal feelings as to the morality and efficacy of the death penalty, and be confined to the meaning and applicability of the uncertain language of the Eighth Amendment. . . .

II

Counsel for petitioners properly concede that capital punishment was not impermissibly cruel at the time of the adoption of the Eighth Amendment. Not only do the records of the debates indicate that the Founding Fathers were limited in their concern to the prevention of torture, but it is also clear from the language of the Constitution itself that there was no thought whatever of the elimination of capital punishment. The opening sentence of the Fifth Amendment is a guarantee that the death penalty not be imposed "unless on a presentment or indictment of a Grand Jury." The Double Jeopardy Clause of the Fifth Amendment is a prohibition against being "twice put in jeopardy of life" for the same offense. Similarly, the Due Process Clause commands "due process of law" before an accused can be "deprived of life, liberty, or property." Thus, the explicit language of the Constitution affirmatively acknowledges the legal power to impose capital punishment; it does not expressly or by implication acknowledge the legal power to impose any of the various punishments that have been banned as cruel since 1791. . . .

In the 181 years since the enactment of the Eighth Amendment, not a single decision of this Court has cast the slightest shadow of a doubt on the constitutionality of capital punishment. In rejecting Eighth Amendment attacks on particular modes of execution, the Court has more than once implicitly denied that capital punishment is impermissibly "cruel" in the constitutional sense. . . . It is only 14 years since Mr. Chief Justice Warren, speaking for four members of the Court, stated without equivocation:

> *Whatever the arguments may be against capital punishment, both on moral grounds and in terms of accomplishing the purposes of punishment—and they are forceful—the death penalty has been employed throughout our history, and, in a day when it is still widely accepted, it cannot be said to violate the constitutional concept of cruelty.*

It is only one year since Mr. Justice Black made his feelings clear on the constitutional issue:

> *The Eighth Amendment forbids 'cruel and unusual punishments.' In my view, these words cannot be read to outlaw capital punishment because that penalty was in common use and authorized by law here and in the countries from which our ancestors came at the time the Amendment was adopted. It is inconceivable to me that the framers intended to end capital punishment by the Amendment.*

Before recognizing such an instant evolution in the law, it seems fair to ask what factors have changed that capital punishment should now be "cruel" in the constitutional sense as it has not been in the past. It is apparent that there has been no change of constitutional significance in the nature of the punishment itself. Twentieth century modes of execution surely involve no greater physical suffering than the means employed at the time of the Eighth Amendment's adoption. And although a man awaiting execution must inevitably experience extraordinary mental anguish, no one suggests that this anguish is materially different from that experienced by condemned men in 1791, even though protracted appellate review processes have greatly increased the waiting time on "death row." To be sure, the ordeal of the condemned man may be thought cruel in the sense that all suffering is thought cruel. But if the Constitution proscribed every punishment producing severe emotional stress, then capital punishment would clearly have been impermissible in 1791.

However, the inquiry cannot end here. For reasons unrelated to any change in intrinsic cruelty, the Eighth Amendment prohibition cannot fairly be limited to those punishments thought excessively cruel and barbarous at the time of the adoption of the Eighth Amendment. A punishment is inordinately cruel, in the sense we must deal with it in these cases, chiefly as perceived by the society so characterizing it. The standard of extreme cruelty is not merely descriptive, but necessarily embodies a moral judgment. The standard itself remains the same, but its applicability must change as the basic mores of society change. . . .

III

There are no obvious indications that capital punishment offends the conscience of society to such a degree that our traditional deference to the legislative judgment must be abandoned. It is not a punishment such as burning at the stake that everyone would ineffably find to be repugnant to all civilized standards. Nor is it a punishment so roundly condemned that only a few aberrant legislatures have retained it on the statute books. Capital punishment is authorized by statute in 40 States, the District of Columbia, and in the federal courts for the commission of certain crimes. On four occasions in the last 11 years Congress has added to the list of federal crimes punishable by death. In looking for reliable indicia of contemporary attitude, none more trustworthy has been advanced. . . .

Counsel for petitioners rely on a different body of empirical evidence. They argue, in effect, that the number of cases in which the death penalty is imposed, as compared with the number of cases in which it is statutorily available, reflects a general revulsion toward the penalty that would lead to its repeal if only it were more generally and widely enforced. It cannot be gainsaid that by the choice of juries—and sometimes judges—the death penalty is imposed in far fewer than half the cases in which it is available. To go further and characterize the rate of imposition as "freakishly rare," as petitioners insist, is unwarranted hyperbole. And regardless of its characterization, the rate of imposition does not impel the conclusion that capital punishment is now regarded as intolerably cruel or uncivilized.

IV

Capital punishment has also been attacked as violative of the Eighth Amendment on the ground that it is not needed to achieve legitimate penal aims and is thus "unnecessarily cruel." As a pure policy matter, this approach has much to recommend it, but it seeks to give a dimension to the Eighth Amendment that it was never intended to have and promotes a line of inquiry that this Court has never before pursued. . . .

By pursuing the necessity approach, it becomes even more apparent that it involves matters outside the purview of the Eighth Amendment. Two of the several aims of punishment are generally associated with capital punishment—retribution and deterrence. It is argued that retribution can be discounted because that, after all, is what the Eighth Amendment seeks to eliminate. There is no authority suggesting that the Eighth Amendment was intended to purge the law of its retributive elements, and the Court has consistently assumed that retribution is a legitimate dimension of the punishment of crimes. . . .

Comparative deterrence is not a matter that lends itself to precise measurement; to shift the burden to the States is to provide an illusory solution to an enormously complex problem. If it were proper to put the States to the test of demonstrating the deterrent value of capital punishment, we could just as well ask them to prove the need for life imprisonment or any other punishment. . . .

V

The actual scope of the Court's ruling, which I take to be embodied in these concurring opinions, is not entirely clear. This much, however, seems apparent: if the legislatures are to continue to authorize capital punishment for some crimes, juries and judges can no longer be permitted to make the sentencing determination in the same manner they have in the past. . . .

This application of the words of the Eighth Amendment suggests that capital punishment can be made to satisfy Eighth Amendment values if its rate of imposition is somehow multiplied; it seemingly follows that the flexible sentencing system created by the legislatures, and carried out by juries and judges, has yielded more mercy than the Eighth Amendment can stand. The implications of this approach are mildly ironical. For example, by this measure of the Eighth Amendment, the elimination of death-qualified juries in *Witherspoon v. Illinois*, 391 U.S. 510 (1968), can only be seen in retrospect as a setback to "the evolving standards of decency that mark the progress of a maturing society." . . .

The Eighth Amendment was included in the Bill of Rights to assure that certain types of punishments would never be imposed, not to channelize the sentencing process. The approach of these concurring opinions has no antecedent in the Eighth Amendment cases. It is essentially and exclusively a procedural due process argument.

While I would not undertake to make a definitive statement as to the parameters of the Court's ruling, it is clear that if state legislatures and the Congress wish to maintain the availability of capital punishment, significant statutory changes will have to be made. Since the two pivotal concurring opinions turn on the assumption that the punishment of death is now meted out in a random and unpredictable manner, legislative bodies may seek to bring their laws into compliance with the Court's ruling by providing standards for juries and judges to follow in determining the sentence in capital cases or by more narrowly defining the crimes for which the penalty is to be imposed. . . .

Real change could clearly be brought about if legislatures provided mandatory death sentences in such a way as to deny juries the opportunity to bring in a verdict on a lesser charge; under such a system, the death sentence could only be avoided by a verdict of acquittal. If this is the only alternative that the legislatures can safely pursue under today's ruling, I would have preferred that the Court opt for total abolition. . . .

VI

Since there is no majority of the Court on the ultimate issue presented in these cases, the future of capital punishment in this country has been left in an uncertain limbo. Rather than providing a final and unambiguous answer on the basic constitutional question, the collective impact of the majority's ruling is to demand an undetermined measure of change from the various state legislatures and the Congress. While I cannot endorse the process of decisionmaking that has yielded today's result and the restraints that that result imposes on legislative action, I am not altogether displeased that legislative bodies have been given the opportunity, and indeed unavoidable responsibility, to make a thorough re-evaluation of the entire subject of capital punishment. If today's opinions demonstrate nothing else, they starkly show that this is an area where legislatures can act far more effectively than courts. . . .

APPENDIX E

EXTRACT FROM U.S. SUPREME COURT RULING: *McCLESKEY v. KEMP*, 1987

481 U.S. 279
MCCLESKEY V. KEMP, SUPERINTENDENT, GEORGIA DIAGNOSTIC AND CLASSIFICATION CENTER
CERTIORARI TO THE UNITED STATES COURT OF APPEALS FOR THE ELEVENTH CIRCUIT
NO. 84-6811.

Argued October 15, 1986
Decided April 22, 1987

[Note: selected excerpts given, with footnotes and most references omitted.]

JUSTICE POWELL delivered the opinion of the Court.
This case presents the question whether a complex statistical study that indicates a risk that racial considerations enter [481 U.S. 279, 283] into capital sentencing determinations proves that petitioner McCleskey's capital sentence is unconstitutional under the Eighth or Fourteenth Amendment.

I

McCleskey, a black man, was convicted of two counts of armed robbery and one count of murder in the Superior Court of Fulton County, Georgia, on

October 12, 1978. McCleskey's convictions arose out of the robbery of a furniture store and the killing of a white police officer during the course of the robbery. . . .

In support of his claim, McCleskey proffered a statistical study performed by Professors David C. Baldus, Charles Pulaski, and George Woodworth (the Baldus study) that purports to show a disparity in the imposition of the death sentence in Georgia based on the race of the murder victim and, to a lesser extent, the race of the defendant. The Baldus study is actually two sophisticated statistical studies that examine over 2,000 murder cases that occurred in Georgia during the 1970's. The raw numbers collected by Professor Baldus indicate that defendants charged with killing white persons received the death penalty in 11% of the cases, but defendants charged with killing blacks received the death penalty in only 1% of the cases. The raw numbers also indicate a reverse racial disparity according to the race of the defendant: 4% of the black defendants received the death penalty, as opposed to 7% of the white defendants.

Baldus also divided the cases according to the combination of the race of the defendant and the race of the victim. He found that the death penalty was assessed in 22% of the cases involving black defendants and white victims; 8% of the cases involving white defendants and white victims; 1% of the cases involving black defendants and black victims; and 3% of the cases involving white defendants and black victims. Similarly, Baldus found that prosecutors sought the death penalty in 70% of the cases involving black defendants and white victims; 32% of the cases involving white defendants and white victims; 15% of the cases involving black defendants and black victims; and 19% of the cases involving white defendants and black victims.

Baldus subjected his data to an extensive analysis, taking account of 230 variables that could have explained the disparities on nonracial grounds. One of his models concludes that, even after taking account of 39 nonracial variables, defendants charged with killing white victims were 4.3 times as likely to receive a death sentence as defendants charged with killing blacks. According to this model, black defendants were 1.1 times as likely to receive a death sentence as other defendants. Thus, the Baldus study indicates that black defendants, such as McCleskey, who kill white victims have the greatest likelihood of receiving the death penalty.

II

McCleskey's first claim is that the Georgia capital punishment statute violates the Equal Protection Clause of the Fourteenth Amendment. He argues that race has infected the administration of Georgia's statute in two ways: persons who murder whites are more likely to be sentenced to death than persons who murder blacks, and black murderers are more likely to be sentenced to death than white murderers. As a black defendant who killed a white victim, McCleskey claims that the Baldus study demonstrates that he was discriminated against because of his race and because of the race of his victim. In its broadest form, McCleskey's claim of discrimination extends to every actor in the Georgia capital sentencing process, from the prosecutor who sought the death penalty and the jury that imposed the sentence, to the State itself that enacted the capital punishment statute and allows it to remain in effect despite its allegedly discriminatory application. We agree with the Court of Appeals, and every other court that has considered such a challenge, that this claim must fail.

A

Our analysis begins with the basic principle that a defendant who alleges an equal protection violation has the burden of proving "the existence of purposeful discrimination." A corollary to this principle is that a criminal defendant must prove that the purposeful discrimination "had a discriminatory effect" on him. Thus, to prevail under the Equal Protection Clause, McCleskey must prove that the decisionmakers in his case acted with discriminatory purpose. He offers no evidence specific to his own case that would support an inference that racial considerations played a part in his sentence.

Instead, he relies solely on the Baldus study. McCleskey argues that the Baldus study compels an inference that his sentence rests on purposeful discrimination. McCleskey's claim that these statistics are sufficient proof of discrimination, without regard to the facts of a particular case, would extend to all capital cases in Georgia, at least where the victim was white and the defendant is black.

The Court has accepted statistics as proof of intent to discriminate in certain limited contexts. First, this Court has accepted statistical disparities as proof of an equal protection violation in the selection of the jury venire in a particular district. . . . Second, this Court has accepted statistics in the form of multiple-regression analysis to prove statutory violations under Title VII of the Civil Rights Act of 1964.

But the nature of the capital sentencing decision, and the relationship of the statistics to that decision, are fundamentally different from the corresponding elements in the venire-selection or Title VII cases. Most importantly, each particular decision to impose the death penalty is made by a petit jury selected from a properly constituted venire. Each jury is unique in its composition, and the Constitution requires that its decision rest on consideration of innumerable factors that vary according to the characteristics of the individual defendant and the facts of the particular capital offense. Thus, the application of an inference drawn from the general statistics to a specific decision in a trial and sentencing simply is not comparable to the application of an inference drawn from general statistics to a specific venire-selection or Title VII case. In those cases, the statistics relate to fewer entities, and fewer variables are relevant to the challenged decisions.

Another important difference between the cases in which we have accepted statistics as proof of discriminatory intent and this case is that, in the venire-selection and Title VII contexts, the decisionmaker has an opportunity to explain the statistical disparity. Here, the State has no practical opportunity to rebut the Baldus study. "[C]ontrolling considerations of . . . public policy," dictate that jurors "cannot be called. . . . to testify to the motives and influences that led to their verdict." Similarly, the policy considerations behind a prosecutor's traditionally "wide discretion" suggest the impropriety of our requiring prosecutors to defend their decisions to seek death penalties, "often years after they were made." Moreover, absent far stronger proof, it is unnecessary [481 U.S. 279, 297] to seek such a rebuttal, because a legitimate and unchallenged explanation for the decision is apparent from the record: McCleskey committed an act for which the United States Constitution and Georgia laws permit imposition of the death penalty.

Finally, McCleskey's statistical proffer must be viewed in the context of his challenge. McCleskey challenges decisions at the heart of the State's criminal justice system. "[O]ne of society's most basic tasks is that of protecting the lives of its citizens and one of the most basic ways in which it achieves the task is through criminal laws against murder." Implementation of these laws necessarily requires discretionary judgments. Because discretion is essential to the criminal justice process, we would demand exceptionally clear proof before we would infer that the discretion has been abused. The unique nature of the decisions at issue in this case also counsels against adopting such an inference from the disparities indicated by the Baldus study. Accordingly, we hold that the Baldus study is clearly insufficient to support an inference that any of the decisionmakers in McCleskey's case acted with discriminatory purpose.

B

McCleskey also suggests that the Baldus study proves that the State as a whole has acted with a discriminatory purpose. He appears to argue that the

Appendix E

State has violated the Equal [481 U.S. 279, 298] Protection Clause by adopting the capital punishment statute and allowing it to remain in force despite its allegedly discriminatory application. But "'[d]iscriminatory purpose' . . . implies more than intent as volition or intent as awareness of consequences. It implies that the decisionmaker, in this case a state legislature, selected or reaffirmed a particular course of action at least in part 'because of,' not merely 'in spite of,' its adverse effects upon an identifiable group." . . . For this claim to prevail, McCleskey would have to prove that the Georgia Legislature enacted or maintained the death penalty statute because of an anticipated racially discriminatory effect. In *Gregg v. Georgia*, supra, this Court found that the Georgia capital sentencing system could operate in a fair and neutral manner. There was no evidence then, and there is none now, that the Georgia Legislature enacted the capital punishment statute to further a racially discriminatory purpose. . . .

III

McCleskey also argues that the Baldus study demonstrates that the Georgia capital sentencing system violates the Eighth Amendment. We begin our analysis of this claim by reviewing the restrictions on death sentences established by our prior decisions under that Amendment. . . .

A

In sum, our decisions since *Furman* have identified a constitutionally permissible range of discretion in imposing the death penalty. First, there is a required threshold below which the death penalty cannot be imposed. In this context, the State must establish rational criteria that narrow the decisionmaker's judgment as to whether the circumstances of a particular defendant's case meet the threshold. Moreover, a societal consensus that the death penalty is disproportionate [481 U.S. 279, 306] to a particular offense prevents a State from imposing the death penalty for that offense. Second, States cannot limit the sentencer's consideration of any relevant circumstance that could cause it to decline to impose the penalty. In this respect, the State cannot channel the sentencer's discretion, but must allow it to consider any relevant information offered by the defendant.

IV
A

In light of our precedents under the Eighth Amendment, McCleskey cannot argue successfully that his sentence is "disproportionate to the crime in the traditional sense." He does not deny that he committed a murder in the course of a planned robbery, a crime for which this Court has determined that the death penalty constitutionally may be imposed. His disproportionality claim "is of a different sort." McCleskey argues that the sentence in his case is disproportionate to the sentences in other murder cases. On the one hand, he cannot base a constitutional claim on an argument that his case differs from other cases in which defendants did receive the death penalty. On automatic appeal, the Georgia Supreme Court found that McCleskey's death sentence was not disproportionate to other death sentences imposed in the State. The court supported this conclusion with an appendix containing citations to 13 cases involving generally similar murders. Moreover, where the statutory procedures adequately channel the sentencer's discretion, such proportionality review is not constitutionally required.

On the other hand, absent a showing that the Georgia capital punishment system operates in an arbitrary and capricious manner, McCleskey cannot prove a constitutional violation by demonstrating that other defendants who may be similarly situated did not receive the death penalty. In *Gregg*, the Court confronted the argument that "the opportunities for discretionary action that are inherent in the processing of any murder case under Georgia law," specifically the opportunities for discretionary leniency, rendered the capital sentences imposed arbitrary and capricious. We rejected this contention. . . .

Because McCleskey's sentence was imposed under Georgia sentencing procedures that focus discretion "on the particularized nature of the crime and the particularized characteristics of the individual defendant," id., at 206, we lawfully may presume that McCleskey's death sentence was not "wantonly and freakishly" imposed, id., at 207, and thus that the sentence is not disproportionate within any recognized meaning under the Eighth Amendment.

B

Although our decision in *Gregg* as to the facial validity of the Georgia capital punishment statute appears to foreclose McCleskey's disproportionality argument, he further contends that the Georgia capital punishment system is arbitrary and capricious in application, and therefore his sentence is excessive, because racial considerations may influence capital sentencing decisions in Georgia. We now address this claim.

To evaluate McCleskey's challenge, we must examine exactly what the Baldus study may show. Even Professor Baldus does not contend that his statistics prove that race enters into any capital sentencing decisions or that race was a factor in McCleskey's particular case. Statistics at most may show only a likelihood that a particular factor entered into some decisions. There is, of course, some risk of racial prejudice influencing a jury's decision in a criminal case. There are similar risks that other kinds of prejudice will influence other criminal trials. . . . The question "is at what point that risk becomes constitutionally unacceptable," McCleskey asks us to accept the likelihood allegedly shown by the Baldus study as the constitutional measure of an unacceptable risk of racial prejudice influencing capital sentencing decisions. This we decline to do. . . .

C

At most, the Baldus study indicates a discrepancy that appears to correlate with race. Apparent disparities in sentencing are an inevitable part of our criminal justice system. The discrepancy indicated by the Baldus study is "a far cry from the major systemic defects identified in *Furman*." As this Court has recognized, any mode for determining guilt or punishment "has its weaknesses and the potential for misuse." . . . Specifically, "there can be 'no perfect procedure for deciding in which cases governmental authority should be used to impose death.'" . . . Where the discretion that is fundamental to our criminal process is involved, we decline to assume that what is unexplained is invidious. In light of the safeguards designed to minimize racial bias in the process, the fundamental value of jury trial in our criminal justice system, and the benefits that discretion provides to criminal defendants, we hold that the Baldus study does not demonstrate a constitutionally significant risk of racial bias affecting the Georgia capital sentencing process.

V

Two additional concerns inform our decision in this case. First, McCleskey's claim, taken to its logical conclusion, [481 U.S. 279, 315] throws into serious question the principles that underlie our entire criminal justice system. The Eighth Amendment is not limited in application to capital punishment, but applies to all penalties. Thus, if we accepted McCleskey's claim that racial bias has impermissibly tainted the capital sentencing decision, we could soon be faced with similar claims as to other types of penalty. Moreover, the claim that his sentence rests on the irrelevant factor of race easily could be extended to apply to claims based on unexplained discrepancies that correlate to membership in other minority groups, and even to gender.

Second, McCleskey's arguments are best presented to the legislative bodies. It is not the responsibility—or indeed even the right—of this Court to determine the appropriate punishment for particular crimes. It is the legislatures, the elected representatives of the people, that are "constituted to respond to the will and consequently the moral values of the people." . . .

VI

Accordingly, we affirm the judgment of the Court of Appeals for the Eleventh Circuit.
It is so ordered.

JUSTICE BRENNAN, with whom JUSTICE MARSHALL joins, and with whom JUSTICE BLACKMUN and JUSTICE STEVENS join in all but Part I, dissenting.

I

Adhering to my view that the death penalty is in all circumstances cruel and unusual punishment forbidden by the Eighth and Fourteenth Amendments, I would vacate the decision below insofar as it left undisturbed the death sentence imposed in this case. The Court observes that "[t]he *Gregg*-type statute imposes unprecedented safeguards in the special context of capital punishment," which "ensure a degree of care in the imposition of the death penalty that can be described only as unique." Notwithstanding these efforts, murder defendants in Georgia with white victims are more than four times as likely to receive the death sentence as are defendants with black victims. . . . Nothing could convey more powerfully the intractable reality of the death penalty: "that the effort to eliminate arbitrariness in the infliction of that ultimate sanction is so plainly doomed to failure that it—and the death penalty—must be abandoned altogether."

Even if I did not hold this position, however, I would reverse the Court of Appeals, for petitioner McCleskey has clearly demonstrated that his death sentence was imposed in violation of the Eighth and Fourteenth Amendments. . . .

II

. . . The Court today holds that Warren McCleskey's sentence was constitutionally imposed. It finds no fault in a system in which lawyers must tell their clients that race casts a large shadow on the capital sentencing process. The Court arrives at this conclusion by stating that the Baldus study cannot "prove that race enters into any capital sentencing decisions or that race was a factor in McCleskey's particular case." Ante, at 308 (emphasis in original). Since, according to Professor Baldus, we cannot say "to a moral certainty" that race influenced a decision, we can identify only "a likelihood that a particular factor entered into some decisions," and "a discrepancy that appears to correlate with race." This "likelihood" and "discrepancy," holds the Court, is insufficient to establish a constitutional violation. . . .

III

A

It is important to emphasize at the outset that the Court's observation that McCleskey cannot prove the influence of race on any particular sentencing decision is irrelevant in evaluating his Eighth Amendment claim. Since *Furman v. Georgia*, 408 U.S. 238 (1972), the Court has been concerned with the risk of the imposition of an arbitrary sentence, rather than the proven fact of one. Furman held that the death penalty "may not be imposed under sentencing procedures that create a substantial risk that the punishment will be inflicted in an arbitrary and capricious manner." . . . This emphasis on risk acknowledges the difficulty of divining the jury's motivation in an individual case. In addition, it reflects the fact that concern for arbitrariness focuses on the rationality of the system as a whole, and that a system that features a significant probability that sentencing decisions are influenced by impermissible considerations cannot be regarded as rational . . .

Defendants challenging their death sentences thus never have had to prove that impermissible considerations have actually infected sentencing decisions. We have required instead that they establish that the system under which they were sentenced posed a significant risk of such an occurrence. McCleskey's claim does differ, however, in one respect from these earlier cases: it is the first to base a challenge not on speculation about how a system might operate, but on empirical documentation of how it does operate.

The Court assumes the statistical validity of the Baldus study, and acknowledges that McCleskey has demonstrated a risk that racial prejudice plays a role in capital sentencing in Georgia. Nonetheless, it finds the probability of prejudice insufficient to create constitutional concern. Close analysis of the Baldus study, however, in light of both statistical principles and human experience, reveals that the risk that race influenced McCleskey's sentence is intolerable by any imaginable standard.

B

The Baldus study indicates that, after taking into account some 230 nonracial factors that might legitimately influence a sentencer, the jury more likely than not would have spared McCleskey's life had his victim been black. . . .

Furthermore, even examination of the sentencing system as a whole, factoring in those cases in which the jury exercises little discretion, indicates the influence of race on capital sentencing. For the Georgia system as a whole, race accounts for a six percentage point difference in the rate at which capital punishment is imposed. Since death is imposed in 11% of all white-victim cases, the rate in comparably aggravated black-victim cases is 5%. The rate of capital sentencing in a white-victim case is thus 120% greater than the rate in a black-victim case. Put another way, over half—55%—of defendants in white-victim crimes in Georgia would not have been sentenced to die if their victims had been black. Of the more than 200 variables potentially relevant to a sentencing decision, race of the victim is a powerful explanation for variation in death sentence rates—as powerful as nonracial aggravating factors such as a prior murder conviction or acting as the principal planner of the homicide. . . .

C

Evaluation of McCleskey's evidence cannot rest solely on the numbers themselves. We must also ask whether the conclusion suggested by those numbers is consonant with our understanding of history and human experience. Georgia's legacy of a race-conscious criminal justice system, as well as this Court's own recognition of the persistent danger that racial attitudes may affect criminal proceedings, indicates that McCleskey's claim is not a fanciful product of mere statistical artifice. . . .

The majority thus misreads our Eighth Amendment jurisprudence in concluding that McCleskey has not demonstrated a degree of risk sufficient to raise constitutional concern. . . . It is true that every nuance of decision cannot be statistically captured, nor can any individual judgment be plumbed with absolute certainty. Yet the fact that we must always act without the illumination of complete knowledge cannot induce paralysis when we confront what is literally an issue of life and death. Sentencing data, history, and experience all counsel that Georgia has provided insufficient assurance of the heightened rationality we have required in order to take a human life.

Appendix E

IV

The Court cites four reasons for shrinking from the implications of Mc-Cleskey's evidence: the desirability of discretion for actors in the criminal justice system, the existence of statutory safeguards against abuse of that discretion, the potential consequences for broader challenges to criminal sentencing, and an understanding of the contours of the judicial role. While these concerns underscore the need for sober deliberation, they do not justify rejecting evidence as convincing as McCleskey has presented.

The Court maintains that petitioner's claim "is antithetical to the fundamental role of discretion in our criminal justice system." It states that "[w]here the discretion that is fundamental to our criminal process is involved, we decline to assume that what is unexplained is invidious." Ante, at 313.

Reliance on race in imposing capital punishment, however, is antithetical to the very rationale for granting sentencing discretion. Discretion is a means, not an end. It is bestowed in order to permit the sentencer to "trea[t] each defendant in a capital case with that degree of respect due the uniqueness of the individual." . . .

The Court also declines to find McCleskey's evidence sufficient in view of "the safeguards designed to minimize racial bias in the [capital sentencing] process." . . . *Gregg v. Georgia*, 428 U.S., at 226, upheld the Georgia capital sentencing statute against a facial challenge which JUSTICE WHITE described in his concurring opinion as based on "simply an assertion of lack of faith" that the system could operate in a fair manner. JUSTICE WHITE observed that the claim that prosecutors might act in an arbitrary fashion was "unsupported by any facts," and that prosecutors must be assumed to exercise their charging duties properly "[a]bsent facts to the contrary." . . .

It has now been over 13 years since Georgia adopted the provisions upheld in *Gregg*. Professor Baldus and his colleagues have compiled data on almost 2,500 homicides committed during the period 1973–1979. They have taken into account the influence of 230 nonracial variables, using a multitude of data from the State itself, and have produced striking evidence that the odds of being sentenced to death are significantly greater than average if a defendant is black or his or her victim is white. The challenge to the Georgia system is not speculative or theoretical; it is empirical. As a result, the Court cannot rely on the statutory safeguards in discounting McCleskey's evidence, for it is the very effectiveness of those safeguards that such evidence calls into question. . . .

The Court next states that its unwillingness to regard petitioner's evidence as sufficient is based in part on the fear that recognition of McCleskey's claim would open the door to widespread challenges to all aspects of criminal sentencing. Taken on its face, such a statement seems to suggest a fear of too much justice. . . .

The Court also maintains that accepting McCleskey's claim would pose a threat to all sentencing because of the prospect that a correlation might be demonstrated between sentencing outcomes and other personal characteristics. Again, such a view is indifferent to the considerations that enter into a determination whether punishment is "cruel and unusual." Race is a consideration whose influence is expressly constitutionally proscribed. We have expressed a moral commitment, as embodied in our fundamental law, that this specific characteristic should not be the basis for allotting burdens and benefits. . . .

Finally, the Court justifies its rejection of McCleskey's claim by cautioning against usurpation of the legislatures' role in devising and monitoring criminal punishment. The Court is, of course, correct to emphasize the gravity of constitutional intervention and the importance that it be sparingly employed. The fact that "[c]apital punishment is now the law in more than two thirds of our States," however, does not diminish the fact that capital punishment is the most awesome act that a State can perform. The judiciary's role in this society counts for little if the use of governmental power to extinguish life does not elicit close scrutiny.

V

It is tempting to pretend that minorities on death row share a fate in no way connected to our own, that our treatment of them sounds no echoes beyond the chambers in which they die. Such an illusion is ultimately corrosive, for the reverberations of injustice are not so easily confined. "The destinies of the two races in this country are indissolubly linked together," and the way in which we choose those who will die reveals the depth of moral commitment among the living. . . .

INDEX

Page numbers in *italic* indicate illustrations (charts, graphs). **Boldface** page numbers refer to definitions. Page numbers followed by *t* indicate tables.

A

Abolitionist Action Committee 227–228
abolitionists 4, 18–19, **127**
  on barbarity 18
  on deterrence 14–15
  on expense of capital punishment 22
  on fairness 20–21
  on irreversibility 19–20
  on proportionality 17
  on retribution 17
  on social protection 16
  web sites by 133, 134–135
abolition movement(s). *See also* Legal Defense and Education Fund
  first, in the United States 8–9
  history of 91–116
  international 38–39
  1920s 10
  1980s–1990s 13–14
Abu-Jamal, Mumia 14, 114, 115
academic organizations 225–227
accomplices, capital punishment for 27, 69–70

ACLU. *See* American Civil Liberties Union
actual innocence 88–89, **127**
Adams, Randall Dale 109
Adams v. Texas 57
adultery 7, 91
advocacy groups
  international 245–246
  national 227–234
  state 235–245
advocacy web sites 134–135
advocates of capital punishment. *See* retentionists
affirm **127**
African Americans. *See* blacks
age 30, 45, 48, 83–84
aggravating circumstance (factor) 27, 33, 41, 42–44, 67–68, **127**
Aikens v. California 58
Alabama, capital punishment in 48
Alaska, abolishment of capital punishment in 11
Allen, Jerome 111
American Bar Association (ABA) 97, 103, 105, 113, 228

American Civil Liberties Union (ACLU) 12, 13, 98, 107, 135, 228
American colonies, criminal laws of 7, 22, 91
American Federation of Labor (AFL) 93
American Friends Service Committee 228
American Law Institute 11
American League to Abolish Capital Punishment 10, 94, 95, 121, 123
American Medical Association (AMA) 105
American Society for the Abolition of Capital Punishment 9, 92, 121
Amnesty International 38, 104, 105, 108, 135, 228
Amsterdam, Anthony G. 12, 117
Anaya, Toney 108
ancient world, death sentence in 5–6, 90
appeals 25–26, 28, 33–35, 70–73
arbitrary and capricious 29, 40, 113, **127**

291

Arizona
    advocacy groups in 235
    capital punishment in
        48
Arkansas
    advocacy groups in
        235
    capital punishment in
        48–49
arson **42**
Askew, Reuben 102
assistance of counsel,
    effective 81–83, **128**
Athens, ancient, death
    sentence in 6, 90

B

Bailey, William C. 259,
    260
Baldus, David 21, 76, 78,
    261
barbarity 18
Barefoot v. Estelle 70–73,
    106
Barfield, Margie Velma
    107
battery **42**
Beccaria, Cesare 6–7, 91,
    117, 125
Bedau, Hugo Adam 19,
    108, 117, 262
Belli, Melvin 98
Bentham, Jeremy 7,
    117–118
Berns, Walter 118
Bethea, Rainey 94
bibliographic resources
    137–140
bifurcated trial 33, 40, 57,
    60, **127**
Bill of Rights 28, 92
Bird, Rose 108, 118
Blackmun, Harry Andrew
    34, 35, 82, 87, 88, 112,
    113, 118, 119

blacks, and capital
    punishment 20–21,
    31–32, 260–261
blasphemy 5, 7, 91
"Bloody Code" 6
Blystone v. Pennsylvania 64
Boggs, J. Caldo 96
Booth v. Maryland 33,
    79–81, 87, 108, 125
Bosler, SueZann 118
Bovee, Marvin H. 9,
    118–119
Bradford, William 8
Branch v. Texas 58
Brennan, William J. 59,
    97, 119
Bright, Stephen B. 119
Brooks, Charlie 106
Brown, Edmund G.
    96–97, 101, 119
brutalization **127**, 260
Bryant, William Cullen 9
Bryan v. Moore 115
Buchanan v. Angelone 67
Bullington v. Missouri 106
Bundy, Theodore R. 105,
    109, 119
Bureau of Justice Statistics
    136, 225–226
Burger, Warren Earl 60,
    66, 102, 119
Burger v. Kemp 81–83
burglary **42**
Bush, George, H. W. 13,
    37–38, 109, 111,
    119–120, 121
Bush, George W. 116
Byrd, James, Jr. 115

C

California
    abolitionist movement
        in 11
    advocacy groups in 235
    capital punishment in
        49, 98, 99

California v. Brown 41
Callins v. Collins 34, 113,
    118
Campaign to End the
    Death Penalty 228–229
Camus, Albert 120
capital offense 24, 25,
    26–27, **127**
    in 1897 93
    federal 45–47
    kidnapping as 10, 94
    skyjacking as 11
    by state 47–54
capital punishment
    abolishment of
        (1972–1976) 3,
        12–13, 39, 59–60,
        102–104
    for accomplice 27,
        69–70
    as cruel and unusual
        punishment. *See*
        Eighth Amendment
    effectiveness of 14–22
    expense of 21–22,
        261–262
    future of 35–39
    history of 5–14,
        90–116
    law of 24–35, 40–89
    for non-murder crime
        27, 30, 64–65, 95,
        97, 104
    religion and 22–24
    researching 133–149,
        258–265
    by state 47–54
capital punishment
    jurisdiction **128**
Capital Punishment
    Project 13
Capital Punishment
    Research Project 229
Capote, Truman 99, 120
carjacking **42**
Carnahan, Mel 114
Carvel, Elbert N. 97

Index

"case-in-chief" 40
Cassell, Paul G. 263
Catholic Church 23, 103,
  105
Catholics Against Capital
  Punishment 229
Cell 2455 Death Row
  (Chessman) 10–11
Center for Constitutional
  Rights 229
certiorari **128**
Cheever, George 120
Chessman, Caryl 10–11,
  37, 95, 97, 120
Chiles, Lawton 114
China 38
Christianity 23
Citizens United for
  Alternatives to the
  Death Penalty 229
Citizens United for
  Rehabilitation of Errants
  (CURE) 229
civil rights movement
  11–12, 31, 77
Civil War, U.S. 9
Clark, Ramsey 37, 120
class, and capital
  punishment 20–21
clemency **128**
Clinton, Bill 13, 115
codefendant spared death
  penalty **45**
Cohen, Lande 120
Coker v. Georgia 64–65, 74,
  104
Coleman, Roger Keith
  111, 112
Coleman v. Thompson 111
Colorado
  advocacy groups in
    235–236
  capital punishment in
    49, 98
common law 24
commutation **128**

Comprehensive Violent
  Crime Control Act
  (1991) 111
concurring opinion **128**
Congregationalists 23
Congress 25
Connecticut
  advocacy groups in 236
  capital punishment in
    49, 101
conservative religious
  groups 23
Constitution
  Bill of Rights 28, 92
  Eighth Amendment.
    See Eighth
    Amendment
  Fifth Amendment 25
  First Amendment 22
  Fourteenth
    Amendment. *See*
    Fourteenth
    Amendment
  Sixth Amendment 55
Coolidge, Calvin 94
Cooper, Paula R. 110
Copeland, Ray 111
Cornell Law School Death
  Penalty Project 226
court-appointed counsel
  128
court of appeals 25–26,
  128
crime rate 14, 18, 36
criminal justice system
  24–26
criminal laws 16
  early reforms of 7
  first 5
  in Great Britain 6, 7,
    91, 100
cruel and unusual
  punishment **128**. *See also*
  Eighth Amendment
culpability 17, 30, 41
Cuomo, Mario 38, 113,
  120–121

Curtis, Newton M. 9, 121

D

Dallas, George Mifflin 121
Darden, Willie Jasper 109
Darrow, Clarence 10, 93,
  94, 121, 123
databases 138–140
Davis, Angela 102
Davis v. Georgia 57
Dead Man Walking
  (Prejean) 124
death penalty. *See* capital
  punishment
Death Penalty Act (1996)
  115
*The Death Penalty in
  America* (Bedau) 117
Death Penalty Information
  Center 37, 134,
  229–230, 263
Death Penalty Net 230
death qualified jury **128**
Death Row (documentary)
  99, 120
death row population
  demographic
    characteristics of
    251*t*
  growth of 34
  mental impairment
    and 86
  1953–1999 *249*
  1990s 3, *114*
  by race 21, *250*
Death Row Support
  Project 230
defendants, capital, future
  dangerousness of **45**,
  70–73
defense counsel
  court-appointed **128**
  effective assistance of
    81–83, **128**
  quality of 20
  role of 27, 28, 40, 41

Defense of Capital Punishment (Cheever) 120

Delaware
  abolishment of capital punishment in 11, 96
  advocacy groups in 236
  capital punishment in 49
  restoring capital punishment in 11, 97

The Deliberate Stranger (Bundy) 119

democracy, capital punishment and 18–19

deterrence 14–15, **128**, 258–260

Dieter, Richard C. 263

diminished capacity **128**

dissent **128**

Dodd, Westley Allan 112

double jeopardy 106

Douglas, William O. 12, 59, 97, 125

Draco 6, 90

drug trafficking **42**

due process **128**. *See also* Fourteenth Amendment

Dugger v. Adams 109

Dukakis, Michael 13, 37–38, 109, 120, 121

E

Eberheart v. Georgia 65

Eddings v. Oklahoma 67

effective assistance of counsel 81–83, **128**

Egypt, ancient, death sentence in 6

Ehrlich, Isaac 259

Ehrmann, Herbert B. 121

Eighth Amendment 25, 35, 91, 92, **129**
  violation of
    Aikens v. California 58

Booth v. Maryland 80

Coker v. Georgia 65

Enmund v. Florida 69

execution methods and 31

Ford v. Wainwright 75

Furman v. Georgia 29, 58, 59

Herrera v. Collins 88

Lockett v. Ohio 66

McCleskey v. Kemp 78

Payne v. Tennessee 87

Penry v. Lynaugh 85

Thompson v. Oklahoma 83, 84

Wilkerson v. Utah 93

Woodson v. North Carolina 63

electrocution 18, 31, 93, 94, 115

Enlightenment 6–7

Enmund v. Florida 27, 69–70, 106

An Enquiry into the Effects of Public Punishments upon Criminals and upon Society (Rush) 125

Equal Justice USA 230

equal protection **129**

error **129**
  "harmless" **129**
  reversible **130**

escape **42**

espionage 10, 30, 45, 96, 108, 125

Essay on Crimes and Punishment (Beccaria) 6–7, 91, 117

Evangelium Vitae 23, 113

evidence 33, 41

execution(s)
  barbarity of 18
  extrajudicial **129**
  freeze on (1968) 12
  of innocent people 19–20, 107, 108, 114, 262–263
  as institutionalized violence 18
  of juveniles 83–84, 109
  of mentally retarded 30–31, 74–76, 84–86, 110
  methods of
    early 6
    guillotine 91–92, 122
    modern 31
    by state 47–54
  number of
    1930–1998 *252*
    1990s 3, 34
    by region *254*
    by state 253*t*
  during pending appeal 70–73
  private 8
  public 7, 8, 93, 94, 95

Executioner: Pierrepoint (Pierrepoint) 124

The Executioner's Song (Mailer) 105, 121

expense of capital punishment 21–22, 261–262

extrajudicial execution **129**

extreme duress **45**

F

factfinder 42, **129**

fairness 19–20

Faulkner, Daniel 114

Federal Bureau of Investigation (FBI) 226

Federal Bureau of Prisons 226

Index

federal courts **129**
federal law 25
Fellowship of
Reconciliation 230
felony **129**
felony-murder 26–27, 41,
69, 127, **129**
Feminists for Life of
America 230
Feuger, Victor 97
Fifth Amendment 25
First Amendment 22
first-degree murder 15, 26,
92, **129**
Florida
advocacy groups in
236
capital punishment in
49, 102, 103
*For Capital Punishment:
Crime and the Morality of
the Death Penalty* (Berns)
118
Ford v. Wainwright 74–76,
108
Fourteenth Amendment
25, 29, 92–93, 129
violation of
Ford v. Wainwright
75
Furman v. Georgia
58
Herrera v. Collins
88
Lockett v. Ohio 66
McCleskey v. Kemp
31, 77, 78
Franklin, Benjamin 7
Friends Committee on
National Legislation 230
Friends Committee to
Abolish the Death
Penalty 231
Furman v. Georgia 12,
29–30, 40, 54, 57–60,
77, 102, 118, 127,
266–278

G
gender, and opinion on
capital punishment 36
Georgia
advocacy groups in
236
capital punishment in
49–50, 97
Gilmore, Gary 13, 104,
105, 121
Godfrey v. Georgia 67–68,
105
Goldberg, Arthur J. 97
Gottlieb, Gerald 97
government agencies
135–137, 225–227
Great Britain 6, 7, 91, 100
Greeley, Horace 9,
121–122
Greenberg, Jack 11, 99,
100, 122
Gregg v. Georgia 13, 30,
54, 60–62, 103, 118
Guillotin, Joseph-Ignace
91–92, 122
"guilt phase" 40

H
habeas corpus 81, 111,
129
Hammarskjold, Dag 97
Hammurabi Code 5–6, 90
Ham v. South Carolina 77
hanging 31, 94, 97, 112
"harmless error" **129**
Harris, Robert Alton 112
hate crime 17, **43**, 115
Hauptmann, Bruno
Richard 94
Hawaii, abolishment of
capital punishment in
11, 96
Henry VIII (king of
England) 6, 91
Herrera v. Collins 34,
88–89, 112

hijacking **43**
Hinman, Lawrence M.
135
homicide 15, 30, **129**. *See
also* murder(s)
Horton, Willie 38
House Judiciary
Committee 226
Hugo, Victor 122
Humphrey, Hubert H. 37,
97

I
Idaho, capital punishment
in 50
Illinois
advocacy groups in
237
capital punishment in
50
income, and opinion on
capital punishment 36
indexes 138–139, 141–145
Indiana
advocacy groups in
237
capital punishment in
50
individualized
consideration **129**
Ingle, Joe 122
innocence, actual 88–89,
127
innocent people, execution
of 19–20, 107, 108, 114,
262–263
international abolitionist
movements 38–39
international advocacy
groups 245–246
Internet. *See* World Wide
Web
Iowa, advocacy groups in
237
Iran 38
irrevocability 19–20, **129**

J

Jackson, Andrew 123
Jackson, Roscoe 95
Jackson v. Georgia 58
Jehovah's Witnesses 23
Jesus Christ, execution of 6, 90
Jewish Peace Fellowship 231
Johans, Mike 115
John, Gee 93
John Paul II (pope) 23, 106, 108, 113, 114
Johnson, Lyndon B. 37, 99
Journey of Hope 231
Jurek v. Texas 60
jury 27–28, 41–42
  death qualified **128**
jury override **129**
jury selection 27, 55–57
Justice for All 231
Justice Research and Statistics Association 226
juveniles, capital punishment for 30, 83–84, 109

K

Kansas
  advocacy groups in 237–238
  capital punishment in 50
  restoring death penalty in (1932) 10, 35, 94
Kennedy, Robert F. 102
Kentucky
  advocacy groups in 238
  capital punishment in 50
kidnapping 10, 27, 30, **43**, 65, 94, 95, 97, 104
Kindler, Joseph 111
King, John William 115
Koestler, Arthur 96, 122

L

law, components of 24
Lawes, Lewis E. 10, 94, 122–123
Law without Order: Capital Punishment and the Liberals (Cohen) 120
Legal Defense and Education Fund (LDF) 11–12, 57, 76, 95, 99, 117, 122, 123, 231–232
legal issues of capital punishment 24–35
legal research 145–149
Legal Services Corporation 226
Leopold, Nathan 10, 93, 121, 123
lethal gas 31, 93
lethal injection 18, 31, 106, 107
library catalogs 137–138
Liebman, James S. 116
Life Plus 99 Years (Leopold) 123
life without possibility of parole 15, 16, 33, **129**
Lindbergh, Charles A. 94
Livingston, Edward 8, 92, 123
local courts 25
Lockett v. Ohio 65–67, 85, 105
Lockhart v. McRee 57
Loeb, Richard 10, 93, 121, 123
Louisiana
  advocacy groups in 238
  capital punishment in 50
Louisiana ex rel Francis v. Resweber 95
Lutheran Church 98

M

Mailer, Norman 105, 121
Maine
  advocacy groups in 238
  moratorium on executions (1837) 9
majority opinion **130**
mandatory death statutes 33, 61, 62–64, 104, **130**
Manson, Charles 102
Markman, Stephen J. 263
Marshall, Thurgood 36–37, 59, 75, 87, 123
"Marshall hypothesis" 36–37
Maryland
  advocacy groups in 238
  capital punishment in 51
Massachusetts
  advocacy groups in 238
  colonial, criminal law of 7, 91
Massachusetts Council for the Abolition of the Death Penalty 94
Maxwell, William L. 100
Maxwell v. Bishop 100
McCleskey v. Kemp 31, 76–79, 108, 111, 261, 279–290
McGinn, Ricky Nolen 116
McKoy v. North Carolina 67
McMillen, Walter 112–113
McVeigh, Timothy 114
Mease, Darrell J. 114
Medina, Pedro 18, 113
Meese, Edwin, III 123
Mennonite Central Committee 231
mental impairment 45, 128
  execution and 30–31, 74–76, 84–86, 110
Methodist Church 102

Index

Michigan
  abolishment of capital
    punishment (1846)
    9, 92
  advocacy groups in
    239
Middle Ages, capital
  punishment in 6
Mills v. Maryland 67
"mini-trial" 27, 40, 262
Minnesota, advocacy
  groups in 239
minorities, and capital
  punishment 20–21. *See
  also* race
minor participation **45**
Mississippi, capital
  punishment in 51, 95
Missouri
  advocacy groups in
    239–240
  capital punishment in
    51
mitigating circumstance
  (factor) 27, 41, 42,
  44–45, 66–67, **130**
Model Penal Code 11
Monge, Luis Jose 98
Monroe, Ronald 110
Montana
  advocacy groups in
    240
  capital punishment in
    51
moral justification **45**
More, Sir Thomas 6
Mormons 23
Morris, Errol 109
murder(s) **130**
  as capital offense 7, 25,
    26–27, 91
  capital punishment and
    rate of 14
  felony-murder 26–27,
    41, 127, **129**
  first-degree 15, 26, 92,
    129
  victim of 15, 43–44

Murder Victim Families
  for Reconciliation 231

N

NAACP LDF. *See* Legal
  Defense and Education
  Fund
national advocacy groups
  227–234
National Association of
  Criminal Defense
  Lawyers (NACDL) 232
National Bar Association
  232
National Black Police
  Association 232
National Coalition to
  Abolish the Death
  Penalty (NCADP) 13,
  134–135, 232
National Conference of
  Black Lawyers 232
National Council on
  Crime and Delinquency
  232–233
National Institute of
  Justice 226–227
National Lawyers Guild
  233
National Legal Aid &
  Defender Association
  233
NCADP. *See* National
  Coalition to Abolish the
  Death Penalty
Nebraska
  advocacy groups in
    240
  capital punishment in
    51
netnews 140–141
Nevada
  advocacy groups in
    240
  capital punishment in
    51
New Hampshire

advocacy groups in
    240
  capital punishment in
    51
New Jersey
  abolitionist movement
    in 11
  advocacy groups in
    240
  capital punishment in
    52
New Mexico
  advocacy groups in
    240
  capital punishment in
    52
news 140–141
newspapers 140–141
New York
  advocacy groups in
    240–241
  capital punishment in
    52
Ng, Charles 111
Nixon, Richard 12, 59,
  97, 100, 102, 103, 124
non-murder crime,
  capital punishment for
  27, 30, 64–65, 95, 97,
  104
North Carolina
  advocacy groups in
    241
  capital punishment in
    52
Nuremberg trials 95

O

O'Connor, Sandra Day 41,
  84, 85, 86
Ohio
  abolitionist movement
    in 11
  advocacy groups in
    241–242
  capital punishment in
    52

Oklahoma
  advocacy groups in 242
  capital punishment in 52
opening statements 27, 40
opponents of capital punishment. *See* abolitionists
Oregon
  abolitionist movement in 11, 98
  advocacy groups in 242
  capital punishment in 52–53
organizations 145, 225–246
O'Sullivan, John L. 8, 123–124

P

Parents of Murdered Children 233
Partisan Defense Committee 233
Pataki, George 35, 36, 113
Payne v. Tennessee 33, 81, 86–87, 111
penal system 28
penalty phase 27, **130**
Pennsylvania
  advocacy groups in 242–243
  capital punishment in 53
  colonial, criminal law of 7, 91
Penry v. Lynaugh 84–86, 110
people, finding 145
People v. Anderson 101–102
periodical indexes 139–140
Peterson, Ruth D. 260
Pierrepoint, Albert 124
Pius XII (pope) 95
plurality opinion **130**

police officer, killing 15, 260
politics, capital punishment in 37–38
polls 18, 19, 36, 100, 102, 103, 105, 107, 255–257
Porter, Anthony 114
Powell, Lewis F., Jr. 61, 72, 78, 80, 106, 110, 124
Powell v. Alabama 94
Prejean, Helen 124
Presbyterian Church Criminal Justice Program 233
Presbyterians 23
Prison Radio Project 233–234
prison system, development of 7–8
private executions 8
private offenses 5
Profitt v. Florida 60
Progressive Era 9
Prohibition period 10
Project Hope to Abolish the Death Penalty 234
proponents of capital punishment. *See* retentionists
proportionality 17–18
proportionality review 73–74, 107, **130**
prosecution
  evidence 33
  role of 27, 28, 40, 41
public executions 7, 8, 93, 94, 95
Public Justice, Private Mercy: A Governor's Education on Death Row (Brown) 119
public offenses 5
public opinion 18–19, 35–37, 100, 102, 103, 105, 107, 255–257
Pulaski, Charles 21, 261
Pulley v. Harris 73–74, 107

Q

Quakers 23, 91

R

race
  and capital punishment 20–21, 31–32, 76–79, 260–261, 279–290
  and opinion on capital punishment 36
Radelet, Michael L. 19, 108, 262
Rantoul, Robert, Jr. 8, 124
rape 27, 30, 43, 64–65, 77, 97, 99, 100, 104
Reagan, Ronald 12, 59, 102, 107, 108, 123, 124
recidivist **130**
Rector, Ricky Ray 13
Reflections on Hanging (Koestler) 96, 122
Rehnquist, William H. 34, 72, 87, 88, 109, 110, 124
Religious Debate 22–24
Religious Organizing Against the Death Penalty Project 234
remand **130**
Renaissance, capital punishment in 6
reprieve **130**
researching 133–149, 258–265
retentionists 4, 19, **130**
  on deterrence 14–15
  on expense of capital punishment 22
  on fairness 20–21
  on proportionality 17–18
  on retribution 16–17
  on social protection 16
retribution 16–17, **130**

reversible error **130**
Ristaino v. Ross 77
Roach, James Terry 107
robbery **43**
Robertson, Pat 24
Roberts v. Louisiana 63
Rockefeller, Nelson 98
Rockefeller, Winthrop 101
Roemer, Buddy 110
Romilly, Samuel 7, 125
Rosenberg, Ethel 10, 96, 125
Rosenberg, Julius 10, 96, 125
Rudolph v. Alabama 97
Rumbaugh, Charles 107
Rush, Benjamin 7, 8, 125
Russia 38
Ryan, George 115

S

Sacco, Nicola 10, 94, 125
St. Valentine's Day Massacre 10
sanction **130**
Sawyer v. Whittley 112
Scalia, Antonin 81, 125–126
Schwarzchild, Henry 126
search engines 143–144
Sellin, Thorsten 126, 258–259
Senate Judiciary Committee 227
sentencing phase 57, **130**
Sentencing Project 234
sexual assault 27, 30, **43**. *See also* rape
Shaheen, Jeanne 116
Shapp, Milton 101
Shaw, Bernard 109
Simmons v. South Carolina 73
Sixth Amendment 55
Skipper v. South Carolina 67
skyjacking 11, 27, 43

Slovik, Eddie D. 95, 126
Smith, Susan 113
Snyder, Ruth 10
social protection, capital punishment as means of 15–16
Socrates 6, 90
Sourcebook of Criminal Justice Statistics 136
Souter, David 112
South Carolina
  advocacy groups in 243
  capital punishment in 53
  restoring capital punishment in (1932) 10
South Carolina v. Gathers 81, 87, 110
South Dakota
  advocacy groups in 243
  capital punishment in 53
Southern Center for Human Rights 234
Spaziano v. Florida 118
Spenkelink, John A. 105, 126
split trial. *See* bifurcated trial
Stanford Law Review (Bedau and Radelet) 19
state advocacy groups 235–245
statistics 15, 16, 21, 31, 94, 99, 100, 106, 135–137, 249–254
statutory aggravating circumstances 42–44
statutory law 24
statutory mitigating circumstances 44–45
Stevens, John Paul 61, 82, 84, 112
Stewart, Potter 56, 59, 61, 68, 126

Strickland v. Washington 82
Summer v. Shuman 63
Supreme Court 26, 28, 227. *See also specific court cases*
  procedural issues 32–35
  rulings on capital punishment 30–31, 54–89

T

Tarver, Robert Lee 115
Tennessee
  advocacy groups in 243–244
  capital punishment in 53
Texas
  advocacy groups in 244
  capital punishment in 53
The Thin Blue Line (movie) 109
Thomas, Clarence 125
Thompson v. Oklahoma 48, 83–84, 109
three-tier system **130**
Tison v. Arizona 70
Torah 6
train wrecking **43**
traumatic-stress syndrome **45**
treason 7, 30, 45, 91
Truman, Harry S 95
Truth in Justice 234
Tucker, Karla Faye 14, 23–24, 114
Turner v. Murray 77

U

Ukraine 38
United Nations 38, 96, 97, 102, 110, 114

U.S. Commission on Civil Rights 227
U.S. Department of Justice 227
U.S. Sentencing Commission 227
U.S. Supreme Court. *See* Supreme Court
Utah, capital punishment in 53
utilitarianism 117

V

van den Haag, Ernest 126
Vanzetti, Bartolomeo 10, 94, 125
Vermont, advocacy groups in 244
victim, identity of 43–44
victim impact statements 33, 79–81, 86–87, 110
victim's consent **45**

Virginia
    advocacy groups in 244
    capital punishment in 53–54
    colonial, capital punishment in 91
voir dire 27

W

Wainwright v. Witt 57
Washington
    advocacy groups in 244–245
    capital punishment in 54
Weems v. United States 93
West Virginia, advocacy groups in 245
White, Byron R. 59, 69, 71, 74
Whitman, Walt 9
Whittier, John Greenleaf 8–9

Wilkerson v. Utah 93
Williams, Michael 115
witchcraft 5, 7, 22, 91
Witherspoon v. Illinois 55–57, 99
witness 40, 43
women. *See* gender
Woodson v. North Carolina 60, 61, 62–64, 103
Woodworth, George 21, 261
World Medical Association 106
World War I, capital punishment and 9–10
World War II, capital punishment and 10
World Wide Web 133, 134–137
    searching 141–145
Wyoming, capital punishment in 54